DETROIT LAKES & OTTER TAIL AREAS

Detroit Lakes & Otter Tail Area Fishing Map Guide
Table of Contents

See back cover for alphabetical index of lakes

MAPS IN THIS GUIDE ARE NOT FOR NAVIGATION

(Continued on next page)

Detroit Lakes & Otter Tail Area Fishing Map Guide
by Sportsman's Connection

Editor: James F. Billig
Editorial/Research: Jack Tyllia, Steve Meyer, Jon Wisniewski, Chuck Hartley
Cartography: Hart Graphics, Janet Billig
Typesetting/Layout: Shelly Wisniewski

Sportsman's Connection
Superior, Wisconsin

See back cover for alphabetical index of lakes

Your complete guide to over 145 lakes in the Detroit Lakes & Otter Tail Areas

SPORTSMAN'S connection®

Leading Publisher of Fishing Map Guides

The lakes selected for this guide are confined to those that are accessible to the public. Test surveys were performed by Minnesota Department of Natural Resource personnel to assist in their evaluation of fisheries. Note that some lakes test with more reliability than others and weather and other factors can skew results. Secchi disk readings indicated are typically averaged over a period of time, and actual water clarity may vary according to season. Information regarding public access is based upon sources available at time of publication, and is subject to change. Maps are not intended for navigation. Publisher is not responsible for errors or omissions.

Length to weight conversion scale

Northern Pike

Inches	24	25	26	27	28	29	30	31	32	33	34	35	36	37	38	39	40	41	42
Pounds	3.9	4.4	5.0	5.6	6.2	7.0	7.7	8.5	9.3	10.2	11.2	12.2	13.3	14.5	15.7	16.9	18.3	19.6	21.2

Walleye

Inches	14	15	16	17	18	19	20	21	22	23	24	25	26	27	28	29
Pounds	1.0	1.2	1.5	1.8	2.2	2.5	3.0	3.4	3.9	4.5	5.1	5.7	6.5	7.2	8.1	9.0

Largemouth Bass

Inches	12	13	14	15	16	17	18	19	20	21	22	23
Pounds	1.0	1.3	1.7	2.1	2.5	3.0	3.6	4.2	5.0	5.7	6.6	7.6

Crappie

Inches	8	9	10	11	12	13	14	15	16	17
Pounds	0.4	0.6	0.8	1.1	1.4	1.8	2.2	2.8	3.4	4.1

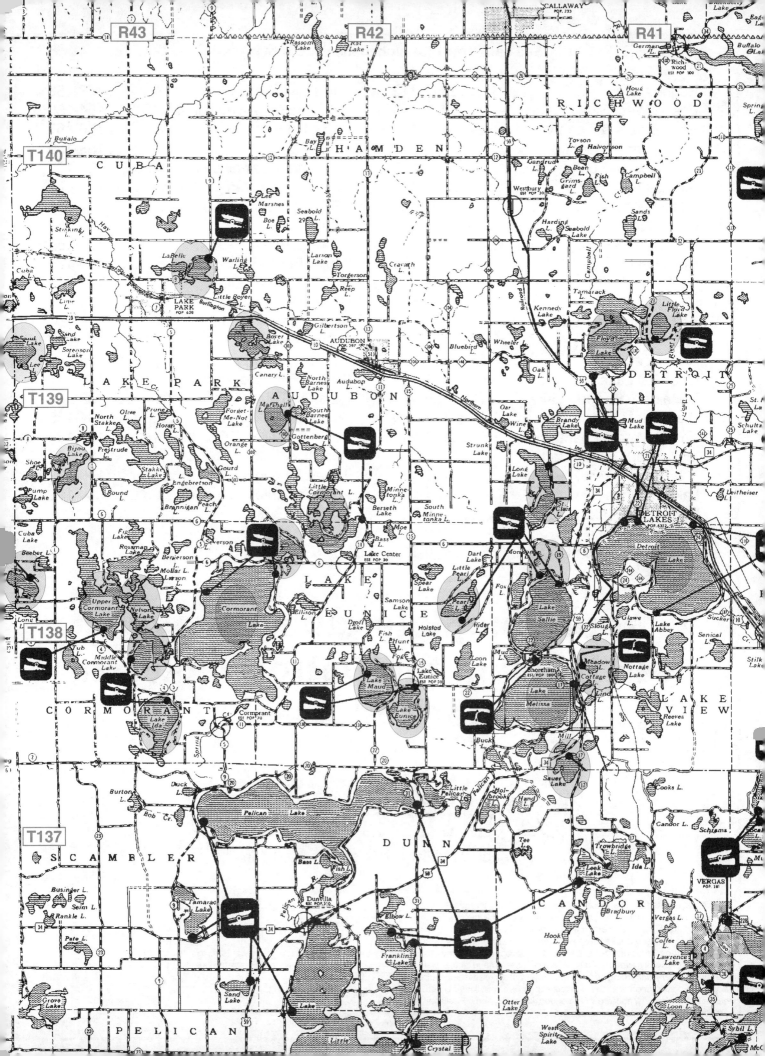

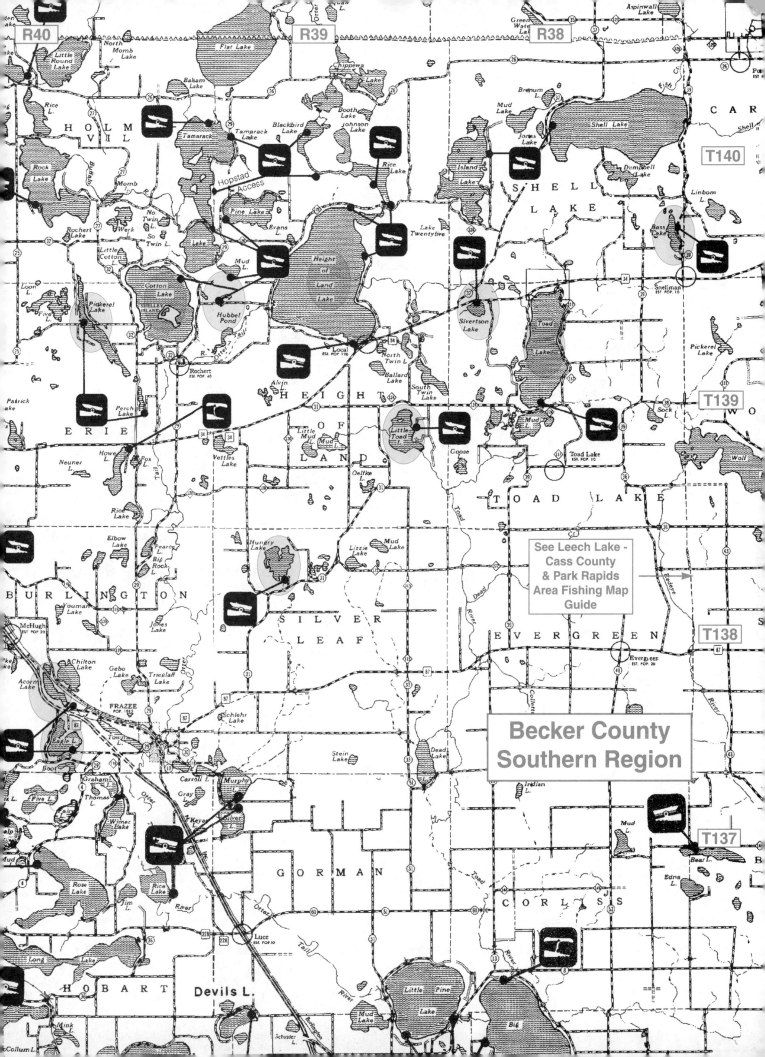

Becker County
Southern Region

See Leech Lake -
Cass County
& Park Rapids
Area Fishing Map
Guide

DETROIT LAKE
Becker County

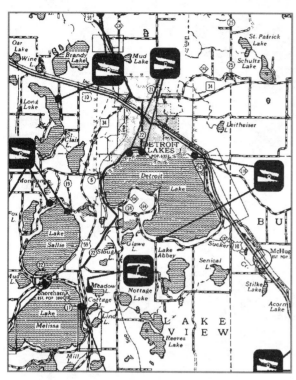

Location: Township 138, 139 Range 41
Watershed: Otter Tail
Surface Water Area: 3,083 Acres
Shorelength: 12.4 Miles
Secchi disk (water clarity): 6.0 Ft.
Water color: Green
Cause of water color: Algae

Maximum depth: 82 Ft.
Median depth: NA
Accessibility: Public accesses on northeast shore, northwest shore and south shore (see map)
Boat Ramp: Concrete
Accommodations: Resort; motel; campground

Shoreland zoning classification: General Development
Dominant forest/soil type: Deciduous/Sand
Management class: Walleye-Centrarchid
Ecological type: Centrarchid-Walleye

FISH STOCKING DATA

year	species	size	# released
90	Muskellunge	Fingerling	3,014
90	Muskellunge	Yearling	5
90	Walleye	Fingerling	28,648
90	Walleye	Yearling	615
94	Muskellunge	Fingerling	3,000
95	Walleye	Fingerling	43,422
95	Walleye	Yearling	5
95	Muskellunge	Fingerling	3,000
96	Muskellunge	Fingerling	3,010

NET CATCH DATA

survey date: 8/8/94

species	Gill Nets # per net	Gill Nets avg fish wt. (lbs.)	Trap Nets # per set	Trap Nets avg fish wt. (lbs.)
Black Bullhead	10.5	0.66	0.5	0.59
Black Crappie	0.1	0.29	0.4	0.36
Bluegill	13.4	0.16	59.9	0.16
Bowfin (Dogfish)	-	-	0.1	5.73
Brown Bullhead	6.6	0.70	1.8	0.48
Green Sunfish	-	-	0.3	0.05
Hybrid Sunfish	0.4	0.19	4.8	0.20
Largemouth Bass	-	-	0.5	0.81
Muskellunge	trace	2.56	-	-
Northern Pike	6.4	1.44	0.9	1.93
Pumpkin. Sunfish	1.9	0.13	3.6	0.15
Rock Bass	trace	0.66	trace	0.56
Tullibee (Cisco)	2.4	0.87	-	-
Walleye	6.9	1.57	0.2	2.62
White Sucker	1.4	2.62	0.2	1.94
Yellow Bullhead	26.3	0.49	10.4	0.43
Yellow Perch	2.4	0.08	2.6	0.10

LENGTH OF SELECTED SPECIES SAMPLED FROM ALL GEAR
Number of fish caught for the following length categories (inches):

species	0-5	6-8	9-11	12-14	15-19	20-24	25-29	>30	Total
Black Bullhead	-	7	149	-	-	-	-	-	156
Black Crappie	-	7	2	-	-	-	-	-	9
Bluegill	314	260	-	-	-	-	-	-	574
Brown Bullhead	-	9	110	8	-	-	-	-	127
Green Sunfish	6	-	-	-	-	-	-	-	6
Hybrid Sunfish	48	49	-	-	-	-	-	-	97
Largemouth Bass	4	-	-	4	1	-	-	-	9
Muskellunge	-	-	-	-	-	1	-	-	1
Northern Pike	-	-	4	15	50	22	15	1	107
Pumpkin. Sunfish	67	27	-	-	-	-	-	-	94
Rock Bass	-	-	2	-	-	-	-	-	2
Tullibee (Cisco)	-	12	7	4	10	-	-	-	33
Walleye	-	-	5	33	49	10	3	-	100
Yellow Bullhead	6	158	249	2	-	-	-	-	415
Yellow Perch	54	28	1	-	-	-	-	-	83

DNR COMMENTS: Lake holds good populations of Northern Pike, Black Crappie, Largemouth Bass and Walleye, and a trophy population of Muskellunge is being established. Bluegills are overabundant, slow-growing and small.

FISHING INFORMATION: Perhaps due to the nearness of the town or because it's in the middle of a vast recreational area, Detroit Lake is often overlooked. In fact, it is a very good Walleyes spot, an early source for Largemouth Bass and an excellent panfish lake. Detroit is a 3,083 acre expanse with a shore length of 12.4 miles and a water clarity of about 6 feet. The more shallow eastern section of the lake, Little Detroit, generally warms up faster than the western section and is a good spot to try for early Bass and panfish in the emergent weedbeds at the Pelican River outlet and along the southern shore, particularly in holes along the sandbar at mid-lake. (Not the same as the shallow bar that separates Little from Big Detroit to the west.) Another good early spot is just off the Pelican River inlet on the north end of Big Detroit. For one more early Bass spot, head to the southwest corner of Big Detroit and fish the narrows going into Deadshot Bay. Then fish the bay itself, casting into the weedbreaks. In summer, use live bait rigs with shiners, nightcrawlers or leeches. For Walleyes, drift the bars and humps along the eastern shore of Big Detroit and jig the 15-20 foot breaks in the 60- to 80-foot holes along the southern shore. In summer, find the sunken hump out from the southwestern point at the start of the narrows leading to Deadshot. Detroit's many Northerns will find you in any of these spots as well.

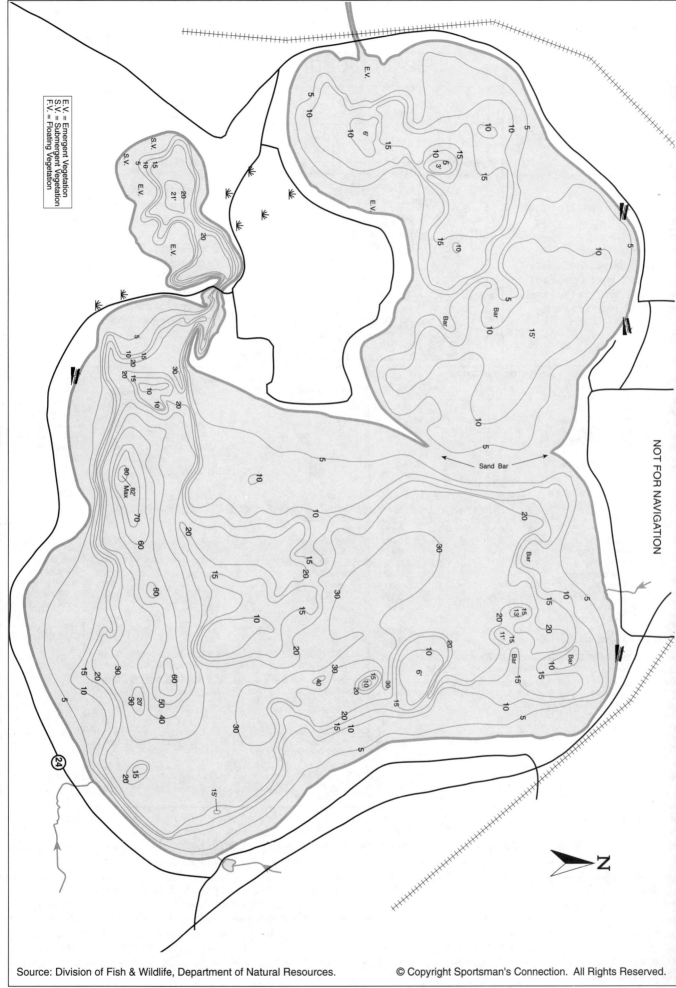

E.V. = Emergent Vegetation
S.V. = Submergent Vegetation
F.V. = Floating Vegetation

N

FLOYD LAKE

Becker County

Location: Township 139 Range 41
Watershed: Otter Tail
Surface Water Area: 1,212 Acres
Shorelength: 5.8 Miles
Secchi disk (water clarity): 14.0 Ft.
Water color: Clear
Cause of water color: NA
Maximum depth: 34 Ft.
Median depth: 9 Ft.
Accessibility: Public access on southeast shore
Boat Ramp: Concrete
Accommodations: Resort
Shoreland zoning classif.: Rec. Dev.
Dominant forest/soil type: Decid/Sand
Management class: Walleye-Centrarchid
Ecological type: Centrarchid-Walleye

LITTLE FLOYD LAKE

Location: Township 139 Range 41
Watershed: Otter Tail
Surface Water Area: 205 Acres
Shorelength: 2.2 Miles
Secchi disk (water clarity): 8.5 Ft.
Water color: Green
Cause of water color: Moderate algae bloom
Maximum depth: 32 Ft.
Median depth: 17 Ft.
Accessibility: Public access on south shore
Boat Ramp: Concrete
Accommodations: Resorts
Shoreland zoning classif.: Rec. Dev.
Dominant forest/soil type: Decid/Sand
Management class: Walleye-Centrarchid
Ecological type: Centrarchid-Walleye

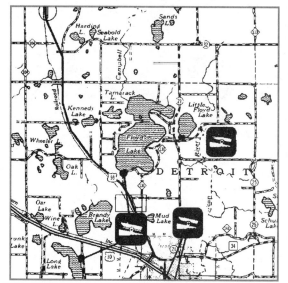

FLOYD LAKE

DNR COMMENTS:
Northern Pike catch is lowest ever recorded but near third quartile range for lake class; mean weight up and 20 percent above statewide average; 83 percent of sample less than 25 inches. Walleye numbers near bottom of normal range; mean weight is up to 2.6 lb.; growth rate about average; natural reproduction occurring. Largemouth Bass and Black Crappie populations stable; growth rates normal. Bluegill numbers above normal range; growth slow. Yellow Perch population about average for lake class. Yellow Bullhead numbers lowest since 1950s.

FISH STOCKING DATA

year	species	size	# released
87	Walleye	Fingerling	11,626
89	Walleye	Fingerling	33,066
93	Walleye	Fingerling	31,645
95	Walleye	Yearling	1,687
95	Walleye	Fingerling	2,325
95	Walleye	Adult	17
96	Walleye	Fingerling	28,545

survey date: 6/24/96

NET CATCH DATA

	Gill Nets		Trap Nets	
species	# per net	avg fish wt. (lbs)	# per set	avg fish wt. (lbs)
Black Crappie	0.4	0.98	0.5	0.16
Bluegill	13.0	0.24	76.4	0.21
Green Sunfish	0.3	0.06	0.9	0.12
Hybrid Sunfish	1.9	0.11	8.1	0.23
Largemouth Bass	-	-	0.8	0.48
Northern Pike	8.0	2.36	0.2	2.03
Pumpkin. Sunfish	1.8	0.07	3.2	0.13
Rock Bass	2.0	0.41	3.1	0.36
Tullibee (Cisco)	0.1	3.08	-	-
Walleye	4.5	2.61	0.4	1.39
Yellow Perch	23.1	0.19	0.2	0.06

LENGTH OF SELECTED SPECIES SAMPLED FROM ALL GEAR
Number of fish caught for the following length categories (inches):

species	0-5	6-8	9-11	12-14	15-19	20-24	25-29	>30	Total
Black Crappie	2	4	2	1	-	-	-	-	9
Bluegill	125	199	-	-	-	-	-	-	324
Green Sunfish	13	-	-	-	-	-	-	-	13
Hybrid Sunfish	44	68	-	-	-	-	-	-	112
Largemouth Bass	-	5	3	2	-	-	-	-	10
Northern Pike	-	-	-	1	25	25	9	6	66
Pumpkin. Sunfish	38	14	-	-	-	-	-	-	52
Rock Bass	14	27	12	-	-	-	-	-	53
Tullibee (Cisco)	-	-	-	-	-	1	-	-	1
Walleye	2	1	3	5	12	17	1	-	41
Yellow Perch	49	101	14	-	-	-	-	-	164

LITTLE FLOYD LAKE

FISH STOCKING DATA

year	species	size	# released
88	Walleye	Fingerling	7,500
88	Walleye	Yearling	48
90	Walleye	Fingerling	3,000
94	Walleye	Fingerling	6,270
96	Walleye	Fingerling	2,310

survey date: 6/17/96

NET CATCH DATA

	Gill Nets		Trap Nets	
species	# per net	avg fish wt. (lbs)	# per set	avg fish wt. (lbs)
Black Crappie	-	-	0.3	0.38
Bluegill	3.4	0.18	83.7	0.20
Green Sunfish	0.2	0.19	25.3	0.07
Hybrid Sunfish	-	-	18.3	0.16
Largemouth Bass	-	-	0.7	0.76
Northern Pike	26.0	1.83	0.1	2.20
Pumpkin. Sunfish	-	-	4.9	0.14
Rock Bass	-	-	0.4	0.63
Tullibee (Cisco)	5.2	2.33	-	-
Walleye	2.8	2.58	0.4	2.31
Yellow Perch	21.8	0.15	3.3	0.41

LENGTH OF SELECTED SPECIES SAMPLED FROM ALL GEAR
Number of fish caught for the following length categories (inches):

species	0-5	6-8	9-11	12-14	15-19	20-24	25-29	>30	Total
Black Crappie	-	2	1	-	-	-	-	-	3
Bluegill	112	96	-	-	-	-	-	-	208
Green Sunfish	141	4	-	-	-	-	-	-	145
Hybrid Sunfish	74	46	-	-	-	-	-	-	120
Largemouth Bass	-	3	2	-	1	-	-	-	6
Northern Pike	-	-	-	2	62	55	10	2	131
Pumpkin. Sunfish	23	21	-	-	-	-	-	-	44
Rock Bass	-	1	3	-	-	-	-	-	4
Tullibee (Cisco)	-	-	1	2	23	-	-	-	26
Walleye	-	-	6	-	5	4	3	-	18
Yellow Perch	30	80	14	4	-	-	-	-	128

DNR COMMENTS:
Northern Pike, Largemouth Bass, and Panfish populations high. Walleyes numbers about average, but size structure very good; this species is stocked regularly, but numbers actually were higher during 1960s, when stocking was not taking place. Ciscoes present. Black Bullheads scarce, reflecting relatively good water quality.

FISHING INFORMATION: These lakes two miles north of Detroit Lakes are dominated by Northern Pike and panfish but also have good Largemouth Bass populations and some Walleyes. They are also loaded with Yellow Bullheads. **Floyd Lake** is relatively shallow, particularly the well weeded south end. Fish for Crappies over the weeds with minnows under a slip bobber; sometimes the weeds can run down to 20 feet. Or, use a jig with something juicy on it to get Bass coming your way. The broad flats extending over most of the south end can be very productive for Northerns. Anglers we spoke with in Detroit Lakes advised fishing with a bottom rig and live bait, such as leeches, in the spring. The north end of the lake is fairly deep but has good weeds that can be fished for Bluegills and Bass. The narrow area between the bays is often excellent. There isn't great Walleye habitat in the lake, but the rock piles in the opening between the bays holds promise bet early in the season. In summer, bigger fish will head into deeper water during the day. **Little Floyd** is smaller, but quite similar: a deep weedline, relatively shallow water and good populations of Northerns and panfish, with some nice Largemouth Bass. The vegetation on all four sides of the lake is where you're going to find the Bass and panfish. The water is clear and the weeds deep, so you may want to use a slip bobber to put your bait down to the weed tops. The Northerns are at the deep weed edges. You can troll these slowly with leeches or shiner minnows.

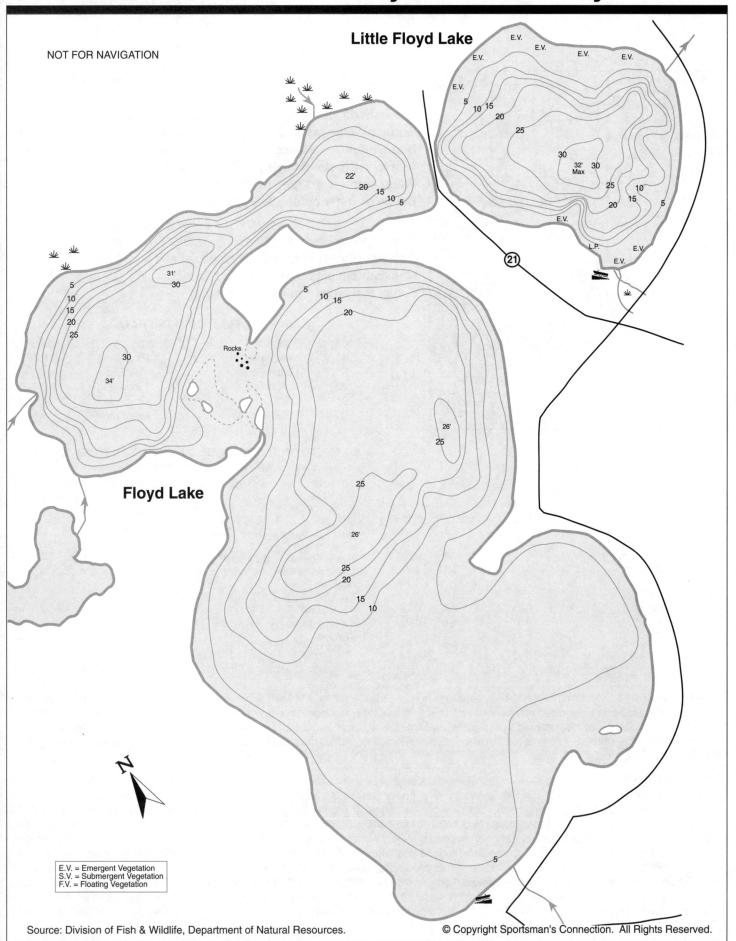

Little Floyd Lake

NOT FOR NAVIGATION

Floyd Lake

N

E.V. = Emergent Vegetation
S.V. = Submergent Vegetation
F.V. = Floating Vegetation

LONG LAKE
Becker County

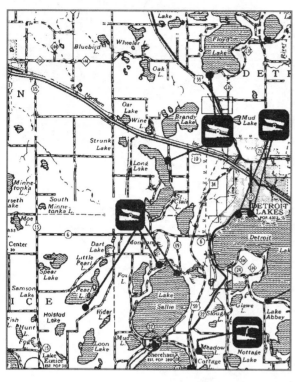

Location: Township 138, 139 Range 41
Watershed: Otter Tail
Surface Water Area: 357 Acres
Shorelength: 5.9 Miles
Secchi disk (water clarity): 12.0 Ft.
Water color: Light green
Cause of water color: Very light algae

Maximum depth: 61 Ft.
Median depth: 20 Ft.
Accessibility: State-owned public access near city park on northeast shore
Boat Ramp: Concrete
Accommodations: Resorts; campground

Shoreland zoning classification: Natural Environment
Dominant forest/soil type: Deciduous/Sand
Management class: Walleye-Centrarchid
Ecological type: Centrarchid-Walleye

FISH STOCKING DATA

year	species	size	# released
88	Walleye	Fingerling	6,685
88	Walleye	Yearling	96
90	Walleye	Fingerling	2,475
94	Walleye	Fingerling	4,160
96	Walleye	Fingerling	3,100

NET CATCH DATA

survey date: 6/26/95

species	Gill Nets # per net	Gill Nets avg fish wt. (lbs.)	Trap Nets # per set	Trap Nets avg fish wt. (lbs.)
Black Crappie	-	-	0.2	0.42
Bluegill	4.5	0.13	107.4	0.19
Green Sunfish	-	-	1.4	0.07
Hybrid Sunfish	0.3	0.31	9.8	0.25
Largemouth Bass	0.3	0.79	1.3	0.18
Northern Pike	31.5	1.20	0.5	1.20
Pumpkin. Sunfish	1.1	0.29	2.9	0.24
Rock Bass	3.9	0.41	4.3	0.41
Tullibee (Cisco)	3.1	1.17	-	-
Walleye	3.6	2.10	0.3	1.61
Yellow Perch	2.5	0.14	-	-

LENGTH OF SELECTED SPECIES SAMPLED FROM ALL GEAR

Number of fish caught for the following length categories (inches):

species	0-5	6-8	9-11	12-14	15-19	20-24	25-29	>30	Total
Black Bullhead	-	-	3	3	-	-	-	-	6
Black Crappie	-	-	2	-	-	-	-	-	2
Bluegill	151	220	-	-	-	-	-	-	371
Brown Bullhead	-	-	7	9	-	-	-	-	16
Green Sunfish	17	-	-	-	-	-	-	-	17
Hybrid Sunfish	33	87	-	-	-	-	-	-	120
Largemouth Bass	7	7	4	-	-	-	-	-	18
Northern Pike	-	-	9	68	131	37	11	2	258
Pumpkin. Sunfish	8	36	-	-	-	-	-	-	44
Rock Bass	5	74	4	-	-	-	-	-	83
Tullibee (Cisco)	-	6	7	7	5	-	-	-	25
Walleye	-	1	-	-	26	5	-	-	32
Yellow Perch	4	16	-	-	-	-	-	-	20

DNR COMMENTS: Northern Pike numbers unusually high, nearly four times the level expected for lake class; majority of Pike are age 2 to 4; growth rate normal. Walleye numbers down but still normal for lake class; average size is up to 18.2 inches. Largemouth Bass not adequately sampled, but test nets did indicate a significant number of year-old Bass; growth appears fast, and this species should offer good angling opportunities in the future. Black Crappie, Cisco, Rock Bass and Bullheads present in modest numbers. Angling for all these species can be good at times.

FISHING INFORMATION: Long Lake, in the western suburbs of Detroit Lakes, is a nice amenity for a back yard; thus most of the homes around this lake are permanent. Long stretches out over nearly 6 miles of shore. It's is very clear, with a secchi reading of 12 feet. One of the features here is shore fishing at the city park on the northeast shore. Otherwise there are patches of cattails and weedbeds all around the shoreline and a series of drops and holes, descending as deep as 60 feet. Long is stocked regularly with Walleyes even though the DNR also reports that natural reproduction is high. Walleyes number around the local median-level, and Northern Pike are *four times* the local median. This, of course, is both good and bad. The Northerns have depleted the Yellow Perch population, resulting in average Walleye and Northern size smaller than it has been historically. On the plus side, the Bluegill population has grown steadily, and the Crappies are decent-size. All this means that Long works fine as a city recreational and family lake. For panfish, Bass and Crappies, anglers cast along the shoreline weedbeds or move off to 10 to 15 feet and drop live bait on a slip bobber, adding a sucker minnow if the target is a roving Northern. Later in spring, Walleye anglers probe the slopes of the holes with jigs carrying shiners, nightcrawlers or leeches.

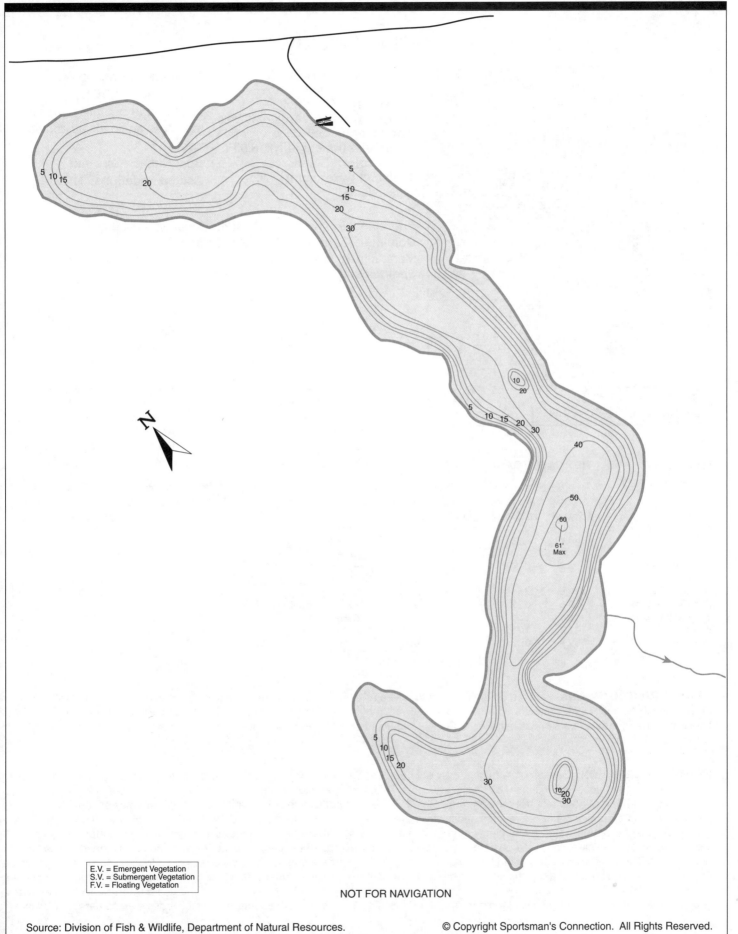

E.V. = Emergent Vegetation
S.V. = Submergent Vegetation
F.V. = Floating Vegetation

NOT FOR NAVIGATION

Source: Division of Fish & Wildlife, Department of Natural Resources.

LAKE SALLIE
Becker County

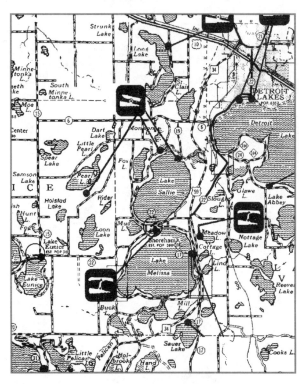

Location: Township 138 Range 41
Watershed: Otter Tail
Surface Water Area: 1,246 Acres
Shorelength: 5.6 Miles
Secchi disk (water clarity): 13.0 Ft.
Water color: Green
Cause of water color: Mild algae bloom

Maximum depth: 50 Ft.
Median depth: 16 Ft.
Accessibility: State-owned public access on northeast and northwest shores
Boat Ramp: Concrete
Accommodations: NA

Shoreland zoning classification: General Development
Dominant forest/soil type: Decid/Sand
Management class: Walleye-Centrarchid
Ecological type: Centrarchid-Walleye

FISH STOCKING DATA

year	species	size	# released
93	Walleye	Fry	3,313,887
93	Walleye	Fingerling	23,020
94	Walleye	Fry	4,071,100
94	Walleye	Fingerling	16,520
95	Walleye	Fry	3,993,000
95	Walleye	Fingerling	4,135
95	Walleye	Yearling	577
95	Walleye	Adult	56
96	Walleye	Fry	8,186,745
96	Walleye	Fingerling	21,213

NET CATCH DATA

survey date: 7/18/94

species	Gill Nets # per net	Gill Nets avg fish wt. (lbs.)	Trap Nets # per set	Trap Nets avg fish wt. (lbs.)
Black Crappie	0.6	0.81	-	-
Bluegill	3.4	0.35	1.2	0.12
Green Sunfish	-	-	0.3	0.01
Hybrid Sunfish	0.9	0.24	3.4	0.12
Largemouth Bass	-	-	0.3	1.64
Northern Pike	2.8	3.54	trace	2.33
Pumpkin. Sunfish	0.5	0.22	0.2	0.08
Tullibee (Cisco)	12.1	1.01	-	-
Walleye	11.9	1.75	1.6	1.30
Yellow Perch	63.3	0.13	12.7	0.10

LENGTH OF SELECTED SPECIES SAMPLED FROM ALL GEAR

Number of fish caught for the following length categories (inches):

species	0-5	6-8	9-11	12-14	15-19	20-24	25-29	>30	Total
Black Crappie	-	-	4	1	-	-	-	-	5
Bluegill	12	29	-	-	-	-	-	-	41
Green Sunfish	4	-	-	-	-	-	-	-	4
Hybrid Sunfish	29	19	-	-	-	-	-	-	48
Largemouth Bass	-	2	-	1	1	-	-	-	4
Northern Pike	-	-	-	2	3	7	7	4	23
Pumpkin. Sunfish	4	2	-	-	-	-	-	-	6
Tullibee (Cisco)	-	47	1	17	32	-	-	-	97
Walleye	-	34	14	8	32	23	3	-	114
Yellow Perch	149	188	-	-	-	-	-	-	337

DNR COMMENTS: Walleye numbers up significantly to well above the normal range for lake class; average weight a healthy 1.7 lb; growth good. Northern Pike numbers up to low end of normal range; large numbers of yearling pike captured at spawn may indicate a future increase in the numbers of catchable fish. Bluegill numbers low. Yellow Perch numbers increasing. All three species of Bullheads present and increasing in number.

FISHING INFORMATION: Because of a huge supply of forage like Yellow Perch or other favorable conditions, the Northern Pike population in a lake will explode. This happened a few years ago at Lake Sallie, and lots of big fish are still being pulled out. Northerns average 2.5 pounds, and 7- to 8-pounders are reported regularly. The Walleye population is very abundant, and, strangely enough, size is fairly good, averaging around 1 3/4 lb. Crappies, meanwhile, are big and fairly numerous, but Bluegill numbers are way down. Sallie is a classic Detroit Lakes-area water: it has plenty of bars, sunken humps, a shoreline with large bulrush patches and water clarity up to 13 feet. Walleyes are mainly found in the eastern end of the lake, especially at 15 to 20 feet around the sunken island a quarter-mile straight out from the Pelican River inlet and in the bars and sunken humps just off the northern shore. Bass will be found along the bulrushes on that same northern shore and along the southern bulrushes as well. The main Northern site is the big bar reaching out from the southern shore at mid lake. Drift a live bait rig with a sucker minnow near the bottom at 10 to 15 feet around this bar for the lunker Northerns. Drop a crawler or leech on a light line at the bulrushes for Bass. Or jig shiners, crawlers and leeches off those sunken bars for Walleyes.

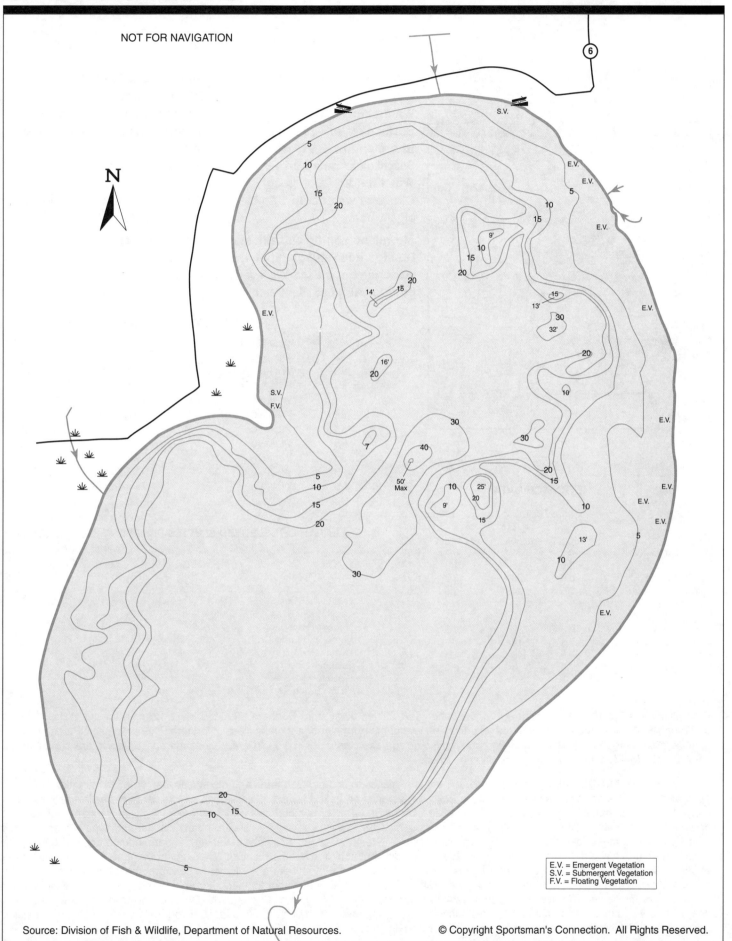

SPORTSMAN'S Connection®

NOT FOR NAVIGATION

N

E.V. = Emergent Vegetation
S.V. = Submergent Vegetation
F.V. = Floating Vegetation

Source: Division of Fish & Wildlife, Department of Natural Resources.

LAKE MELISSA
Becker County

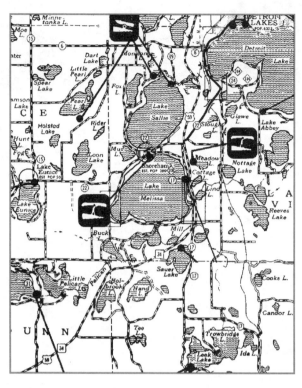

Location: Township 138 Range 41, 42
Watershed: Otter Tail
Surface Water Area: 1,830 Acres
Shorelength: 6.9 Miles
Secchi disk (water clarity): 7.0 Ft.
Water color: Light green
Cause of water color: Light algal bloom

Maximum depth: 43 Ft.
Median depth: NA
Accessibility: State-owned public access on east central shore and carry down on north shore
Boat Ramp: Concrete; carry down
Accommodations: Resorts and campgrounds

Shoreland zoning classification: General Development
Dominant forest/soil type: Deciduous/Sand
Management class: Walleye-Centrarchid
Ecological type: Centrarchid-Walleye

FISH STOCKING DATA

year	species	size	# released
93	Walleye	Fry	1,980,000
93	Walleye	Fingerling	32,224
93	Walleye	Yearling	354
94	Walleye	Fry	1,104,000
94	Walleye	Fingerling	20,667
95	Walleye	Fry	2,044,900
95	Walleye	Fingerling	5,358
95	Walleye	Yearling	1,099
95	Walleye	Adult	55
96	Walleye	Fingerling	24,335
96	Walleye	Adult	77

NET CATCH DATA

survey date: 7/18/94

species	Gill Nets # per net	Gill Nets avg fish wt. (lbs.)	Trap Nets # per set	Trap Nets avg fish wt. (lbs.)
Black Crappie	0.5	0.51	0.4	0.33
Bluegill	59.6	0.15	101.8	0.14
Hybrid Sunfish	0.8	0.26	8.8	0.15
Largemouth Bass	0.6	0.94	0.9	0.83
Northern Pike	3.8	2.44	0.4	1.31
Pumpkin. Sunfish	2.9	0.12	1.4	0.14
Rock Bass	0.3	0.22	0.7	0.28
Tullibee (Cisco)	5.6	1.14	-	-
Walleye	7.9	1.46	1.4	1.65
Yellow Perch	20.8	0.10	2.0	0.12

LENGTH OF SELECTED SPECIES SAMPLED FROM ALL GEAR
Number of fish caught for the following length categories (inches):

species	0-5	6-8	9-11	12-14	15-19	20-24	25-29	>30	Total
Black Crappie	-	4	5	-	-	-	-	-	9
Bluegill	306	204	-	-	-	-	-	-	510
Hybrid Sunfish	75	36	-	-	-	-	-	-	111
Largemouth Bass	2	4	4	5	1	-	-	-	16
Northern Pike	-	-	3	9	7	4	12	-	35
Pumpkin. Sunfish	29	11	-	-	-	-	-	-	40
Rock Bass	3	7	-	-	-	-	-	-	10
Tullibee (Cisco)	-	14	-	12	19	-	-	-	45
Walleye	-	8	18	14	27	12	1	-	80
Yellow Perch	67	91	-	-	-	-	-	-	158

DNR COMMENTS: During the last decade, the fishery has shifted away from Northern Pike and Black Crappie toward Walleye, Cisco and Bluegill. Walleye and Cisco numbers near the high end of the normal range for lake class. Northern Pike and Yellow Perch numbers near normal. Largemouth Bass population about average for lake class, but spawning areas endangered. Bluegills are abundant but small in Lake Melissa; mean length is less than 6 inches.

FISHING INFORMATION: In recent years one of the surest places to find big Northerns and nice Walleyes in the Detroit Lakes area has been along the bars and breaks just south of the Pelican River inlet on Lake Melissa. Melissa has a broad area of shallow flats along its eastern shore that harbor a good supply of forage fish. There also are some nice holes up to 37 feet, along with bars and humps, that provide gamefish with good mid-summer structure. This is an 1,830 acre lake with 6.9 miles of nearly circular shoreline, water clarity of over 7 feet and a mostly sandy bottom. Walleyes like it here. A depthfinder will be helpful in finding the bars, humps and holes that generally run west of a line directly from the Pelican River inlet to its outlet on the southern shore. There is another patch of similar structure about a half mile northwest of the outlet. Jig the slopes of these bars with shiners and nightcrawlers from springtime onward, moving steadily outward into the holes as the water warms. Without a depthfinder, stay about 20 feet out from the weedlines. Cast a slip bobber with a sucker minnow for Northerns or drop a leech or crawler on a light line just off the reeds for Bass, Crappies or fat Bluegills. For a change of pace, motor over to the bay in the southwest corner and drop a live bait rig with a leech along the sides of the hole just inside the point that sticks up from the southern shore. You should find Bass.

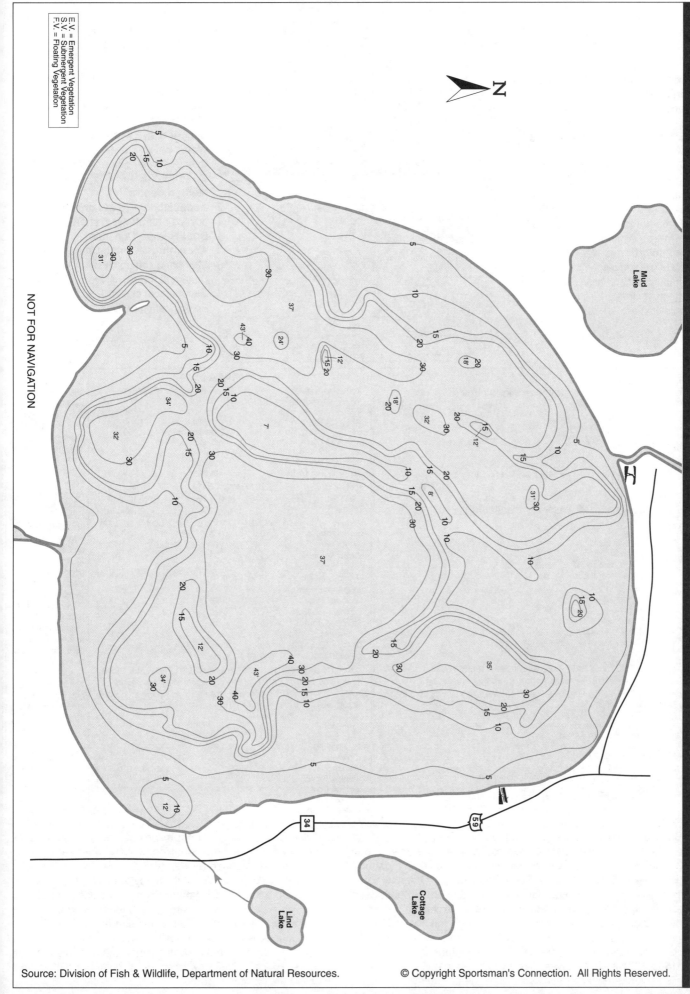

E.V. = Emergent Vegetation
S.V. = Submergent Vegetation
F.V. = Floating Vegetation

NOT FOR NAVIGATION

N

Mud Lake

Cottage Lake

Lind Lake

34

59

Source: Division of Fish & Wildlife, Department of Natural Resources.

SAUER LAKE

MEADOW LAKE

Becker County

Location: Township 137, 138 Range 41
Watershed: Otter Tail
Surface Water Area: 212 Acres
Shorelength: 2.8 Miles
Secchi disk (water clarity): 12.0 Ft.
Water color: Green
Cause of water color: Algae bloom
Maximum depth: 39 Ft.
Median depth: NA
Accessibility: State-owned public access on north shore, off U.S. #59
Boat Ramp: Asphalt
Accommodations: NA
Shoreland zoning classif.: Rec. Dev.
Dominant forest/soil type: NA
Management class: Walleye-Centrarchid
Ecological type: Centrarchid

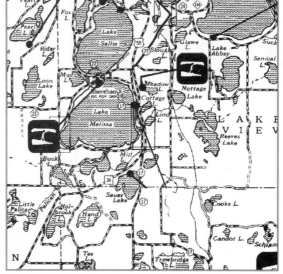

Location: Township 138 Range 41
Watershed: Otter Tail
Surface Water Area: 66 Acres
Shorelength: NA
Secchi disk (water clarity): 9.3 Ft.
Water color: Green
Cause of water color: Algae bloom
Maximum depth: 72 Ft.
Median depth: NA
Accessibility: State-owned public access on northwest shore, off U.S. #59
Boat Ramp: Concrete
Accommodations: Campground
Shoreland zoning classif.: Nat. Env.
Dominant forest/soil type: NA
Management class: Trout
Ecological type: Unclassified

DNR COMMENTS:
Northern Pike, Yellow Perch and Largemouth Bass numbers up to above normal range for lake class. Walleye numbers likewise high; the population consists mainly of stocked fish. Bluegill population stable and near high end of the normal range. Black Crappie and Black Bullhead, two species which favor turbid water, are less numerous; both populations below normal. Channel Catfish sampled in low numbers; mean weight 3.3 lb.; this species originally stocked illegally; then population was supplemented by DNR stockings in the 1980s.

FISH STOCKING DATA

year	species	size	# released
93	Walleye	Fingerling	2,520
95	Walleye	Fingerling	2,650
96	Walleye	Fingerling	2,805

survey date: 6/19/95

NET CATCH DATA

	Gill Nets		Trap Nets	
species	# per net	avg fish wt. (lbs)	# per set	avg fish wt. (lbs)
Black Crappie	-	-	0.1	0.07
Bluegill	13.0	0.29	37.7	0.24
Channel Catfish	1.5	3.28	-	-
Green Sunfish	-	-	0.9	0.05
Hybrid Sunfish	1.8	0.37	12.7	0.22
Largemouth Bass	2.3	0.59	1.8	0.62
Northern Pike	22.8	2.10	-	-
Pumpkin. Sunfish	1.0	0.28	2.7	0.17
Walleye	7.5	1.13	0.3	3.28
White Sucker	0.5	3.21	-	-
Yellow Bullhead	5.3	0.59	8.3	0.45
Yellow Perch	56.0	0.14	0.6	0.21

LENGTH OF SELECTED SPECIES SAMPLED FROM ALL GEAR
Number of fish caught for the following length categories (inches):

species	0-5	6-8	9-11	12-14	15-19	20-24	25-29	>30	Total
Black Crappie	1	-	-	-	-	-	-	-	1
Bluegill	47	173	-	-	-	-	-	-	220
Channel Catfish	-	-	-	4	1	1	-	-	6
Green Sunfish	8	-	-	-	-	-	-	-	8
Hybrid Sunfish	35	80	-	-	-	-	-	-	115
Largemouth Bass	1	6	13	5	-	-	-	-	25
Northern Pike	-	-	-	-	55	28	3	5	91
Pumpkin. Sunfish	15	13	-	-	-	-	-	-	28
Walleye	-	-	16	1	13	2	1	-	33
Yellow Bullhead	1	29	65	1	-	-	-	-	96
Yellow Perch	24	87	-	-	-	-	-	-	111

FISH STOCKING DATA

year	species	size	# released
93	Rainbow Trout	Yearling	1,500
93	Brown Trout	Yearling	750
94	Rainbow Trout	Yearling	1,500
94	Brown Trout	Yearling	750
95	Rainbow Trout	Yearling	1,500
95	Brown Trout	Yearling	750
96	Rainbow Trout	Yearling	1,500
06	Brown Trout	Yearling	750

survey date: 7/11/94

NET CATCH DATA

	Gill Nets		Trap Nets	
species	# per net	avg fish wt. (lbs)	# per set	avg fish wt. (lbs)
Black Crappie	0.3	0.23	1.3	0.46
Bluegill	3.8	0.14	100.2	0.15
Brown Trout	1.5	0.38	-	-
Green Sunfish	-	-	1.9	0.05
Hybrid Sunfish	5.3	0.10	28.1	0.10
Largemouth Bass	-	-	1.1	0.32
Northern Pike	1.8	3.72	0.2	1.12
Pumpkin. Sunfish	0.3	0.29	9.2	0.10
Rainbow Trout	5.3	0.45	-	-
Rock Bass	-	-	0.1	0.28
Tullibee (Cisco)	40.8	0.46	-	-
Yellow Perch	0.8	0.12	1.3	0.25

LENGTH OF SELECTED SPECIES SAMPLED FROM ALL GEAR
Number of fish caught for the following length categories (inches):

species	0-5	6-8	9-11	12-14	15-19	20-24	25-29	>30	Total
Black Crappie	-	5	8	-	-	-	-	-	13
Bluegill	180	64	-	-	-	-	-	-	244
Brown Trout	-	1	5	-	-	-	-	-	6
Green Sunfish	16	1	-	-	-	-	-	-	17
Hybrid Sunfish	167	37	-	-	-	-	-	-	204
Largemouth Bass	1	7	1	1	-	-	-	-	10
Northern Pike	-	-	-	-	2	3	3	1	9
Pumpkin. Sunfish	76	8	-	-	-	-	-	-	84
Rainbow Trout	-	-	17	4	-	-	-	-	21
Rock Bass	-	1	-	-	-	-	-	-	1
Tullibee (Cisco)	-	-	91	6	-	-	-	-	97
Yellow Perch	1	12	2	-	-	-	-	-	15

DNR COMMENTS:
Lake is managed as a two-story Trout lake; Rainbow and Brown Trout yearlings stocked annually. Cisco numbers up substantially and above normal range for lake class. Rapid growth rates for scarce Northern Pike, which prey on Ciscoes. Bluegill numbers good, but size structure has deteriorated; only 26 percent of fish reach 6- to 8-inch range. Largemouth Bass numbers within normal range. Black Crappie population likewise normal; half of population larger than 10 inches.

FISHING INFORMATION: Down Hwy. 59, outside Detroit Lakes, are big lakes with familiar names. Four miles out, you pass little Meadow Lake before you know it. Then there's big Lake Melissa on your right and, right after that, another small one called Sauer Lake. Don't overlook these little waters. **Meadow**, at 66 acres, is basically just one hole of 72 feet surrounded by weedy shoreline. Within the hole, though, is a slew of Ciscoes, Yellow Perch and panfish. Given all those forage fish and some regular stocking by the DNR, Meadow has thriving populations of Brown and Rainbow Trout, and Largemouth Bass. And there are a few large Northern Pike. All species are well fed. You're going to have to convince them to make an exception for you. The Bass will stay in the shore area and deeper weedbreaks but the Northerns and Trout will suspend. Cast lures or drift live bait like a sucker minnow at 10 to 20 feet along the shore and 15 to 20 feet or deeper farther out. Meadow is a challenge but there's a payoff. **Sauer**, at 212 acres, is best known for Largemouth Bass, but it provides good size in nearly all gamefish. The lake is not hard to read. There is a big sunken hump just off the north shore. Jig live bait there at 15 to 20 feet for Walleyes. Then traverse the entire lake - it's 2.8 miles - at 20 feet. Cast toward shore or trail a live bait rig until you find fish. Northerns tend to find you. Pay attention to the shoreline in the bay at the northwest corner.

NOT FOR NAVIGATION

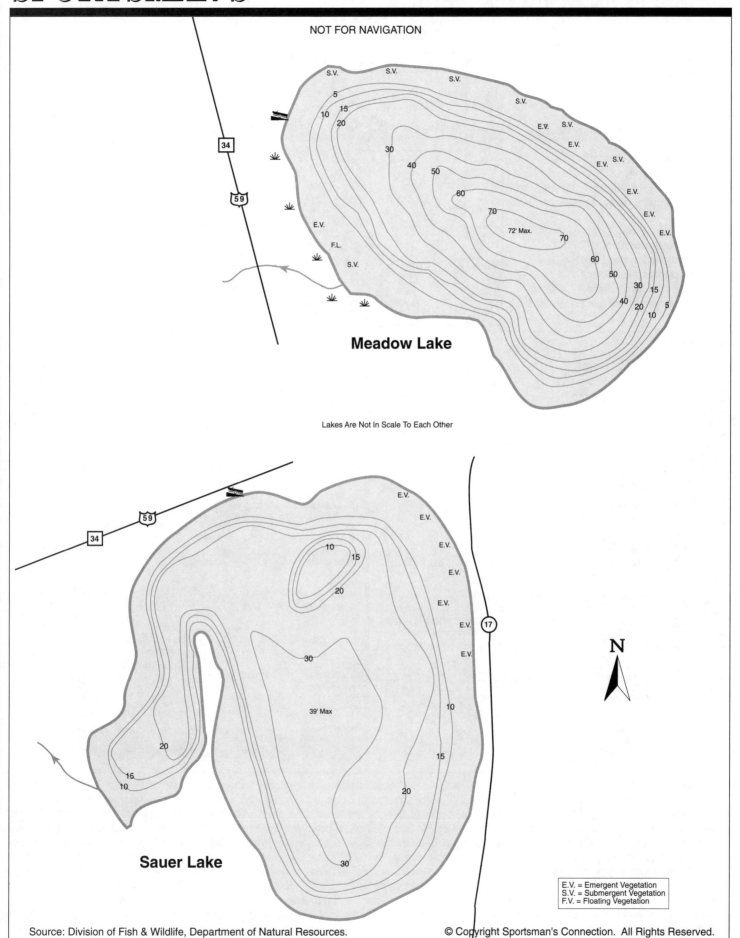

Meadow Lake

Lakes Are Not In Scale To Each Other

Sauer Lake

N

E.V. = Emergent Vegetation
S.V. = Submergent Vegetation
F.V. = Floating Vegetation

Source: Division of Fish & Wildlife, Department of Natural Resources.

MUNSON LAKE

Becker County

PEARL LAKE

Location: Township 138   Range 41
Watershed: Otter Tail
Surface Water Area: 123 Acres
Shorelength: NA
Secchi disk (water clarity): 7.0 Ft.
Water color: Green
Cause of water color: Moderate algae bloom
Maximum depth: 26 Ft.
Median depth: NA
Accessibility: State-owned public access on the southeast corner of the lake
Boat Ramp: Earth
Accommodations: NA
Shoreland zoning classif.: Rec. Dev.
Dominant forest/soil type: NA
Management class: Walleye-Centrarchid
Ecological type: Centrarchid-Walleye

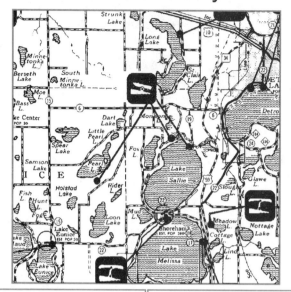

Location: Township 138   Range 42
Watershed: Otter Tail
Surface Water Area: 237 Acres
Shorelength: 3.7 Miles
Secchi disk (water clarity): NA
Water color: NA
Cause of water color: NA
Maximum depth: 54 Ft.
Median depth: 14 Ft.
Accessibility: State-owned public access on south shore
Boat Ramp: Concrete
Accommodations: NA
Shoreland zoning classif.: Rec. Dev.
Dominant forest/soil type: Decid/Wet
Management class: Walleye-Centrarchid
Ecological type: Centrarchid

DNR COMMENTS:
Northern Pike numbers below normal for lake class; size structure has improved, however, with the average fish weighing 4.9 lb. Walleye population about normal; good average size of 3.3 lb. Largemouth Bass numbers about normal. Black Crappie population down to below normal range; size range decreasing, indicating larger fish are being "cropped off" by anglers. Bluegill numbers high; angler cropping occurring. Yellow Perch numbers normal.

FISH STOCKING DATA

year	species	size	# released
90	Walleye	Fingerling	700
90	Walleye	Yearling	71
94	Walleye	Fingerling	525
94	Walleye	Yearling	80

survey date: 8/1/94

NET CATCH DATA

	Gill Nets		Trap Nets	
species	# per net	avg fish wt. (lbs)	# per set	avg fish wt. (lbs)
Black Crappie	-	-	0.6	0.15
Bluegill	1.3	0.21	80.2	0.11
Brown Bullhead	0.5	1.30	-	-
Green Sunfish	-	-	1.0	0.06
Hybrid Sunfish	26.3	trace	12.9	0.15
Largemouth Bass	0.3	1.44	0.3	0.13
Northern Pike	2.0	4.91	-	-
Pumpkin. Sunfish	-	-	1.6	0.15
Walleye	2.0	3.31	0.2	4.35
White Sucker	1.0	2.56	-	-
Yellow Bullhead	5.0	0.57	4.0	0.64
Yellow Perch	35.8	0.10	1.0	0.12

LENGTH OF SELECTED SPECIES SAMPLED FROM ALL GEAR
Number of fish caught for the following length categories (inches):

species	0-5	6-8	9-11	12-14	15-19	20-24	25-29	>30	Total
Black Crappie	2	3	-	-	-	-	-	-	5
Bluegill	242	52	-	-	-	-	-	-	294
Brown Bullhead	-	-	-	2	-	-	-	-	2
Green Sunfish	9	-	-	-	-	-	-	-	9
Hybrid Sunfish	68	34	-	-	-	-	-	-	102
Largemouth Bass	1	2	-	1	-	-	-	-	4
Northern Pike	-	-	-	-	-	2	4	2	8
Pumpkin. Sunfish	8	6	-	-	-	-	-	-	14
Walleye	-	-	-	-	4	5	1	-	10
Yellow Bullhead	-	11	37	8	-	-	-	-	56
Yellow Perch	45	62	-	-	-	-	-	-	107

FISH STOCKING DATA

year	species	size	# released
90	Walleye	Fingerling	6,000
90	Walleye	Yearling	180
93	Walleye	Yearling	336
95	Walleye	Fingerling	1,700
96	Walleye	Fingerling	5,610

survey date: 8/16/93

NET CATCH DATA

	Gill Nets		Trap Nets	
species	# per net	avg fish wt. (lbs)	# per set	avg fish wt. (lbs)
Black Bullhead	31.8	0.57	3.6	0.50
Black Crappie	4.5	0.20	2.2	0.36
Bluegill	59.5	0.21	89.5	0.18
Brown Bullhead	2.0	0.66	1.4	0.57
Largemouth Bass	1.8	0.61	1.0	0.82
Northern Pike	5.5	1.82	1.1	1.39
Pumpkin. Sunfish	2.3	0.10	3.9	0.11
Walleye	1.0	0.83	0.4	0.49
White Sucker	0.8	2.76	-	-
Yellow Perch	17.3	0.09	0.4	0.15

LENGTH OF SELECTED SPECIES SAMPLED FROM ALL GEAR
Number of fish caught for the following length categories (inches):

species	0-5	6-8	9-11	12-14	15-19	20-24	25-29	>30	Total
Black Bullhead	-	11	125	2	-	-	-	-	138
Black Crappie	12	15	13	-	-	-	-	-	40
Bluegill	161	257	-	-	-	-	-	-	418
Brown Bullhead	-	1	19	2	-	-	-	-	22
Largemouth Bass	-	5	6	6	-	-	-	-	17
Northern Pike	-	-	2	2	16	11	-	2	33
Pumpkin. Sunfish	42	6	-	-	-	-	-	-	48
Walleye	-	-	3	4	1	-	-	-	8
Yellow Perch	51	22	-	-	-	-	-	-	73

DNR COMMENTS:
Northern Pike population has fluctuated widely and is now high; size structure generally poor, however. Walleye numbers down significantly but still within normal range for lake class; natural reproduction marginal. Largemouth Bass population appears to be thriving. Bluegill numbers up and abnormally high; growth below average, and size structure has suffered. Yellow Perch population moderate and stable.

FISHING INFORMATION: Although Northern Pike is still the main gamefish in **Pearl Lake** and Largemouth Bass and Crappies are increasing, Walleye numbers are down sharply. There are still decent numbers of the goggle eyes, but the population is nothing like what it was a few years back. Natural reproduction appears to have dropped off, and most of the population is from stocked year classes. Pearl is an oval lake of 237 acres with a shoreline of 3.7 miles. There's good Walleye structure, including a varied bottom with sunken bars, humps and holes that drop as deep as 54 feet. Early in the season, the slender northern bay draws anglers to the edges of emerging vegetation because of the healthy Bass and Crappie population. The same is true with the reed beds in the main lake, where surface lures cast into the weedbreaks and live bait rigs with shiners augmented with spinners tossed along the weeds can draw fish. As the water warms, move to the 10- to 15-foot drops off the island at the eastern side and the point at the northern bay. Drift a live bait rig with a sucker minnow in the deeper breaks along the cattails for Northerns. In **Munson**, you'll find fair numbers of Walleyes and a few Northerns of exceptional size, along with about a zillion small panfish. Try the emergent vegetation early for Crappies. Later, hit the weedlines with live bait rigs for goggle eyes and alligators.

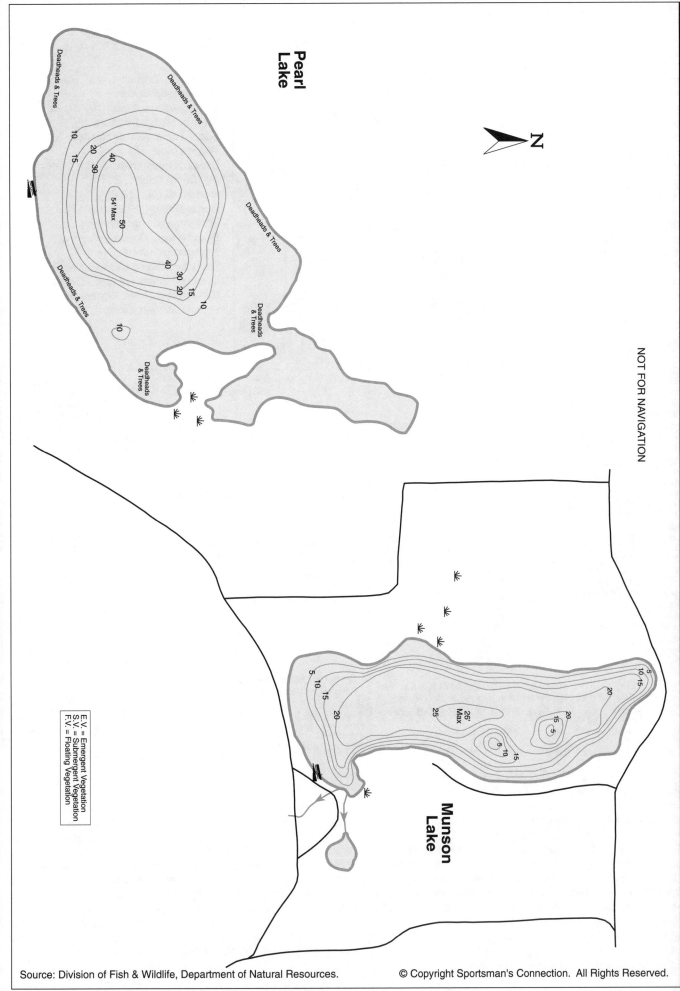

Munson & Pearl Lakes

N

NOT FOR NAVIGATION

Pearl
Lake

Deadheads & Trees
Deadheads & Trees
Deadheads & Trees
Deadheads & Trees
Deadheads & Trees
Deadheads & Trees

10
20
15
40
30
54' Max
50
40
30 20
15
10
10

Munson
Lake

5
10 15
20
25
26' Max
20
15 5
5 10
15
15
5
10
15
20
10
5

E.V. = Emergent Vegetation
S.V. = Submergent Vegetation
F.V. = Floating Vegetation

LaBELLE LAKE   MARSHALL LAKE
Becker County

Location: Township 139, 140 Range 43
Watershed: Buffalo
Surface Water Area: 146 Acres
Shorelength: 2.5 Miles
Secchi disk (water clarity): 5.0 Ft.
Water color: Light green
Cause of water color: Algae bloom
Maximum depth: 19 Ft.
Median depth: 10 Ft.
Accessibility: State-owned public access on north shore
Boat Ramp: Concrete
Accommodations: NA
Shoreland zoning classif.: Nat. Env.
Dominant forest/soil type: No tree/Wet
Management class: Game
Ecological type: Roughfish-Gamefish

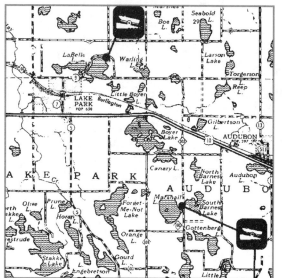

Location: Township 139 Range 42
Watershed: Buffalo
Surface Water Area: 159 Acres
Shorelength: 1.9 Miles
Secchi disk (water clarity): 3.4 Ft.
Water color: Light green
Cause of water color: Algae bloom
Maximum depth: 20 Ft.
Median depth: 15 Ft.
Accessibility: State-owned public access on the east shore
Boat Ramp: Concrete
Accommodations: NA
Shoreland zoning classif.: Rec. Develop.
Dominant forest/soil type: Decid/Loam
Management class: Warm-water Gamefish
Ecological type: Roughfish-Gamefish

DNR COMMENTS:
Lake is susceptible to occasional winterkill. Walleye numbers normal for lake class; average weight of 4.4 lb. reflects preponderance of older fish. Northern Pike numbers down, possibly a result of poor spawning success during years of low water levels. Bluegill population low. Black Bullhead numbers down dramatically; this species is the most resistant to low oxygen levels and its population exploded during winterkill years.

FISH STOCKING DATA

year	species	size	# released
94	Walleye	Fry	77,000
96	Walleye	Fry	77,000

NET CATCH DATA
survey date: 6/28/93

	Gill Nets		Trap Nets	
species	# per net	avg fish wt. (lbs)	# per set	avg fish wt. (lbs)
Black Bullhead	34.3	0.52	27.9	0.49
Bluegill	-	-	3.9	0.12
Golden Shiner	-	-	0.9	0.03
Northern Pike	1.3	4.60	0.2	3.24
Pumpkin. Sunfish	-	-	0.9	0.08
Walleye	3.3	4.38	-	-
White Sucker	1.8	2.31	0.1	3.46
Yellow Perch	54.8	0.14	6.3	0.09

LENGTH OF SELECTED SPECIES SAMPLED FROM ALL GEAR
Number of fish caught for the following length categories (inches):

species	0-5	6-8	9-11	12-14	15-19	20-24	25-29	>30	Total
Black Bullhead	2	93	171	-	-	-	-	-	266
Bluegill	36	3	-	-	-	-	-	-	39
Northern Pike	-	-	-	-	5	1	1	-	7
Pumpkin. Sunfish	9	-	-	-	-	-	-	-	9
Walleye	-	-	-	-	1	11	1	-	13
Yellow Perch	127	81	8	-	-	-	-	-	216

FISH STOCKING DATA

year	species	size	# released
90	Walleye	Fingerling	180
90	Walleye	Yearling	80
94	Walleye	Fingerling	2,730
96	Walleye	Fingerling	2,860

NET CATCH DATA
survey date: 6/5/95

	Gill Nets		Trap Nets	
species	# per net	avg fish wt. (lbs)	# per set	avg fish wt. (lbs)
Black Bullhead	5.5	0.48	29.6	0.42
Brown Bullhead	2.8	0.54	34.9	0.53
Hybrid Sunfish	0.4	0.36	-	-
Largemouth Bass	-	-	1.0	0.10
Northern Pike	5.0	2.75	0.6	2.71
Pumpkin. Sunfish	0.3	0.25	2.8	0.23
Walleye	9.0	2.89	-	-
White Sucker	1.8	2.39	0.1	2.09
Yellow Perch	161.8	0.15	21.1	0.13

LENGTH OF SELECTED SPECIES SAMPLED FROM ALL GEAR
Number of fish caught for the following length categories (inches):

species	0-5	6-8	9-11	12-14	15-19	20-24	25-29	>30	Total
Black Bullhead	-	71	150	-	-	-	-	-	221
Brown Bullhead	-	1	195	-	-	-	-	-	196
Hybrid Sunfish	-	4	-	-	-	-	-	-	4
Largemouth Bass	4	5	-	-	-	-	-	-	9
Northern Pike	-	-	-	3	8	5	6	3	25
Pumpkin. Sunfish	4	22	-	-	-	-	-	-	26
Walleye	-	-	-	-	25	10	1	-	36
Yellow Perch	65	197	1	-	-	-	-	-	263

DNR COMMENTS:
Lake is subject to periodic, partial winterkill. Northern Pike numbers near lower end of normal range for lake class; average length 22 inches; growth above average; spawning habitat in short supply for this species. Walleye population very high for lake class; average length 19.2 inches; good growth. Yellow Perch abundant. Largemouth Bass stocked in 1989 apparently have survived to reproduce; nine yearlings sampled; above average growth for this species. No Bluegills sampled in this survey.

FISHING INFORMATION: The campaign to stem Black Bullhead domination in **LaBelle** is gaining ground. Their numbers have declined considerably in the past decade. Meanwhile, Walleyes have not only become more numerous but larger. The DNR reports an average size over 4 pounds. LaBelle has 2.5 miles of shoreline that winds from a large lobe on the east and a small lobe in the middle to an extended bay in the far western end. This is a shallow lake with a number of dips and holes along the bottom but a maximum depth of only 16 feet. Most of the fishing is in the extensive weedbeds and just off the channels between the lake sections where Northerns hover in the traffic lanes. As the water warms, locate the holes in the main lake and jig live bait - shiners, nightcrawlers or leeches - at the 10- to 15-foot breaks and along the deep weedlines. **Marshall** is a 159-acre lake south of LaBelle with a shoreline of 1.9 miles. It, too, is a shallow lake with a maximum depth of 20 feet, but its water is a little murkier than LaBelle's, with a secchi reading of just 3.4 feet. The lake is stocked with Walleyes which reach good size, aided by a big supply of Yellow Perch. Northerns are not in great abundance, but their size is exceptional, with a few trophies pulled out every year. Go for the Walleyes and Northerns here with leeches or sucker minnows at the 10- to 15-foot breaks and in the holes.

LaBelle & Marshall Lakes

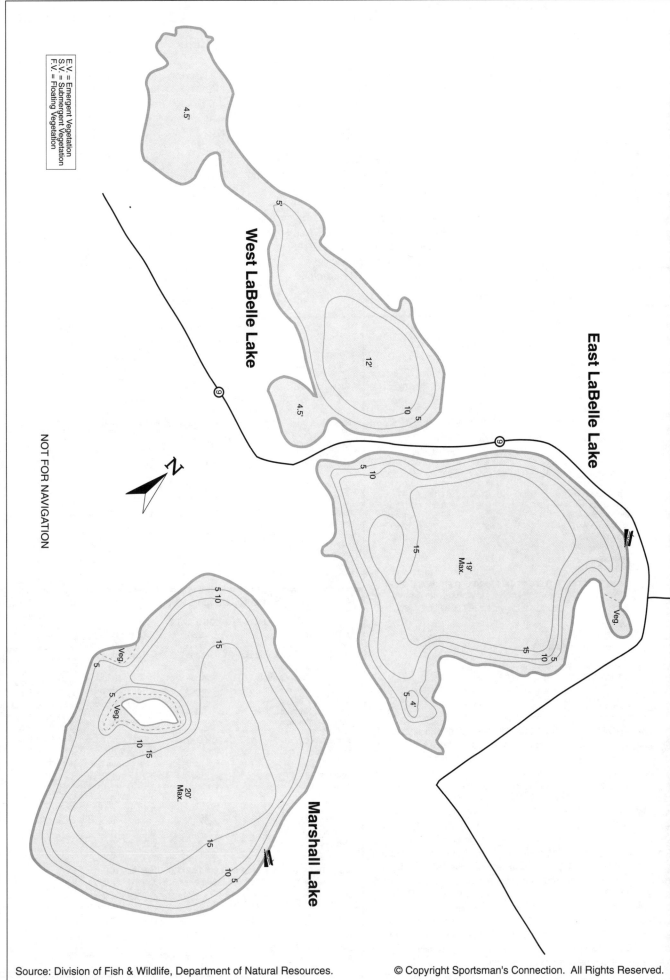

E.V. = Emergent Vegetation
S.V. = Submergent Vegetation
F.V. = Floating Vegetation

West LaBelle Lake

4.5'

5'

12'

4.5'

5

10

East LaBelle Lake

5

10

19'
Max.

15

Veg.

15

10

5

5

10

5 4'

N

NOT FOR NAVIGATION

Marshall Lake

5 10

15

Veg.

5

Veg.

5

10 15

20'
Max.

15

10 5

Location: Township 139 Range 42-44
Watershed: Otter Tail

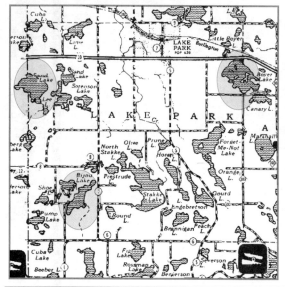

Becker County

Size of lake: 226 Acres		310 Acres	197 Acres
Shorelength: NA		NA	NA
Secchi disk (water clarity): 12.0 Ft.		4.0 Ft.	6.0 Ft.
Water color: clear		NA	NA
Cause of water color: NA		NA	NA
Maximum depth: 27 Ft.		26 Ft.	28 Ft.
Median depth: NA		NA	NA
Accessibility: Public access on south shore of northwest bay		Unknown	Public access on northwest shore
Boat Ramp: Gravel		Unknown	Gravel
Accommodations: NA		NA	NA
Shoreland zoning classif.: Nat. Environ.		Nat. Environ.	Nat. Environ.
Dominant forest/soil type: NA		NA	NA
Management class: Walleye		Walleye	Walleye
Ecological type: Centrarchid		Centrarchid	Centrarchid

DNR COMMENTS:
Lake experienced severe winterkill in 1994. Fish community is rebounding quickly after restocking. Aeration system installed in 1995 to help prevent oxygen depletion.

Beseau Lake

FISH STOCKING DATA

year	species	size	# released
93	Walleye	Fingerling	5,000
94	Bluegill	Adult	24
94	Yellow Perch	Adult	24
95	Largemouth Bass	Adult	15
95	Walleye	Yearling	192
95	Walleye	Fingerling	288

survey date: 6/10/96

NET CATCH DATA

	Gill Nets		Trap Nets	
		avg fish		avg fish
species	# per net	wt. (lbs)	# per set	wt. (lbs)
Black Crappie	0.3	0.47	19.3	0.11
Green Sunfish	0.2	0.06	1.1	0.06
Hybrid Sunfish	-	-	0.9	0.16
Largemouth Bass	0.3	0.07	10.6	0.11
Northern Pike	7.5	2.65	1.3	2.86
Pumpkin. Sunfish	-	-	0.2	0.09
Rock Bass	0.2	0.76	-	-
Walleye	0.2	1.79	-	-
Yellow Perch	0.7	0.34	0.7	0.06

LENGTH OF SELECTED SPECIES SAMPLED FROM ALL GEAR

Number of fish caught for the following length categories (inches):

species	0-5	6-8	9-11	12-14	15-19	20-24	25-29	>30	Total
Black Crappie	85	74	-	2	-	-	-	-	161
Bluegill	268	7	3	-	-	-	-	-	278
Green Sunfish	14	-	-	-	-	-	-	-	14
Hybrid Sunfish	8	3	-	-	-	-	-	-	11
Largemouth Bass	100	6	5	-	1	-	-	-	112
Northern Pike	-	-	-	-	2	49	10	-	61
Pumpkin. Sunfish	2	-	-	-	-	-	-	-	2
Rock Bass	-	-	1	-	-	-	-	-	1
Walleye	-	-	-	-	1	-	-	-	1
Yellow Perch	10	-	2	-	-	-	-	-	12

Boyer Lake

FISH STOCKING DATA

year	species	size	# released
95	Walleye	Fry	204,000

survey date: 8/16/93

NET CATCH DATA

	Gill Nets		Trap Nets	
		avg fish		avg fish
species	# per net	wt. (lbs)	# per set	wt. (lbs)
Bluegill	-	-	0.1	0.95
Green Sunfish	0.2	0.05	-	-
Walleye	3.2	1.23	-	-
Yellow Perch	22.0	0.10	6.9	0.08

LENGTH OF SELECTED SPECIES SAMPLED FROM ALL GEAR

Number of fish caught for the following length categories (inches):

species	0-5	6-8	9-11	12-14	15-19	20-24	25-29	>30	Total
Black Bullhead	-	192	50	1	-	-	-	-	243
Bluegill	-	1	-	-	-	-	-	-	1
Brown Bullhead	-	9	31	1	-	-	-	-	41
Green Sunfish	1	-	-	-	-	-	-	-	1
Walleye	-	-	12	-	5	2	-	-	19
Yellow Perch	122	47	-	-	-	-	-	-	169

DNR COMMENTS:
Lake is subject to periodic winterkill. Fish community typical of winterkill lakes and composed primarily of stocked Walleye, Yellow Perch and Bullheads.

Sand (Stump) Lake

FISH STOCKING DATA

year	species	size	# released
94	Walleye	Fry	104,000
94	Largemouth Bass	Adult	9
94	Bluegill	Adult	20
94	Black Crappie	Adult	16
94	Yellow Perch	Adult	20
95	Walleye	Fry	52,000
96	Northern Pike	Adult	49
96	Walleye	Fry	52,000

survey date: 6/14/93

NET CATCH DATA

	Gill Nets		Trap Nets	
		avg fish		avg fish
species	# per net	wt. (lbs)	# per set	wt. (lbs)
Bluegill	-	-	0.1	1.13
Hybrid Sunfish	-	-	0.2	0.12
Largemouth Bass	-	-	0.1	0.15
Northern Pike	1.3	5.39	-	-
Pumpkin. Sunfish	-	-	0.1	0.09
Walleye	5.0	2.70	0.2	3.94
Yellow Perch	17.7	0.21	4.3	0.04

LENGTH OF SELECTED SPECIES SAMPLED FROM ALL GEAR

Number of fish caught for the following length categories (inches):

species	0-5	6-8	9-11	12-14	15-19	20-24	25-29	>30	Total
Bluegill	-	-	1	-	-	-	-	-	1
Hybrid Sunfish	2	-	-	-	-	-	-	-	2
Largemouth Bass	-	1	-	-	-	-	-	-	1
Northern Pike	-	-	-	-	-	5	3	-	8
Pumpkin. Sunfish	1	-	-	-	-	-	-	-	1
Walleye	-	-	-	4	18	10	-	-	32
Yellow Perch	42	89	14	-	-	-	-	-	145

DNR COMMENTS:
Lake is subject to widely fluctuating water levels, as much as 10 feet in one year, or 20 feet over time. Winterkill is a problem in years of low water levels. Lake winterkilled severely in 1994, and has been restocked game and forage species.

FISHING INFORMATION: You'll want to check with local bait and tackle shops before heading to any of these lakes to make sure there's something to fish for. All are subject to periodic winterkill, and their fish communities can literally disappear overnight. That's particularly true of **Sand Lake** (a.k.a. Stump), whose water level can fluctuate 10 feet or so in a season, due to its proximity to an aquifer. Sand killed in 1994, and has been restocked with Walleye, Largemouth Bass, Crappies, Northern Pike and forage species. Gary Bakken of Bakken Bait Station, Highway 10, Audubon (218) 439-6125, says locals have begun taking decent Walleyes and Northerns, along with some OK panskis. So all is not lost. **Beseau** (a.k.a. Bijou) also killed in 1994-95, and Bakken says its fish community, too, is returning. Walleyes, Bass, and Northerns should be fishable in 1999 and beyond, he says. **Boyer** likewise is rebounding from a kill. Currently there's a "little bit of everything" in catchable quantities and sizes, says Bakken. Trouble is, access is in doubt. Currently, there is no public site on the lake, Bakken notes, though one property owner opened his gate to ice anglers during 1998-99. Better check with local bait shop or DNR on current access situation before heading out to this one.

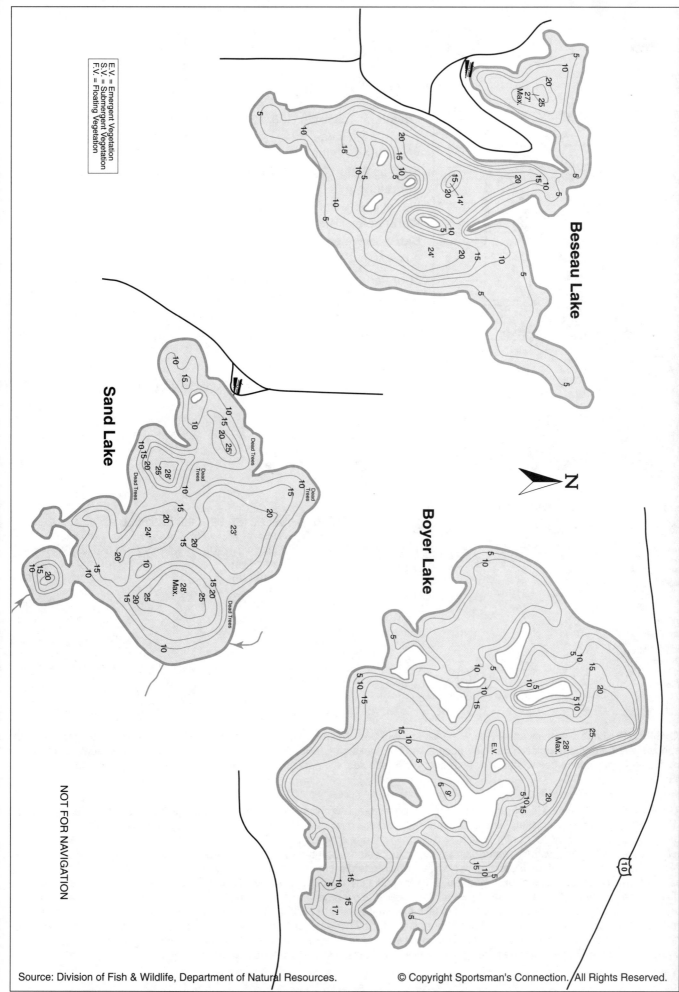

Beseau, Boyer & Sand Lakes

Beseau Lake

Sand Lake

Boyer Lake

N

E.V. = Emergent Vegetation
S.V. = Submergent Vegetation
F.V. = Floating Vegetation

NOT FOR NAVIGATION

27' Max.

24'

14'

28' Max.

23'

24'

28' Max.

25'

9'

17'

E.V.

Dead Trees

10

LITTLE CORMORANT LAKE
Becker County

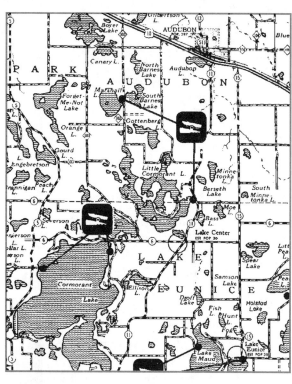

Location: Township 138, 139
Range 42
Watershed: Otter Tail
Surface Water Area: 924 Acres
Shorelength: 19 Miles
Secchi disk (water clarity): 3.0 Ft.
Water color: Brownish green
Cause of water color: Suspended algae and silt

Maximum depth: 34 Ft.
Median depth: 20 Ft.
Accessibility: State-owned access on east shore off County Highway 11
Boat Ramp: Concrete
Accommodations: NA

Shoreland zoning classification: Recreational Development
Dominant forest/soil type: No Tree/Wet
Management class: Walleye-Centrarchid
Ecological type: Centrarchid-Walleye

FISH STOCKING DATA

year	species	size	# released
88	Walleye	Fry	770,000
89	Walleye	Fry	619,000
94	Walleye	Fry	619,000
96	Walleye	Fry	619,000

NET CATCH DATA

survey date: 6/22/92

	Gill Nets		Trap Nets	
species	# per net	avg fish wt. (lbs.)	# per set	avg fish wt. (lbs.)
Yellow Perch	119.9	0.09	27.9	0.08
White Sucker	1.0	1.88	-	-
Walleye	5.9	2.47	0.4	2.54
Pumpkin. Sunfish	4.3	0.16	21.2	0.11
Northern Pike	6.0	3.04	-	-
Largemouth Bass	0.4	0.67	0.2	0.90
Brown Bullhead	8.0	0.21	29.3	0.20
Black Crappie	2.5	0.28	6.6	0.19
Black Bullhead	212.6	0.13	155.2	0.13
Hybrid Sunfish	-	-	0.8	0.23
Bluegill	-	-	15.1	0.12

LENGTH OF SELECTED SPECIES SAMPLED FROM ALL GEAR

Number of fish caught for the following length categories (inches):

species	0-5	6-8	9-11	12-14	15-19	20-24	25-29	>30	Total
Black Bullhead	80	231	5	-	-	-	-	-	316
Black Crappie	13	85	7	-	-	-	-	-	105
Bluegill	129	34	-	-	-	-	-	-	163
Brown Bullhead	2	95	9	-	-	-	-	-	106
Hybrid Sunfish	5	6	1	-	-	-	-	-	12
Largemouth Bass	1	-	3	2	-	-	-	-	6
Northern Pike	-	-	-	-	2	31	14	1	48
Pumpkin. Sunfish	112	5	-	-	-	-	-	-	117
Walleye	-	-	-	1	37	16	-	-	54
Yellow Perch	142	56	1	-	-	-	-	-	199

DNR COMMENTS: Lake experienced severe winterkill in 1985-86. Walleye population has increased to nearly double the statewide average; however, the entire population can be traced to the fry stocking of 1986. Northern Pike and Yellow Perch present. Largemouth Bass and Bluegill populations below statewide average; these species are particularly susceptible to winterkill. Brown and Black Bullheads present.

FISHING INFORMATION: Little Cormorant came back strong from a 1986 winterkill, but you should check at a local tackle shop for the latest information on this complex lake. Little Cormorant's 924 acres cover over 19 miles of shoreline. Essentially, this lake is a series of pools, each having a 20- to 34-foot hole, linked by a narrow channels which sometimes are choked with vegetation. Median depth throughout the lake is 20 feet, with the water being on the murky side. Clarity reading is about 3 feet. Sound like a lake to stay away from? Not if you like the idea of an interesting exploration which offers a chance at a limit in Northern Pike or Walleyes. Northerns and Crappies were unaffected by the winterkill, and the DNR immediately restocked Walleyes which were recently reported at double the statewide average. Because the weeds can choke off the many shallow bays, the best fishing in Little Cormorant tends to be in the early spring or late fall. Even then you are going to have to take the weedbeds into account, because that's where the fish are. Use crankbaits along with weedlines or sucker minnows on a slip bobber just off the channels for Northerns. Bass and Crappies will respond to surface baits and spinners, and when the water warms, you can switch to leeches at the 10-foot breaks. Little Cormorant doesn't offer the leisurely day on the water, but the nice gamefish population will reward the skilled boater/adventurous angler.

NOT FOR NAVIGATION

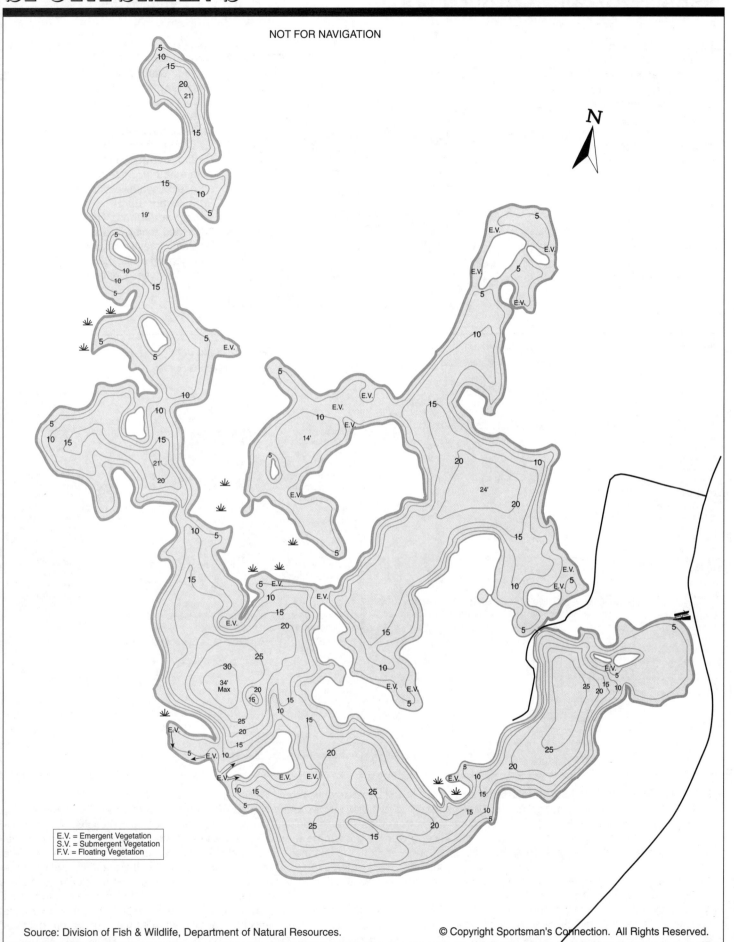

E.V. = Emergent Vegetation
S.V. = Submergent Vegetation
F.V. = Floating Vegetation

Source: Division of Fish & Wildlife, Department of Natural Resources.

BIG CORMORANT LAKE

Becker County

Location: Township 138 Range 42, 43
Watershed: Otter Tail
Surface Water Area: 3,421 Acres
Shorelength: 9.1 Miles
Secchi disk (water clarity): 12.0 Ft.
Water color: Light green
Cause of water color: Suspended algae
Maximum depth: 75 Ft.
Median depth: 10 Ft.
Accessibility: Public access on northeast shore and west shore
Boat Ramp: Concrete (both)
Accommodations: NA
Shoreland zoning classif.: Rec. Dev.
Dominant forest/soil type: Decid/Wet
Management class: Walleye
Ecological type: Hard-Water Walleye

LEIF LAKE

Location: Township 138 Range 42, 43
Watershed: Otter Tail
Surface Water Area: 488 Acres
Shorelength: 9.5 Miles
Secchi disk (water clarity): 7.0 Ft.
Water color: Green
Cause of water color: Algae bloom
Maximum depth: 26 Ft.
Median depth: 15 Ft.
Accessibility: State-owned public access on southwest corner of the lake
Boat Ramp: Earth
Accommodations: NA
Shoreland zoning classif.: Rec. Dev.
Dominant forest/soil type: Decid/Wet
Management class: Centrarchid
Ecological type: Centrarchid

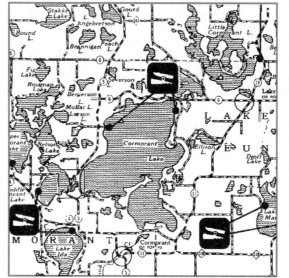

BIG CORMORANT LAKE

DNR COMMENTS: Walleye numbers stable and relatively high; population mainly composed of 3- and 4-year-old fish averaging 1.2 lb. average growth for this species. Northern Pike numbers lower than normal for lake class. Largemouth and Smallmouth Bass numbers probably near the normal range for lake class; growth rates slow for Largemouth. Bluegill numbers low; growth slow. Carp population about normal for lake class.

FISH STOCKING DATA

No record of stocking since 1985.

NET CATCH DATA

survey date: 8/8/94

species	Gill Nets # per net	avg fish wt. (lbs)	Trap Nets # per set	avg fish wt. (lbs)
Black Bullhead	0.7	1.09	0.5	0.73
Black Crappie	-	-	0.5	0.17
Bluegill	-	-	0.9	0.20
Brown Bullhead	0.3	1.63	0.4	1.47
Common Carp	0.6	6.60	0.4	3.98
Green Sunfish	0.1	0.06	0.6	0.06
Hybrid Sunfish	-	-	1.1	0.16
Largemouth Bass	-	-	3.5	0.05
Northern Pike	1.3	1.32	0.2	1.46
Pumpkin. Sunfish	0.6	0.10	0.1	0.10
Rock Bass	3.8	0.43	6.1	0.33
Smallmouth Bass	0.1	0.86	0.6	0.74
Walleye	22.1	1.24	0.8	1.05
Yellow Perch	31.9	0.16	15.0	0.11

LENGTH OF SELECTED SPECIES SAMPLED FROM ALL GEAR
Number of fish caught for the following length categories (inches):

species	0-5	6-8	9-11	12-14	15-19	20-24	25-29	>30	Total
Black Bullhead	-	2	8	4	-	-	-	-	14
Black Crappie	5	1	1	-	-	-	-	-	7
Bluegill	4	8	-	-	-	-	-	-	12
Brown Bullhead	-	-	-	8	-	-	-	-	8
Green Sunfish	10	-	-	-	-	-	-	-	10
Hybrid Sunfish	12	4	-	-	-	-	-	-	16
Largemouth Bass	49	-	-	-	-	-	-	-	49
Northern Pike	-	-	4	4	5	2	-	1	16
Pumpkin. Sunfish	7	1	-	-	-	-	-	-	8
Rock Bass	30	65	14	-	-	-	-	-	109
Smallmouth Bass	1	2	3	3	-	-	-	-	9
Walleye	-	9	28	94	93	7	1	-	232
Yellow Perch	97	208	5	-	-	-	-	-	310

LEIF LAKE

FISH STOCKING DATA

No record of stocking since 1984.

NET CATCH DATA

survey date: 8/2/93

species	Gill Nets # per net	avg fish wt. (lbs)	Trap Nets # per set	avg fish wt. (lbs)
Black Bullhead	1.3	0.71	-	-
Black Crappie	2.2	0.15	0.7	0.20
Bluegill	76.3	0.15	44.1	0.14
Brown Bullhead	0.2	0.43	0.3	0.57
Common Carp	0.3	9.17	0.9	6.96
Green Sunfish	-	-	0.3	0.03
Hybrid Sunfish	2.8	0.14	19.5	0.08
Largemouth Bass	0.8	2.15	-	-
Northern Pike	12.7	2.08	1.5	1.14
Pumpkin. Sunfish	5.2	0.12	2.1	0.08
Walleye	1.8	4.24	-	-
White Sucker	0.7	2.06	0.1	3.20
Yellow Bullhead	11.0	0.39	7.7	0.40
Yellow Perch	0.8	0.09	0.4	0.17

LENGTH OF SELECTED SPECIES SAMPLED FROM ALL GEAR
Number of fish caught for the following length categories (inches):

species	0-5	6-8	9-11	12-14	15-19	20-24	25-29	>30	Total
Black Bullhead	-	1	6	1	-	-	-	-	8
Black Crappie	8	10	2	-	-	-	-	-	20
Bluegill	229	153	-	-	-	-	-	-	382
Brown Bullhead	-	1	3	-	-	-	-	-	4
Green Sunfish	3	-	-	-	-	-	-	-	3
Hybrid Sunfish	53	25	-	-	-	-	-	-	78
Largemouth Bass	-	1	1	3	-	-	-	-	5
Northern Pike	-	2	2	7	32	37	11	-	91
Pumpkin. Sunfish	45	7	-	-	-	-	-	-	52
Walleye	-	-	-	2	7	2	-	-	11
Yellow Bullhead	-	86	57	-	-	-	-	-	143
Yellow Perch	3	6	-	-	-	-	-	-	9

DNR COMMENTS: Walleye numbers low; population primarily composed of large old fish left over from earlier stocking efforts; average weight 4.6 lb. Northern Pike slow-growing. Yellow Perch scarce. Bluegills very numerous and slow-growing. Carp numbers up, but this species does not appear to have significantly affected water quality or the rest of the fish community.

FISHING INFORMATION: Big Cormorant is a favorite not just because of its robust Walleye population but because of its long-standing reputation as Smallmouth Bass producer. Big Cormorant covers 3,421 acres and has a varied shoreline of 9.1 miles. The lake is fairly clear and has holes as deep as 78 feet. Structure varies from the visible to sunken islands, sandbars, points and dropoffs. Anglers dispute whether the shorelines of the upper or shallower lower lake are more productive, but there is little argument that the channel between the two and the slopes along the southern shore west from the channel and around the two small islands in the upper lake are prime Walleye and Bass territory. The islands and point vary with water levels, but find and work the 10- to 20-foot breaks between the islands with shiners, crawlers and leeches. Do the same at the point and the western side of the channel. Mid-channel is good for Northern Pike traffic and just inside the lower lake both shores are good for Crappies. **Leif**, meanwhile, is 488 acres of ragged shoreline that wanders for 9.5 miles. While there are lots of slow-growing Northerns and a few Walleyes to be found, Leif is chiefly where Bass, Crappie and panfish anglers come every spring to prowl the many bays and bars. They are seldom disappointed. Leif has a maximum depth of 26 feet but a median of just 15 and water clarity of 7.0 feet. Drop a leech on a light line just off weeds and reeds for some good action.

Big Cormorant & Leif Lakes

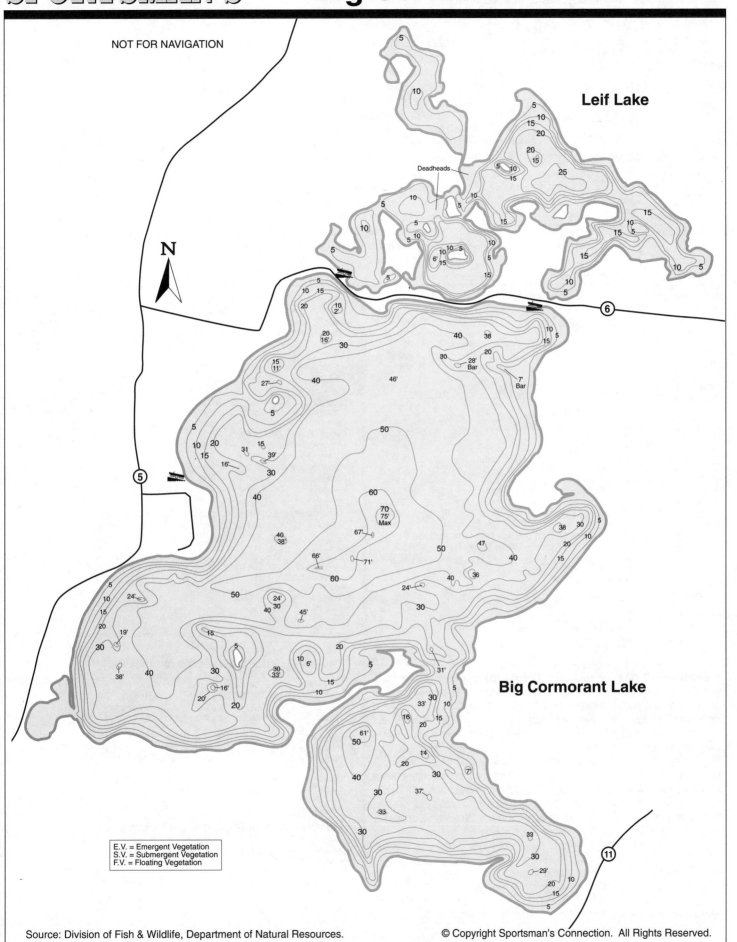

NOT FOR NAVIGATION

Leif Lake

Deadheads

Big Cormorant Lake

E.V. = Emergent Vegetation
S.V. = Submergent Vegetation
F.V. = Floating Vegetation

Source: Division of Fish & Wildlife, Department of Natural Resources.

Becker County

	Upper Cormorant	Middle Cormorant	Nelson
Size of lake:	856 Acres	360 Acres	241 Acres
Shorelength:	9.8 Miles	3.2 Miles	3.5 Miles
Secchi disk (water clarity):	6.0 Ft.	8.6 Ft.	7.0 Ft.
Water color:	Green	Light green	Brown-green
Cause of water color:	Algae	Algae bloom	Suspended plankton
Maximum depth:	29 Ft.	39 Ft.	16 Ft.
Median depth:	13 Ft.	25 Ft.	10 Ft.
Accessibility:	State-owned public access on southwest shore	Public access on west & east shores	From Middle or Upper Cormorant
Boat Ramp:	Earth	Concrete	None
Accommodations:	Resort	NA	NA
Shoreland zoning classif.:	Rec. Dev.	Rec. Dev.	Rec. Dev.
Dominant forest/soil type:	Decid/Loam	Decid/Loam	Decid/Loam
Management class:	Walleye-Centrarchid	Walleye-Centrarchid	Centrarchid
Ecological type:	Centrarchid-Walleye	Centrarchid	Centrarchid

DNR COMMENTS:
Although sample sizes of Northern Pike and Walleye have not changed drastically since 1963, average size of both species has declined significantly; age groups over 4 absent. Yellow Perch rare. Bluegill numbers up but average size is down. Yellow Bullheads abundant, large and grub-infested. Carp numbers up significantly.

Upper Cormorant Lake

FISH STOCKING DATA

year	species	size	# released
90	Walleye	Fingerling	8,625
90	Walleye	Yearling	260
93	Walleye	Yearling	2,080
95	Walleye	Fingerling	10,384

survey date: 8/8/88

NET CATCH DATA

	Gill Nets		Trap Nets	
		avg fish		avg fish
species	# per net	wt. (lbs)	# per set	wt. (lbs)
White Sucker	1.3	1.66	-	-
Walleye	6.0	0.49	0.3	3.03
Pumpkin. Sunfish	0.2	0.20	3.0	0.16
Northern Pike	3.7	1.05	1.7	1.65
Largemouth Bass	0.2	0.50	0.8	0.61
Hybrid Sunfish	0.3	0.30	4.0	0.22
Common Carp	0.3	5.55	1.4	0.59
Brown Bullhead	4.7	0.46	1.4	0.59
Bluegill	5.2	0.19	57.9	0.18
Black Crappie	0.3	0.30	2.6	0.45

LENGTH OF SELECTED SPECIES SAMPLED FROM ALL GEAR
Number of fish caught for the following length categories (inches):

species	0-5	6-8	9-11	12-14	15-19	20-24	25-29	>30	Total
Black Crappie	-	8	20	-	-	-	-	-	28
Bluegill	48	53	-	-	-	-	-	-	101
Brown Bullhead	-	4	33	5	-	-	-	-	42
Hybrid Sunfish	16	26	-	-	-	-	-	-	42
Largemouth Bass	1	4	3	-	1	-	-	-	9
Northern Pike	-	-	1	6	21	8	2	1	39
Pumpkin. Sunfish	22	9	-	-	-	-	-	-	31
Walleye	-	-	20	15	3	-	1	-	39
Yellow Bullhead	-	49	66	1	-	-	-	-	116
Yellow Perch	-	1	1	-	-	-	-	-	2

Middle Cormorant Lake

FISH STOCKING DATA

year	species	size	# released
90	Walleye	Fingerling	3,875
93	Walleye	Fingerling	5,800
96	Walleye	Fingerling	3,770

survey date: 8/5/96

NET CATCH DATA

	Gill Nets		Trap Nets	
		avg fish		avg fish
species	# per net	wt. (lbs)	# per set	wt. (lbs)
Black Crappie	2.5	0.17	1.9	0.20
Bluegill	31.7	0.20	58.6	0.16
Hybrid Sunfish	0.3	0.14	1.2	0.18
Largemouth Bass	2.7	0.58	2.2	0.36
Northern Pike	11.0	1.49	1.1	1.08
Pumpkin. Sunfish	3.7	0.16	2.8	0.16
Rock Bass	0.2	0.29	0.1	0.28
Walleye	2.0	2.31	0.8	2.95
Yellow Perch	2.2	0.19		

LENGTH OF SELECTED SPECIES SAMPLED FROM ALL GEAR
Number of fish caught for the following length categories (inches):

species	0-5	6-8	9-11	12-14	15-19	20-24	25-29	>30	Total
Black Crappie	12	16	4	-	-	-	-	-	32
Bluegill	170	179	-	-	-	-	-	-	349
Hybrid Sunfish	7	6	-	-	-	-	-	-	13
Largemouth Bass	-	-	16	18	2	-	-	-	36
Northern Pike	-	-	2	13	37	19	3	1	75
Pumpkin. Sunfish	37	10	-	-	-	-	-	-	47
Rock Bass	-	2	-	-	-	-	-	-	2
Walleye	-	-	7	3	6	3	-	-	19
Yellow Perch	2	11	-	-	-	-	-	-	13

DNR COMMENTS:
The diverse fish community reflects relatively good water quality. Black Bullheads are relatively scarce. Walleye population about average with good size structure. Northern Pike numerous and small. Bluegills abundant. Largemouth Bass, Black Crappie, and Yellow Perch present.

Nelson Lake

FISH STOCKING DATA: NO RECORD OF STOCKING

survey date: 7/13/66

NET CATCH DATA

	Gill Nets		Trap Nets	
		avg fish		avg fish
species	# per net	wt. (lbs)	# per set	wt. (lbs)
Yellow Perch	8.0	0.16	0.9	0.10
Walleye	2.5	2.68	6.7	1.67
Pumpkin. Sunfish	5.0	0.17	26.6	0.22
Northern Pike	7.0	0.74	6.6	1.08
Hybrid Sunfish	1.5	0.17	60.4	0.25
Bluegill	8.0	0.49	97.1	0.32
Black Crappie	1.5	0.30	1.4	0.51
Rock Bass	-	-	0.1	0.90
Largemouth Bass	-	-	7.4	0.77

LENGTH OF SELECTED SPECIES SAMPLED FROM ALL GEAR
Number of fish caught for the following length categories (inches):

species	0-5	6-8	9-11	12-14	15-19	20-24	25-29	>30	Total
Black Crappie	-	5	8	-	-	-	-	-	13
Bluegill	47	138	1	-	-	-	-	-	186
Hybrid Sunfish	43	132	-	-	-	-	-	-	175
Largemouth Bass	-	11	40	7	1	-	-	-	59
Northern Pike	-	-	3	17	36	3	1	-	60
Pumpkin. Sunfish	29	108	-	-	-	-	-	-	137
Rock Bass	-	-	1	-	-	-	-	-	1
Walleye	-	-	-	3	44	5	-	-	52
Yellow Perch	9	13	-	-	-	-	-	-	22

DNR COMMENTS:

NOT AVAILABLE

FISHING INFORMATION: Upper Cormorant is a fishery in a bind. There are good numbers of Walleye and Northern Pike, but the species on which these gamefish prefer to feed, Yellow Perch, has been all but wiped out. It's not surprising, then, that average size of the Wallies and alligators caught has been decreasing. That doesn't mean it's not worthwhile to fish here; just be aware that a little patience will be required. Fish the points, bars and sunken islands for Walleyes and Northerns, and work the weeds for Largemouth Bass. **Middle Cormorant** offers quite-decent Walleyes and fairly nice Largemouth, in addition to loads of snake Northerns. Bass anglers concentrate on the rubble of trees along the western and south shores, and the weedbeds around the inlet from Cormorant Lake. Surface lures and shallow-running spinners will serve nicely. For Northerns and Walleyes, try around the 3-foot hump in the shelf just off the south shore. Or fish the 10- to 15-foot breaks just before the channel into Nelson Lake. The snakes watch the traffic in this latter area for forage. **Nelson**, meanwhile, is mostly just a thoroughfare. In it, you'll find many of the small snakes and some Crappies. Cast to the weedbeds or jig the one small, 16-foot hole almost at the lake's center for what action this lake's going to allow you.

NOT FOR NAVIGATION

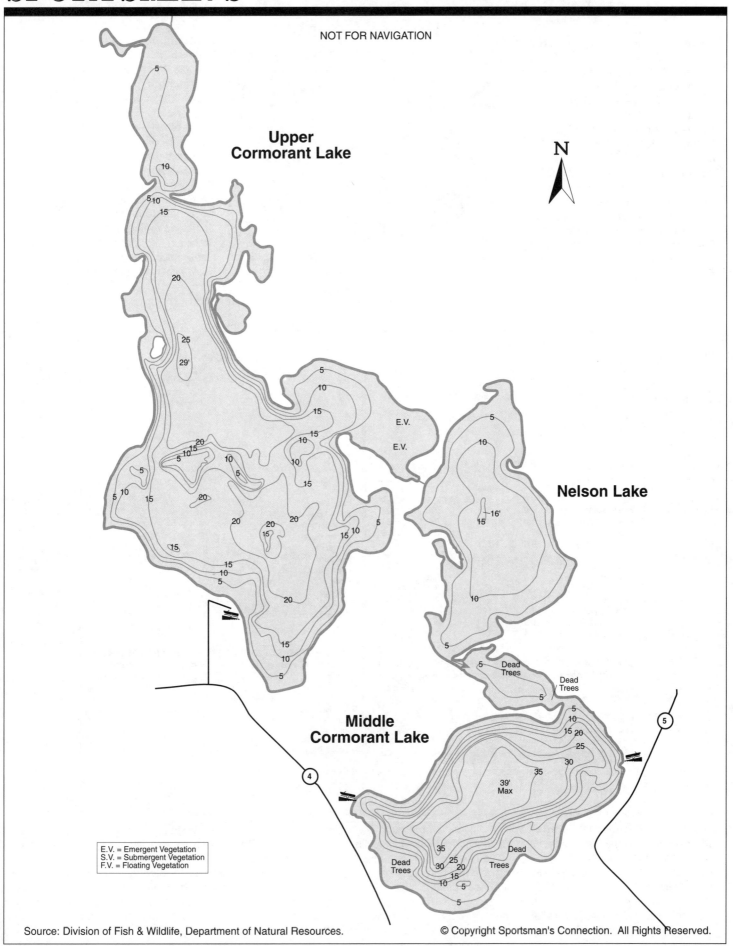

Upper Cormorant Lake

N

E.V. = Emergent Vegetation
S.V. = Submergent Vegetation
F.V. = Floating Vegetation

Nelson Lake

Middle Cormorant Lake

E.V.

Dead Trees

Dead Trees

Dead Trees

Dead Trees

39' Max

Source: Division of Fish & Wildlife, Department of Natural Resources.

IDA LAKE

Location: Township 137, 138 Range 43
Watershed: Otter Tail
Surface Water Area: 580 Acres
Shorelength: 5.6 Miles
Secchi disk (water clarity): 8.0 Ft.
Water color: Green
Cause of water color: Mild algae bloom
Maximum depth: 20 Ft.
Median depth: 10 Ft.
Accessibility: State-owned public access on north shore
Boat Ramp: Concrete
Accommodations: NA
Shoreland zoning classif.: Rec. Dev.
Dominant forest/soil type: Decid/Sand
Management class: Walleye-Centrarchid
Ecological type: Centrarchid

Becker County

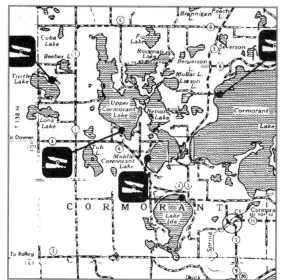

TURTLE LAKE

Location: Township 138 Range 43, 44
Watershed: Buffalo
Surface Water Area: 147 Acres
Shorelength: 2.2 Miles
Secchi disk (water clarity): 19.0 Ft.
Water color: Clear
Cause of water color: NA
Maximum depth: 73 Ft.
Median depth: 20 Ft.
Accessibility: State-owned public access on east shore
Boat Ramp: Concrete
Accommodations: NA
Shoreland zoning classif.: Rec. Dev.
Dominant forest/soil type: NA
Management class: Walleye-Centrarchid
Ecological type: Centrarchid

DNR COMMENTS:
Northern Pike numbers about normal for lake class; average size 2.2 lb. and 21 inches. Walleye numbers above average for lake class; average size good at 17.1 inches and 2 lb.; natural reproduction appears to be occurring sporadically. Black Crappie population down. Bluegill population increasing, but size structure diminishing; average size 5.6 inches. Yellow Perch population up; mean length 6.3 inches; growth rate normal for lake class.

FISH STOCKING DATA

year	species	size	# released
90	Walleye	Fingerling	7,200
90	Walleye	Yearling	405
93	Walleye	Fingerling	8,248
93	Walleye	Yearling	28
95	Walleye	Fingerling	14,989
96	Walleye	fingerling	14,355

survey date: 6/28/93

NET CATCH DATA

	Gill Nets		Trap Nets	
species	# per net	avg fish wt. (lbs)	# per set	avg fish wt. (lbs)
Black Bullhead	1.0	1.38	0.1	1.03
Black Crappie	1.0	0.30	0.5	0.24
Bluegill	39.5	0.30	60.4	0.18
Brown Bullhead	8.6	1.21	-	-
Hybrid Sunfish	1.5	0.33	1.5	0.35
Largemouth Bass	0.4	1.49	0.1	2.70
Northern Pike	6.5	2.16	0.3	1.40
Pumpkin. Sunfish	2.8	0.33	5.0	0.25
Walleye	5.5	1.97	0.4	4.34
White Sucker	1.1	3.18	-	-
Yellow Bullhead	18.8	0.64	4.5	0.63
Yellow Perch	14.4	0.12	0.5	0.08

LENGTH OF SELECTED SPECIES SAMPLED FROM ALL GEAR
Number of fish caught for the following length categories (inches):

species	0-5	6-8	9-11	12-14	15-19	20-24	25-29	>30	Total
Black Bullhead	-	-	3	6	-	-	-	-	9
Black Crappie	7	4	1	1	-	-	-	-	13
Bluegill	219	278	2	-	-	-	-	-	499
Brown Bullhead	-	1	14	53	1	-	-	-	69
Hybrid Sunfish	10	18	-	-	-	-	-	-	28
Largemouth Bass	-	-	-	3	1	-	-	-	4
Northern Pike	-	1	-	1	20	29	3	1	55
Pumpkin. Sunfish	30	47	-	-	-	-	-	-	48
Yellow Bullhead	-	28	147	24	-	-	-	-	199
Yellow Perch	32	61	-	-	-	-	-	-	93

FISH STOCKING DATA

year	species	size	# released
89	Walleye	Fingerling	2,625
93	Walleye	Fingerling	2,800
95	Walleye	Fingerling	840

survey date: 6/27/94

NET CATCH DATA

	Gill Nets		Trap Nets	
species	# per net	avg fish wt. (lbs)	# per set	avg fish wt. (lbs)
Black Bullhead	1.3	1.30	-	-
Bluegill	5.0	0.14	70.8	0.10
Brown Bullhead	1.0	0.97	0.1	0.88
Green Sunfish	-	-	0.4	0.05
Hybrid Sunfish	5.0	0.09	79.2	0.06
Largemouth Bass	0.5	0.93	2.7	0.21
Northern Pike	14.0	2.12	1.2	1.76
Pumpkin. Sunfish	1.5	0.05	5.6	0.07
Rock Bass	3.8	0.26	12.0	0.19
Walleye	5.5	2.52	1.0	0.42
White Sucker	5.3	2.61	-	-
Yellow Perch	18.0	0.12	1.3	0.20

LENGTH OF SELECTED SPECIES SAMPLED FROM ALL GEAR
Number of fish caught for the following length categories (inches):

species	0-5	6-8	9-11	12-14	15-19	20-24	25-29	>30	Total
Black Bullhead	-	-	1	4	-	-	-	-	5
Bluegill	226	64	3	-	-	-	-	-	293
Brown Bullhead	-	-	3	2	-	-	-	-	5
Green Sunfish	4	-	-	-	-	-	-	-	4
Hybrid Sunfish	222	35	-	-	-	-	-	-	257
Largemouth Bass	1	20	4	1	-	-	-	-	26
Northern Pike	-	-	2	2	19	40	4	-	67
Pumpkin. Sunfish	55	1	-	-	-	-	-	-	56
Rock Bass	63	60	-	-	-	-	-	-	123
Walleye	-	6	1	6	8	9	1	-	31
Yellow Perch	27	50	7	-	-	-	-	-	84

DNR COMMENTS:
Northern Pike population above average for lake class; maximum size has declined for this species. Walleye numbers high; average size relatively large at 18.7 inches and 2.5 lb. Largemouth Bass appear to be abundant. Rock Bass and Hybrid Sunfish very numerous. Black Crappie population has crashed for an unknown reason; none sampled in latest survey.

FISHING INFORMATION: Turtle Lake is fairly small, but quite deep and very clear. It is also a good place to fish for Northern Pike, Walleyes and Largemouth Bass. And you'll also find lots of Bluegills and Rock Bass. Tempt the Bass and panfish with live bait fished under a slip bobber over the weed tops. The Northerns will be outside the weeds, cruising deep at the outer edges. Because the water is so clear, you may want to attract them with live bait bumped along on a bottom rig. If that doesn't work, switch to your conventional lures. Nearby **Ida Lake** is larger than Turtle but doesn't provide quite as good fishing. It holds a lot of small Northerns and Largemouths as well as big populations of large Yellow Bullheads and small Bluegills. It's a fairly weedy lake, slightly cloudy and shallow. Fish the weeds with a jig combined with worms, smaller minnows or pork rinds early in the season. Troll the outer edges with a spoon for Northerns, moving slowly along the weeds. Or, if you want, check with a local bait shop; the Pike may be biting better on live bait.

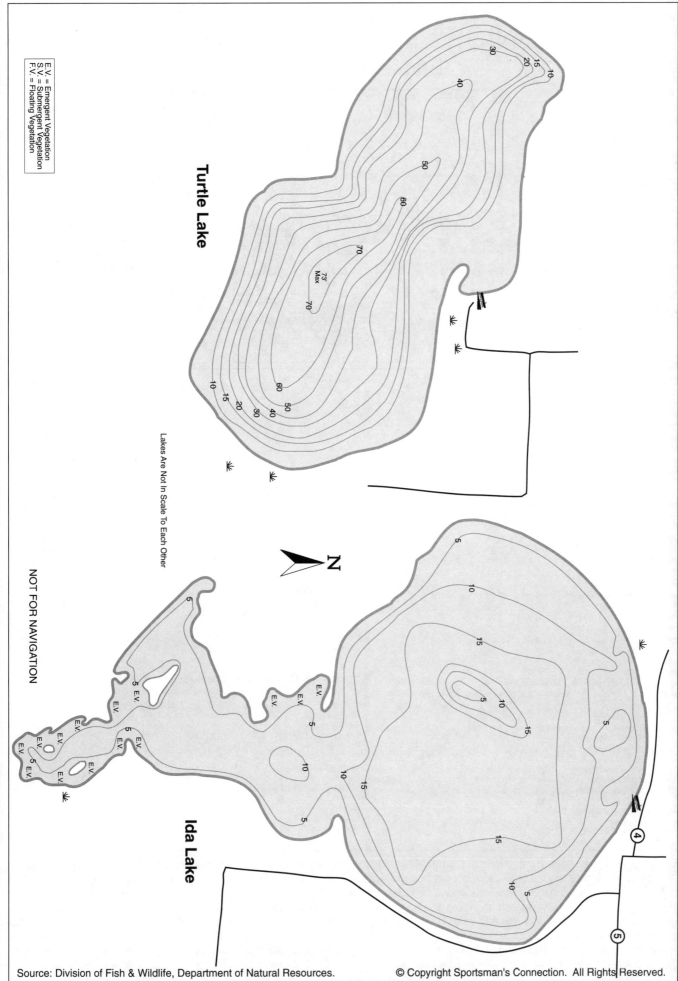

Ida & Turtle Lakes

Turtle Lake

73' Max

Ida Lake

E.V. = Emergent Vegetation
S.V. = Submergent Vegetation
F.V. = Floating Vegetation

Lakes Are Not In Scale To Each Other

NOT FOR NAVIGATION

N

Source: Division of Fish & Wildlife, Department of Natural Resources.

LAKE EUNICE

Becker County

LAKE MAUD

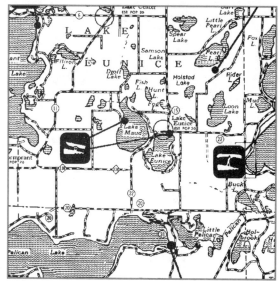

Location: Township 138 Range 42
Watershed: Otter Tail
Surface Water Area: 324 Acres
Shorelength: 3.2 Miles
Secchi disk (water clarity): 9.0 Ft.
Water color: Light green
Cause of water color: NA
Maximum depth: 30 Ft.
Median depth: 12 Ft.
Accessibility: Public access on north shore
Boat Ramp: Concrete
Accommodations: NA
Shoreland zoning classif.: Gen. Dev.
Dominant forest/soil type: Decid/Sand
Management class: Walleye-Centrarchid
Ecological type: Centrarchid

Location: Township 138 Range 42
Watershed: Otter Tail
Surface Water Area: 547 Acres
Shorelength: 4.3 Miles
Secchi disk (water clarity): 12.0 Ft.
Water color: Light green
Cause of water color: Light algae bloom
Maximum depth: 30 Ft.
Median depth: 15 Ft.
Accessibility: State-owned public access midway on the west shore
Boat Ramp: Concrete
Accommodations: NA
Shoreland zoning classif.: Rec. Dev.
Dominant forest/soil type: No Tree/Wet
Management class: Walleye-Centrarchid
Ecological type: Centrarchid

DNR COMMENTS:
Northern Pike numbers within normal range for lake class; small Pike dominate the population, but about 10 percent of sample was larger than 30 inches. Walleye population low, despite high-density fingerling stocking. Largemouth Bass and Rock Bass populations appear to be above normal range. Black Crappie numbers very low. Bluegill and Yellow Perch populations within normal range, but Bluegill size structure has deteriorated. Cisco numbers about average for lake class.

FISH STOCKING DATA

year	species	size	# released
94	Walleye	Fingerling	4,165
96	Walleye	Fingerling	6,270

survey date: 6/13/94

NET CATCH DATA

	Gill Nets		Trap Nets	
species	# per net	avg fish wt. (lbs)	# per set	avg fish wt. (lbs)
Black Bullhead	0.2	0.71	-	-
Bluegill	6.2	0.17	38.2	0.22
Bowfin (Dogfish)	-	-	0.1	4.08
Brown Bullhead	0.2	0.73	-	-
Green Sunfish	0.2	0.07	3.7	0.04
Hybrid Sunfish	8.0	0.25	26.7	0.24
Largemouth Bass	3.7	1.01	3.6	0.31
Northern Pike	9.3	1.41	1.4	0.71
Pumpkin. Sunfish	1.0	0.17	2.9	0.22
Rock Bass	3.0	0.37	6.2	0.28
Tullibee (Cisco)	0.8	3.77	-	-
Walleye	0.5	2.45	-	-
White Sucker	0.5	2.13	-	-
Yellow Perch	17.0	0.33	-	-

LENGTH OF SELECTED SPECIES SAMPLED FROM ALL GEAR
Number of fish caught for the following length categories (inches):

species	0-5	6-8	9-11	12-14	15-19	20-24	25-29	>30	Total
Black Bullhead	-	-	1	-	-	-	-	-	1
Bluegill	105	234	-	-	-	-	-	-	339
Brown Bullhead	-	-	1	-	-	-	-	-	1
Green Sunfish	34	-	-	-	-	-	-	-	34
Hybrid Sunfish	67	171	-	-	-	-	-	-	238
Largemouth Bass	-	20	23	10	1	-	-	-	54
Northern Pike	-	-	12	20	24	5	4	4	69
Pumpkin. Sunfish	9	23	-	-	-	-	-	-	32
Rock Bass	18	52	4	-	-	-	-	-	74
Tullibee (Cisco)	-	-	-	-	5	-	-	-	5
Walleye	-	-	-	-	2	1	-	-	3
Yellow Perch	14	38	50	-	-	-	-	-	102

FISH STOCKING DATA

year	species	size	# released
94	Walleye	Fingerling	6,480
96	Walleye	Fingerling	10,750

survey date: 8/1/94

NET CATCH DATA

	Gill Nets		Trap Nets	
species	# per net	avg fish wt. (lbs)	# per set	avg fish wt. (lbs)
Black Bullhead	2.7	1.01	-	-
Black Crappie	0.2	0.36	-	-
Bluegill	17.0	0.16	42.4	0.20
Bowfin (Dogfish)	-	-	0.5	5.81
Brown Bullhead	2.2	1.60	0.1	1.05
Hybrid Sunfish	3.5	0.22	7.0	0.28
Largemouth Bass	3.3	0.89	0.8	0.66
Northern Pike	8.0	1.99	1.4	0.74
Pumpkin. Sunfish	9.0	0.21	5.5	0.21
Rock Bass	0.5	0.24	1.4	0.26
Walleye	3.3	3.08	-	-
White Sucker	0.3	2.41	-	-
Yellow Bullhead	2.3	1.27	1.3	1.19
Yellow Perch	7.7	0.16	0.1	0.30

LENGTH OF SELECTED SPECIES SAMPLED FROM ALL GEAR
Number of fish caught for the following length categories (inches):

species	0-5	6-8	9-11	12-14	15-19	20-24	25-29	>30	Total
Black Bullhead	-	1	10	5	-	-	-	-	16
Black Crappie	-	1	-	-	-	-	-	-	1
Bluegill	106	177	-	-	-	-	-	-	283
Brown Bullhead	-	-	-	14	-	-	-	-	14
Hybrid Sunfish	15	62	-	-	-	-	-	-	77
Largemouth Bass	-	2	17	7	-	-	-	-	26
Northern Pike	-	-	5	21	16	8	2	7	59
Pumpkin. Sunfish	26	72	-	-	-	-	-	-	98
Rock Bass	5	8	1	-	-	-	-	-	14
Walleye	-	-	-	4	8	6	1	1	20
Yellow Bullhead	-	-	8	16	-	-	-	-	24
Yellow Perch	17	29	1	-	-	-	-	-	47

DNR COMMENTS:
Northern Pike numbers about normal to lake class; population is dominated by small fish, but about 15 percent of sample was over 30 inches. Walleye population low, but average size is large; about 40 percent of sample was longer than 20 inches. Bluegill numbers within normal range, but average size has declined. Largemouth Bass, Rock Bass and Yellow perch populations within normal ranges for lake class.

FISHING INFORMATION: Lake Eunice is known primarily as a Northern Pike and panfish lake as well as one offering a decent number of Largemouth Bass. There are Walleyes, too, but not in large numbers, as DNR stocking has been only partially successful. Over half the shoreline has good vegetation for smaller fish and Largemouth Bass. The water is relatively clear, so you can use worms or small minnows on a bare hook to attract panfish and a pig and jig for the Bass. Northerns will be cruising the outer edges of the weeds where you can troll slowly or throw a spoon. Nearby **Lake Maud**, meanwhile, offers good numbers of small Northerns and some decent Largemouth and panfish. Fish the weedlines with worms or minnows for the nice spring Crappies. The Bass, of course, will be in the same weeds, somewhat inactive after spawning, but hungry early in June. Jigs armed with pork rinds or minnows should get their attention quickly. As in Eunice, there are Walleyes in Maud, stocked periodically by the DNR without great success. The population is below area averages, but the average size is pretty fair, with over 40 percent of the fish topping 20 inches. Fish the weedlines with live bait.

NOT FOR NAVIGATION

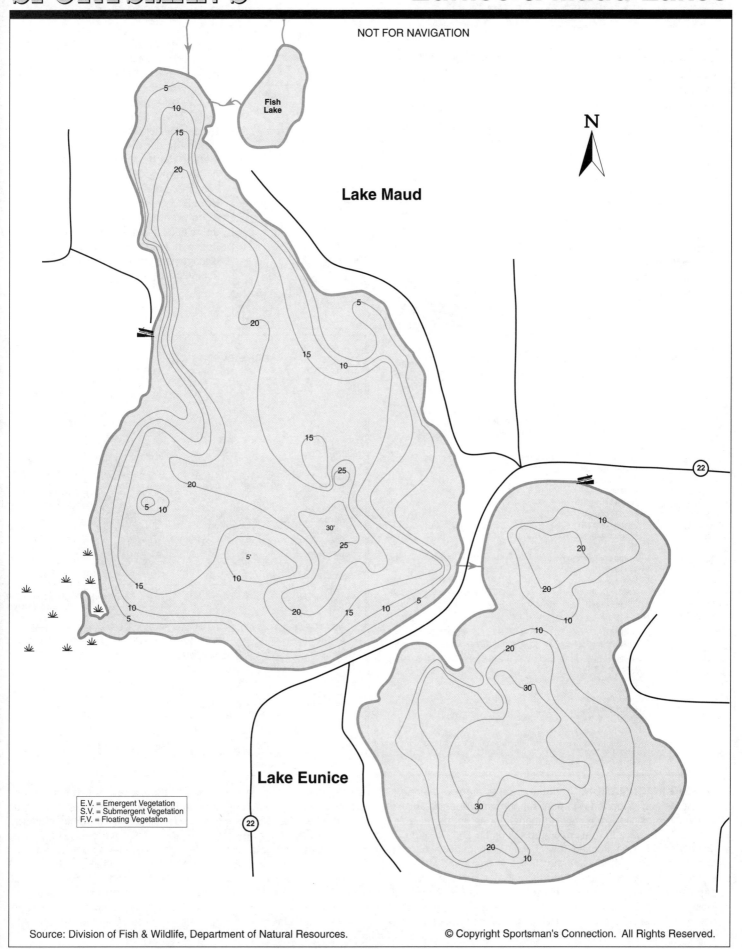

Fish Lake

Lake Maud

N

Lake Eunice

22

E.V. = Emergent Vegetation
S.V. = Submergent Vegetation
F.V. = Floating Vegetation

22

ACORN LAKE

Becker County

Location: Township 138 Range 40
Watershed: Otter Tail
Surface Water Area: 112 Acres
Shorelength: NA
Secchi disk (water clarity): NA
Water color: NA
Cause of water color: NA
Maximum depth: 55 Ft.
Median depth: NA
Accessibility: Access on southeast corner of the lake
Boat Ramp: Concrete
Accommodations: Motel; bed and breakfast inn
Shoreland zoning classif.: Rec. Dev.
Dominant forest/soil type: NA
Management class: Walleye-Centrarchid
Ecological type: Centrarchid

EAGLE LAKE

Location: Township 138 Range 40
Watershed: Otter Tail
Surface Water Area: 313 Acres
Shorelength: 3.7 Miles
Secchi disk (water clarity): 5.0 Ft.
Water color: Green
Cause of water color: Algae bloom
Maximum depth: 29 Ft.
Median depth: 17 Ft.
Accessibility: Public access on southeast shore of lake
Boat Ramp: Concrete
Accommodations: NA
Shoreland zoning classif.: Rec.Dev.
Dominant forest/soil type: Decid/Sand
Management class: Walleye-Centrarchid
Ecological type: Centrarchid

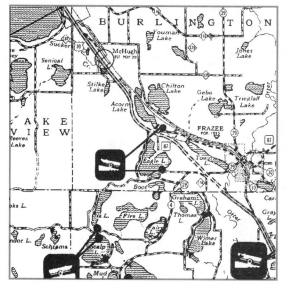

ACORN LAKE

DNR COMMENTS:
Cisco and Rock Bass populations have disappeared. Northern Pike numbers relatively stable; fast growth. Walleye numbers low, despite heavy stocking; growth well below average; virtually no natural reproduction.. Bluegill population has declined to low levels for no apparent reason; majority of fish younger than 7 and growing at average rate. Yellow Perch numbers extremely high at 121.3/gill-net set. Anglers occasionally reporting good Black Crappie fishing.

FISH STOCKING DATA

year	species	size	# released
93	Walleye	Fingerling	2,960
95	Walleye	Fingerling	1,435

NET CATCH DATA
survey date: 6/21/93

	Gill Nets		Trap Nets	
species	# per net	avg fish wt. (lbs)	# per set	avg fish wt. (lbs)
Black Bullhead	0.3	0.75	0.1	0.10
Black Crappie	-	-	0.1	0.10
Bluegill	0.5	0.27	5.1	0.32
Bowfin (Dogfish)	0.3	3.57	0.4	3.88
Brown Bullhead	-	-	0.1	2.37
Hybrid Sunfish	-	-	0.3	0.31
Largemouth Bass	0.3	3.31	-	-
Northern Pike	3.5	2.58	0.1	0.23
Pumpkin. Sunfish	-	-	1.0	0.32
Walleye	5.8	1.50	-	-
White Sucker	2.8	2.27	0.1	2.87
Yellow Bullhead	1.0	0.78	4.0	0.81
Yellow Perch	121.3	0.17	8.7	0.11

LENGTH OF SELECTED SPECIES SAMPLED FROM ALL GEAR
Number of fish caught for the following length categories (inches):

species	0-5	6-8	9-11	12-14	15-19	20-24	25-29	>30	Total
Black Bullhead	-	1	1	-	-	-	-	-	2
Black Crappie	1	-	-	-	-	-	-	-	1
Bluegill	4	44	-	-	-	-	-	-	48
Brown Bullhead	-	-	-	1	-	-	-	-	1
Hybrid Sunfish	-	3	-	-	-	-	-	-	3
Largemouth Bass	-	-	-	1	3	10	-	1	15
Pumpkin. Sunfish	2	7	-	-	-	-	-	-	9
Walleye	-	-	2	13	5	1	2	-	23
Yellow Bullhead	-	2	36	2	-	-	-	-	40
Yellow Perch	50	131	1	-	-	-	-	-	182

EAGLE LAKE

FISH STOCKING DATA

year	species	size	# released
93	Walleye	Fingerling	5,640
95	Walleye	Fingerling	5,195
96	Walleye	Fingerling	4,686

NET CATCH DATA
survey date: 8/8/88

	Gill Nets		Trap Nets	
species	# per net	avg fish wt. (lbs)	# per set	avg fish wt. (lbs)
Yellow Perch	29.5	0.19	3.0	0.14
Yellow Bullhead	13.8	0.45	14.2	0.43
White Sucker	0.8	2.10	-	-
Walleye	5.5	1.41	0.8	2.21
Northern Pike	8.8	1.61	2.7	1.33
Largemouth Bass	0.3	0.50	0.8	0.38
Brown Bullhead	2.0	0.54	-	-
Bluegill	41.0	0.21	67.6	0.15
Black Crappie	2.3	0.27	2.7	0.29
Pumpkin. Sunfish	-	-	3.0	0.15
Hybrid Sunfish	-	-	0.9	0.17

LENGTH OF SELECTED SPECIES SAMPLED FROM ALL GEAR
Number of fish caught for the following length categories (inches):

species	0-5	6-8	9-11	12-14	15-19	20-24	25-29	>30	Total
Black Crappie	-	34	7	-	-	-	-	-	41
Bluegill	11	97	-	-	-	-	-	-	108
Brown Bullhead	-	1	8	3	-	-	-	-	12
Hybrid Sunfish	1	8	-	-	-	-	-	-	9
Largemouth Bass	1	6	2	-	1	-	-	-	10
Northern Pike	-	-	9	46	16	6	3	80
Pumpkin. Sunfish	7	23	-	-	-	-	-	-	30
Walleye	-	-	16	12	3	8	3	-	42
Yellow Bullhead	1	24	73	9	-	-	-	-	107
Yellow Perch	2	103	1	-	-	-	-	-	106

DNR COMMENTS:
Walleye numbers above state and local medians, with the majority of fish being 9 to 12 inches in length. Northern Pike numbers likewise above average; population has been increasing continuously since 1956 without any apparent effects on the forage base. Bluegill numbers extremely high for lake class; young of year very numerous, but survey found no fish ages 1-3, Yellow Perch numbers continue strong, almost double the local average.

FISHING INFORMATION: Acorn and Eagle are two members of a small group of lakes on the outskirts of Frazee. **Acorn** is a slender 144 acres and is loaded with panfish, primarily Bluegills and Yellow Perch. Northern Pike, Largemouth Bass and Walleyes also show up in the DNR test nets, but only Northerns appear in appreciable quantity. (Largemouth are frequently under counted in the nets, however, and could be here in reasonably good numbers.) Although fingerlings are stocked here by the DNR, Walleyes have been showing up downstream in non-stocked Town Lake, which might account for the low Walleye count in Acorn. Best chance here is early in the year, casting the edges of the weedbeds with spinners and shiners. You might also try a sucker minnow for the roving Northern, or toss nightcrawlers and catch a load of panskis. **Eagle** is bigger than Acorn, at 313 acres. It has a shoreline of 3.7 miles and a good, varied fish population. Bluegills and Perch are here in quantity as well but Walleyes, Northern Pike are also present in numbers above the state and local medians. Walleyes are stocked, but population has not matched the Northerns'. The latter species has increased steadily in number and size since the 1950s. Best strategy is to work the waters off the weedbeds in the spring and jig the 10- to 15-foot levels along the shoreline and, as the water warms, along the slopes of the 29-foot hole.

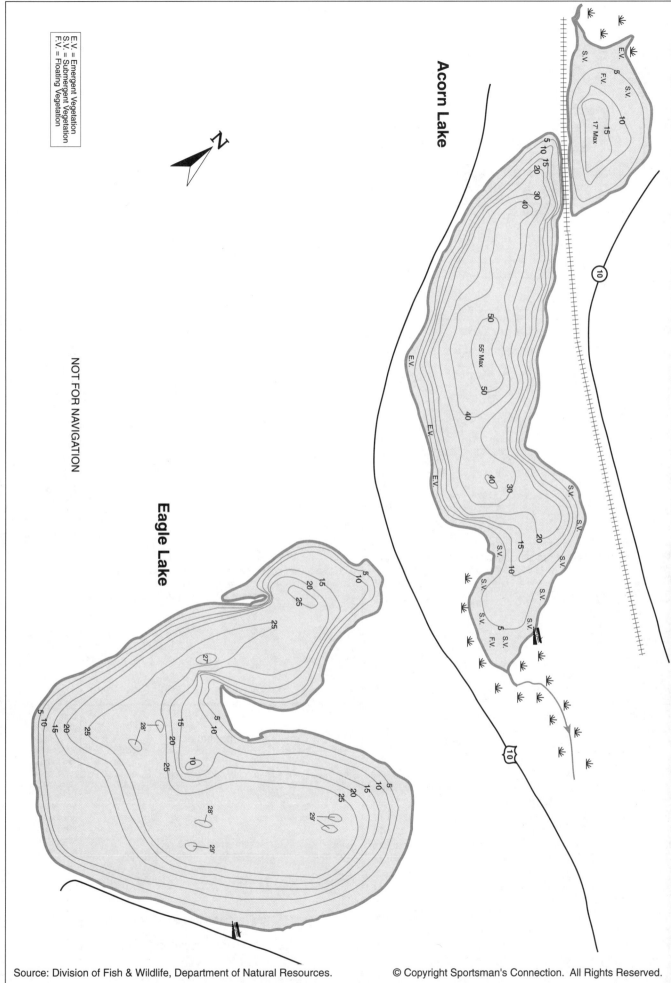

SPORTSMAN'S *Connection*®

Acorn & Eagle Lakes

Acorn Lake

Eagle Lake

N

NOT FOR NAVIGATION

E.V. = Emergent Vegetation
S.V. = Submergent Vegetation
F.V. = Floating Vegetation

Source: Division of Fish & Wildlife, Department of Natural Resources.

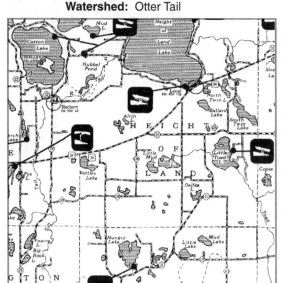

	Hungry	Little Toad	Hanson
Size of lake:	240 Acres	345 Acres	33 Acres
Shorelength:	3.8 Miles	3.4 Miles	NA
Secchi disk (water clarity):	14.0 Ft.	20.0 Ft.	10.0 Ft.
Water color:	Light green	Blue-green	Green
Maximum depth:	50 Ft.	65 Ft.	30 Ft.
Median depth:	5 Ft.	25 Ft.	NA
Accessibility:	Public access on south shore, off County Road #31	Public access on east shore	Public access on southwest shore
Boat Ramp:	Gravel	Earth	Concrete
Accommodations:	NA	Resort, campground	NA
Shoreland zoning classif.:	Nat. Env.	Recreational Dev.	Natural Environment
Dominant forest/soil type:	Decid./Loam	Decid./Sand	NA
Cause of water color:	Algae bloom	Light algae bloom	Light algae bloom
Management class:	Walleye-Centrarchid	Walleye-Centrarchid	Trout
Ecological type:	Centrarchid	Centrarchid-Walleye	Unclassified

DNR COMMENTS:
Northern Pike numbers up and well above what would be expected for lake class; mean length 17.9 inches; growth slower than average. High Northern Pike numbers have depleted the Yellow Perch population. Bluegills abundant; growth has slowed, and mean size has dropped from 7 inches to 6.2 inches. Largemouth Bass and Black Crappies present in modest numbers. Walleye population likewise modest and supported by stocking.

Hungry Lake

FISH STOCKING DATA

year	species	size	# released
93	Walleye	Fingerling	4,290
95	Walleye	Fingerling	2,190
96	Walleye	Fingerling	6,105

survey date: 6/12/95

NET CATCH DATA

	Gill Nets		Trap Nets	
species	# per net	avg fish wt. (lbs)	# per set	avg fish wt. (lbs)
Black Crappie	-	-	0.3	0.56
Bluegill	3.0	0.15	63.9	0.23
Hybrid Sunfish	-	-	0.6	0.35
Largemouth Bass	0.3	1.10	0.5	1.17
Northern Pike	18.3	1.33	1.0	0.68
Pumpkin. Sunfish	-	-	2.9	0.20
Walleye	1.8	1.94	-	-
Yellow Perch	7.5	0.14	0.1	0.05

LENGTH OF SELECTED SPECIES SAMPLED FROM ALL GEAR
Number of fish caught for the following length categories (inches):

species	0-5	6-8	9-11	12-14	15-19	20-24	25-29	>30	Total
Black Crappie	-	-	2	-	-	-	-	-	2
Bluegill	93	149	-	-	-	-	-	-	242
Hybrid Sunfish	-	5	-	-	-	-	-	-	5
Largemouth Bass	-	-	1	4	-	-	-	-	5
Northern Pike	-	-	6	24	25	23	3	-	81
Pumpkin. Sunfish	12	11	-	-	-	-	-	-	23
Walleye	-	-	-	4	1	1	1	-	7
Yellow Perch	8	23	-	-	-	-	-	-	31

Little Toad Lake

FISH STOCKING DATA

year	species	size	# released
90	Walleye	Fingerling	3,885
94	Walleye	Fingerling	2,771
96	Walleye	Fingerling	2,510

survey date: 6/14/93

NET CATCH DATA

	Gill Nets		Trap Nets	
species	# per net	avg fish wt. (lbs)	# per set	avg fish wt. (lbs)
Black Crappie	0.5	0.08	-	-
Bluegill	2.0	0.65	10.3	0.24
Hybrid Sunfish	-	-	0.9	0.32
Largemouth Bass	0.2	1.76	-	-
Northern Pike	8.5	2.31	0.1	0.88
Pumpkin. Sunfish	0.2	0.31	9.9	0.26
Rock Bass	6.7	0.66	4.1	0.57
Walleye	7.0	1.50	0.2	5.24
Yellow Perch	37.7	0.14	1.0	0.15

LENGTH OF SELECTED SPECIES SAMPLED FROM ALL GEAR
Number of fish caught for the following length categories (inches):

species	0-5	6-8	9-11	12-14	15-19	20-24	25-29	>30	Total
Black Crappie	1	2	-	-	-	-	-	-	3
Bluegill	44	62	9	-	-	-	-	-	115
Hybrid Sunfish	2	7	-	-	-	-	-	-	9
Largemouth Bass	-	-	-	-	1	-	-	-	1
Northern Pike	-	-	-	11	36	5	-	-	52
Pumpkin. Sunfish	25	75	-	-	-	-	-	-	100
Rock Bass	3	43	35	-	-	-	-	-	81
Walleye	-	-	-	28	7	8	1	-	44
Yellow Perch	117	104	15	-	-	-	-	-	236

DNR COMMENTS:
Overstocking has damaged this lake's fish population. Northern Pike numbers down but still high; average size small. Walleye numbers have rebounded to above normal for lake class; good average size of 16 inches. Yellow Perch population appears to be rebounding. Largemouth Bass present in modest numbers. Anglers report excellent Black Crappie fishing at times. Bluegill population variable, but currently within normal range; 38 percent of fish reaching 8 inches.

Hanson Lake

FISH STOCKING DATA

year	species	size	# released
90	Rainbow Trout	Yearling	1,000
90	Rainbow Trout	Fingerling	2,500
93	Rainbow Trout	Fingerling	2,500
94	Rainbow Trout	Fingerling	2,500
95	Rainbow Trout	Fingerling	2,500
96	Rainbow Trout	Fingerling	2,500

survey date: 8/9/93

NET CATCH DATA

	Gill Nets		Trap Nets	
species	# per net	avg fish wt. (lbs)	# per set	avg fish wt. (lbs)
Rainbow Trout	6.0	0.93	-	-

LENGTH OF SELECTED SPECIES SAMPLED FROM ALL GEAR
Number of fish caught for the following length categories (inches):

species	0-5	6-8	9-11	12-14	15-19	20-24	25-29	>30	Total
Rainbow Trout	-	-	1	11	-	-	-	-	12

DNR COMMENTS:
Lake was chemically reclaimed for a second time in 1989 and restocked with Rainbow Trout. Current Rainbow population composed of yearling fish 13 inches in length. No other species sampled.

FISHING INFORMATION: A 35-acre pond between Cotton and Height of Land Lakes, **Hanson** is a rarity: the domain of fly fisherman and the Rainbow Trout. The was chemically reclaimed by the DNR in 1989 and restocked with Rainbows. These fish were reported in good supply, averaging about 13 inches in 1995. For current information, call the DNR in Detroit Lakes at (218) 847-1579. **Hungry,** meanwhile, is a very clear lake of 240 acres, with a shoreline of 3.8 miles. It has wide, shallow weedbeds in the south and north and a series of steady drops to a 50-foot hole at mid lake. Stocked Walleye fingerlings have to hustle to escape the large population of Northern Pike.   Fortunately some Walleyes survive, and so do Largemouth Bass and Crappies. Fish the weedbeds in the south and the far north in the spring. As the water warms, jig live bait at the 15- to 20-foot drops along and off the tip of the northern point. **Little Toad** is similar. It's a fine lake for gamefish, and all populations are above state and local median levels, including that of Walleyes. Most fishing centers on the shoreline, including that of the small island. Fish the 10- to 15-foot drops in the Toad River inlet bay at the south end, the weedbeds around the outlet on the western shore, and the sunken points at 10 to 20 feet to the south and west of the island.

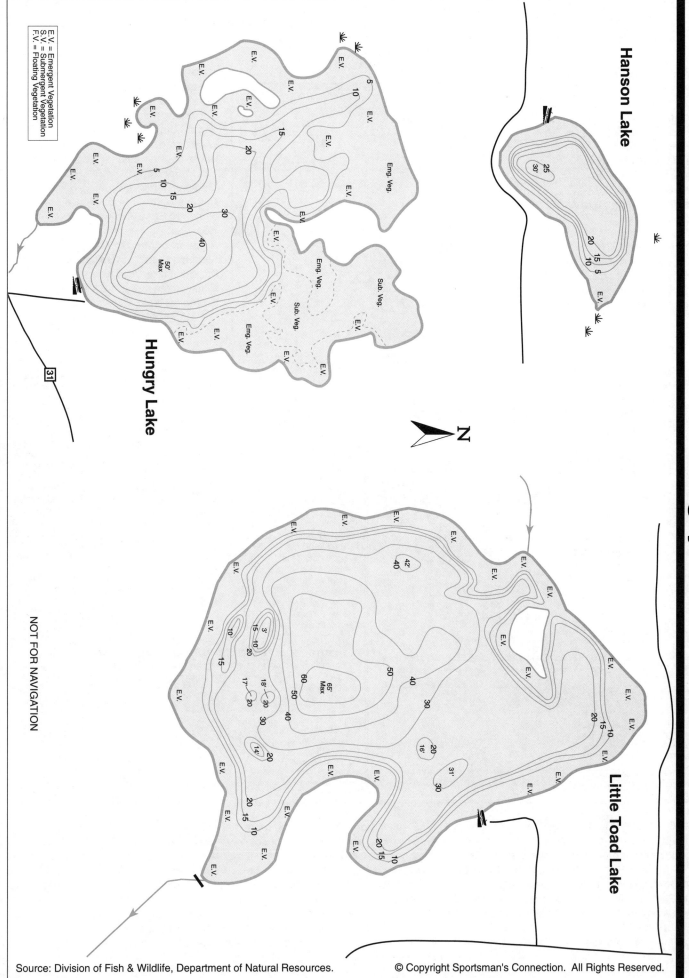

SPORTSMAN'S Connection®

E.V. = Emergent Vegetation
S.V. = Submergent Vegetation
F.V. = Floating Vegetation

Hanson Lake

Hungry Lake

Little Toad Lake

N

NOT FOR NAVIGATION

Source: Division of Fish & Wildlife, Department of Natural Resources.

BASS LAKE

SIEVERSON LAKE

Becker County

Location: Township 140 Range 38
Watershed: Crow Wing
Surface Water Area: 135 Acres
Shorelength: NA
Secchi disk (water clarity): 9.0 Ft.
Water color: Brown
Cause of water color: NA
Maximum depth: 35 Ft.
Median depth: NA
Accessibility: Public access in Chilton Park on east shore
Boat Ramp: Earth
Accommodations: NA
Shoreland zoning classif.: Nat. Env.
Dominant forest/soil type: NA
Management class: Walleye-Centrarchid
Ecological type: Centrarchid-Walleye

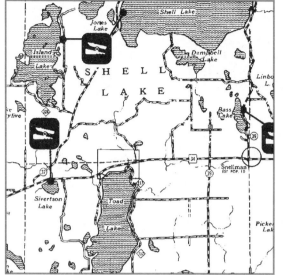

Location: Township 139 Range 38
Watershed: Buffalo
Surface Water Area: 77 Acres
Shorelength: NA
Secchi disk (water clarity): 13.0 Ft.
Water color: Brown
Cause of water color: Bog stain, algae
Maximum depth: 48 Ft.
Median depth: NA
Accessibility: Public access on north shore, off State Highway #34
Boat Ramp: Asphalt
Accommodations: NA
Shoreland zoning classif.: Nat. Env.
Dominant forest/soil type: NA
Management class: Centrarchid
Ecological type: Centrarchid

FISH STOCKING DATA

year	species	size	# released
89	Walleye	Fingerling	5,519

survey date: 7/1/96

NET CATCH DATA

	Gill Nets		Trap Nets	
species	# per net	avg fish wt. (lbs)	# per set	avg fish wt. (lbs)
Black Crappie	1.3	0.09	0.7	0.29
Bluegill	1.5	0.18	43.2	0.21
Brown Bullhead	0.8	0.92	0.3	0.44
Hybrid Sunfish	-	-	0.8	0.25
Largemouth Bass	0.5	0.43	0.7	0.30
Northern Pike	15.8	1.96	0.4	0.79
Pumpkin. Sunfish	0.8	0.18	15.7	0.15
Walleye	0.5	3.03	-	-
White Sucker	1.5	2.18	-	-
Yellow Bullhead	4.3	0.23	3.8	0.35
Yellow Perch	2.8	0.19	0.6	0.12

LENGTH OF SELECTED SPECIES SAMPLED FROM ALL GEAR
Number of fish caught for the following length categories (inches):

species	0-5	6-8	9-11	12-14	15-19	20-24	25-29	>30	Total
Black Crappie	4	5	2	-	-	-	-	-	11
Bluegill	39	172	-	-	-	-	-	-	211
Brown Bullhead	1	1	1	3	-	-	-	-	6
Hybrid Sunfish	2	5	-	-	-	-	-	-	7
Largemouth Bass	-	7	1	-	-	-	-	-	8
Northern Pike	-	-	-	8	30	19	10	-	67
Pumpkin. Sunfish	96	28	-	-	-	-	-	-	124
Walleye	-	-	-	-	1	1	-	-	2
Yellow Bullhead	7	19	25	-	-	-	-	-	51
Yellow Perch	3	13	-	-	-	-	-	-	16

FISH STOCKING DATA

year	species	size	# released
90	Walleye	Fingerling	680
94	Walleye	Fingerling	2,280
96	Walleye	Fingerling	1,050

survey date: 7/25/94

NET CATCH DATA

	Gill Nets		Trap Nets	
species	# per net	avg fish wt. (lbs)	# per set	avg fish wt. (lbs)
Black Bullhead	1.0	0.46	-	-
Black Crappie	0.3	0.19	0.4	0.40
Bluegill	1.7	0.20	34.2	0.20
Brown Bullhead	-	-	0.1	0.80
Hybrid Sunfish	1.3	0.16	4.4	0.14
Largemouth Bass	0.7	0.94	3.0	1.06
Northern Pike	2.0	2.51	0.7	0.82
Pumpkin. Sunfish	0.7	0.10	3.3	0.13
Walleye	2.7	3.25	0.2	2.02
White Sucker	0.3	2.39	-	-
Yellow Bullhead	7.7	0.27	6.0	0.28
Yellow Perch	63.0	0.16	0.3	0.21

LENGTH OF SELECTED SPECIES SAMPLED FROM ALL GEAR
Number of fish caught for the following length categories (inches):

species	0-5	6-8	9-11	12-14	15-19	20-24	25-29	>30	Total
Black Bullhead	-	3	-	-	-	-	-	-	3
Black Crappie	-	1	4	-	-	-	-	-	5
Bluegill	59	117	-	-	-	-	-	-	176
Brown Bullhead	-	-	1	-	-	-	-	-	1
Hybrid Sunfish	33	11	-	-	-	-	-	-	44
Largemouth Bass	-	3	11	13	2	-	-	-	29
Northern Pike	-	-	-	2	4	5	1	-	12
Pumpkin. Sunfish	27	5	-	-	-	-	-	-	32
Walleye	-	-	-	1	3	5	1	-	10
Yellow Bullhead	1	67	9	-	-	-	-	-	77
Yellow Perch	7	72	-	-	-	-	-	-	79

FISHING INFORMATION: These are two small lakes on either side of Toad Lake along Minn. Hwy. 34. Both are undeveloped holes, worth a look when the wind is up on the bigger lakes or when you want a change of scenery. **Sieverson** is just 77 acres of very clear water with a slight brownish tint of bog stain. The DNR has been stocking Walleyes, and numbers of this species are about normal for the area.   Northern Pike, Largemouth Bass and Crappies also show up in the test nets here. A stop early in the season, to cast a few spoons and spinners, or to drop some shiners or a sucker minnow on a slip bobber, might provide an entertaining morning. **Bass** is bigger at 135 acres and may be an even better bet as a short side trip. Where Sieverson is nearly round, Bass long and slender with a water clarity reading of nine feet.   Bluegills are numerous, and Northern Pike numbers, too, are very high. This lake is an easy read. If it's early in the season, cast along the weedbreaks in the emerging beds on the north end. If it's summer and the wind is right, trail a live bait rig down the western shore out about 20 feet from the vegetation. Your best chance is with Northerns.

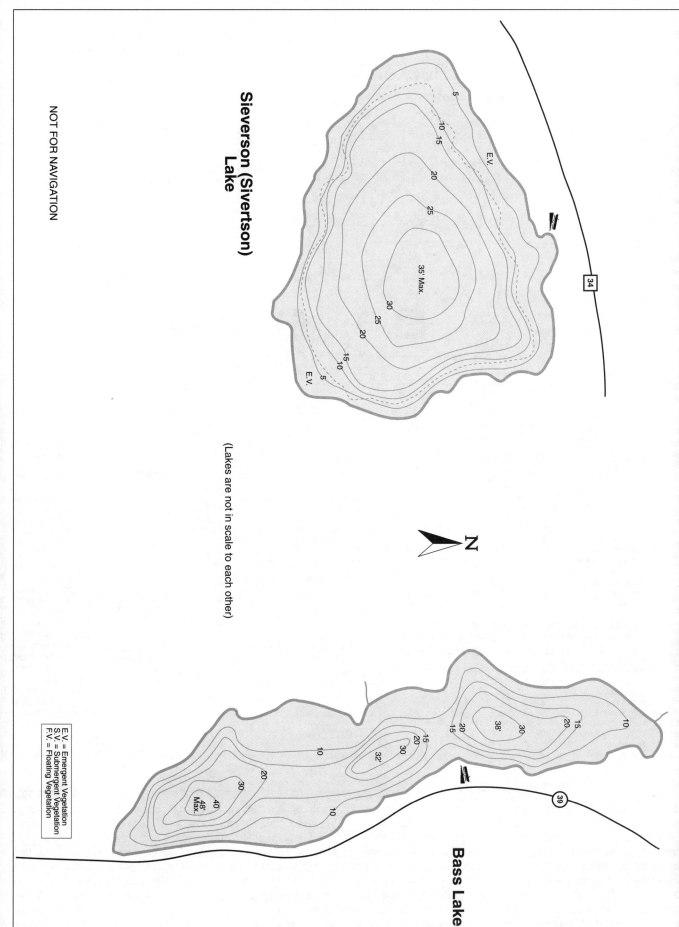

Sieverson (Sivertson) Lake

NOT FOR NAVIGATION

E.V.

34

(Lakes are not in scale to each other)

N

Bass & Sieverson Lakes

Bass Lake

39

E.V. = Emergent Vegetation
S.V. = Submergent Vegetation
F.V. = Floating Vegetation

COTTON LAKE   PICKEREL LAKE
Becker County

Location: Township 139, 140
      Range 40
Watershed: Otter tail
Surface Water Area: 1,668 Acres
Shorelength: 7.9 Miles
Secchi disk (water clarity): 10.0 Ft.
Water color: Slightly green
Cause of water color: Suspended algae
Maximum depth: 28 Ft.
Median depth: 19 Ft.
Accessibility: Federally-owned public access on northeast corner of the lake
Boat Ramp: Concrete
Accommodations: Resorts
Shoreland zoning classif.: Rec. Dev.
Dominant forest/soil type: NA
Management class: Walleye-Centrarchid
Ecological type: Centrarchid-Walleye

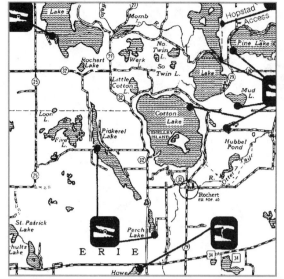

Location: Township 139, 140
      Range 40
Watershed: Otter Tail
Surface Water Area: 332 Acres
Shorelength: 6.7 Miles
Secchi disk (water clarity): 19.0 Ft.
Water color: Green
Cause of water color: Suspended algae
Maximum depth: 74 Ft.
Median depth: 21 Ft.
Accessibility: State-owned access on west shore of the lake
Boat Ramp: Asphalt
Accommodations: NA
Shoreland zoning classif.: Rec. Dev.
Dominant forest/soil type: Decid/Loam
Management class: Walleye-Centrarchid
Ecological type: Centrarchid

DNR COMMENTS:
Walleye survey catch rate within normal range for lake class; strong natural reproduction is producing the best year classes. Northern Pike numerous but small; some fish over 12 lb. taken, however; mean size 15.8 inches and 1.1 lb. Good angling for Largemouth Bass and Black Crappies. Bluegill population up substantially; and very high; average size 6.4 inches; growth slow, with no fish over 8 inches captured. Mercury advisory in effect for larger gamefish; year-around residents should not eat larger Walleyes or Northern Pike more often than once each week.

FISH STOCKING DATA

year	species	size	# released
90	Walleye	Fingerling	13,469
93	Walleye	Fingerling	18,315
93	Walleye	Yearling	480
95	Walleye	Fingerling	13,896

survey date: 7/15/96

NET CATCH DATA

	Gill Nets		Trap Nets	
species	# per net	avg fish wt. (lbs)	# per set	avg fish wt. (lbs)
Black Crappie	0.5	0.55	0.3	0.16
Bluegill	44.3	0.20	106.1	0.21
Hybrid Sunfish	0.3	0.20	2.8	0.26
Largemouth Bass	0.6	1.63	1.1	0.62
Northern Pike	8.5	1.14	1.1	0.48
Pumpkin. Sunfish	4.5	0.18	2.3	0.18
Rock Bass	3.7	0.56	3.4	0.45
Tullibee (Cisco)	0.8	1.09	-	-
Walleye	4.3	2.36	trace	0.34
Yellow Perch	20.9	0.22	0.3	0.21

LENGTH OF SELECTED SPECIES SAMPLED FROM ALL GEAR
Number of fish caught for the following length categories (inches):

species	0-5	6-8	9-11	12-14	15-19	20-24	25-29	>30	Total
Black Bullhead	1	2	4	-	-	-	-	-	7
Black Crappie	2	4	3	1	-	-	-	-	10
Bluegill	271	602	-	-	-	-	-	-	873
Brown Bullhead	-	-	3	5	-	-	-	-	8
Hybrid Sunfish	12	35	-	-	-	-	-	-	47
Largemouth Bass	2	7	6	6	3	-	-	-	24
Northern Pike	-	-	34	46	14	18	6	1	119
Pumpkin. Sunfish	51	39	-	-	-	-	-	-	90
Rock Bass	6	61	32	-	-	-	-	-	99
Tullibee (Cisco)	-	4	1	4	-	-	-	-	10
Walleye	-	1	4	6	22	17	2	-	52
Yellow Bullhead	-	1	69	21	-	-	-	-	91
Yellow Perch	41	177	38	-	-	-	-	-	256

FISH STOCKING DATA

year	species	size	# released
94	Walleye	Fingerling	7,980
96	Walleye	Fingerling	2,860

survey date: 7/8/96

NET CATCH DATA

	Gill Nets		Trap Nets	
species	# per net	avg fish wt. (lbs)	# per set	avg fish wt. (lbs)
Black Crappie	0.7	0.20	2.3	0.23
Bluegill	2.0	0.21	14.5	0.21
Brown Bullhead	0.3	0.97	-	-
Largemouth Bass	0.8	0.41	1.1	0.26
Northern Pike	3.5	3.65	0.2	3.25
Pumpkin. Sunfish	0.2	0.16	0.3	0.15
Walleye	16.0	0.74	0.1	3.64
White Sucker	12.2	1.58	0.2	0.77
Yellow Bullhead	0.2	0.16	0.5	0.95
Yellow Perch	12.5	0.13	0.6	0.13

LENGTH OF SELECTED SPECIES SAMPLED FROM ALL GEAR
Number of fish caught for the following length categories (inches):

species	0-5	6-8	9-11	12-14	15-19	20-24	25-29	>30	Total
Black Crappie	-	28	1	-	-	-	-	-	29
Bluegill	45	104	-	-	-	-	-	-	149
Brown Bullhead	-	2	-	1	-	-	-	-	3
Largemouth Bass	1	10	6	-	-	-	-	-	17
Northern Pike	-	-	-	-	-	13	6	4	23
Pumpkin. Sunfish	3	1	-	-	-	-	-	-	4
Walleye	-	24	39	22	6	6	-	-	97
Yellow Bullhead	-	2	2	3	-	-	-	-	7
Yellow Perch	14	68	-	-	-	-	-	-	82

DNR COMMENTS:
Northern Pike at highest levels ever for Pickerel Lake, but only slightly above third-quartile range for lake class; mean length 25.4 inches; growth faster than statewide average. Walleye numbers triple third-quartile value; young fish dominate the population; mean length 11.7 inches; strong 1994 year class of stocked fish; population dependent on stocking; growth faster than average. Largemouth Bass numbers stable. Black Crappie population variable, with spawning success; mean length 6.1 inches. Bluegill numbers normal for lake class; mean length 6.4 inches.

FISHING INFORMATION: Cotton Lake, about nine miles northeast of Detroit Lakes and fairly close to Rochert, offers a nice variety of fishing for visiting anglers. There are good populations of Northern Pike, Walleyes, Largemouth Bass, and Crappies, as well as a lot of Yellow Perch to keep them well fed. Walleyes, stocked here by the Department of Natural Resources, have some excellent early season feeding spots at the four sunken islands along the west side. The steep downward breaks crossing mid lake are also good. Fish the bottoms at these places with a leech or shiner minnow on a bottom rig, bumping your rig along the bottom slowly. Bass and panfish will be in the weeds at the northeast, southeast and south end of the lake near the outlet to the Otter Tail River. The water is quite clear in the spring, so you can do just fine with a jig and pig for the bass and with worms or small minnows on a bare hook for the panskis. Later, when the water has warmed, you'll do better with plastic worms or weedless lures. That outlet to the river is a fine place for Northerns. So are the flats at the northeast corner where there is an unnamed inlet carrying nutrients into the lake. Nearby **Pickerel Lake** has an outstanding number of Walleye. They are stocked by the DNR and also show good natural reproduction. The water is very clear, so you can see them feeding along the points and steep dropoffs. Offer leeches or shiner minnows early in the season. Later, the marble eyes will head deep to escape the warm water and bright sun of summer. There are some dandy Largemouths in Pickerel. Go into the weeds after them following the spawn with a pig and jig. Or, fish the weed edges with sucker minnows for the numerous Northerns.

Cotton & Pickerel Lakes

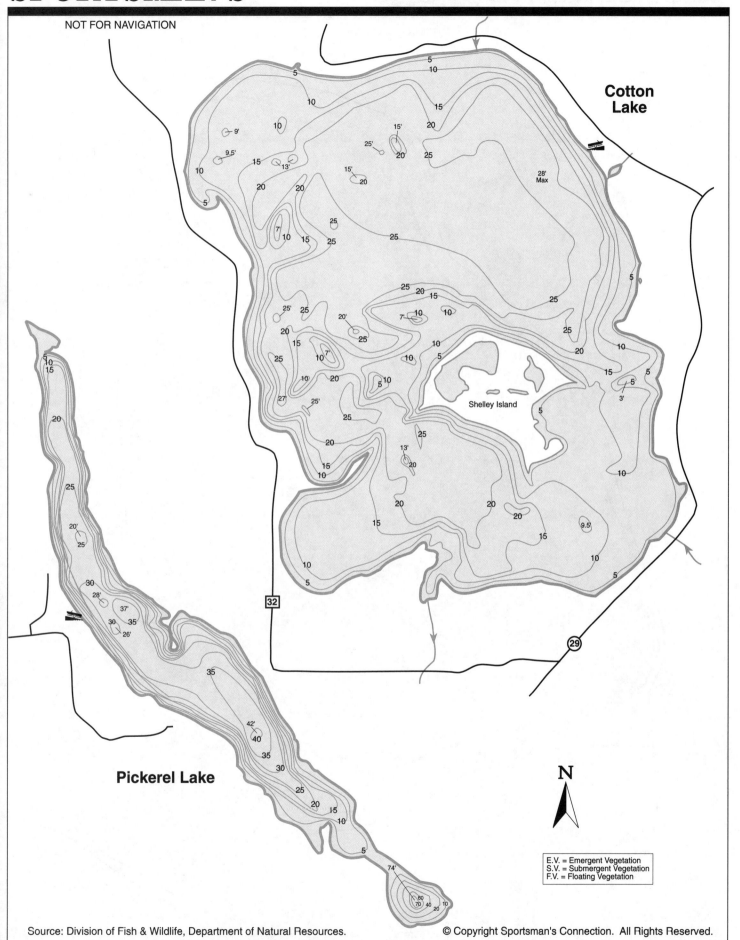

Cotton Lake

Shelley Island

Pickerel Lake

28' Max

N

E.V. = Emergent Vegetation
S.V. = Submergent Vegetation
F.V. = Floating Vegetation

NOT FOR NAVIGATION

E.V. = Emergent Vegetation
S.V. = Submergent Vegetation
F.V. = Floating Vegetation

Source: Division of Fish & Wildlife, Department of Natural Resources.

NOT FOR NAVIGATION

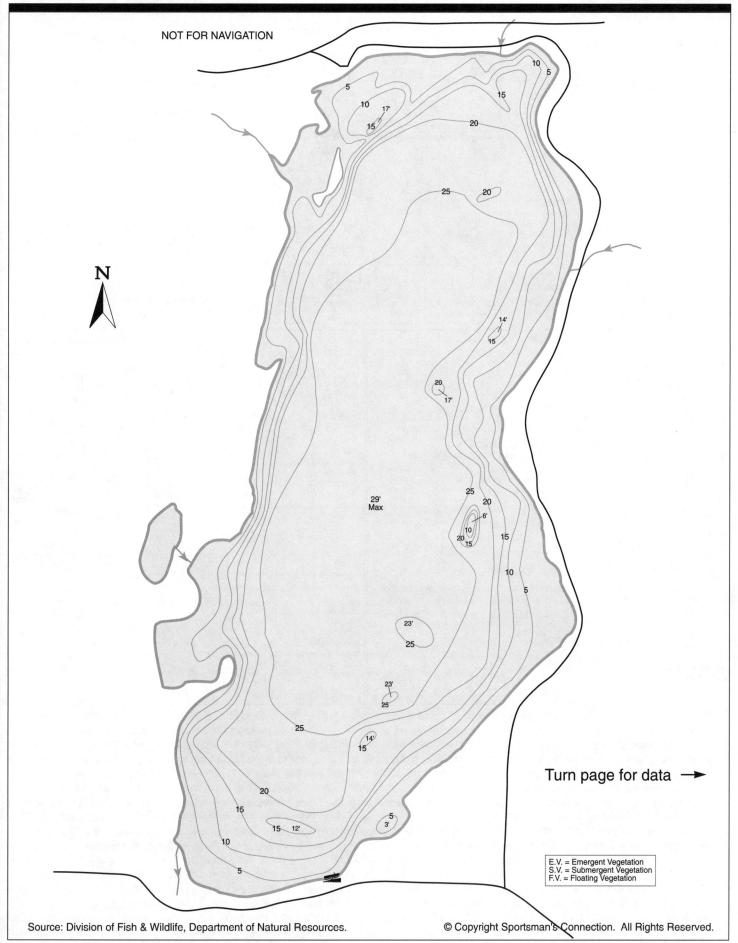

Turn page for data ➡

E.V. = Emergent Vegetation
S.V. = Submergent Vegetation
F.V. = Floating Vegetation

HEIGHT OF LAND LAKE   TOAD LAKE
Becker County

Location: Township 139, 140
Range 39
Watershed: Otter Tail
Surface Water Area: 3,520 Acres
Shorelength: 11.5 Miles
Secchi disk (water clarity): 6.0 Ft.
Water color: Green
Cause of water color: Moderate algae bloom
Maximum depth: 21 Ft.
Median depth: 7 Ft.
Accessibility: Public access on east, south and north shores of the lake
Boat Ramp: Concrete (E & S); Gravel (N)
Accommodations: NA
Shoreland zoning classif.: Rec. Dev.
Dominant forest/soil type: No Tree/Wet
Management class: Walleye-Centrarchid
Ecological type: Centrarchid-Walleye

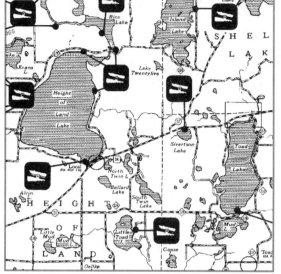

Location: Township 139
Range 38
Watershed: Otter Tail
Surface Water Area: 1,666 Acres
Shorelength: 5.7 Miles
Secchi disk (water clarity): 4.5 Ft.
Water color: Light green
Cause of water color: Slight algae bloom
Maximum depth: 29 Ft.
Median depth: 21 Ft.
Accessibility: Public access on south shore of the lake
Boat Ramp: Concrete
Accommodations: Resort and private campground
Shoreland zoning classif.: Rec. Dev.
Dominant forest/soil type: Decid/Loam
Management class: Walleye-Centrarchid
Ecological type: Centrarchid-Walleye

DNR COMMENTS:
Lake is subject to periodic, partial winterkill. No. Pike population dominated by small, young fish; mean size 17.2 inches and 1 lb. Walleye population fluctuates with winter oxygen conditions; avg. length 14.4 inches; growth slightly faster than normal. LM Bass numbers about normal. Yellow Perch abundant and relatively large; about 10 percent of fish larger than 10 inches. Bluegill numbers low; few young fish present; avg. size 8.1 inches. Black and Brown Bullheads abundant; Yellow Bullhead numbers normal for lake class.

FISH STOCKING DATA

year	species	size	# released
90	Walleye	Fry	3,190,000
93	Walleye	Fry	3,190,000
96	Walleye	Fry	3,190,000
96	Largemouth Bass	Adult	16
96	Black Crappie	Adult	2
96	Bluegill	Adult	540
96	Walleye	Fingerling	60,350

survey date: 6/19/95

NET CATCH DATA

	Gill Nets		Trap Nets	
		avg fish		avg fish
species	# per net	wt. (lbs)	# per set	wt. (lbs)
Bluegill	0.1	0.48	0.5	0.52
Hybrid Sunfish	0.5	0.48	3.6	0.45
Largemouth Bass	-	-	0.5	0.64
Northern Pike	18.6	1.04	1.0	0.75
Pumpkin. Sunfish	0.1	0.47	2.1	0.37
Rock Bass	-	-	trace	0.63
Walleye	3.4	1.30	-	-
Yellow Perch	15.6	0.28	0.7	0.15

LENGTH OF SELECTED SPECIES SAMPLED FROM ALL GEAR
Number of fish caught for the following length categories (inches):

species	0-5	6-8	9-11	12-14	15-19	20-24	25-29	>30	Total
Bluegill	1	5	2	-	-	-	-	-	8
Hybrid Sunfish	3	54	1	-	-	-	-	-	58
Largemouth Bass	-	6	-	1	1	-	-	-	8
Northern Pike	-	-	8	20	122	12	2	-	164
Pumpkin. Sunfish	2	30	-	-	-	-	-	-	32
Rock Bass	-	-	1	-	-	-	-	-	1
Walleye	-	9	-	1	16	1	-	-	27
Yellow Perch	29	66	40	-	-	-	-	-	135

FISH STOCKING DATA

year	species	size	# released
93	Walleye	Fingerling	10,170
95	Walleye	fingerling	14,770

survey date: 8/12/96

NET CATCH DATA

	Gill Nets		Trap Nets	
		avg fish		avg fish
species	# per net	wt. (lbs)	# per set	wt. (lbs)
Black Crappie	0.3	0.50	0.5	1.16
Bluegill	2.3	0.35	5.2	0.20
Largemouth Bass	0.3	1.03	2.5	0.34
Northern Pike	7.5	1.62	0.9	1.40
Pumpkin. Sunfish	1.0	0.19	4.1	0.14
Rock Bass	7.3	0.50	1.1	0.44
Walleye	11.5	1.76	0.2	4.37
Yellow Perch	0.3	0.19	1.0	0.09

LENGTH OF SELECTED SPECIES SAMPLED FROM ALL GEAR
Number of fish caught for the following length categories (inches):

species	0-5	6-8	9-11	12-14	15-19	20-24	25-29	>30	Total
Black Crappie	1	1	1	6	-	-	-	-	9
Bluegill	24	63	-	-	-	-	-	-	87
Largemouth Bass	7	18	9	2	1	-	-	-	37
Northern Pike	-	-	-	-	30	21	2	1	54
Pumpkin. Sunfish	42	22	-	-	-	-	-	-	64
Rock Bass	6	34	20	-	-	-	-	-	60
Walleye	-	8	5	7	32	17	2	-	71
Yellow Perch	12	3	1	-	-	-	-	-	16

DNR COMMENTS:
Northern Pike numbers high, but declining toward a normal level for lake class; few older Pike present, likely because anglers "cropping off" the larger fish. Yellow Perch numbers very low. Bluegill population has soared; many fish over 6 inches. Walleye numbers above normal for lake class; average size nearly 2 lb.; natural reproduction taking place. Black Crappie numbers modest; good numbers of large fish, including some over 1 lb. Largemouth Bass, rock Bass, and Pumpkinseed present, and populations are self-sustaining.

FISHING INFORMATION: Before giving **Height of Land** a try for the first time, it's a good idea to check on its seasonal status with the DNR office in Osage or nearby tackle shops. Ask about recent winterkill. If there's no problem, and you like to fish Northern Pike, this is a good lake. One look and you know this is a hunter's lake as well as the angler's: plenty of weeds and wild rice beds. Water clarity is about 7 feet, which is just about median depth so it's best to stay offshore and cast to the edges of the weed and rice beds with crankbaits and spinners. Because this is a shallow lake, it is most heavily fished early in the season. There is a hole almost dead center, and its slopes and several surrounding humps are the main Walleye hangouts. Jig the edges of the deep weedlines or drift at 10 to 15 feet with Lindy rigs armed with shiners or nightcrawlers. Northerns are all over the place, especially around the outlet. In contrast, the unusual characteristic of **Toad Lake** is its lack of structure. It's like fishing in a soup bowl. Even so, many lakes a lot more complex than Toad don't have its abundant gamefish populations. While there is some irregularity to the shoreline, a few small bays and points, the main lake drops down in steady breaks to a pan of 29 feet that is fully half of the lake's bottom area. Walleye numbers are above average and Perch, Largemouth Bass and Bluegill populations, too, are all above statewide medians. The problem is how to locate the fish given the near-absence of structure. For starters, try the sunken island 7 feet below the surface just off the eastern shore at mid-lake. All sides of this structure are Walleye territory. Jig or drift the slopes with shiners or crawlers. Take advantage of any weedbed or shoreline structure you find, such as the two small inlets on the northwest and far north ends of the lake. Largemouth favor the broad bay on the lower eastern shore. The favored style of fishing in Toad is to locate a variation in the lake's bottom tand drop a leech, shiner or nightcrawler down on a slip bobber or drift the 15-foot breaks. This lake is a real challenge in angling finesse, but those who solve the riddle go home with heavy stringers.

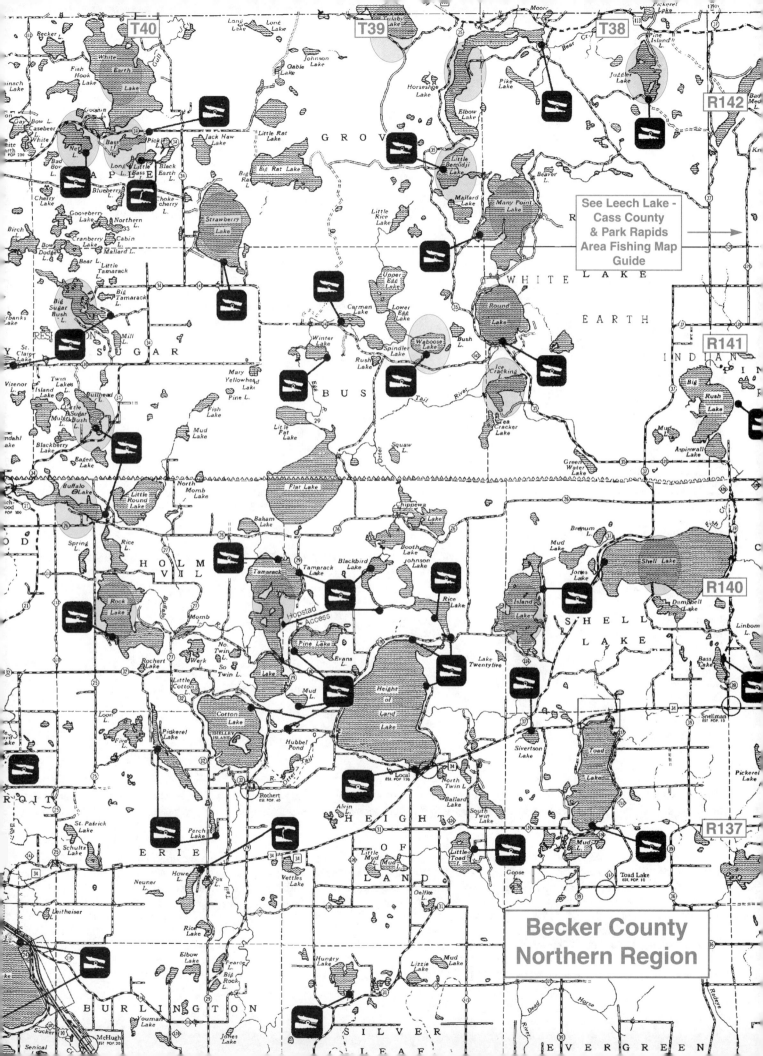

Becker County
Northern Region

See Leech Lake -
Cass County
& Park Rapids
Area Fishing Map
Guide

SHELL LAKE
Becker County

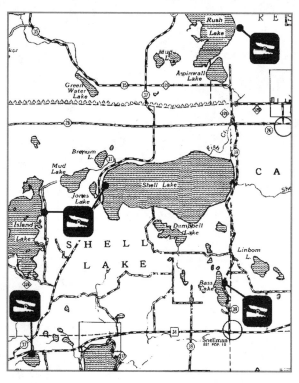

Location: Township 140 Range 37, 38
Watershed: Crow Wing
Surface Water Area: 3,140 Acres
Shorelength: 10.3 Miles
Secchi disk (water clarity): 5.0 Ft.
Water color: Light green
Cause of water color: Slight algae bloom and bog stain

Maximum depth: 16 Ft.
Median depth: 7 Ft.
Accessibility: Public access on west shore of lake
Boat Ramp: Concrete
Accommodations: Resorts and campgrounds

Shoreland zoning classification: Recreational Development
Dominant forest/soil type: Deciduous/Wet
Management class: Warm-Water Gamefish
Ecological type: Roughfish-Gamefish

FISH STOCKING DATA

year	species	size	# released
93	Walleye	Fry	3,070,000
94	Walleye	Fry	3,086,400
96	Walleye	Fry	3,070,000
96	Bluegill	Adult	500
96	Black Crappie	Adult	6
96	Largemouth Bass	Adult	6

NET CATCH DATA

survey date: 8/14/95

species	Gill Nets # per net	Gill Nets avg fish wt. (lbs.)	Trap Nets # per set	Trap Nets avg fish wt. (lbs.)
Black Bullhead	41.8	0.14	56.1	0.13
Black Crappie	1.3	0.36	0.3	0.34
Bluegill	5.5	0.30	14.7	0.26
Brown Bullhead	20.3	0.19	15.9	0.20
Common Carp	-	-	0.2	5.52
Hybrid Sunfish	-	-	0.3	0.14
Largemouth Bass	0.1	0.29	0.2	0.25
Northern Pike	4.0	1.09	0.7	2.18
Pumpkin. Sunfish	2.9	0.20	8.3	0.04
Walleye	4.6	1.70	0.1	5.06
White Sucker	1.4	2.29	1.5	1.97
Yellow Bullhead	0.5	0.62	2.9	0.37
Yellow Perch	7.8	0.11	6.6	0.09

LENGTH OF SELECTED SPECIES SAMPLED FROM ALL GEAR

Number of fish caught for the following length categories (inches):

species	0-5	6-8	9-11	12-14	15-19	20-24	25-29	>30	Total
Black Bullhead	14	323	-	-	-	-	-	-	337
Black Crappie	2	6	7	-	-	-	-	-	15
Bluegill	50	171	-	-	-	-	-	-	221
Brown Bullhead	-	262	5	-	-	-	-	-	267
Hybrid Sunfish	2	2	-	-	-	-	-	-	4
Largemouth Bass	-	4	-	-	-	-	-	-	4
Northern Pike	-	-	-	9	21	8	4	-	42
Pumpkin. Sunfish	112	25	-	-	-	-	-	-	137
Walleye	-	5	7	4	15	6	2	-	39
Yellow Bullhead	2	34	12	-	-	-	-	-	48
Yellow Perch	45	80	-	-	-	-	-	-	125

DNR COMMENTS: Lake experienced a severe winterkill in 1995-96. Walleye, Largemouth Bass, and Panfish populations were devastated. Those species were restocked in spring 1996, and a fishery recovery was expected in three to five years, barring further winterkills.

FISHING INFORMATION: Shell is a 3,140-acre lake with a smooth shoreline of 10.3 miles but with a maximum depth of only 16 feet and a median depth of just 7 feet. Because it's shallow, Shell is subject to occasional winterkill. In fact, the lake's number came up in 1995-96, and the fish population was devastated. Ignore, therefore, the data above. But be aware that the lake has been restocked with Walleye, Largemouth Bass, and panfish, and those populations should offer good angling starting about 1999, barring further kills. The lake, of course, warms up early and is, therefore, most active in spring, late fall and in winter. In the spring, interest centers on the 5- to 10-foot breaks out from the Shell River outlet at the east end, the Fish Creek inlet on the north shore and the inlet from Dumbbell Lake on the southern shore. In the late fall and winter, interest shifts to the 13-foot trough just off the eastern shore and the scattered holes from 12 to 16 feet across the center of the lake. In mid-summer, with a water clarity of five feet and a median depth of seven, the lake warms considerably and becomes a recreational playground. Early open water mainly draws panfish, Crappie and Bass anglers.

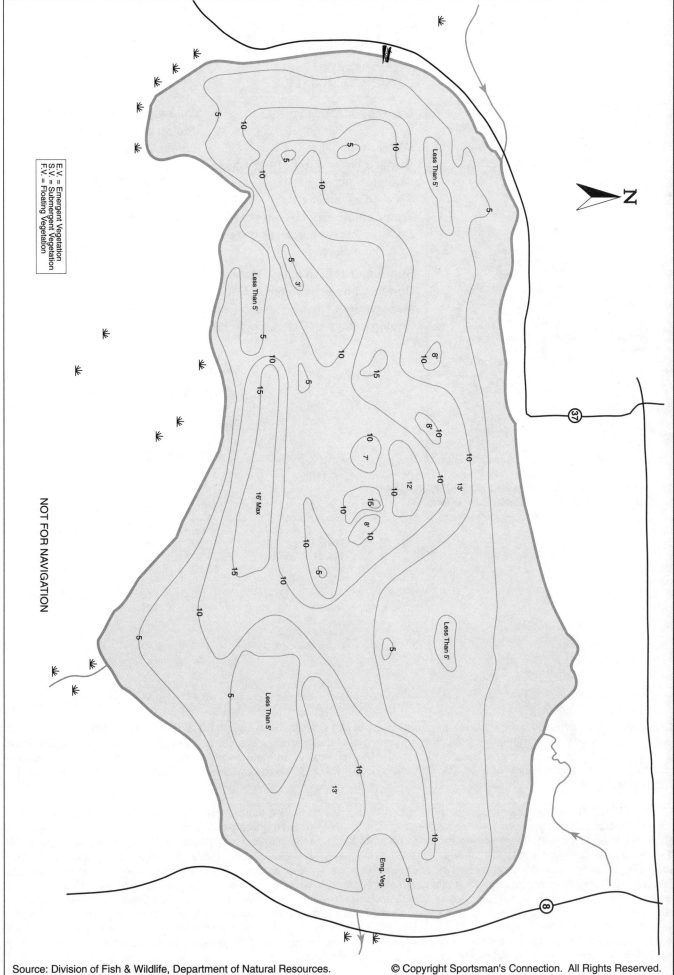

N

E.V. = Emergent Vegetation
S.V. = Submergent Vegetation
F.V. = Floating Vegetation

NOT FOR NAVIGATION

Less Than 5'

Less Than 5'

3'

16' Max

15

8'

15

8' 10

12'

13'

10

7

15

8'

Less Than 5'

Less Than 5'

Emg. Veg.

37

8

ISLAND LAKE
Becker County

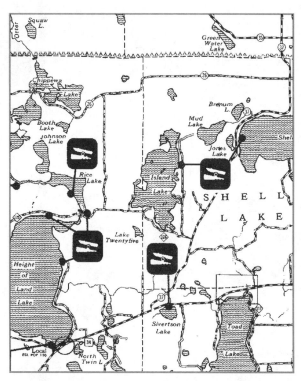

Location: Township 140 Range 38, 39
Watershed: Otter Tail
Surface Water Area: 1,142 Acres
Shorelength: 9.7 Miles
Secchi disk (water clarity): 6.5 Ft.
Water color: Light brown-green
Cause of water color: Bog stain, mild algae bloom

Maximum depth: 38 Ft.
Median depth: 20 Ft.
Accessibility: State-owned public access on east shore
Boat Ramp: Concrete
Accommodations: Resorts and campgrounds

Shoreland zoning classification: Recreational Development
Dominant forest/soil type: Deciduous/Loam
Management class: Walleye-Centrarchid
Ecological type: Centrarchid-Walleye

FISH STOCKING DATA

No record of stocking since 1985.

LENGTH OF SELECTED SPECIES SAMPLED FROM ALL GEAR
Number of fish caught for the following length categories (inches):

species	0-5	6-8	9-11	12-14	15-19	20-24	25-29	>30	Total
Black Bullhead	54	70	12	-	-	-	-	-	136
Black Crappie	1	23	2	-	-	-	-	-	26
Bluegill	93	8	1	-	-	-	-	-	102
Brown Bullhead	-	-	6	2	-	-	-	-	8
Green Sunfish	8	3	-	-	-	-	-	-	11
Hybrid Sunfish	17	16	-	-	-	-	-	-	33
Largemouth Bass	3	-	-	-	-	-	-	-	3
Northern Pike	-	-	-	-	2	5	1	-	8
Pumpkin. Sunfish	3	4	-	-	-	-	-	-	7
Rock Bass	5	9	-	-	-	-	-	-	14
Smallmouth Bass	1	13	7	2	-	-	-	-	23
Walleye	-	26	43	36	19	7	2	-	133
Yellow Bullhead	-	2	1	7	-	-	-	-	10
Yellow Perch	1	31	41	1	-	-	-	-	74

NET CATCH DATA
survey date: 8/11/89

species	Gill Nets # per net	Gill Nets avg fish wt. (lbs.)	Trap Nets # per set	Trap Nets avg fish wt. (lbs.)
Yellow Perch	15.3	0.47	1.0	0.33
Yellow Bullhead	0.3	0.30	0.8	1.13
White Sucker	0.3	2.90	0.2	4.50
Pumpkin. Sunfish	-	-	0.6	0.27
Walleye	27.8	0.79	2.1	0.81
Largemouth Bass	-	-	0.3	0.12
Smallmouth Bass	3.8	0.46	0.8	0.30
Rock Bass	0.3	0.20	1.1	0.35
Hybrid Sunfish	-	-	2.8	0.28
Northern Pike	1.0	1.88	0.3	3.10
Brown Bullhead	1.0	0.70	0.3	1.10
Bluegill	2.0	0.25	21.7	0.10
Green Sunfish	-	-	0.9	0.12
Black Crappie	0.5	0.35	2.0	0.38
Black Bullhead	61.8	0.39	10.0	0.22

DNR COMMENTS: Northern Pike numbers low; fast growth rates for this species. Smallmouth Bass, Bluegill and Black Crappie populations are rebounding from lows in the early 1980s, and the numbers of these species are above average for lake class. Yellow Perch numbers down but about average for lake class. Walleye numbers several times state and local median levels; natural reproduction excellent; population composed mainly of ages 1 to 3; growth good. Black Bullhead numbers well above average for lake class; this species first sampled in 1975.

FISHING INFORMATION: Island is for anglers who like lots of structure and for fish that like lots of structure as well, namely Walleyes and Smallmouth Bass. Island comprises 1,142 acres and 9.7 miles of highly irregular shoreline. It's spring-fed and is fairly clear with secchi disk readings of up to 10 feet. There are several holes up to 43 feet, and the lake reaches 30 feet fairly quickly. Median depth is 20 feet, which means most of the action is just offshore or around the several bars and sunken islands. For your best chance, you'll make good use of a depthfinder. Earliest fishing is in the far south and far north, areas of shallows and of weedbeds. Fishing heats up in June, when the bars that reach out from the southern and eastern shores begin to provide weed cover. Same with a small sunken island that rises to within 4 feet of the surface at mid lake. Toss spinners and shallow-running lures along the inner weedbreaks of this structure, particularly the network of bars and humps that reach mid-lake about three quarters of the way up off the eastern shore. You can also jig this area with shiners and nightcrawlers or, as the water warms, put a leech on a light line with a split shot and let it settle along the deep weedbreaks. Also try the drop-offs in the small bay midway up the western shore, and jig the sunken island at the bay's center. A campground on the southwest shore and abundant fish make this a favorite family lake.

SPORTSMAN'S Connection®

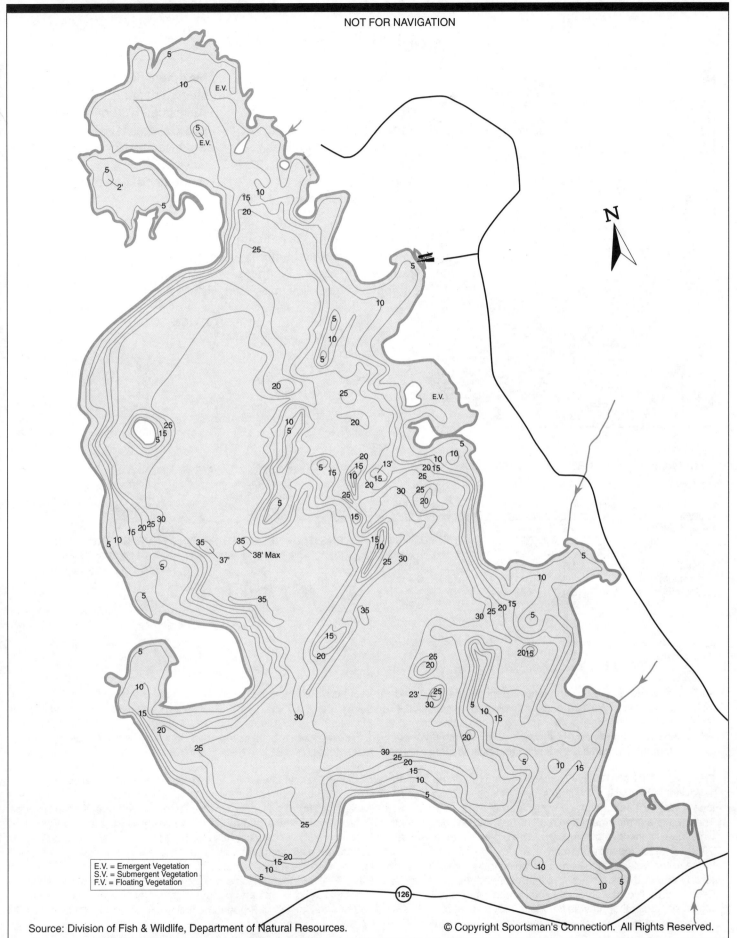

E.V. = Emergent Vegetation
S.V. = Submergent Vegetation
F.V. = Floating Vegetation

38' Max

126

TAMARACK LAKE
Becker County

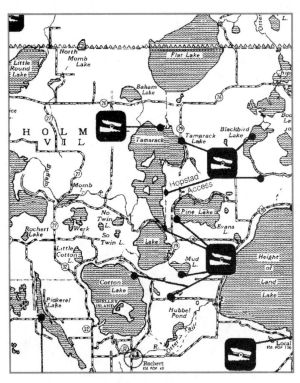

Location: Township 140
Range 39, 40
Watershed: Otter Tail
Surface Water Area: 1,431 Acres
Shorelength: 13.7 Miles
Secchi disk (water clarity): 3.3 Ft.
Water color: Green
Cause of water color: Moderate algae bloom

Maximum depth: 16 Ft.
Median depth: 5 Ft.
Accessibility: Four points of public access (see map)
Boat Ramp: Concrete (N & NE) Gravel (SE)
Accommodations: NA

Shoreland zoning classification: Natural Environment
Dominant forest/soil type: NA
Management class: Warm-Water Gamefish
Ecological type: Roughfish-Gamefish

FISH STOCKING DATA

year	species	size	# released
90	Walleye	Fry	1,390,000
93	Walleye	Fry	1,390,000
94	Walleye	Fry	1,390,000
94	Bluegill	Adult	300
94	Black Crappie	Adult	56
94	Largemouth Bass	Adult	39
95	Walleye	Fry	695,000
95	Largemouth Bass	Adult	74
96	Walleye	Fry	1,390,000
96	Bluegill	Adult	1,040
96	Black Crappie	Adult	8
96	Largemouth Bass	Adult	27
96	Walleye	Fingerling	31,555

NET CATCH DATA

survey date: 8/9/93

species	Gill Nets # per net	Gill Nets avg fish wt. (lbs.)	Trap Nets # per set	Trap Nets avg fish wt. (lbs.)
Black Bullhead	0.3	1.32	-	-
Black Crappie	1.0	0.35	3.5	0.64
Bluegill	4.0	0.21	11.3	0.37
Brown Bullhead	1.3	1.16	4.2	0.93
Largemouth Bass	2.3	1.41	0.1	0.44
Northern Pike	18.3	2.49	0.9	1.86
Pumpkin. Sunfish	3.5	0.23	2.8	0.28
Walleye	7.8	1.73	0.5	3.70
White Sucker	3.5	2.47	-	-
Yellow Bullhead	6.3	0.97	20.3	0.88
Yellow Perch	33.8	0.11	0.1	0.11

LENGTH OF SELECTED SPECIES SAMPLED FROM ALL GEAR
Number of fish caught for the following length categories (inches):

species	0-5	6-8	9-11	12-14	15-19	20-24	25-29	>30	Total
Black Crappie	-	24	7	10	-	-	-	-	41
Bluegill	44	72	21	-	-	-	-	-	137
Largemouth Bass	-	-	5	9	1	-	-	-	15
Northern Pike	-	1	-	2	35	46	34	1	119
Pumpkin. Sunfish	13	36	-	-	-	-	-	-	49
Walleye	-	-	4	9	29	7	3	-	52
Yellow Perch	102	62	-	-	-	-	-	-	164

DNR COMMENTS: Lake experiences periodic, partial winterkill. Northern Pike population above normal for lake class; mean size 22 inches and 2.5 lb.. Walleye numbers about average; good average weight of 1.7 lb. Black Crappie population about normal; fish are large, with mean length of nearly 10 inches and some fish up to 14 inches present. Bluegills abundant; average size over 7 inches, with some fish measuring nearly 11 inches. Yellow Perch numbers high. Yellow Bullheads have replaced Black Bullheads as the most abundant bottom feeder; numbers are high, and average length is nearly 12 inches.

FISHING INFORMATION: Tamarack is another of the shallow lakes in the Detroit Lakes area that experiences occasional winterkill, so it is advisable to check at Walther's Tackle Shop in Detroit Lakes or at the DNR office there for the most current information. Tamarack is a long 2,227 acre lake (surface water area of 1,431 acres) with 13.7 miles of shoreline located in the Tamarack National Wildlife Refuge. The lake has a maximum depth of 16 feet and a median depth of 5 feet which means that much of its surface is covered with wild rice, water lilies, cattails and bulrushes. The big bay in the northeast section of the lake, however, has a sizable pond that dropping down from 10 to 16 feet in a series of broad shelves. This area draws most local anglers, especially when the ice cover forms, because Tamarack is home to the fattest Bluegills and Crappies in the area. In spring, those panfish are there as well. They're just trickier to reach. There are also Northern Pike here, as well as Bass, and the DNR stocks Walleyes. All of these species are available. Cast spinners or weedless lures or drop live bait on a light line into the breaks in the weeds or at the 10-foot drops and deeper as summer progresses. It's not the bigger gamefish that provide the major draw, as much as it is the 1 1/2-pound Sunfish or 2-pound Crappie on a light rod. They're why the anglers came to Tamarack, in the first place, and year after year, why they keep coming back.

Tamarack Lake

NOT FOR NAVIGATION

N

E.V. = Emergent Vegetation
S.V. = Submergent Vegetation
F.V. = Floating Vegetation

BUFFALO LAKE

ROCK LAKE

Becker County

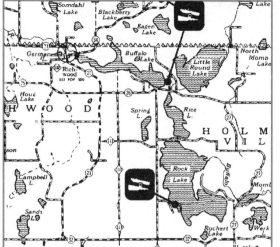

Location: Township 140, 141 Range 40, 41
Watershed: Buffalo
Surface Water Area: 376 Acres
Shorelength: 7.3 Miles
Secchi disk (water clarity): 12.0 Ft.
Water color: Slightly green
Cause of water color: Suspended algae
Maximum depth: 37 Ft.
Median depth: 15 Ft.
Accessibility: State-owned public access on east shore of the lake
Boat Ramp: Asphalt
Accommodations: NA
Shoreland zoning classif.: Rec. Dev.
Dominant forest/soil type: Decid/Loam
Management class: Walleye-Centrarchid
Ecological type: Centrarchid

Location: Township 140 Range 40
Watershed: Buffalo
Surface Water Area: 1,048 Acres
Shorelength: 8.6 Miles
Secchi disk (water clarity): 6.0 Ft.
Water color: Brown-green
Cause of water color: Suspended algae, bog stain
Maximum depth: 18 Ft.
Median depth: 8 Ft.
Accessibility: State-owned public access on southwest shore of the lake
Boat Ramp: Concrete
Accommodations: NA
Shoreland zoning classif.: Rec. Dev.
Dominant forest/soil type: Decid/Sand
Management class: Walleye-Centrarchid
Ecological type: Centrarchid

DNR COMMENTS:

NOT AVAILABLE

FISH STOCKING DATA

year	species	size	# released
93	Walleye	Fingerling	7,680
95	Walleye	Adult	179
95	Walleye	Fingerling	156
95	Walleye	Yearling	46
96	Walleye	Fingerling	2,340

survey date: 8/19/91

NET CATCH DATA

	Gill Nets		Trap Nets	
		avg fish		avg fish
species	# per net	wt. (lbs)	# per set	wt. (lbs)
Yellow Perch	20.5	0.16	2.4	0.15
Yellow Bullhead	48.3	0.64	3.9	0.43
White Sucker	5.7	2.06	0.1	3.50
Walleye	6.5	0.83	-	-
Tullibee (Cisco)	16.3	1.31	-	-
Rock Bass	1.0	0.43	1.1	0.31
Pumpkin. Sunfish	0.5	0.17	5.3	0.19
Northern Pike	6.0	1.53	1.0	0.72
Largemouth Bass	0.3	0.55	-	-
Brown Bullhead	6.7	0.59	0.1	0.70
Bluegill	1.2	0.26	19.1	0.11
Black Crappie	0.5	0.80	0.1	0.30
Black Bullhead	2.8	0.62	0.1	0.10

LENGTH OF SELECTED SPECIES SAMPLED FROM SURVEY

Not Available.

FISH STOCKING DATA

year	species	size	# released
90	Walleye	Fry	1,001,000
93	Walleye	Fry	1,001,000
95	Walleye	Fry	1,001,000
96	Walleye	Fry	1,001,000
96	Largemouth Bass	Adult	29
96	Bluegill	Adult	560
96	Black Crappie	Adult	6
96	Walleye	Fingerling	29,485

survey date: 7/17/95

NET CATCH DATA

	Gill Nets		Trap Nets	
		avg fish		avg fish
species	# per net	wt. (lbs)	# per set	wt. (lbs)
Black Crappie	0.5	0.05	6.8	0.04
Bluegill	4.1	0.33	22.1	0.25
Largemouth Bass	0.1	0.41	2.3	0.20
Northern Pike	8.0	1.56	0.6	2.76
Pumpkin. Sunfish	1.1	0.21	2.4	0.25
Walleye	7.4	1.67	0.1	3.86
Yellow Perch	14.1	0.15	2.0	0.11

LENGTH OF SELECTED SPECIES SAMPLED FROM ALL GEAR

Number of fish caught for the following length categories (inches):

species	0-5	6-8	9-11	12-14	15-19	20-24	25-29	>30	Total
Black Crappie	48	1	-	-	-	-	-	-	49
Bluegill	29	196	-	-	-	-	-	-	225
Largemouth Bass	5	21	-	-	-	-	-	-	26
Northern Pike	-	-	-	3	43	19	5	1	71
Pumpkin. Sunfish	13	22	-	-	-	-	-	-	35
Walleye	-	-	22	8	21	7	2	-	60
Yellow Perch	27	93	1	-	-	-	-	-	121

DNR COMMENTS: Rock Lake sustained a major winterkill in 1995-96. Only Bullheads and White Suckers, plus a few Northern Pike and Yellow Perch survived. Bluegill, Black Crappie, Largemouth Bass, and Walleye stocking were planned for 1996. The lake should be fishable in 1999 and beyond, barring any further winterkills.

FISHING INFORMATION: Buffalo Lake, twelve miles north of Detroit Lakes, is pretty much a natural for panfish and Northerns, but it also holds some nice Walleyes, thanks to DNR stocking. A number of spots promise panfish: nearly anywhere you see a weedline is decent, but the far west end near the outlet to the Buffalo River and the east end near the inlet from Rice Lake are very good. The two shallow bays on the north side also are good. Offer worms or small minnows on a bare hook. Northerns are in the same areas, feeding on Yellow Perch and smaller panskis. Live bait can get their attention quickly enough, but you may want to consider an injured minnow lure. There aren't a lot of Walleye in the lake, but you can catch them off points on both the north and south shores. Steep dropoffs just off the middle of the south shore can be good also. Use minnows or leeches on a bottom rig in the spring. Later, go deep for the Walleyes as well as the bigger Northerns and Crappies. Nearby **Rock Lake** experienced a major winterkill in 1995-96. Most gamefish populations were nearly wiped out. The lake was restocked in 1996 with Walleyes, Largemouth Bass, Bluegills and Crappies, and these species – together with the Northern Pike which survived the kill – should offer good angling opportunities starting in about 1999, barring further dieoffs. Try the spawning grounds in the northeast bay for panfish. Northerns will be off the lake's weedlines early and can be attracted by spinnerbaits and spoons. Start at the area around the dam on the west side and near the boat access area on the south side. Walleyes will be off points on the south side and the hump located at the southeast end.

Buffalo & Rock Lakes

NOT FOR NAVIGATION

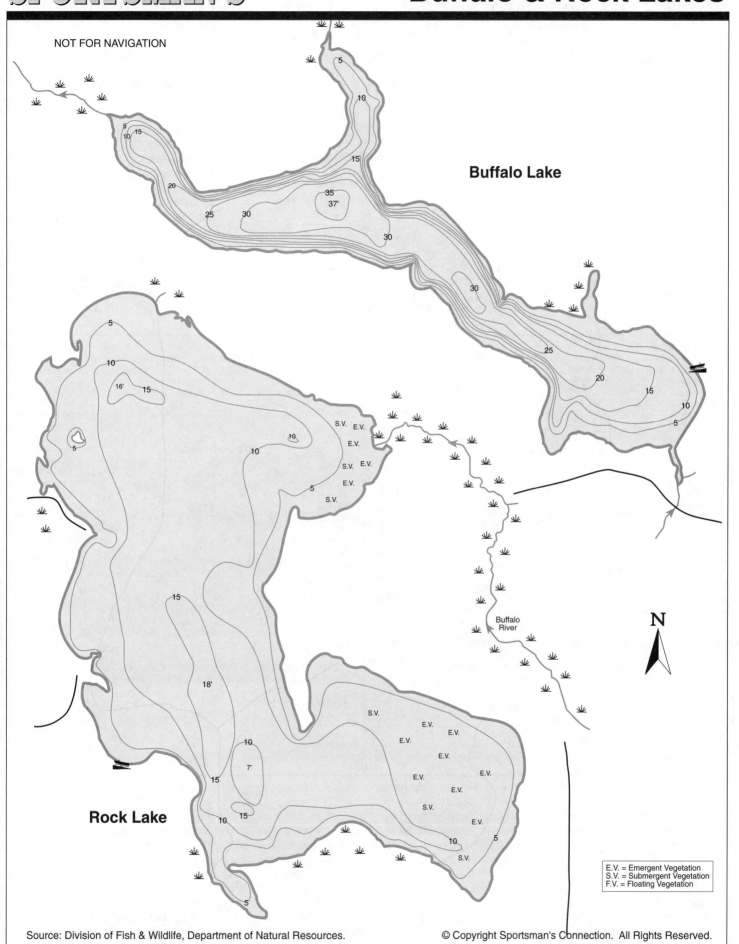

Buffalo Lake

5
10
15
15
10
5
10
15
20
35
37'
30
25
30
30
25
20
15
10
5

Rock Lake

5
10
16'
15
5
10
10
15
5
15
18'
10
7'
15
10
15
5
5

S.V. E.V.
E.V.
S.V. E.V.
E.V.
S.V.

S.V.
E.V. E.V.
E.V.
E.V.
E.V. E.V.
E.V.
S.V.
E.V.
10 5
S.V.

Buffalo
River

N

E.V. = Emergent Vegetation
S.V. = Submergent Vegetation
F.V. = Floating Vegetation

BIG SUGARBUSH LAKE   LITTLE SUGARBUSH LAKE
Becker County

Location: Township 141 Range 40
Watershed: Buffalo
Surface Water Area: 472 Acres
Shorelength: 7.4 Miles
Secchi disk (water clarity): 15.0 Ft.
Water color: Clear
Cause of water color: NA
Maximum depth: 42 Ft.
Median depth: 15 Ft.
Accessibility: County-owned public access on east shore of the northeast bay of the lake
Boat Ramp: Concrete
Accommodations: NA
Shoreland zoning classif.: Rec. Dev.
Dominant forest/soil type: Decid/Loam
Management class: Walleye-Centrarchid
Ecological type: Centrarchid

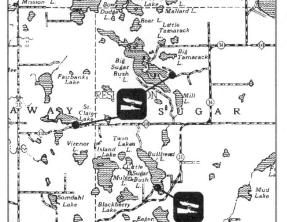

Location: Township 141 Range 40
Watershed: Buffalo
Surface Water Area: 202 Acres
Shorelength: 3.3 Miles
Secchi disk (water clarity): 6.5 Ft.
Water color: Green
Cause of water color: Suspended algae
Maximum depth: 29 Ft.
Median depth: 17 Ft.
Accessibility: State-owned public access on southwest shore of the lake
Boat Ramp: Concrete
Accommodations: Resorts; campgrounds
Shoreland zoning classif.: Rec. Dev.
Dominant forest/soil type: Decid/Loam
Management class: Walleye-Centrarchid
Ecological type: Centrarchid

DNR COMMENTS:
Walleye numbers up somewhat, but not above normal for lake class; natural reproduction very sporadic. Northern Pike, Largemouth Bass, Bluegill and Yellow Bullhead numbers remain strong. Black Crappies captured for first time; numbers and size structure good. Yellow Perch numbers up but still below average for lake class.

FISH STOCKING DATA

year	species	size	# released
90	Walleye	Fingerling	13,450
93	Walleye	Fry	300,000
94	Walleye	Fry	300,000
96	Walleye	Fry	298,000

NET CATCH DATA
survey date: 6/24/87

| | Gill Nets | | Trap Nets | |
| | | avg fish | | avg fish |
species	# per net	wt. (lbs)	# per set	wt. (lbs)
Yellow Perch	4.3	0.12	0.3	0.13
Yellow Bullhead	40.5	0.39	22.9	0.32
White Sucker	0.3	2.25	-	-
Walleye	3.0	1.26	0.3	0.83
Pumpkin. Sunfish	7.0	0.15	5.0	0.17
Northern Pike	5.2	1.23	0.7	0.93
Largemouth Bass	1.2	0.91	2.1	0.27
Brown Bullhead	0.2	0.50	0.3	0.77
Bluegill	6.8	0.21	40.3	0.17
Black Crappie	2.7	0.27	2.2	0.33

LENGTH OF SELECTED SPECIES SAMPLED FROM ALL GEAR
Number of fish caught for the following length categories (inches):

species	0-5	6-8	9-11	12-14	15-19	20-24	25-29	>30	Total
Black Crappie	-	17	1	-	-	-	-	-	18
Brown Bullhead	-	-	1	-	-	-	-	-	1
Largemouth Bass	3	2	4	3	-	-	-	-	12
Northern Pike	-	-	-	8	17	5	-	1	31
Pumpkin. Sunfish	24	24	-	-	-	-	-	-	48
Walleye	-	-	1	7	8	2	-	-	18
Yellow Bullhead	-	9	7	1	-	-	-	-	17
Yellow Perch	7	19	2	-	-	-	-	-	28

FISH STOCKING DATA

year	species	size	# released
93	Walleye	Fingerling	3,366
95	Walleye	Fingerling	4,598
95	Walleye	Yearling	9
96	Walleye	Fingerling	13,350

NET CATCH DATA
survey date: 6/15/87

| | Gill Nets | | Trap Nets | |
| | | avg fish | | avg fish |
species	# per net	wt. (lbs)	# per set	wt. (lbs)
Yellow Perch	55.0	0.13	2.3	0.14
Walleye	2.5	1.32	0.1	5.70
White Sucker	1.3	2.32	-	-
Yellow Bullhead	-	-	3.4	0.54
Pumpkin. Sunfish	0.3	0.20	6.3	0.20
Hybrid Sunfish	-	-	16.3	0.22
Northern Pike	8.8	1.95	-	-
Green Sunfish	-	-	0.6	0.15
Largemouth Bass	0.5	0.10	2.7	0.08
Golden Shiner	-	-	0.3	0.05
Bluegill	0.8	0.17	104.4	0.18
Brown Bullhead	-	-	0.7	0.78
Black Bullhead	1.3	0.26	0.7	0.76

LENGTH OF SELECTED SPECIES SAMPLED FROM ALL GEAR
Number of fish caught for the following length categories (inches):

species	0-5	6-8	9-11	12-14	15-19	20-24	25-29	>30	Total
Yellow Perch	42	54	-	-	-	-	-	-	96
Walleye	-	-	3	3	3	1	-	-	10
Northern Pike	-	-	-	8	14	7	5	1	35
Largemouth Bass	2	-	-	-	-	-	-	-	2
Black Bullhead	2	2	1	-	-	-	-	-	5

DNR COMMENTS:
Walleye population substantially unchanged since 1976; numbers are about half the local median level; some natural reproduction taking place. Northern Pike numbers high, with acceptable range of sizes. Largemouth Bass numbers good. Yellow Perch abundant. Bluegill numbers about six times the local median; this population has varied considerably in recent years.

FISHING INFORMATION: Big Sugarbush is best known for its Largemouth Bass, Northern Pike and Black Crappie as well as a lot of Yellow Bullheads and a decent number of Walleyes. The northwest end of the lake is relatively shallow and heavy with weeds and bulrushes, perfect structure for Bass spawning. Early in the season, you can do well enough with a pig and jig, but you will need topwater lures later. Try for Crappies in the northwest end early in the season. The water is clear so use small minnows on a bare hook. Panfish are at other locations in the lake: the southeast corner is good as well as the back end of most of the small bays where you see emerging vegetation. Northerns will be cruising these same weeds at either end of the lake. The area around the outlet into small Mill Lake in the southeast corner is usually a good producer. Walleyes are at the many points early in the season. Use leeches or shiner minnows early. Later they will be in deep water, but usually return at night to the points and islands. Smaller than its neighbor, **Little Sugarbush** is every bit as good for Largemouth Bass and Northerns. It's also full of Bluegills. After the Bass have spawned, you can do very well in these weeds with a pig and jig, but you'll want to use spinnerbaits, weedless spoons and plastic worms by July at the latest. There are fine panfish in the weeds, too, Crappies as well as Bluegills. Northerns will be at the outer edges of weeds, showing preference for the north and south ends, but the east shoreline is often productive.

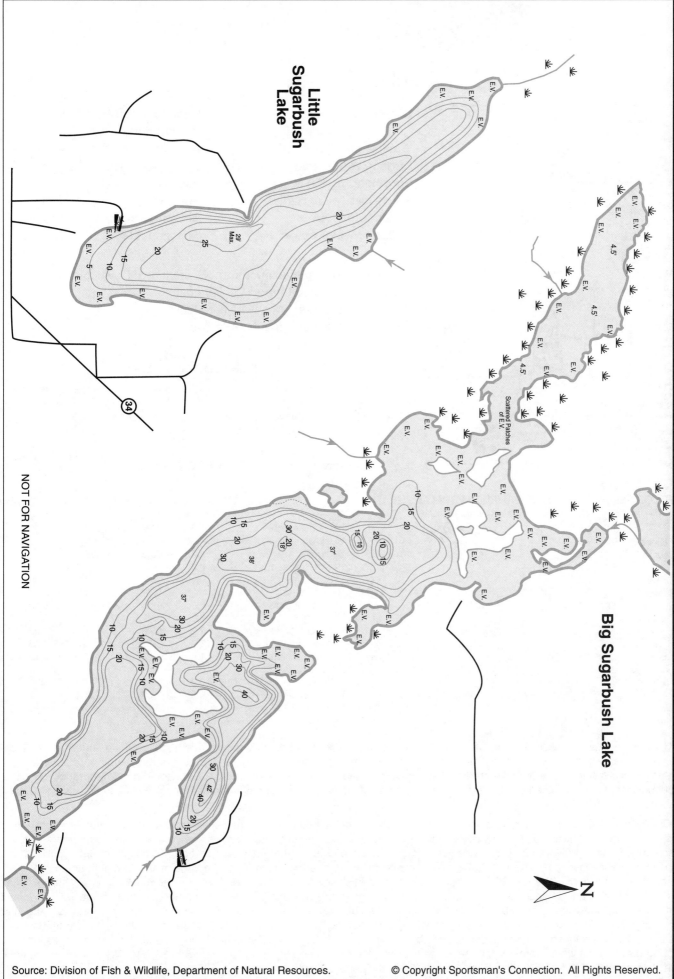

Little
Sugarbush
Lake

Big Sugarbush Lake

Big & Little Sugarbush Lakes

NOT FOR NAVIGATION

N

STRAWBERRY LAKE
Becker County

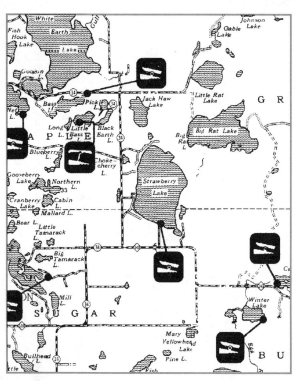

Location: Township 141, 142 Range 40
Watershed: Eastern Wild Rice
Surface Water Area: 1,522 Acres
Shorelength: 6.6 Miles
Secchi disk (water clarity): NA
Water color: NA
Cause of water color: NA

Maximum depth: 40 Ft.
Median depth: NA
Accessibility: State-owned public access on south shore of the lake
Boat Ramp: Concrete
Accommodations: Resort and campgrounds

Shoreland zoning classification: Recreational Development
Dominant forest/soil type: Conifer/Loam
Management class: Walleye-Centrarchid
Ecological type: Centrarchid-Walleye

FISH STOCKING DATA

year	species	size	# released
94	Walleye	Fingerling	13,815
96	Walleye	Fingerling	14,690

NET CATCH DATA

survey date: 7/22/96

	Gill Nets		Trap Nets	
species	# per net	avg fish wt. (lbs.)	# per set	avg fish wt. (lbs.)
Black Bullhead	4.3	0.73	0.4	0.39
Black Crappie	-	-	trace	0.90
Bluegill	3.3	0.28	7.5	0.12
Brown Bullhead	0.3	0.83	1.0	0.56
Green Sunfish	-	-	trace	0.06
Hybrid Sunfish	0.2	0.28	7.0	0.14
Largemouth Bass	0.2	1.63	3.8	0.19
Northern Pike	8.2	1.47	0.4	1.78
Pumpkin. Sunfish	2.2	0.08	0.8	0.07
Rock Bass	13.7	0.38	11.9	0.19
Smallmouth Bass	1.8	1.23	2.4	0.15
Tullibee (Cisco)	0.5	1.58	-	-
Walleye	16.0	2.23	0.5	3.26
White Sucker	9.8	2.09	0.9	2.21
Yellow Bullhead	3.0	0.76	2.7	0.90
Yellow Perch	10.5	0.12	1.4	0.10

LENGTH OF SELECTED SPECIES SAMPLED FROM ALL GEAR

Number of fish caught for the following length categories (inches):

species	0-5	6-8	9-11	12-14	15-19	20-24	25-29	>30	Total
Black Bullhead	-	4	27	-	-	-	-	-	31
Black Crappie	-	-	1	-	-	-	-	-	1
Bluegill	59	50	1	-	-	-	-	-	110
Brown Bullhead	-	5	6	3	-	-	-	-	14
Green Sunfish	1	-	-	-	-	-	-	-	1
Hybrid Sunfish	59	26	-	-	-	-	-	-	85
Largemouth Bass	7	37	-	1	1	-	-	-	46
Northern Pike	-	-	-	2	32	18	1	1	54
Pumpkin. Sunfish	19	4	-	-	-	-	-	-	23
Rock Bass	75	112	14	-	-	-	-	-	201
Smallmouth Bass	16	13	5	2	4	-	-	-	40
Tullibee (Cisco)	-	-	1	-	2	-	-	-	3
Walleye	-	-	11	6	60	21	4	-	102
Yellow Bullhead	-	1	35	14	-	-	-	-	50
Yellow Perch	33	46	1	-	-	-	-	-	80

DNR COMMENTS: Lake contains a good Cisco population. Northern Pike numbers and growth rate good, but Pike larger than 30 inches are rare, probably because of "cropping" by anglers; catch-and-release angling recommended to restore the numbers of large Pike. Walleye population stable and well above normal range; good average size at 18.1 inches and 2.2 lb.; some natural reproduction taking place, but population is maintained by stocking. Yellow Perch numbers within normal range for lake class. Smallmouth Bass population self-sustaining.

FISHING INFORMATION: Strawberry is a fine family lake because of an abundance of gamefish and huge population of panfish from Bluegills, Perch and Pumpkinseeds to Rock Bass. Although Northern Pike numbers have been somewhat down in recent years, this is a stable source for *niiiiiice* Walleyes and for Largemouth Bass. Strawberry is also an easy lake to learn. A couple of times out and you should have the spots down pat. This is a 1,522-acre lake with 6.6 miles of shoreline in roughly a large oval. Maximum depth is 40 feet, but most of the center of the lake is a 35-foot shelf, so most of the fishing involves the shoreline. The north has a broad, shallow shelf that has two pools of 8 and 10 feet you should locate early in the year for Bass and panfish. Otherwise stay just off the weedlines and cast surface and shallow-running crankbaits and spinners in the weedbreaks or use live bait, either on a slip bobber or on a light line. Let the bait settle slowly. Try shiners and crawlers in the spring, and then switch over to leeches. The southern shore is more of the same with the exception of a sunken island on a center line about a half-mile offshore. This is prime Walleye territory. Jig the slopes with live bait, moving down as the water warms. Both the eastern and western shores drop off steeply from 5 to 35 feet. When the wind is right, drift both shores at 15 to 20 feet with Lindy Rigs armed with leeches or a sucker minnow.

NOT FOR NAVIGATION

N

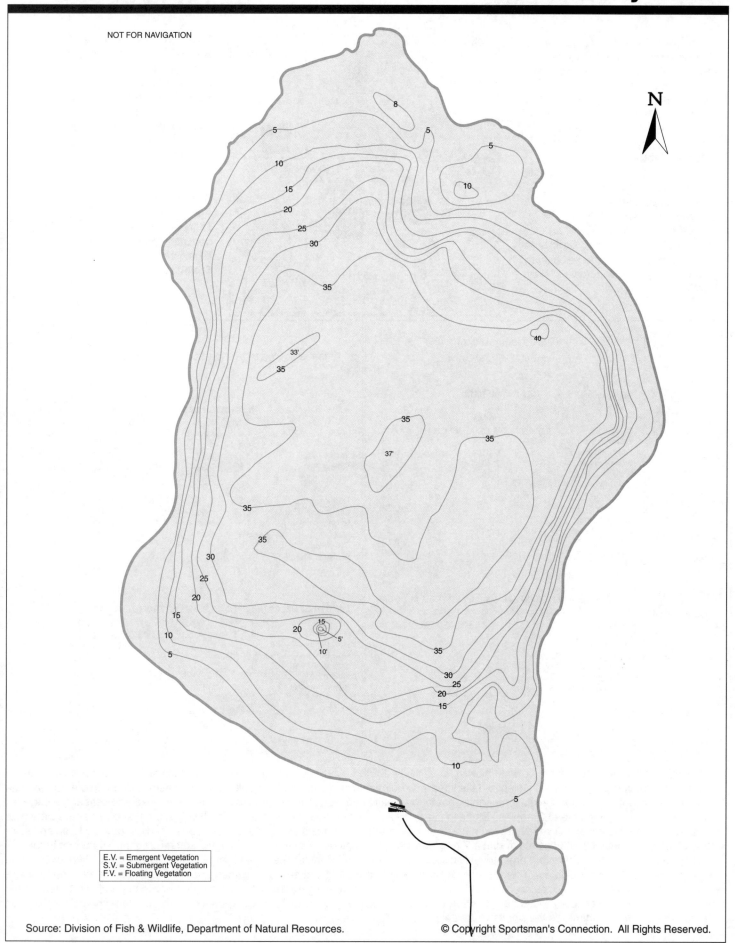

E.V. = Emergent Vegetation
S.V. = Submergent Vegetation
F.V. = Floating Vegetation

Source: Division of Fish & Wildlife, Department of Natural Resources.

NET LAKE

BASS LAKE

Becker County

Location: Township 142 Range 40
Watershed: Eastern Wild Rice
Surface Water Area: 213 Acres
Shorelength: 3.4 Miles
Secchi disk (water clarity): 6.5 Ft.
Water color: Light green
Cause of water color: Algae bloom
Maximum depth: 47 Ft.
Median depth: NA
Accessibility: County-owned public access on south shore
Boat Ramp: Earth
Accommodations: NA
Shoreland zoning classif.: Rec. Dev.
Dominant forest/soil type: Decid/Loam
Management class: Walleye-Centrarchid
Ecological type: Centrarchid-Walleye

Location: Township 142 Range 40
Watershed: Eastern Wild Rice
Surface Water Area: 123 Acres
Shorelength: NA
Secchi disk (water clarity): 11.7 Ft.
Water color: Light green
Cause of water color: Algae
Maximum depth: 50 Ft.
Median depth: NA
Accessibility: County-owned public access on north shore, off Cty. Rd. 34
Boat Ramp: Earth
Accommodations: NA
Shoreland zoning classif.: Nat. Env.
Dominant forest/soil type: NA
Management class: Centrarchid
Ecological type: Centrarchid

DNR COMMENTS:
Quite a substantial Northern population with gill net average of 10.3 compared to state wide average - 2.67. Northerns were small, averaging 1.15 pounds per fish. Panfish population were slightly below state average and this reflected in the fishing reports from locals. Large Bullhead populations with Blacks, Yellow and Brown population was low having gill net average of 3.6. These Walleyes were small and average 0.75 of a pound.

FISH STOCKING DATA

No record of stocking since 1982.

survey date: 7/23/75

NET CATCH DATA

	Gill Nets		Trap Nets	
species	# per net	avg fish wt. (lbs)	# per set	avg fish wt. (lbs)
Yellow Perch	8.7	0.13	1.0	0.23
Yellow Bullhead	6.7	0.31	9.6	0.39
White Sucker	1.0	2.33	0.3	2.50
Walleye	1.7	0.76	0.3	1.75
Rock Bass	0.7	0.50	0.1	0.80
Northern Pike	10.3	1.16	0.4	1.58
Largemouth Bass	0.7	0.85	0.6	0.52
Black Crappie	2.0	0.31	0.9	0.42
Black Bullhead	4.7	0.34	3.8	0.33
Green Sunfish	-	-	3.6	0.17
Brown Bullhead	-	-	7.1	0.36
Bluegill	-	-	10.3	0.20
Pumpkin. Sunfish	-	-	3.6	0.23

LENGTH OF SELECTED SPECIES SAMPLED FROM ALL GEAR

Number of fish caught for the following length categories (inches):

species	0-5	6-8	9-11	12-14	15-19	20-24	25-29	>30	Total
Black Bullhead	-	25	13	-	-	-	-	-	38
Black Crappie	2	7	-	1	-	-	-	-	10
Bluegill	55	26	-	-	-	-	-	-	81
Brown Bullhead	-	29	26	2	-	-	-	-	57
Green Sunfish	17	10	-	-	-	-	-	-	27
Largemouth Bass	-	-	4	4	-	-	-	-	8
Northern Pike	-	-	-	6	26	3	-	-	35
Pumpkin. Sunfish	13	16	-	-	-	-	-	-	29
Rock Bass	-	3	1	-	-	-	-	-	4
Walleye	-	1	2	1	3	-	-	-	7
Yellow Bullhead	-	77	20	-	-	-	-	-	97
Yellow Perch	2	29	3	-	-	-	-	-	34

FISH STOCKING DATA: NO RECORD OF STOCKING

survey date: 8/10/87

NET CATCH DATA

	Gill Nets		Trap Nets	
species	# per net	avg fish wt. (lbs)	# per set	avg fish wt. (lbs)
Yellow Perch	5.0	0.13	0.6	0.20
Yellow Bullhead	12.5	0.32	10.6	0.38
White Sucker	0.5	2.95	-	-
Pumpkin. Sunfish	2.0	0.13	5.9	0.10
Northern Pike	9.3	1.19	0.5	0.95
Largemouth Bass	0.5	1.55	1.3	0.19
Hybrid Sunfish	1.8	0.21	13.5	0.16
Bluegill	5.3	0.13	32.9	0.10
Green Sunfish	-	-	1.5	0.05
Brown Bullhead	-	-	0.3	0.95

LENGTH OF SELECTED SPECIES SAMPLED FROM ALL GEAR

Number of fish caught for the following length categories (inches):

species	0-5	6-8	9-11	12-14	15-19	20-24	25-29	>30	Total
Yellow Perch	8	11	1	-	-	-	-	-	20
Yellow Bullhead	1	30	18	1	-	-	-	-	50
Pumpkin. Sunfish	7	1	-	-	-	-	-	-	8
Northern Pike	-	-	-	3	26	8	-	-	37
Largemouth Bass	-	-	-	2	-	-	-	-	2
Hybrid Sunfish	2	5	-	-	-	-	-	-	7
Bluegill	8	5	-	-	-	-	-	-	13

DNR COMMENTS:
Bluegill, Northern Pike and Largemouth Bass numbers are all above state and local medians. Yellow Bullhead numbers are over twice the state and local averages with Yellow Perch numbers falling below both of the medians.

FISHING INFORMATION: When the wind blows you off White Earth Lake the water may be calm on Bass or Net, two small lakes just to the south. **Bass** is just 138 acres, a slender lake lined with bulrushes with weedbeds at both ends with a steady drop into a 50-foot hole at mid-lake. If water level and vegetation permits, get to the small pond just off the southwestern end of the lake and cast at the edges of the lily pads for Largemouth and Crappies. Same in the weedbeds at the eastern end of the lake. If you're on the lake after the water has warmed and the vegetation thickened, traverse the north and south shorelines staying fifty feet out. Cast medium running lures and spinners along the edges of the bulrushes or drift a live bait rig carrying nightcrawlers or leeches. In mid-summer, jig the 15-20-foot breaks on the southern and eastern shore for Largemouth Bass and Northern Pike. Populations for both fish in Bass, by DNR test count, were higher than the state or local medians. There are fewer Bass in **Net Lake** but Northern Pike came up nearly five times the state median and there is also a varied panfish population. At 243 acres, Net is a basin lake where the shoreline drops down to one hole of 47 feet. Best spots are the southeast shore around the inlet from White Earth Lake and outside the large weedbed on the western shore on either side of the outlet. In summertime, jig the slopes of the deep hole at 15-20 feet.

SPORTSMAN'S connection®

NOT FOR NAVIGATION

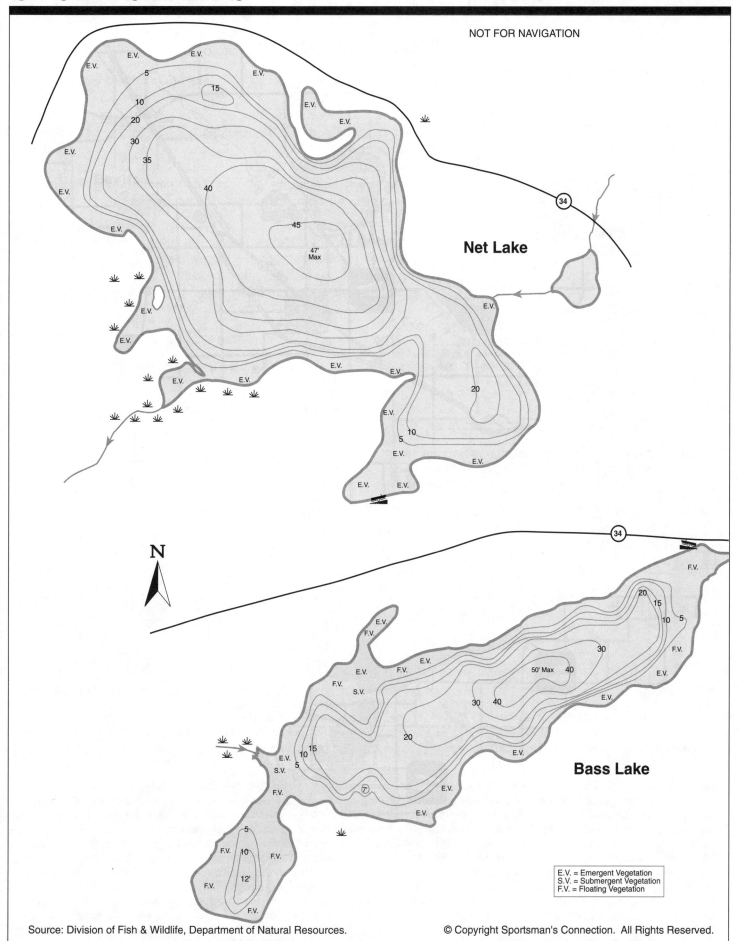

Net Lake

47' Max

34

Bass Lake

50' Max

N

E.V. = Emergent Vegetation
S.V. = Submergent Vegetation
F.V. = Floating Vegetation

Source: Division of Fish & Wildlife, Department of Natural Resources.

WHITE EARTH LAKE

Becker County

Location: Township 142
Range 40
Watershed: Eastern Wild Rice
Surface Water Area: 2,079 Acres
Shorelength: 13.7 Miles
Secchi disk (water clarity): 9.1 Ft.
Water color: Light green
Cause of water color: Suspended algae

Maximum depth: 120 Ft.
Median depth: 25 Ft.
Accessibility: County-owned public access on northeast bay of lake
Boat Ramp: Concrete
Accommodations: Resorts and campgrounds

Shoreland zoning classification: Recreational Development
Dominant forest/soil type: Deciduous/Loam
Management class: Walleye-Centrarchid
Ecological type: Centrarchid-Walleye

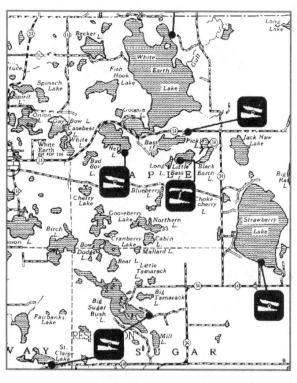

FISH STOCKING DATA

No record of stocking since 1984.

NET CATCH DATA

survey date: 7/18/88	Gill Nets		Trap Nets	
species	# per net	avg fish wt. (lbs.)	# per set	avg fish wt. (lbs.)
Yellow Perch	21.2	0.23	5.3	0.11
Yellow Bullhead	0.8	0.66	3.4	0.68
White Sucker	6.7	1.47	trace	0.20
Walleye	23.7	1.11	0.7	2.25
Tullibee (Cisco)	2.3	1.13	-	-
Smallmouth Bass	0.2	2.00	0.3	0.22
Largemouth Bass	-	-	2.1	0.39
Rock Bass	2.8	0.34	7.8	0.23
Pumpkin. Sunfish	0.3	0.10	1.8	0.12
Hybrid Sunfish	-	-	23.7	0.26
Green Sunfish	-	-	1.1	0.08
Northern Pike	2.8	1.69	0.3	0.60
Burbot	0.2	1.60	-	-
Brown Bullhead	0.8	0.94	1.8	0.95
Black Bullhead	0.8	0.66	-	-
Bluegill	-	-	25.8	0.12

LENGTH OF SELECTED SPECIES SAMPLED FROM ALL GEAR

Number of fish caught for the following length categories (inches):

species	0-5	6-8	9-11	12-14	15-19	20-24	25-29	>30	Total
Black Bullhead	-	-	5	-	-	-	-	-	5
Bluegill	62	42	-	-	-	-	-	-	104
Brown Bullhead	-	-	10	16	-	-	-	-	26
Green Sunfish	13	-	-	-	-	-	-	-	13
Hybrid Sunfish	44	64	-	-	-	-	-	-	108
Largemouth Bass	5	12	7	1	-	-	-	-	25
Northern Pike	-	-	1	3	12	4	-	1	21
Pumpkin. Sunfish	16	8	-	-	-	-	-	-	24
Rock Bass	43	52	5	-	-	-	-	-	100
Smallmouth Bass	-	3	-	1	-	-	-	-	4
Tullibee (Cisco)	-	7	-	2	5	-	-	-	14
Walleye	-	12	25	54	45	9	1	1	147
Yellow Bullhead	-	4	36	6	-	-	-	-	46
Yellow Perch	55	65	1	-	-	-	-	-	121

DNR COMMENTS: Walleye population is over six times the statewide median, averaging 23.67 fish per lift. Northern Pike numbers are slightly over state medians but below the local median. Yellow Perch are very abundant, and Northern Cisco numbers are double that of the local median. Largemouth and Smallmouth Bass numbers were above state and local medians. Bluegill, Pumpkinseed, Hybrid Sunfish and Rock Bass were also well above state and local averages in numbers and pounds per set. Most all species reproduce naturally with enough success to make White Earth Lake self-sustaining and contains one of the broadest qualitative and quantitative fish resources in our area.

FISHING INFORMATION: White Earth is unique among lakes in this area in that it not only has abundant gamefish but it is also self-sustaining. Combine forage fish, lake structure and balanced fishing pressure and the result is Walleye numbers *six times* the statewide median. Northern Pike are over the state median and two major forage fish, Yellow Perch and Northern Cisco, are double the local medians. Largemouth and Smallmouth Bass and most panfish varieties are also numerous. Why so many fish? Two reasons. First, White Earth is somewhat off the beaten path. And, second, it contains structure which abets natural reproduction. This 2,079-acre lake has 13.7 miles of shoreline that provides secluded bays and inlets. Too, the bottom of the broad main lake varies widely, comprising sunken bars, points and islands, as well as holes ranging from 30 to 120 feet deep. Median depth is 25 feet, but, in addition to the holes, you'll also find 5-foot shallows ringing the main basin and the small islands. Needless to say, a depthfinder is a must. Early in the year, try the three bays, in the southwest and on the north shore and just off the inlet on the eastern shore, for Bass, Walleyes and Crappies. Try shallow-running crankbaits and spinners along the emergent weeds. As the water warms, jig the bars coming off both islands toward mid lake, and drift the deep weedbreaks at 15 to 20 feet with live bait rigs. Drop leeches in the pools and breaks along the mature weedbeds.

SPORTSMAN'S® connection

NOT FOR NAVIGATION

N

E.V. = Emergent Vegetation
S.V. = Submergent Vegetation
F.V. = Floating Vegetation

Source: Division of Fish & Wildlife, Department of Natural Resources.

TULABY LAKE
Mahnomen County

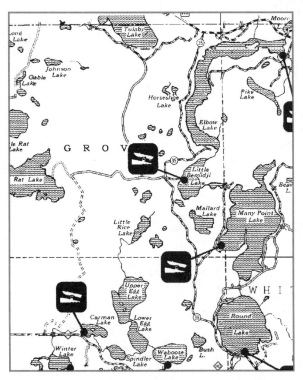

Location: Township 142 Range 38
Watershed: Eastern Wild Rice
Surface Water Area: 773 Acres
Shorelength: NA
Secchi disk (water clarity): 6.0 Ft.
Water color: NA
Cause of water color: NA

Maximum depth: 43 Ft.
Median depth: NA
Accessibility: State-owned public access on north shore
Boat Ramp: Concrete
Accommodations: NA

Shoreland zoning classification: Recreational Development
Dominant forest/soil type: Deciduous/Loam
Management class: Walleye
Ecological type: Centrarchid-Walleye

FISH STOCKING DATA

year	species	size	# released
93	Walleye	Fingerling	9,785
95	Walleye	Fingerling	10,200

NET CATCH DATA

survey date: 7/29/96

	Gill Nets		Trap Nets	
species	# per net	avg fish wt. (lbs.)	# per set	avg fish wt. (lbs.)
Black Crappie	-	-	0.3	0.08
Bluegill	-	-	8.1	0.07
Brown Bullhead	0.2	0.17	trace	1.14
Green Sunfish	-	-	0.6	0.03
Largemouth Bass	-	-	0.2	0.71
Northern Pike	6.3	2.84	0.5	1.70
Pumpkin. Sunfish	0.3	0.06	6.8	0.05
Rock Bass	3.7	0.33	2.8	0.16
Tullibee (Cisco)	6.7	0.90	-	-
Walleye	9.7	2.16	-	-
White Sucker	7.0	2.62	trace	0.11
Yellow Perch	62.5	0.13	7.6	0.09

LENGTH OF SELECTED SPECIES SAMPLED FROM ALL GEAR
Number of fish caught for the following length categories (inches):

species	0-5	6-8	9-11	12-14	15-19	20-24	25-29	>30	Total
Black Crappie	4	-	-	-	-	-	-	-	4
Bluegill	94	3	-	-	-	-	-	-	97
Brown Bullhead	-	1	-	1	-	-	-	-	2
Green Sunfish	7	-	-	-	-	-	-	-	7
Largemouth Bass	-	-	2	-	-	-	-	-	2
Northern Pike	-	2	2	2	5	19	13	1	44
Pumpkin. Sunfish	83	1	-	-	-	-	-	-	84
Rock Bass	40	7	7	-	1	-	-	-	55
Tullibee (Cisco)	-	6	14	14	6	-	-	-	40
Walleye	-	1	10	3	24	18	2	-	58
Yellow Perch	137	144	10	1	-	-	-	-	292

DNR COMMENTS: Northern Pike population at all-time high for this lake, due to strong natural reproduction in 1992 and 1993, but numbers are still within normal range for lake class. Average size 23 inches and 3 pounds. Walleye population stable and within normal range for lake class; average size 17.4 inches and 2.2 lb.; limited natural reproduction. Yellow Perch very abundant, providing adequate forage for gamefish community.

FISHING INFORMATION: Tim Simon of Taylor Baits & Tackle RR 1 Box A175, Waubun (218) 473-3133, says big, old Tulaby is well worth your time if you decide to spend a day – or even a week – on its waters. "Night-fishing is nuts" for Walleyes, he says. And there's good angling, as well, for Northern Pike, big Largemouth Bass, and nice-size Bluegills. For Walleyes, concentrate your efforts on the mid-lake hump toward the northwest end. Use jig/minnow or jig/crawler rigs early, then switch to Shad Raps, say, around the Fourth of July. You can also toss frogs for them. Other good spots to try are the steep drop between the hump and the northeast shoreline and the broad sand flats to the southeast. Simon says you'll find Bass prowling the pads on the west side, toward the south, and again in the outlet bay on the northwest. Toss pig-and-jig combos or plastic worms for a good chance at them. Simon says they run to 7 1/2 pounds, with many in the 4- to 6-pound range, so get set for a thrill if you hook one. Northerns run fair- to decent-size in Tulaby, and they'll be found, of course, patrolling the weedlines looking for a meal. Offer them live sucker minnows, or throw spoons or spinnerbaits. According to Simon, 1-pound Bluegills aren't all that unusual in this lake. They'll be found in the weeds, where they can be taken with worm chunks on a bare hook.

NOT FOR NAVIGATION

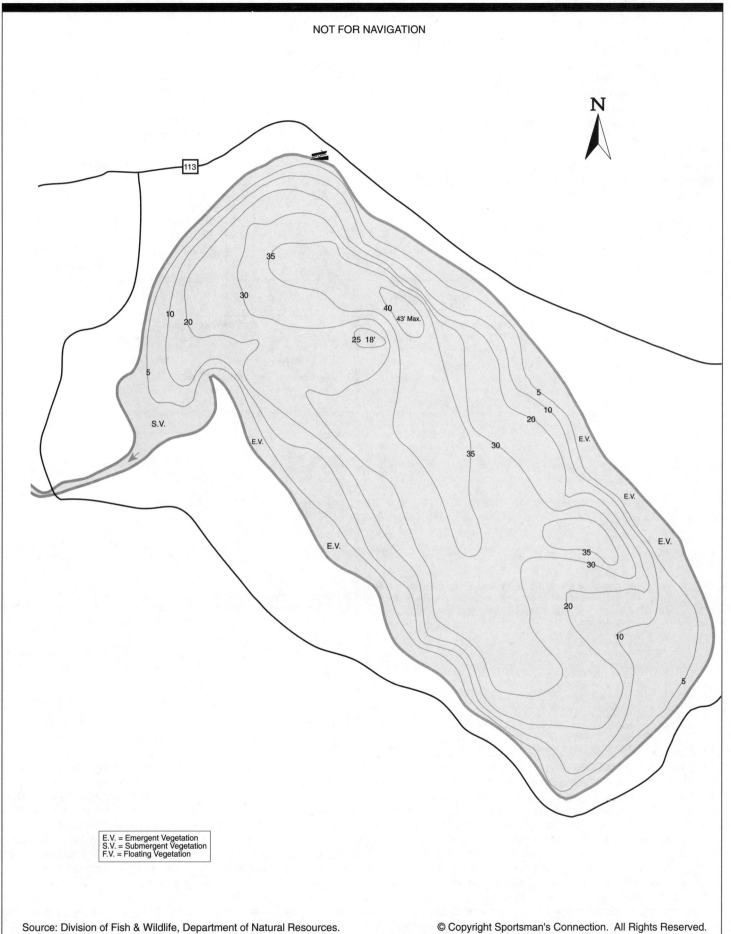

E.V. = Emergent Vegetation
S.V. = Submergent Vegetation
F.V. = Floating Vegetation

ELBOW LAKE LITTLE BEMIDJI LAKE
Becker County

Location: Township 142 Range 38, 39
Watershed: Otter Tail
Surface Water Area: 1,001 Acres
Shorelength: 13.1 Miles
Secchi disk (water clarity): 14.0 Ft.
Water color: Green
Cause of water color: Light algae bloom
Maximum depth: 76 Ft.
Median depth: 31 Ft.
Accessibility: County-owned public access on south shore of extreme northeast bay
Boat Ramp: Earth
Accommodations: NA
Shoreland zoning classif.: Rec. Dev.
Dominant forest/soil type: Conifer/Loam
Management class: Walleye-Centrarchid
Ecological type: Centrarchid-Walleye

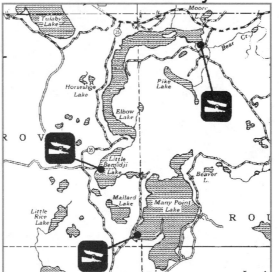

Location: Township 142 Range 39
Watershed: Otter Tail
Surface Water Area: 275 Acres
Shorelength: 3.0 Miles
Secchi disk (water clarity): 10.0 Ft.
Water color: Clear-green
Cause of water color: Suspended algae
Maximum depth: 58 Ft.
Median depth: 29 Ft.
Accessibility: State-owned public access on west shore of lake off County Road 35
Boat Ramp: Earth
Accommodations: NA
Shoreland zoning classif.: Rec. Dev.
Dominant forest/soil type: Decid/Sand
Management class: Walleye-Centrarchid
Ecological type: Centrarchid

DNR COMMENTS:
Walleye population up and high; average size about 1.25 lb. Northern Pike numbers good; most fish are small, but there is a chance at a large one. Largemouth Bass present. Bluegill numbers high; sizes mixed up to 9 inches. Black Crappie and Cisco present. Rock Bass abundant. Abundant and large crayfish are being targeted by anglers.

FISH STOCKING DATA

year	species	size	# released
89	Walleye	Fingerling	7,815

survey date: 7/11/94

NET CATCH DATA

	Gill Nets		Trap Nets	
species	# per net	avg fish wt. (lbs)	# per set	avg fish wt. (lbs)
Black Crappie	-	-	trace	0.34
Bluegill	1.3	0.25	52.9	0.17
Bowfin (Dogfish)	-	-	0.4	6.04
Brown Bullhead	0.1	1.62	0.5	0.84
Green Sunfish	-	-	0.2	0.05
Hybrid Sunfish	0.5	0.26	7.1	0.27
Largemouth Bass	0.1	1.32	-	-
Northern Pike	8.1	1.50	0.5	0.57
Pumpkin. Sunfish	0.3	0.24	1.3	0.20
Rock Bass	3.1	0.45	13.9	0.35
Tullibee (Cisco)	3.6	2.25	-	-
Walleye	21.8	1.21	trace	0.10
White Sucker	4.4	1.92	trace	0.28
Yellow Bullhead	0.4	0.96	1.5	1.06
Yellow Perch	23.4	0.18	8.7	0.22

LENGTH OF SELECTED SPECIES SAMPLED FROM ALL GEAR
Number of fish caught for the following length categories (inches):

species	0-5	6-8	9-11	12-14	15-19	20-24	25-29	>30	Total
Black Crappie	-	1	-	-	-	-	-	-	1
Bluegill	243	165	-	-	-	-	-	-	408
Brown Bullhead	-	-	4	4	-	-	-	-	8
Green Sunfish	3	-	-	-	-	-	-	-	3
Hybrid Sunfish	27	83	-	-	-	-	-	-	110
Largemouth Bass	-	-	-	1	-	-	-	-	1
Northern Pike	-	-	4	11	39	12	4	2	72
Pumpkin. Sunfish	10	12	-	-	-	-	-	-	22
Rock Bass	44	76	28	-	-	-	-	-	148
Tullibee (Cisco)	-	5	-	5	18	1	-	-	29
Walleye	-	5	13	80	73	4	-	-	175
Yellow Bullhead	-	1	15	9	-	-	-	-	25
Yellow Perch	69	201	47	1	-	-	-	-	318

FISH STOCKING DATA

year	species	size	# released
93	Walleye	Fingerling	3,720
95	Walleye	Fingerling	1,010

survey date: 7/19/93

NET CATCH DATA

	Gill Nets		Trap Nets	
species	# per net	avg fish wt. (lbs)	# per set	avg fish wt. (lbs)
Black Crappie	0.2	0.14	-	-
Bluegill	8.0	0.08	47.0	0.14
Bowfin (Dogfish)	-	-	1.8	6.50
Brown Bullhead	0.2	0.75	0.4	1.15
Green Sunfish	-	-	1.1	0.08
Hybrid Sunfish	0.7	0.14	11.0	0.26
Largemouth Bass	0.3	1.27	0.1	1.45
Northern Pike	10.3	1.45	0.7	1.02
Pumpkin. Sunfish	2.5	0.11	9.3	0.18
Rock Bass	1.3	0.39	3.3	0.34
Tullibee (Cisco)	2.8	1.47	-	-
Walleye	1.7	1.88	0.6	1.78
White Sucker	1.3	2.73	-	-
Yellow Bullhead	1.2	0.83	3.0	0.86
Yellow Perch	12.5	0.11	1.8	0.14

LENGTH OF SELECTED SPECIES SAMPLED FROM ALL GEAR
Number of fish caught for the following length categories (inches):

species	0-5	6-8	9-11	12-14	15-19	20-24	25-29	>30	Total
Black Crappie	-	1	-	-	-	-	-	-	1
Bluegill	168	140	-	-	-	-	-	-	308
Brown Bullhead	-	-	2	3	-	-	-	-	5
Green Sunfish	10	1	-	-	-	-	-	-	11
Hybrid Sunfish	25	89	-	-	-	-	-	-	114
Largemouth Bass	-	-	-	3	-	-	-	-	3
Northern Pike	-	1	5	4	42	14	3	-	69
Pumpkin. Sunfish	46	57	-	-	-	-	-	-	103
Rock Bass	4	34	3	-	-	-	-	-	41
Tullibee (Cisco)	-	-	-	5	12	-	-	-	17
Walleye	-	-	1	1	11	3	-	-	16
Yellow Perch	44	48	1	-	-	-	-	-	93

DNR COMMENTS:
Northern Pike population above normal for lake class; small fish dominate; average size about 18 inches and 1.5 lb. Walleye numbers down significantly but within normal range for lake class; average size 18 inches and nearly 2 lb.; sporadic spawning success for this species. Largemouth Bass and Black Crappie samples inadequate for accurate assessment. Yellow Perch numbers down substantially but still in normal range; average length about 6 inches. Bluegills abundant; mean length 5.8 inches, but some fish to 9 inches present.

FISHING INFORMATION: These lakes, tucked in next to the White Earth State Forest and the Tamarack National Wildlife Refuge, offer surprisingly good fisheries. **Elbow Lake** is aptly named; it bends to the right like a dogleg on a golf course fairway. Fortunately for anglers, it's a lot easier to play. It is a Walleye, Northern Pike and panfish lake with plenty of Yellow Perch. The northeast leg is the shallowest part of this deep leg, and it also has the most vegetation. It is a good place to start after Northerns in the spring. You'll spot the reeds easily enough. Follow the weedlines, slowly trolling the outer edges with live bait or a plug. The southernmost end of the lake also has good weeds where the forage fish often are hiding out. Northerns will be looking for them there too. Walleyes, too, have good habitat. The better ones include humps toward the south end and in the north leg. Most of the marble eyes, though, will be at sharp downward breaks off the shorelines. Offer early Walleyes leeches and shiner minnows along the bottom, bouncing your rig to attract fish. Meanwhile, **Little Bemidji** also holds good Walleye, Northern and panfish populations. This, of course, shouldn't be surprising because the two lakes are connected. The southeast end of Little Bemidji is an excellent place to look for Northerns. The alligators head there because forage fish are usually hiding out in the copious weeds. Actually, that bay is named Johnny Cake Lake, and it's an important part of this chain. Walleyes can be found early in the season off the point on the east side, as well as along the steep dropoffs.

Elbow & Little Bemidji Lakes

NOT FOR NAVIGATION

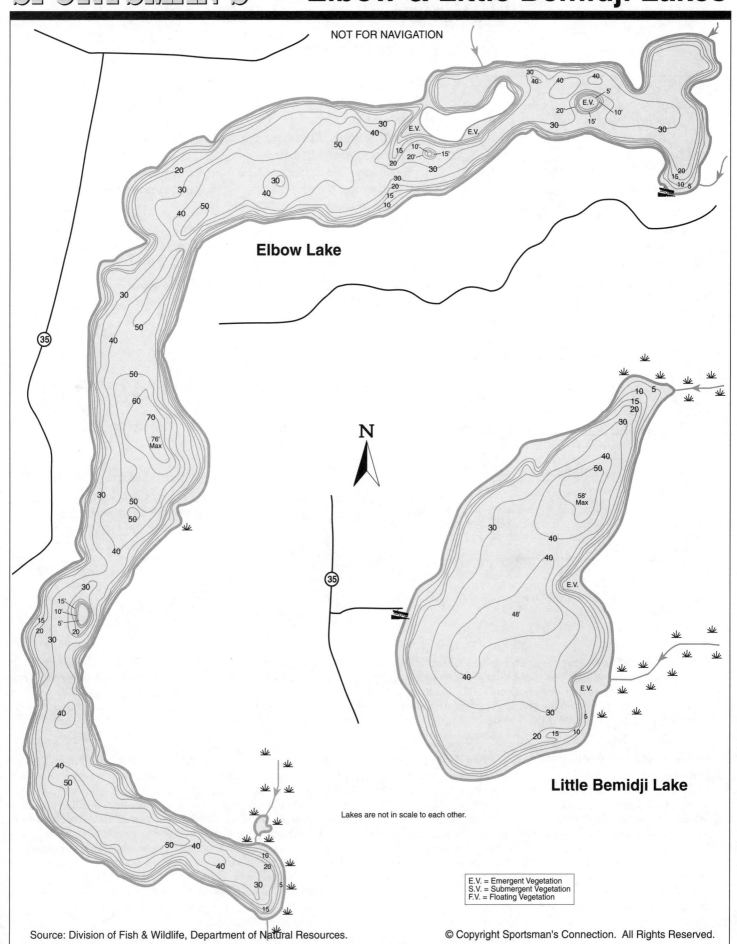

Elbow Lake

Little Bemidji Lake

N

Lakes are not in scale to each other.

E.V. = Emergent Vegetation
S.V. = Submergent Vegetation
F.V. = Floating Vegetation

Source: Division of Fish & Wildlife, Department of Natural Resources.

JUGGLER LAKE
Becker County

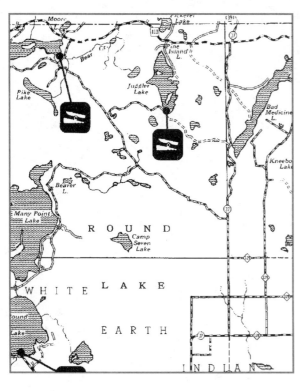

Location: Township 142
Range 38
Watershed: Otter Tail
Surface Water Area: 365 Acres
Shorelength: 4.8 Miles
Secchi disk (water clarity): 13.0 Ft.
Water color: Light green
Cause of water color: Suspended algae

Maximum depth: 78 Ft.
Median depth: 18 Ft.
Accessibility: County-owned public access on southwest corner
Boat Ramp: Gravel
Accommodations: NA

Shoreland zoning classification: Recreational Development
Dominant forest/soil type: Conifer/Loam
Management class: Walleye-Centrarchid
Ecological type: Centrarchid

FISH STOCKING DATA

year	species	size	# released
90	Walleye	Fingerling	1,200
94	Walleye	Fingerling	2,980
96	Walleye	Fingerling	3,360

NET CATCH DATA

survey date: 8/2/93

species	Gill Nets # per net	Gill Nets avg fish wt. (lbs.)	Trap Nets # per set	Trap Nets avg fish wt. (lbs.)
Bluegill	0.5	0.06	3.6	0.08
Largemouth Bass	-	-	0.1	0.07
Northern Pike	1.0	2.14	0.3	1.65
Rock Bass	5.8	0.39	2.4	0.30
Smallmouth Bass	0.5	0.94	0.7	0.16
Walleye	11.7	0.58	0.2	0.76
White Sucker	4.0	2.00	0.2	1.79
Yellow Perch	16.3	0.14	0.1	0.05

LENGTH OF SELECTED SPECIES SAMPLED FROM ALL GEAR

Number of fish caught for the following length categories (inches):

species	0-5	6-8	9-11	12-14	15-19	20-24	25-29	>30	Total
Bluegill	33	2	-	-	-	-	-	-	35
Largemouth Bass	1	-	-	-	-	-	-	-	1
Northern Pike	-	-	-	-	5	4	-	-	9
Rock Bass	13	35	9	-	-	-	-	-	57
Smallmouth Bass	2	5	-	2	-	-	-	-	9
Walleye	-	7	24	33	8	-	-	-	72
Yellow Perch	26	67	6	-	-	-	-	-	99

DNR COMMENTS: Walleye numbers are the highest on record for this lake, but large Walleyes are rare. Northern Pike scarce. Smallmouth Bass, introduced in 1987, are holding their own and offering some opportunities for anglers. Black Crappie and Largemouth Bass numbers have declined significantly since 1960. Yellow Perch population rebounding after lows during the last decade. Crayfish numbers may be decreasing, but the species remains very abundant. Rock Bass, illegally introduced during the 1980s, are abundant and of catchable size. Water quality is good in this lake. Catch-and-release angling should help to restore balance to fish population.

FISHING INFORMATION: This is one of those quiet little spots that don't make the highlight films. A lot of anglers are content to leave it that way. Juggler is a 434-acre lake (surface water area of 365 acres) with 4.8 miles of shoreline, three islands and a series of holes up to 78 feet. It's a spring-fed and has water clarity of nearly 14 feet. Too, there's an area of sharp drop-offs, as well as a shallow area of dense reeds. All of that adds up to above-average Walleye and Smallmouth Bass populations, enough Northerns to keep things interesting and lots of panfish to catch for the fun of it. Moving up the east side of the lake from the southern end, locate the 16-foot hole just at the mouth of a bay on the eastern shore and east of the big island. Early in the year, jig the hole with shiners or drop a nightcrawler on a light line weighted with split shot. Coming back around the island, head over to the western shore and the weedbeds about midway up the lake, staying well off and casting shallow-running crankbaits and spinners for Smallies along the edges of the beds. Then cross back again and trail a live bait rig from the tip of the point around the top north of the small island and along the western shore to the northern end. As the water warms, find the deep holes at the northern end and just north of the large western island. Jig the breaks for Walleyes beginning at 15 feet. Juggler could become a habit for you.

NOT FOR NAVIGATION

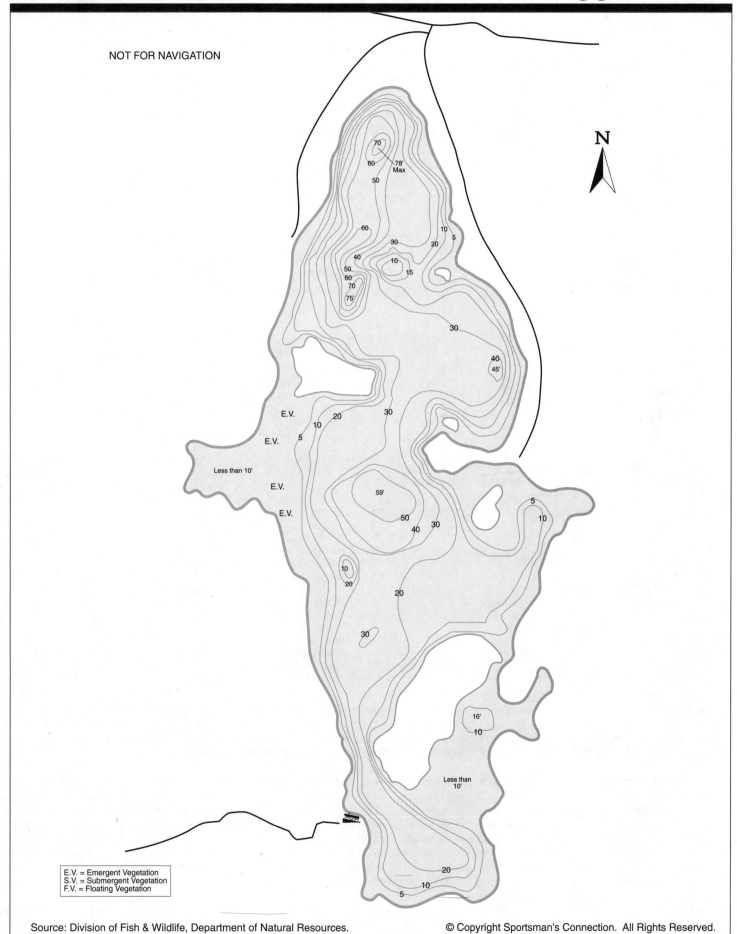

N

70
60 78'
     Max
50

60
      30   10
40   10   20 5
50   15
60
70
75'

                    30

                         40
                         45'

E.V.   20   30
        10
E.V. 5

Less than 10'

E.V.   59'

E.V.   50   30   5
             40   30   10

        10
        20
                  20

        30

                         16'
                         10

                    Less than
                    10'

        20

     10
5

Source: Division of Fish & Wildlife, Department of Natural Resources.

MANY POINT LAKE
Becker County

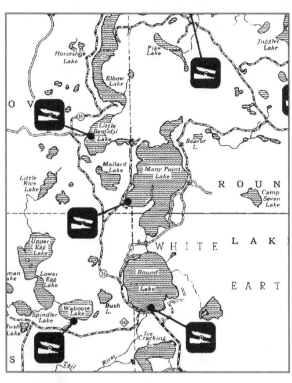

Location: Township 141, 142
Range 38, 39
Watershed: Otter Tail
Surface Water Area: 1,737 Acres
Shorelength: 12.8 Miles
Secchi disk (water clarity): 9.7 Ft.
Water color: Light green
Cause of water color: Suspend-
ed algae

Maximum depth: 92 Ft.
Median depth: NA
Accessibility: Federally-owned
public access on southwest bay of
lake
Boat Ramp: Concrete
Accommodations: Resort and
campgrounds

Shoreland zoning classification: Recreational Development
Dominant forest/soil type: Conifer/Loam
Management class: Walleye-Centrarchid
Ecological type: Centrarchid-Walleye

FISH STOCKING DATA

year	species	size	# released
90	Walleye	Fingerling	3,950
90	Walleye	Yearling	120
94	Walleye	Fingerling	15,080
95	Walleye	Fry	565,000
96	Walleye	Fingerling	14,820

NET CATCH DATA

survey date: 7/12/93

	Gill Nets		Trap Nets	
		avg fish		avg fish
species	# per net	wt. (lbs.)	# per set	wt. (lbs.)
Black Bullhead	trace	0.37	trace	0.39
Black Crappie	trace	0.98	-	-
Bluegill	1.8	0.30	18.7	0.14
Bowfin (Dogfish)	-	-	1.0	5.92
Brown Bullhead	0.2	1.04	1.2	1.33
Hybrid Sunfish	0.3	0.34	4.1	0.25
Largemouth Bass	-	-	trace	2.95
Northern Pike	7.4	1.79	0.3	1.80
Pumpkin. Sunfish	1.0	0.25	2.7	0.14
Rock Bass	3.7	0.44	2.3	0.26
Tullibee (Cisco)	16.6	0.29	-	-
Walleye	6.2	1.55	0.1	2.23
White Sucker	3.6	1.07	-	-
Yellow Bullhead	0.7	1.28	1.4	1.16
Yellow Perch	16.5	0.14	4.5	0.08

LENGTH OF SELECTED SPECIES SAMPLED FROM ALL GEAR

Number of fish caught for the following length categories (inches):

species	0-5	6-8	9-11	12-14	15-19	20-24	25-29	>30	Total
Black Bullhead	-	2	-	-	-	-	-	-	2
Black Crappie	-	-	1	-	-	-	-	-	1
Bluegill	122	94	2	-	-	-	-	-	218
Brown Bullhead	-	-	1	17	2	-	-	-	20
Hybrid Sunfish	25	39	-	-	-	-	-	-	64
Largemouth Bass	-	-	-	-	1	-	-	-	1
Northern Pike	-	-	-	3	54	30	6	1	94
Pumpkin. Sunfish	34	19	-	-	-	-	-	-	53
Rock Bass	17	48	13	-	-	-	-	-	78
Tullibee (Cisco)	-	54	18	27	-	-	-	-	99
Walleye	-	2	5	19	46	4	-	-	76
Yellow Bullhead	-	-	15	14	-	-	-	-	29
Yellow Perch	110	121	4	-	-	-	-	-	235

DNR COMMENTS: Walleye population within normal range for lake class; size structure is excellent for this species, with 68 percent of fish sampled exceeding 15 inches; average weight is 1.5 lb.; natural reproduction is contributing to population. Northern Pike abundant but small; fish 16 to 20 inches make up the majority of sample; some larger fish reported by anglers. Bluegill population modest; growth slow, but some 8- and 9-inch fish are present. Large Black Crappies are occasionally taken by anglers.

FISHING INFORMATION: Many Point is a scenic lake with some sections that remain undeveloped and natural. It comprises over 1700 acres and 12.8 miles of shoreline that includes several large bays. The main body of the lake has a bottom that provides bars, sunken humps and holes that range down to 90 feet. The water is a light green, with a clarity reading of nearly 10 feet. The Northern Pike popu-lation has tripled in size over the past decade. Walleyes continue to be stocked annually by the DNR, and the population remains in the normal range, despite the fact that there is little or no natural reproduction. Yellow Perch, remain numerous., but the Bluegill population is modest for a lake like this. Bass and Crappies, too, are available, albeit not in great numbers. In spring, anglers tend toward the emerg-ing weedbeds in the far northern and southwestern bays. These areas offer early Crappie and Bass activity. Surface lures, plastics and spinners are used both over the weeds and in the breaks and points. Early Northerns are in the 10- to 15-foot depths off the weeds. Use crankbaits or live bait rigs. Early Walleyes are in the breaks and bars off the long slender point that rises from the southern shore and extends nearly to mid-lake. As the water warms, the Walleyes go deeper to the slopes of holes in the main lake. Jigs with leeches will bring them up.

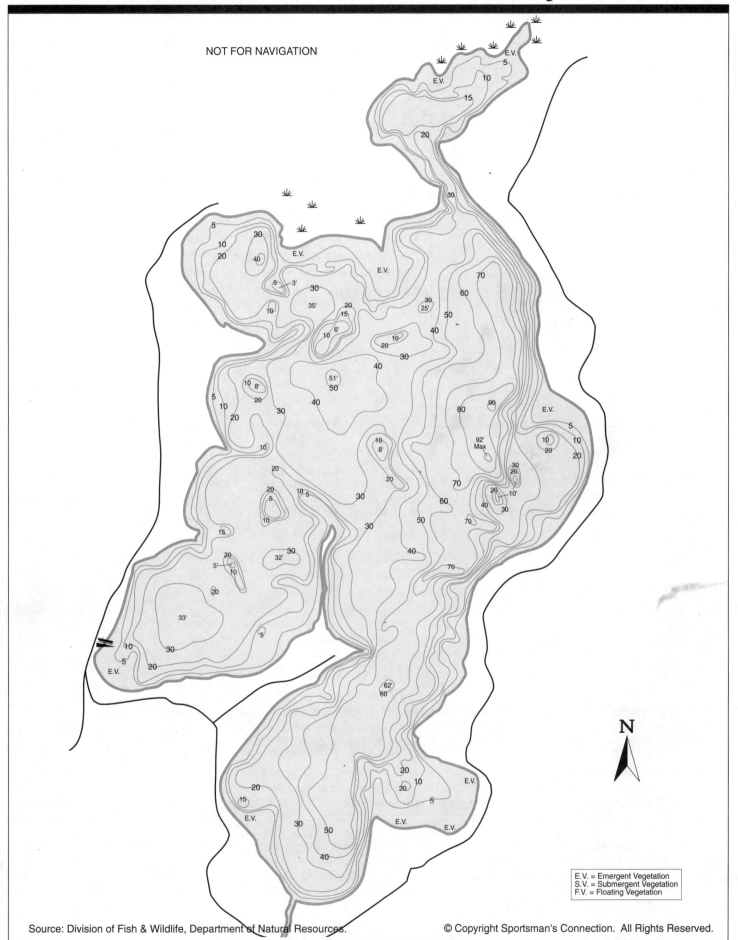

SPORTSMAN'S®

NOT FOR NAVIGATION

N

E.V. = Emergent Vegetation
S.V. = Submergent Vegetation
F.V. = Floating Vegetation

ROUND LAKE
Becker County

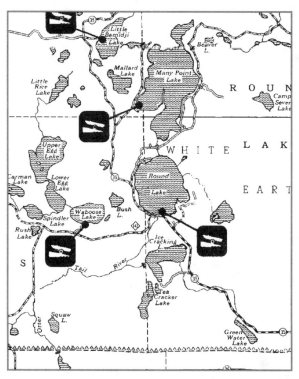

Location: Township 141 Range 38, 39

Watershed: Otter Tail

Surface Water Area: 1,086 Acres

Shorelength: 5.5 Miles

Secchi disk (water clarity): 7.0 Ft.

Water color: Light green

Cause of water color: Algae

Maximum depth: 69 Ft.

Median depth: 19 Ft.

Accessibility: State-owned public access on south shore

Boat Ramp: Metal

Accommodations: NA

Shoreland zoning classification: Recreational Development

Dominant forest/soil type: No Tree/Wet

Management class: Walleye-Centrarchid

Ecological type: Centrarchid-Walleye

FISH STOCKING DATA

year	species	size	# released
90	Walleye	Fingerling	11,530
94	Walleye	Fingerling	13,265
96	Walleye	Fingerling	10,329

NET CATCH DATA

survey date: 7/10/95

species	Gill Nets # per net	Gill Nets avg fish wt. (lbs.)	Trap Nets # per set	Trap Nets avg fish wt. (lbs.)
Black Bullhead	0.1	0.75	-	-
Bluegill	3.2	0.29	75.8	0.25
Bowfin (Dogfish)	0.1	3.58	1.9	5.00
Brown Bullhead	0.2	0.84	0.4	0.71
Golden Shiner	-	-	trace	0.07
Green Sunfish	-	-	trace	0.10
Hybrid Sunfish	-	-	9.2	0.31
Largemouth Bass	0.3	0.95	1.7	0.77
Northern Pike	14.2	1.41	1.3	1.05
Pumpkin. Sunfish	0.3	0.33	5.3	0.21
Rock Bass	2.3	0.47	1.4	0.45
Tullibee (Cisco)	4.4	0.75	-	-
Walleye	6.6	1.36	0.2	0.12
White Sucker	6.1	2.18	-	-
Yellow Bullhead	23.3	0.69	2.3	0.68
Yellow Perch	5.9	0.15	0.3	0.18

LENGTH OF SELECTED SPECIES SAMPLED FROM ALL GEAR

Number of fish caught for the following length categories (inches):

species	0-5	6-8	9-11	12-14	15-19	20-24	25-29	>30	Total
Black Bullhead	-	-	1	-	-	-	-	-	1
Bluegill	44	284	-	-	-	-	-	-	328
Brown Bullhead	-	-	4	3	-	-	-	-	7
Green Sunfish	1	-	-	-	-	-	-	-	1
Hybrid Sunfish	6	103	1	-	-	-	-	-	110
Largemouth Bass	-	16	2	1	4	-	-	-	23
Northern Pike	-	-	-	21	93	33	10	1	158
Pumpkin. Sunfish	24	42	-	-	-	-	-	-	66
Rock Bass	1	28	11	-	-	-	-	-	40
Tullibee (Cisco)	-	11	12	15	6	-	-	-	44
Walleye	-	4	19	15	21	9	-	-	68
Yellow Bullhead	-	-	140	25	-	-	-	-	165
Yellow Perch	17	44	2	-	-	-	-	-	63

DNR COMMENTS: Northern Pike very abundant due to strong 1992 and 1993 year classes; some large fish present. Walleye population relatively stable and within normal range for lake class; average size 15.1 inches and 1.4 lb.; natural reproduction minimal; population maintained by stocking. Yellow Perch scarce. Bluegill numbers up sharply; growth rates for this species have decreased.

FISHING INFORMATION: Round is a well-established Walleye, Largemouth Bass and panfish lake. Round is a 1086-acre lake with a mostly circular shoreline of over five miles. The Otter tail River enters from Many Point Lake on the north and departs at a spillway on the southern shore. In between is relatively easy structure to read with the aid of a depthfinder. The lake is bordered with a wide band of shallows that drop down to a series of points at 20 feet – midsummer Walleye territory – and a single deep hole of 69 feet at the center. There is also an important sunken island rising to about eight feet below the surface just west of the lake's center. Given the lake's water clarity of 7 feet, the top of the island may be visible to anglers not equipped with a depthfinder. It's worth finding, because when you jig the slopes, moving gradually deeper as the water warms, you will find a major Walleye hangout. Otherwise, trace the lake's perimeter at 1O to 15 feet, jigging with live bait, trailing Lindy Rigs or casting spinners and crankbaits along with weedlines. You will find a good supply of Walleyes, Bass, and Northern. The DNR stocked Muskie fingerlings here in the past. True: there've been more sightings than hookings, there's the possibility of hooking a Muskie.

NOT FOR NAVIGATION

N

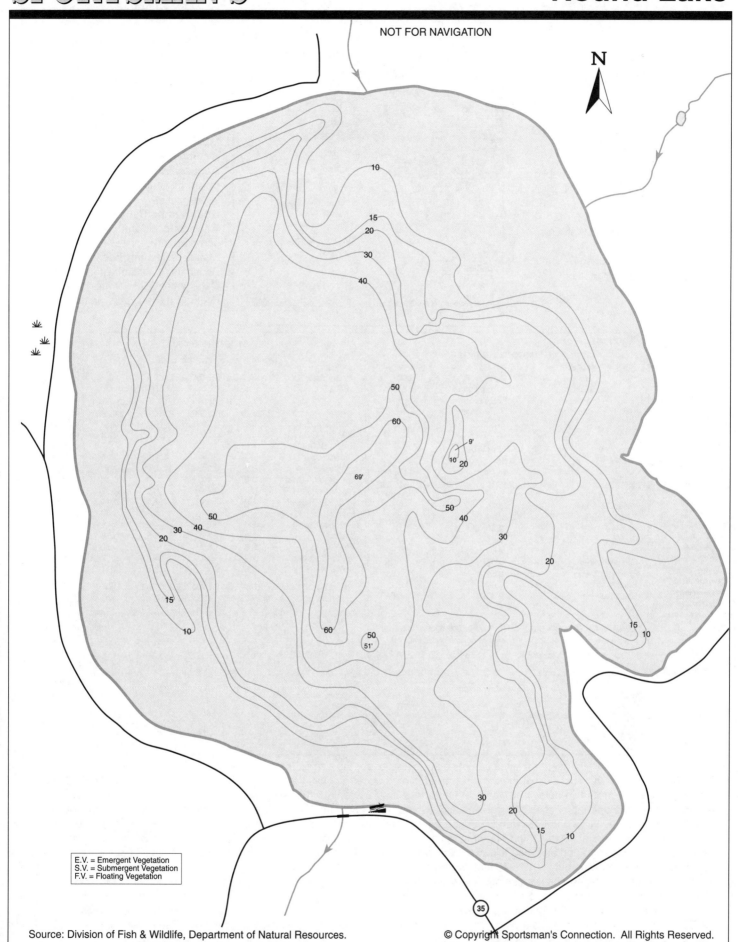

E.V. = Emergent Vegetation
S.V. = Submergent Vegetation
F.V. = Floating Vegetation

35

Source: Division of Fish & Wildlife, Department of Natural Resources.

WABOOSE LAKE   ICE CRACKING LAKE
Becker County

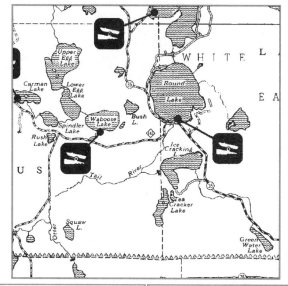

Location: Township 141 Range 39
Watershed: Otter Tail
Surface Water Area: 225 Acres
Shorelength: NA
Secchi disk (water clarity): 4.0 Ft.
Water color: Greenish-brown
Cause of water color: Silt, algal bloom
Maximum depth: 15 Ft.
Median depth: NA
Accessibility: USFS-owned public access on south shore
Boat Ramp: Concrete
Accommodations: Picnic area
Shoreland zoning classif.: Nat. Env.
Dominant forest/soil type: NA
Management class: Walleye-Centrarchid
Ecological type: Centrarchid

Location: Township 141 Range 38, 39
Watershed: Otter Tail
Surface Water Area: 331 Acres
Shorelength: 3.7 Miles
Secchi disk (water clarity): 14.0 Ft.
Water color: Light green
Cause of water color: Light algae bloom
Maximum depth: 73 Ft.
Median depth: 35 Ft.
Accessibility: Public access (carry-down) off County Road on northeast shore
Boat Ramp: Carry-down
Accommodations: Resort and private campground
Shoreland zoning classif.: Rec. Dev.
Dominant forest/soil type: Decid/Loam
Management class: Walleye-Centrarchid
Ecological type: Centrarchid-Walleye

DNR COMMENTS:
Northern Pike population above both state and local median values; acceptable range of sizes present. Walleye numbers down; evidence of natural reproduction only for the years 1980-83. Black Crappie numbers well over both state and local medians; majority of fish in the 6- to 8-inch length range. Yellow Perch numbers above state and local medians. Black Bullhead numbers four times the local average.

FISH STOCKING DATA

year	species	size	# released
93	Walleye	Fingerling	7,000
95	Walleye	Fingerling	3,564
95	Walleye	Yearling	24
96	Walleye	Fingerling	5,610

survey date: 7/27/87
NET CATCH DATA

	Gill Nets		Trap Nets	
species	# per net	avg fish wt. (lbs)	# per set	avg fish wt. (lbs)
Yellow Perch	66.8	0.08	22.1	0.08
Yellow Bullhead	1.5	0.25	0.9	0.50
White Sucker	3.5	2.12	0.1	3.10
Walleye	1.8	2.56	-	-
Pumpkin. Sunfish	29.8	0.24	36.1	0.05
Northern Pike	9.5	2.60	0.6	0.83
Golden Shiner	2.3	0.07	0.1	0.05
Brown Bullhead	10.5	0.34	3.1	0.29
Black Crappie	64.3	0.07	20.0	0.12
Black Bullhead	27.0	0.30	0.3	0.55

LENGTH OF SELECTED SPECIES SAMPLED FROM ALL GEAR
Number of fish caught for the following length categories (inches):

species	0-5	6-8	9-11	12-14	15-19	20-24	25-29	>30	Total
Yellow Perch	124	27	-	-	-	-	-	-	151
Yellow Bullhead	-	1	5	-	-	-	-	-	6
Walleye	-	-	-	1	2	4	-	-	7
Pumpkin. Sunfish	26	80	-	-	-	-	-	-	106
Northern Pike	-	-	-	1	12	20	4	1	38
Brown Bullhead	-	22	20	-	-	-	-	-	42
Black Crappie	15	109	-	1	-	-	-	-	125
Black Bullhead	-	96	12	-	-	-	-	-	108

FISH STOCKING DATA
No record of stocking since 1985.

survey date: 8/7/95
NET CATCH DATA

	Gill Nets		Trap Nets	
species	# per net	avg fish wt. (lbs)	# per set	avg fish wt. (lbs)
Black Crappie	0.6	0.35	0.7	0.08
Bluegill	4.6	0.15	38.4	0.13
Brown Bullhead	1.0	0.94	-	-
Green Sunfish	-	-	2.2	0.05
Hybrid Sunfish	0.3	0.24	5.2	0.16
Largemouth Bass	0.6	1.40	2.2	0.24
Northern Pike	9.4	3.48	0.1	2.62
Pumpkin. Sunfish	1.0	0.13	3.1	0.14
Rock Bass	-	-	0.8	0.39
Tullibee (Cisco)	5.0	0.69	-	-
Walleye	2.9	1.19	0.5	0.68
White Sucker	2.8	1.80	0.1	0.12
Yellow Bullhead	4.3	0.76	3.6	0.77
Yellow Perch	5.3	0.12	7.0	0.11

LENGTH OF SELECTED SPECIES SAMPLED FROM ALL GEAR
Number of fish caught for the following length categories (inches):

species	0-5	6-8	9-11	12-14	15-19	20-24	25-29	>30	Total
Black Crappie	9	-	3	-	-	-	-	-	12
Bluegill	152	61	-	-	-	-	-	-	213
Brown Bullhead	-	-	3	5	-	-	-	-	8
Green Sunfish	22	-	-	-	-	-	-	-	22
Hybrid Sunfish	32	22	-	-	-	-	-	-	54
Largemouth Bass	4	13	7	-	3	-	-	-	27
Northern Pike	-	-	-	-	9	45	16	6	76
Pumpkin. Sunfish	25	14	-	-	-	-	-	-	39
Rock Bass	2	3	3	-	-	-	-	-	8
Tullibee (Cisco)	-	-	8	32	-	-	-	-	40
Walleye	-	1	8	6	12	1	-	-	28
Yellow Bullhead	-	-	57	13	-	-	-	-	70
Yellow Perch	38	69	-	-	-	-	-	-	107

DNR COMMENTS:
Northern Pike numbers slightly above normal range for lake class; some large fish present. Walleye numbers about normal; some larger fish sampled; spawning habitat rare; most of population believed to be composed of stocked fish. Largemouth Bass numbers slightly above normal; size about average for lake class. Black Crappie numbers normal; some large fish captured. Cisco population about average for lake class. Bluegill, Yellow Perch and Yellow Bullheads present in near-normal numbers.

FISHING INFORMATION: These two lakes offer nice opportunities for the angler. **Ice Cracking** is out of the way, not easy to access once you're there, and not very big. Other than that it's great. It's produced trophy Walleyes, as well as big Northerns, Largemouth Bass and Crappies. The lake has two holes of 67 and 72 feet and a median depth of 35 feet. Because of the lake's small size, you can move around and try different approaches until you find fish. Start on the east end of the lake and cast surface and shallow-running crankbaits and spinners over the large bar that extends out at a 7-foot depth from the opening to the Otter tail River spillway. At the edge of the bar, jig shiners and crawlers at 10 to 15 feet. Later in the summer work south into the deep bay where the water drops off sharply to the 72-foot hole. In the western portion of the lake work the shallows off the weedbeds on the southeastern shore. There are early Bass and Crappies here and, moving out to 10 to 20 feet, Walleyes and Northerns. Much of the mid-lake bottom is at 40 feet in this basin, so drifting or trolling the shorelines with live bait rigs will work well. So will dropping a live leech down the steep slopes. **Waboose**, meanwhile, is subject to occasional freezeout, but is known as a good producer of Walleyes, Crappies and sunnies in between. Tim Simon of Taylor Baits & Tackle RR 1, Box A175, Waubun (218) 473-3133, says the most recent winterkill occurred in 1994-95, but it's been restocked by the DNR and is now producing some Walleyes and good Crappies. The lake is basically a cereal bowl, says Simon, so you'll be fishing weedlines. Normal live bait techniques apply.

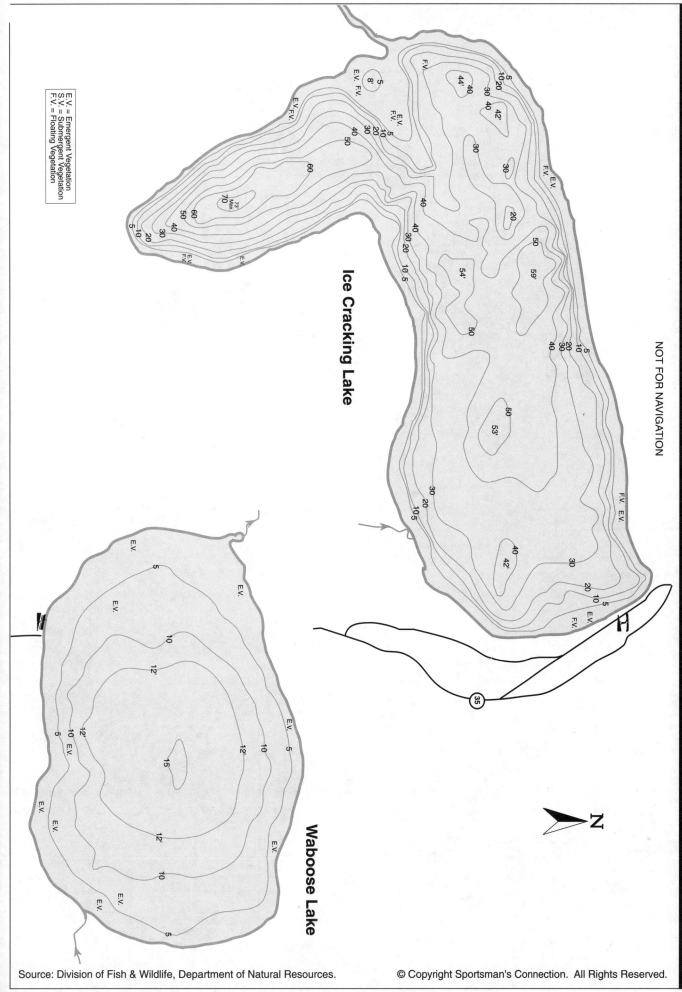

E.V. = Emergent Vegetation
S.V. = Submergent Vegetation
F.V. = Floating Vegetation

Ice Cracking Lake

Waboose Lake

NOT FOR NAVIGATION

N

Source: Division of Fish & Wildlife, Department of Natural Resources.

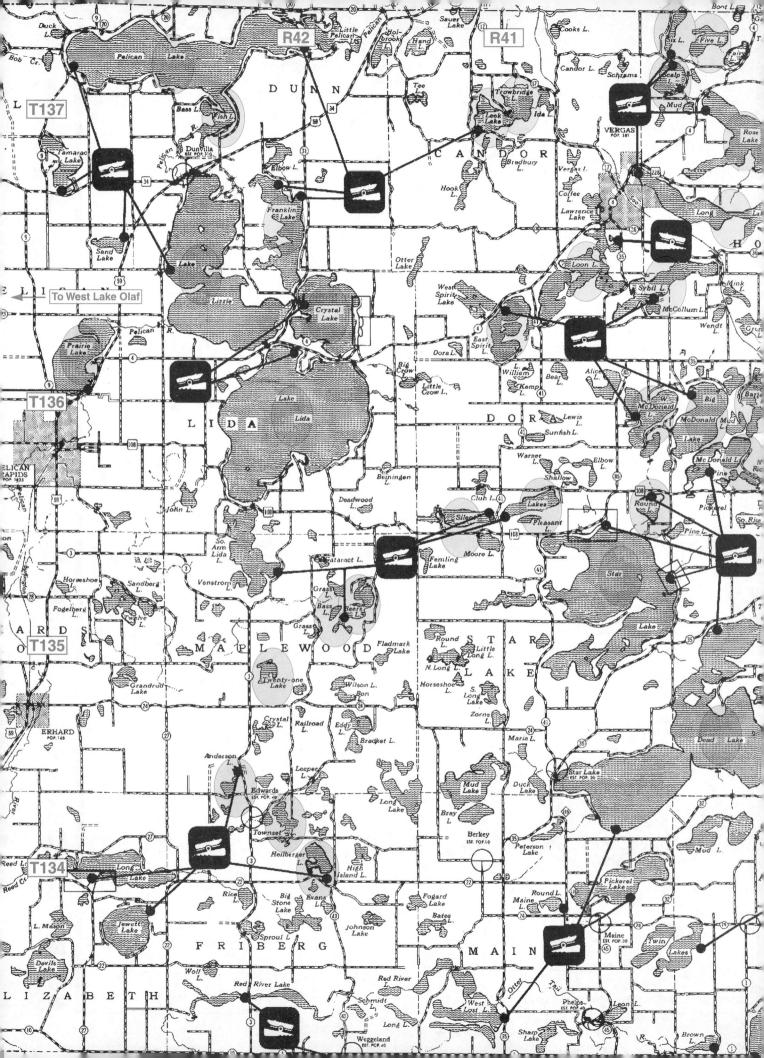

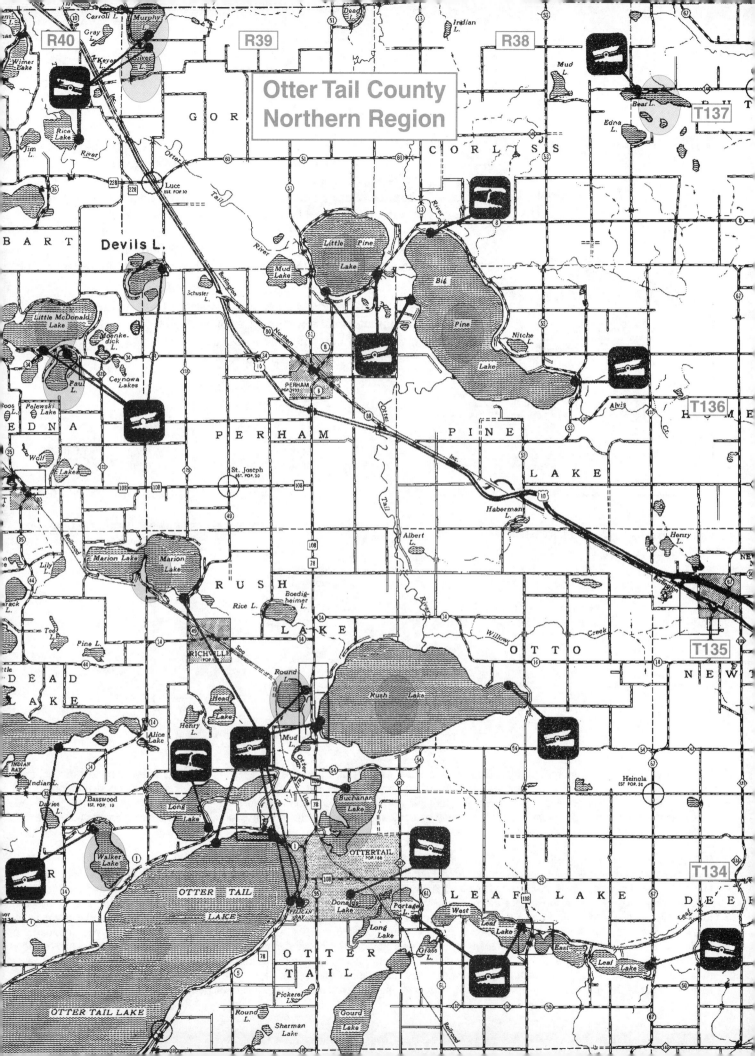

Otter Tail County
Northern Region

PELICAN LAKE
Otter Tail County

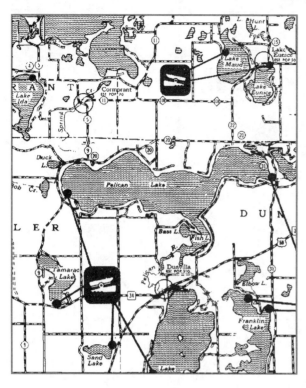

Location: Township 137
Range 42, 43
Watershed: Otter Tail
Surface Water Area: 3,986 Acres
Shorelength: 16.8 Miles
Secchi disk (water clarity): 5.4 Ft.
Water color: Greenish
Cause of water color: Algae

Maximum depth: 64 Ft.
Median depth: NA
Accessibility: Access on east shore off Cty. Hwy. #31 at Pelican Rapids River inlet; also access on southwest shore off Cty. Hwy. #9
Boat Ramp: Concrete (both)
Accommodations: Resorts; campgrounds

Shoreland zoning classification: General Development
Dominant forest/soil type: Deciduous/Sand
Management class: Walleye-Centrarchid
Ecological type: Centrarchid-Walleye

FISH STOCKING DATA

year	species	size	# released
93	Walleye	Fry	1,627,000
93	Muskellunge	Fingerling	1,006
95	Walleye	Fry	1,625,000
95	Muskellunge	Fingerling	1,130
97	Walleye	Fry	1,625,000
97	Muskellunge	Fingerling	1,000

NET CATCH DATA

survey date: 7/29/96

	Gill Nets		Trap Nets	
species	# per net	avg fish wt. (lbs.)	# per set	avg fish wt. (lbs.)
Black Crappie	-	-	trace	1.32
Bluegill	5.9	0.28	18.4	0.22
Freshwater Drum	trace	6.33	trace	8.60
Hybrid Sunfish	0.9	0.17	2.5	0.21
Largemouth Bass	0.3	0.88	0.6	0.42
Northern Pike	6.2	1.57	0.8	1.15
Pumpkin. Sunfish	1.7	0.19	0.4	0.14
Rock Bass	4.1	0.43	2.3	0.38
Smallmouth Bass	-	-	0.3	0.68
Tullibee (Cisco)	0.6	0.57	-	-
Walleye	6.7	1.75	0.3	2.39
Yellow Perch	1.4	0.09	0.2	0.03

LENGTH OF SELECTED SPECIES SAMPLED FROM ALL GEAR

Number of fish caught for the following length categories (inches):

species	0-5	6-8	9-11	12-14	15-19	20-24	25-29	>30	Total
Black Bullhead	-	5	5	3	-	-	-	-	13
Black Crappie	-	-	-	1	-	-	-	-	1
Bluegill	63	248	-	-	-	-	-	-	311
Brown Bullhead	-	-	6	12	-	-	-	-	18
Hybrid Sunfish	23	28	-	-	-	-	-	-	51
Largemouth Bass	-	8	4	1	1	-	-	-	14
Northern Pike	-	-	9	15	38	33	8	2	105
Pumpkin. Sunfish	14	17	-	-	-	-	-	-	31
Rock Bass	8	73	15	-	-	-	-	-	96
Smallmouth Bass	1	3	-	-	1	-	-	-	5
Tullibee (Cisco)	-	3	2	3	1	-	-	-	9
Walleye	-	4	9	29	36	21	2	-	101
Yellow Bullhead	-	-	1	14	-	-	-	-	15
Yellow Perch	5	5	-	-	-	-	-	-	10

DNR COMMENTS: Cisco numbers slightly low for lake class; fish to 15.8 inches sampled. Seven Muskies sampled by test-netting; average size 37.8 inches and 14.1 lb. Northern Pike population stable and within normal range for lake class; average size stable at 18.7 inches and 1.6 lb. Walleye numbers down slightly but still within expected range; average size 16.6 inches and 1.7 lb; 1991 and 1994 year classes appear strong; natural reproduction may be contributing significantly to population. Bluegill numbers down, but 45 percent of fish are 7 inches or larger. Yellow Perch numbers below normal for lake class.

FISHING INFORMATION: Pelican Lake (often referred to as Big Pelican), north of Pelican Rapids, is big (nearly 4,000 acres) and offers a variety of good fishing year around. Northern Pike, Largemouth Bass, panfish and Walleyes are all present in fairly high numbers. The lake also provides really good structure that challenges anglers. Sunken islands at the lake's west end, at mid lake, and near the north side are good places to start looking for early-season Walleyes. A sand-and-rubble bottom gives anglers an opportunity to fish the bottoms at these shallower areas. Use a bottom rig with a leech or minnow, bumping it along the bottom as you retrieve it slowly where the Walleyes feed. You'll also find goggle eyes off the points at the middle of the south and north shores. These same areas, too, can provide good Smallmouth Bass fishing, particularly where there's rubble. Northerns can be found in the flats at the east and south sides of the lake, where they patrol the outer edges of weedlines. You can also find a number of the alligators at the outlet into the Pelican River, near the lake's southeast corner. Panfish, meanwhile, are abundant in the weeds. Bluegills are the most prevalent, but you can find some nice Black Crappie too. As the water warms, of course, the Walleyes and larger panfish will head for deeper waters at mid lake.

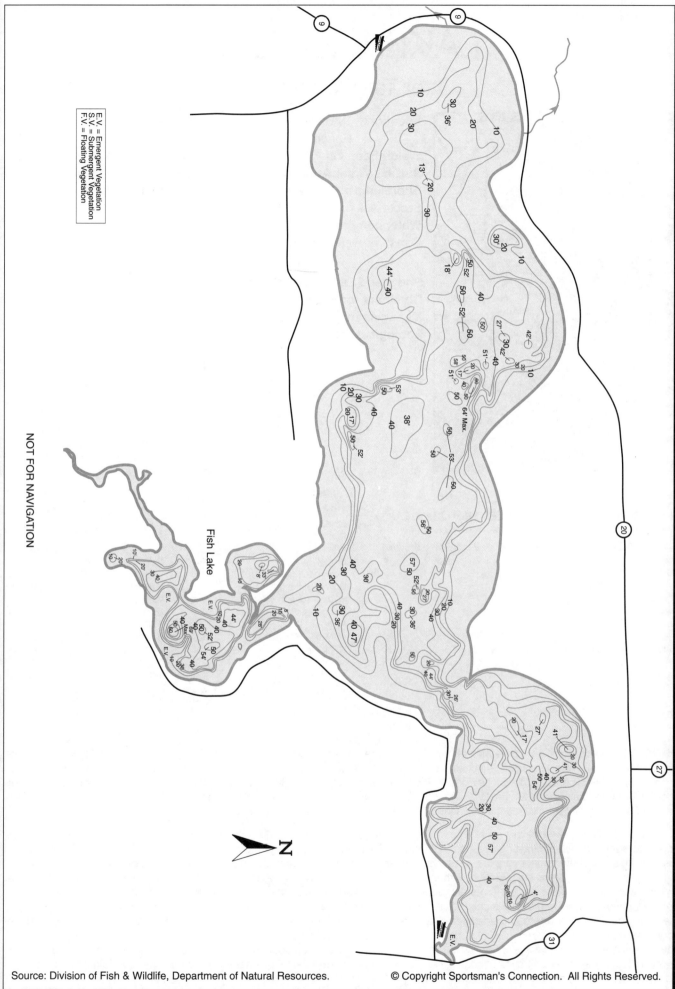

E.V. = Emergent Vegetation
S.V. = Submergent Vegetation
F.V. = Floating Vegetation

NOT FOR NAVIGATION

Fish Lake

N

LAKE LIZZIE
Otter Tail County

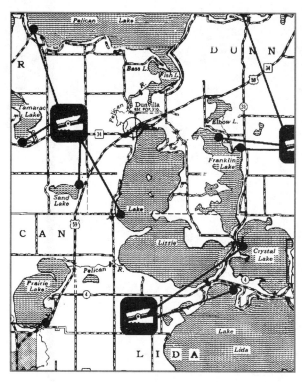

Location: Township 136, 137 Range 42
Watershed: Otter Tail
Surface Water Area: 4,035 Acres
Shorelength: 16.7 Miles
Secchi disk (water clarity): 6.5 Ft.
Water color: Greenish
Cause of water color: Algae

Maximum depth: 66 Ft.
Median depth: 10 Ft.
Accessibility: State-owned public access on west shore, one mile east off State Hwy. #59
Boat Ramp: Concrete
Accommodations: NA

Shoreland zoning classification: Recreational Development
Dominant forest/soil type: Deciduous/Loam
Management class: Walleye-Centrarchid
Ecological type: Centrarchid-Walleye

FISH STOCKING DATA

year	species	size	# released
90	Walleye	Fry	2,504,000
94	Walleye	Fry	2,500,000
96	Walleye	Fry	2,500,000
98	Walleye	Fry	2,500,000

NET CATCH DATA

survey date: 8/28/95

	Gill Nets		Trap Nets	
species	# per net	avg fish wt. (lbs.)	# per set	avg fish wt. (lbs.)
Black Bullhead	0.2	1.09	0.2	1.11
Black Crappie	-	-	0.2	0.10
Bluegill	4.3	0.24	45.4	0.24
Bowfin (Dogfish)	-	-	0.2	5.25
Brown Bullhead	0.2	1.01	0.3	0.92
Hybrid Sunfish	0.4	0.31	1.6	0.28
Largemouth Bass	0.7	0.49	2.1	0.41
Northern Pike	5.9	1.07	0.6	1.70
Pumpkin. Sunfish	1.5	0.22	0.6	0.23
Rock Bass	0.8	0.56	1.4	0.48
Smallmouth Bass	trace	1.91	0.2	0.26
Tullibee (Cisco)	1.9	1.25	-	-
Walleye	6.3	1.05	0.5	2.06
White Sucker	3.5	1.94	0.9	2.77
Yellow Bullhead	2.1	0.79	2.4	0.86
Yellow Perch	5.6	0.12	-	-

LENGTH OF SELECTED SPECIES SAMPLED FROM ALL GEAR

Number of fish caught for the following length categories (inches):

species	0-5	6-8	9-11	12-14	15-19	20-24	25-29	>30	Total
Black Bullhead	-	-	2	4	-	-	-	-	6
Black Crappie	1	2	-	-	-	-	-	-	3
Bluegill	79	289	1	-	-	-	-	-	369
Brown Bullhead	-	-	-	7	-	-	-	-	7
Hybrid Sunfish	3	25	-	-	-	-	-	-	28
Largemouth Bass	2	27	6	6	-	-	-	-	41
Northern Pike	-	-	5	32	38	20	1	2	98
Pumpkin. Sunfish	8	24	-	-	-	-	-	-	32
Rock Bass	5	8	13	1	-	-	-	-	27
Smallmouth Bass	1	1	1	-	1	-	-	-	4
Tullibee (Cisco)	-	3	5	8	12	-	-	-	28
Walleye	-	21	37	2	29	11	2	-	102
Yellow Bullhead	-	1	44	20	-	-	-	-	65
Yellow Perch	19	43	-	-	-	-	-	-	62

DNR COMMENTS: Cisco numbers stable and within normal range; average size 13.8 inches and 1.3 lb. Northern Pike population up and within normal range; average size 16.7 inches and 1.1 lb.; natural reproduction stable. Walleye numbers stable and within normal range for lake class; average size 13.2 inches and 1.3 lb.; natural recruitment limited. Largemouth Bass abundance exceeds normal range; good 1994 year class; mean length 11.7 inches at four years. Bluegill population stable and within normal range; size structure improved, with 39 percent of Bluegills reaching 7 inches. Yellow Perch numbers below normal range.

FISHING INFORMATION: Lake Lizzie is a year-round sporting arena for anglers and duck hunters. The reason is the 4,035-acre lake is almost equally divided into two contrasting sections. The lower lake is almost entirely composed of big, shallow flats mostly full of cattails and bulrushes. This is favorite haunt every fall for Bluegill hunters. In wintertime, meanwhile, the upper lake is home to hordes of anglers harvesting Lizzie's abundant Crappie population. When the ice thaws, a wide variety of anglers head for upper Lizzie. Action begins with early Crappies and panfish in the bay on the south side and in the northwest corner, around the Pelican River channel. Then comes angling for the abundant Bass and Walleye populations. Upper Lizzie has a clarity reading of nearly nine feet and sand-and-rubble bottom. Holes, ranging from 23 to 66 feet, are scattered all over the lake and there are two bars to pay close attention to. One surrounds the island at dead-center-lake and reaches off to the south. The second stands just off the western shore due west of the same island. Both of these bars are prime Walleye territory. Drift east of the island and then on south using minnows and crawlers (early) and leeches (later on) on Lindys or other live-bait rigs. Work the north side of the western bar. For Bass, stand off the weedbeds along the eastern shore and cast the breaks at 10 feet with crankbaits and spinners on a light line.

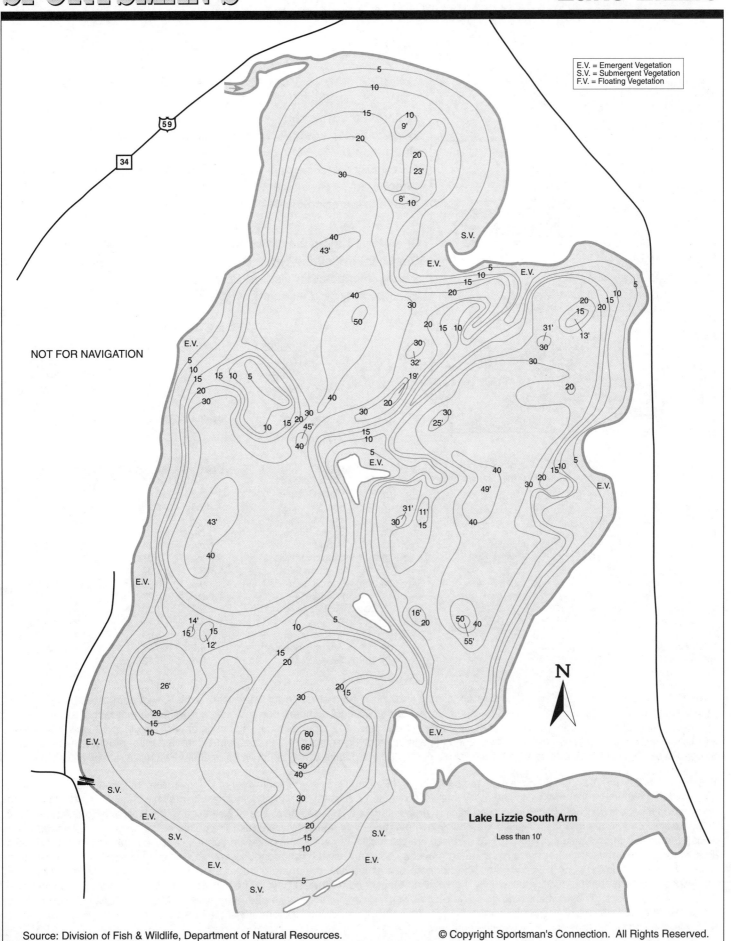

E.V. = Emergent Vegetation
S.V. = Submergent Vegetation
F.V. = Floating Vegetation

NOT FOR NAVIGATION

Lake Lizzie South Arm

Less than 10'

N

LAKE FRANKLIN
Otter Tail County

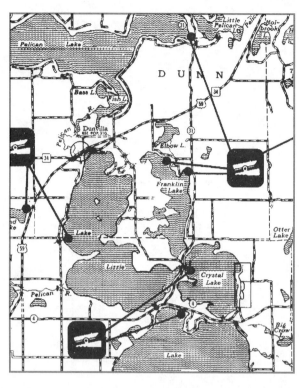

Location: Township 136, 137 Range 42
Watershed: Otter Tail
Surface Water Area: 1,336 Acres
Shorelength: 11.7 Miles
Secchi disk (water clarity): 9.5 Ft.
Water color: NA
Cause of water color: NA

Maximum depth: 48 Ft.
Median depth: NA
Accessibility: State-owned public access on north and northeast shores of lake
Boat Ramp: Concrete (north), Gravel (northeast)
Accommodations: NA

Shoreland zoning classification: Recreational Development
Dominant forest/soil type: Deciduous/Loam
Management class: Walleye-Centrarchid
Ecological type: Centrarchid-Walleye

FISH STOCKING DATA

year	species	size	# released
93	Walleye	Fry	1,123,000
95	Walleye	Fry	1,123,000
97	Walleye	Fry	749,000

NET CATCH DATA

survey date: 7/17/95

species	Gill Nets # per net	avg fish wt. (lbs.)	Trap Nets # per set	avg fish wt. (lbs.)
Black Bullhead	1.0	1.28	0.2	1.09
Black Crappie	0.3	0.47	0.1	0.04
Bluegill	12.4	0.26	56.5	0.25
Bowfin (Dogfish)	-	-	0.6	4.18
Brown Bullhead	0.6	1.31	-	-
Hybrid Sunfish	trace	0.24	2.1	0.29
Largemouth Bass	trace	1.97	0.4	0.21
Northern Pike	13.4	1.07	1.1	1.17
Pumpkin. Sunfish	0.4	0.26	0.8	0.26
Rock Bass	trace	0.77	-	-
Tullibee (Cisco)	3.5	1.30	-	-
Walleye	8.8	1.21	0.2	4.22
White Sucker	0.3	3.00	0.1	3.53
Yellow Bullhead	8.2	0.77	6.8	0.81
Yellow Perch	5.6	0.13	-	-

LENGTH OF SELECTED SPECIES SAMPLED FROM ALL GEAR

Number of fish caught for the following length categories (inches):

species	0-5	6-8	9-11	12-14	15-19	20-24	25-29	>30	Total
Black Bullhead	-	-	1	13	-	-	-	-	14
Black Crappie	1	2	1	-	-	-	-	-	4
Bluegill	72	332	-	-	-	-	-	-	404
Brown Bullhead	-	-	-	7	-	-	-	-	7
Hybrid Sunfish	3	19	-	-	-	-	-	-	22
Largemouth Bass	-	3	1	-	1	-	-	-	5
Northern Pike	-	-	1	49	87	26	7	-	170
Pumpkin. Sunfish	-	13	-	-	-	-	-	-	13
Rock Bass	-	-	1	-	-	-	-	-	1
Tullibee (Cisco)	-	2	-	29	7	-	-	-	38
Walleye	-	13	16	13	51	9	-	-	102
Yellow Bullhead	-	1	137	28	-	-	-	-	166
Yellow Perch	15	27	1	-	-	-	-	-	43

DNR COMMENTS: Northern Pike population up slightly and above normal range for lake class; sample was dominated by small fish; average size 17.1 inches and 1.2 lb.; natural reproduction stable. Bluegill numbers down slightly but within normal range; size structure likewise stable, with 39 percent of fish reaching 7 inches. Well-balanced Largemouth Bass population; fish reaching 13 inches at age 4. Walleye numbers up and above the expected range for lake class; average size 14.7 inches and 1.2 lb.; natural reproduction contributing to population. Yellow Perch numbers stable and within normal range for lake class, but only 7 percent of Perch are reaching 8 inches.

FISHING INFORMATION: Lake Franklin, located northeast of Pelican Rapids and southwest of Detroit Lakes, has good fish populations and the sort of structure that makes fishing really interesting. At least a half-dozen nice points, good small bays, submerged islands and humps and a good weedline all add up to good fishing. In addition, the lake has been liberally stocked with Walleye fry to bolster natural reproduction, and numbers of this species are now above average. For spring Walleye, fish the points on the east side. The long one above the bay on the southeast and the two at mid lake are productive, as are the humps with bulrushes at the north end and at mid lake. The water is clear and the bottom mostly sand and gravel so you can usually fish along the bottom and up the sides of the points with shiner minnows or leeches on a bottom rig. The northern half of the lake is generally better for Largemouth Bass. By mid June, the weedlines there are very productive, especially the small northeast and northwest bays. The two weed-filled bays on the southwest side can also be excellent. Those weeds also hold fine Black Crappies early in the weeks after they spawn. Don't overlook the Northerns in Franklin, either. Though they're generally small, the provide good action. Look for them outside the weeds at the south ends, particularly near the openings to the bays on the west side and the south end.

Lake Franklin

SPORTSMAN'S Connection®

48' Max

E.V. = Emergent Vegetation
S.V. = Submergent Vegetation
F.V. = Floating Vegetation

NOT FOR NAVIGATION

Source: Division of Fish & Wildlife, Department of Natural Resources.

CRYSTAL LAKE
Otter Tail County

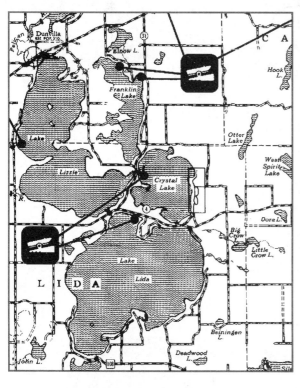

Location: Township 136 Range 42
Watershed: Otter Tail
Surface Water Area: 1,317 Acres
Shorelength: 7.9 Miles
Secchi disk (water clarity): 8.0 Ft.
Water color: Light green
Cause of water color: Algae bloom

Maximum depth: 55 Ft.
Median depth: 20 Ft.
Accessibility: County-owned public access on west shore, off County Road #31
Boat Ramp: Earth
Accommodations: NA

Shoreland zoning classification: Recreational Development
Dominant forest/soil type: Deciduous/Sand
Management class: Walleye-Centrarchid
Ecological type: Centrarchid-Walleye

FISH STOCKING DATA

year	species	size	# released
90	Walleye	Fry	674,000
94	Walleye	Fry	700,000
96	Walleye	Fry	674,000
98	Walleye	Fry	674,000

NET CATCH DATA

survey date: 8/8/94

species	Gill Nets # per net	Gill Nets avg fish wt. (lbs.)	Trap Nets # per set	Trap Nets avg fish wt. (lbs.)
Black Bullhead	0.3	2.33	0.8	1.89
Black Crappie	trace	1.14	trace	0.88
Bluegill	11.3	0.17	38.4	0.18
Bowfin (Dogfish)	-	-	0.3	11.50
Brown Bullhead	-	-	0.2	1.93
Hybrid Sunfish	0.8	0.42	6.1	0.43
Largemouth Bass	0.3	1.30	0.4	1.89
Northern Pike	6.8	1.35	0.2	3.66
Pumpkin. Sunfish	1.3	0.37	1.8	0.38
Rock Bass	0.8	0.62	1.0	0.65
Smallmouth Bass	-	-	0.3	2.48
Tullibee (Cisco)	1.9	1.57	-	-
Walleye	4.4	2.24	trace	2.56
White Sucker	0.3	6.45	-	-
Yellow Bullhead	1.0	1.66	2.3	2.09
Yellow Perch	7.3	0.10	0.4	0.14

LENGTH OF SELECTED SPECIES SAMPLED FROM ALL GEAR

Number of fish caught for the following length categories (inches):

species	0-5	6-8	9-11	12-14	15-19	20-24	25-29	>30	Total
Black Bullhead	-	-	1	12	-	-	-	-	13
Black Crappie	-	-	1	1	-	-	-	-	2
Bluegill	139	250	1	-	-	-	-	-	390
Brown Bullhead	-	-	-	2	-	-	-	-	2
Hybrid Sunfish	29	53	-	-	-	-	-	-	82
Largemouth Bass	-	-	1	5	2	-	-	-	8
Northern Pike	-	1	6	15	35	17	5	2	81
Pumpkin. Sunfish	17	20	-	-	-	-	-	-	37
Rock Bass	4	15	3	-	-	-	-	-	22
Smallmouth Bass	-	-	-	-	3	-	-	-	3
Tullibee (Cisco)	-	9	3	7	4	-	-	-	23
Walleye	1	-	1	4	39	8	1	-	54
Yellow Bullhead	-	-	15	25	-	-	-	-	40
Yellow Perch	35	44	-	-	-	-	-	-	79

DNR COMMENTS: Northern Pike population within normal range for lake class; 10 percent of Northerns exceeded 24 inches. Walleye numbers down but within normal range; mean length 18.3 inches; natural reproduction contributing to population. Largemouth Bass available to anglers; mean length 14.1 inches. Smallmouth Bass also present; mean length 16.3 inches. Black Crappie catch below normal, but trapnet catch may not accurately reflect population.

FISHING INFORMATION: Crystal Lake is located northeast of Pelican Rapids among bigger, more popular fishing lakes. But anglers who want to catch nice Walleyes and Northerns will be making a mistake if they pass it up, for the fishing can be very good. Crystal is managed for Walleyes by the DNR which has been stocking it regularly with fry. The three big points (the north, south and west ends) on this 1,317-acre lake are all productive in the spring. So are some of the quick offshore breaks such as those you'll find at the north end. There are also several exceptional humps: two at mid lake and another in the southeast corner. Use a bottom rig and shiner minnow at these spots in the spring. That's where you'll find old marble eyes feeding, and you can take him by starting about 10 to 15 feet down and retrieving upwards. Spring Northerns will be cruising the outer edges of the weeds waiting to gobble forage fish. Work the flats around the lake, giving special attention to the southeast corner. Trolling with spoons is the best way to work the flats most of the season except during those bright, summer days when Northerns (and Walleyes) suspend deep in the holes. The lake is full of Bluegills which you can take with worms on a bare hook or a jig in the spring. Use a slip bobber in deeper water later on, testing for the right depth. There are some Largemouth and a few Smallmouth Bass in Crystal. They'll be in the weeds early, of course, and, with persistence and good technique, you can haul some in.

NOT FOR NAVIGATION

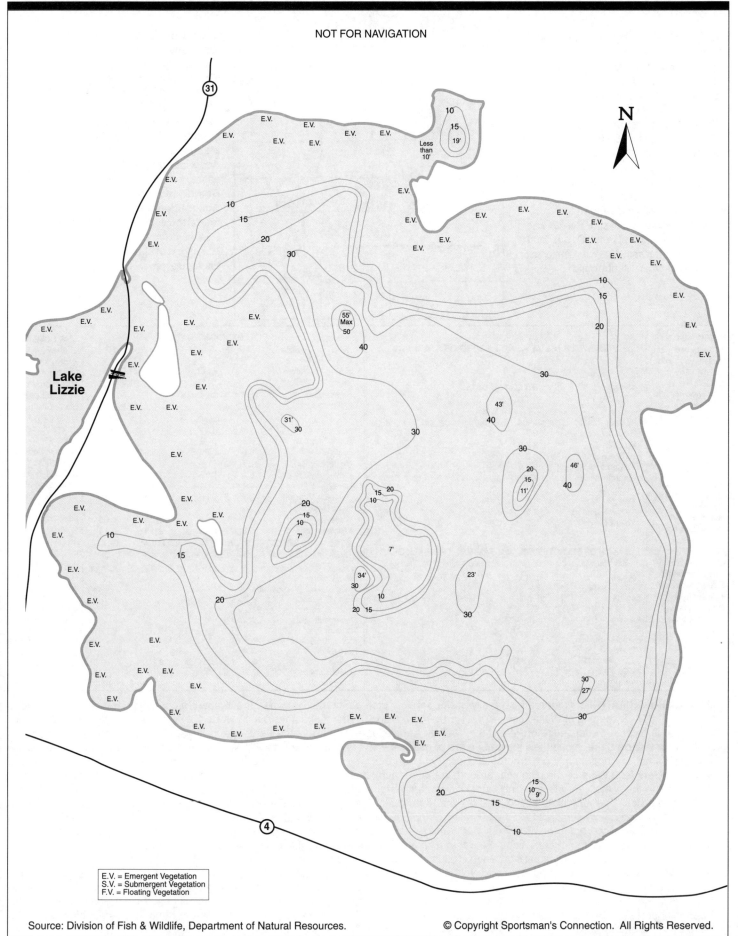

E.V. = Emergent Vegetation
S.V. = Submergent Vegetation
F.V. = Floating Vegetation

WEST OLAF LAKE   PRAIRIE LAKE
Otter Tail County

Location: Township 146 Range 43,44
Watershed: Buffalo
Surface Water Area: 143 Acres
Shorelength: NA
Secchi disk (water clarity): 14.0 Ft.
Water color: Light Green
Cause of water color: Algae
Maximum depth: 61 Ft.
Median depth: NA
Accessibility: State-owned public access on east shore, off Hwy. 30
Boat Ramp: Concrete
Accommodations: NA
Shoreland zoning classif.: Rec. Dev.
Dominant forest/soil type: Decid.-Sand
Management class: Walleye-Centrarchid
Ecological type: Centrarchid

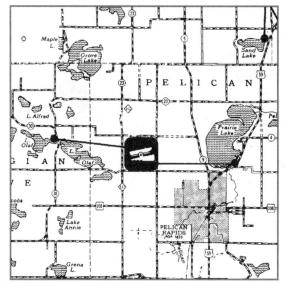

Location: Township 136 Range 43
Watershed: Otter Tail
Surface Water Area: 1,016 Acres
Shorelength: 5.9 Miles
Secchi disk (water clarity): 4.0 Ft.
Water color: Green
Cause of water color: Algae
Maximum depth: 21 Ft.
Median depth: 10 Ft.
Accessibility: Public access on south-east shore
Boat Ramp: Concrete
Accommodations: Resort
Shoreland zoning classif.: Rec. Dev.
Dominant forest/soil type: Decid/Sand
Management class: Walleye-Centrarchid
Ecological type: Centrarchid

DNR COMMENTS:
Northern Pike numbers down slightly and below normal range for lake class; average size 21.4 inches and 2.2 lb.; natural reproduction sporadic. Walleye population down and below normal range; natural reproduction limited. Electrofishing data indicate a healthy Largemouth Bass population. Yellow Perch numbers low; natural reproduction sporadic. Bluegill population within normal range; 10 percent of fish reaching 7 inches.

FISH STOCKING DATA: NO RECORD OF STOCKING

survey date: 7/24/95

NET CATCH DATA

species	Gill Nets # per net	Gill Nets avg fish wt. (lbs)	Trap Nets # per set	Trap Nets avg fish wt. (lbs)
Black Crapple	0.3	0.04	0.2	0.13
Bluegill	3.7	0.17	23.0	0.15
Hybrid Sunfish	0.2	0.27	1.0	0.22
Largemouth Bass	0.2	1.51	0.4	1.40
Northern Pike	2.0	2.05	0.1	1.26
Pumpkin. Sunfish	-	-	2.4	0.21
Walleye	0.8	3.39	0.2	4.41
Yellow Bullhead	9.8	0.63	5.2	0.66
Yellow Perch	3.7	0.08	0.1	0.06

LENGTH OF SELECTED SPECIES SAMPLED FROM ALL GEAR
Number of fish caught for the following length categories (inches):

species	0-5	6-8	9-11	12-14	15-19	20-24	25-29	>30	Total
Black Crappie	2	2	-	-	-	-	-	-	4
Bluegill	88	67	-	-	-	-	-	-	155
Hybrid Sunfish	2	8	-	-	-	-	-	-	10
Largemouth Bass	-	-	2	2	1	-	-	-	5
Northern Pike	-	-	-	-	5	5	1	-	11
Pumpkin. Sunfish	9	13	-	-	-	-	-	-	22
Walleye	-	-	-	-	4	1	2	-	7
Yellow Bullhead	-	7	84	15	-	-	-	-	106
Yellow Perch	9	4	-	-	-	-	-	-	13

FISH STOCKING DATA

year	species	size	# released
94	Walleye	Fry	801,000
96	Walleye	Fry	801,000
98	Walleye	Fry	801,000

survey date: 8/11/97

NET CATCH DATA

species	Gill Nets # per net	Gill Nets avg fish wt. (lbs)	Trap Nets # per set	Trap Nets avg fish wt. (lbs)
Black Crappie	0.5	0.22	0.7	0.15
Bluegill	16.6	0.25	33.5	0.26
Hybrid Sunfish	-	-	2.8	0.26
Largemouth Bass	0.9	0.76	0.7	0.95
Northern Pike	10.1	1.09	0.8	1.11
Pumpkin. Sunfish	8.8	0.20	2.7	0.21
Rock Bass	-	-	trace	0.29
Walleye	4.5	2.15	trace	0.65
Yellow Perch	5.8	0.13	0.2	0.15

LENGTH OF SELECTED SPECIES SAMPLED FROM ALL GEAR
Number of fish caught for the following length categories (inches):

species	0-5	6-8	9-11	12-14	15-19	20-24	25-29	>30	Total
Black Crappie	4	10	-	-	-	-	-	-	14
Bluegill	54	404	-	-	-	-	-	-	458
Brown Bullhead	1	8	5	5	-	-	-	-	19
Hybrid Sunfish	10	23	-	-	-	-	-	-	33
Largemouth Bass	-	1	13	4	1	-	-	-	19
Northern Pike	-	-	6	41	59	16	5	2	129
Pumpkin. Sunfish	59	77	-	-	-	-	-	-	136
Rock Bass	-	1	-	-	-	-	-	-	1
Walleye	-	2	3	20	14	9	7	-	55
Yellow Bullhead	29	42	79	7	-	-	-	-	157
Yellow Perch	24	35	2	-	-	-	-	-	61

DNR COMMENTS:
This lake is best known for excellent Northern Pike, Largemouth Bass, Bluegill and Black Crappie angling. Walleye fry are stocked biennially to supplement natural reproduction which is limited by a shortage of suitable spawning habitat. Other species are able to maintain their levels at or above management goals without stocking. Bluegill and Crappie angling is very popular in winter. The long-term average fish house count is 63.

FISHING INFORMATION: Northern Pike really prefer Yellow Perch as forage, but when the Yellow Perch supply dwindles — as it does during heavy DNR seeding of Walleye fry — the Northern Pike don't suffer much; they simply switch over to Walleyes for food. The problem, then, is that, in the absence of Perch, the Walleye population suffers: only the fleetest and fittest survive. That, then, is why the Walleyes in **Prairie Lake**, though few in number, are of good size, averaging larger than the Northerns. Not bad. Throw in an abundance of Crappies and a good supply of Largemouth Bass, you can see why we say the angler has good prospects on Prairie. Crappie and panfish anglers tend to be on the lake year around, in the northern shallows in the spring, and out on the breaks around the 21-foot maximum depth in the winter. Prairie is on the murky side with a water clarity of four feet. This means bright-colored lures, poppers and buzz baits are in order. The long point jutting out from the northwestern shore is a focus for anglers. In spring, go north around the point to cast into the emergent weedbeds along the shoreline of the bay for Bass and Crappies. Later in the spring, jig the deeper weedbreaks off the southern side of the point for Walleyes. Northerns are all over the lake, but anglers find them often trolling or casting spoons and spinners at the 10- to 15-foot breaks along the western shore. In **West Olaf Lake**, meanwhile, you'll find "a little bit of everything," according to Tim Beiningen of Park Region Sport Shop, 100 N. Broadway, Pelican Rapids (800) 962-8553. Primary quarries, though, are Largemouth, which average around 3 pounds, and Northerns which run 5 pounds and up. Fish the well-weeded bays for the bucketmouths, tossing plastic worms or pig-and-jig combos. Or, you can wait till the sun goes down and the wind drops and cast topwater gear to the openings in the weed tops. For the alligators, work the weedlines with orange and gold spoons. There's good Pike action, too, in the winter, Beiningen says. Set up in the narrows leading to the east bay. The access sports a nice concrete ramp, but recent high water has made its use a bit awkward.

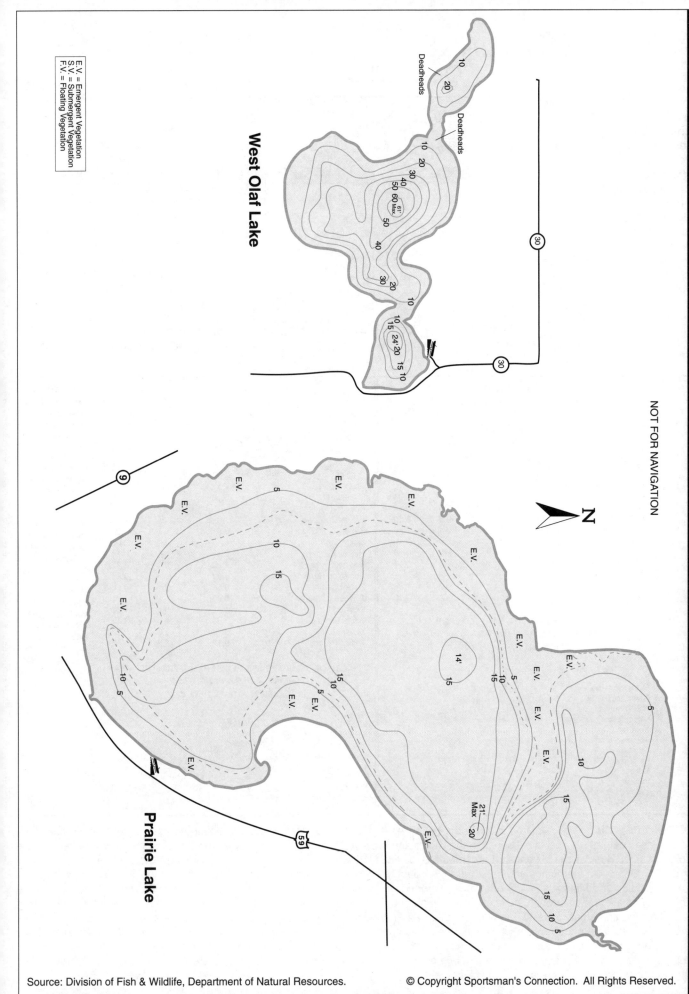

West Olaf & Prairie Lakes

NOT FOR NAVIGATION

N

E.V. = Emergent Vegetation
S.V. = Submergent Vegetation
F.V. = Floating Vegetation

West Olaf Lake

Deadheads

Deadheads

10
20
10
20
30
40
50
60 Max.
61'
50
40
30
20
10
10
15
24 20
15 10
30
30

Prairie Lake

9

E.V.

5
10
15
10
5
15
14'
15
21'
Max
20
15
10
5
15
10
5

59

NORTH LIDA LAKE SOUTH LIDA LAKE
Otter Tail County

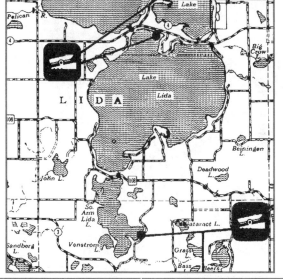

North Lida Lake

Location: Township 135, 136 Range 42
Watershed: Otter Tail
Surface Water Area: 5,564 Acres
Shorelength: 26.1 Miles
Secchi disk (water clarity): 7.9 Ft.
Water color: Light green
Cause of water color: Algae bloom
Maximum depth: 59 Ft.
Median depth: 30 Ft.
Accessibility: State-owned public access on north shore
Boat Ramp: Concrete
Accommodations: Resorts and campground, Maplewood State Park
Shoreland zoning classif.: Gen. Dev.
Dominant forest/soil type: Decid/Loam
Management class: Walleye-Centrarchid
Ecological type: Centrarchid-Walleye

South Lida Lake

Location: Township 135, 136 Range 42
Watershed: Otter Tail
Surface Water Area: 856 Acres
Shorelength: NA
Secchi disk (water clarity): 4.5 Ft.
Water color: Light green
Cause of water color: Algae bloom
Maximum depth: 48 Ft.
Median depth: NA
Accessibility: State-owned public access on southeast shore in Maplewood State Park
Boat Ramp: Concrete
Accommodations: Resorts, campground, Maplewood State Park
Shoreland zoning classif.: Gen. Dev.
Dominant forest/soil type: Decid/Loam
Management class: Walleye-Centrarchid
Ecological type: Centrarchid-Walleye

DNR COMMENTS:
Lake best known for abundant, self-sustaining populations of Walleye, Northern Pike, Black Crappie and Bluegill. Recently the Smallmouth Bass population has been increasing, and anglers are pursuing this species. Average size of Black Crappie has been declining over time, and an 11-inch minimum size limit has been established; this will be evaluated through 2005 to see if it improves the Crappie size structure. No DNR fish stocking takes place in this lake.

FISH STOCKING DATA
No record of stocking since 1986.

NET CATCH DATA

survey date: 8/4/97

species	Gill Nets # per net	Gill Nets avg fish wt. (lbs)	Trap Nets # per set	Trap Nets avg fish wt. (lbs)
Black Crappie	0.1	0.56	1.2	0.48
Bluegill	1.6	0.11	47.0	0.10
Green Sunfish	-	-	0.1	0.04
Hybrid Sunfish	1.3	0.14	7.9	0.12
Largemouth Bass	-	-	0.5	0.50
Northern Pike	5.7	2.14	0.4	1.86
Pumpkin. Sunfish	2.3	0.12	4.0	0.10
Rock Bass	6.2	0.47	2.9	0.36
Smallmouth Bass	1.5	0.71	0.3	0.15
Tullibee (Cisco)	6.7	0.63	-	-
Walleye	10.3	1.54	0.2	1.86
Yellow Perch	27.8	0.10	3.2	0.10

LENGTH OF SELECTED SPECIES SAMPLED FROM ALL GEAR
Number of fish caught for the following length categories (inches):

species	0-5	6-8	9-11	12-14	15-19	20-24	25-29	>30	Total
Black Bullhead	-	1	1	3	-	-	-	-	5
Black Crappie	1	8	10	-	-	-	-	-	19
Bluegill	265	73	-	-	-	-	-	-	338
Brown Bullhead	-	-	-	3	-	-	-	-	3
Green Sunfish	2	-	-	-	-	-	-	-	2
Hybrid Sunfish	98	32	-	-	-	-	-	-	130
Largemouth Bass	-	3	4	-	-	-	-	-	7
Northern Pike	-	-	4	5	31	35	13	2	90
Pumpkin. Sunfish	76	12	-	-	-	-	-	-	88
Rock Bass	23	73	37	-	-	-	-	-	133
Smallmouth Bass	3	5	14	2	2	-	-	-	26
Tullibee (Cisco)	-	47	6	27	10	-	-	-	90
Walleye	-	4	29	52	34	37	-	-	156
Yellow Bullhead	-	10	48	86	-	-	-	-	144
Yellow Perch	195	155	-	-	-	-	-	-	350

FISH STOCKING DATA
No record of stocking since 1986.

NET CATCH DATA

survey date: 7/7/97

species	Gill Nets # per net	Gill Nets avg fish wt. (lbs)	Trap Nets # per set	Trap Nets avg fish wt. (lbs)
Black Crappie	-	-	0.8	0.67
Bluegill	0.8	0.18	9.1	0.22
Bowfin (Dogfish)	-	-	0.2	5.84
Brown Bullhead	0.3	1.38	0.4	1.31
Freshwater Drum	0.3	9.98	0.8	8.32
Golden Shiner	-	-	0.3	0.05
Hybrid Sunfish	0.7	0.25	3.6	0.14
Northern Pike	2.0	2.32	0.3	2.47
Pumpkin. Sunfish	0.7	0.27	0.3	0.24
Rock Bass	2.6	0.38	2.1	0.36
Tullibee (Cisco)	4.3	0.92	-	-
Walleye	8.8	1.15	0.4	1.32
White Sucker	2.5	3.06	0.3	3.17
Yellow Bullhead	2.7	0.74	2.3	0.88
Yellow Perch	19.4	0.12	0.3	0.12

LENGTH OF SELECTED SPECIES SAMPLED FROM ALL GEAR
Number of fish caught for the following length categories (inches):

species	0-5	6-8	9-11	12-14	15-19	20-24	25-29	>30	Total
Black Crappie	-	1	7	1	-	-	-	-	9
Bluegill	66	44	4	-	-	-	-	-	114
Brown Bullhead	-	-	1	7	-	-	-	-	8
Hybrid Sunfish	35	16	-	-	-	-	-	-	51
Northern Pike	-	-	-	-	9	13	6	-	28
Pumpkin. Sunfish	1	11	-	-	-	-	-	-	12
Rock Bass	3	47	6	-	-	-	-	-	56
Tullibee (Cisco)	-	28	-	8	13	-	-	-	49
Walleye	-	1	38	50	6	10	4	-	109
Yellow Bullhead	-	10	31	19	-	-	-	-	60
Yellow Perch	113	101	3	-	-	-	-	-	217

DNR COMMENTS:
Lake is known for abundant, self-sustaining populations of Walleye, Largemouth Bass, Black Crappie and Bluegill. Ciscoes are abundant and pursued by anglers during the winter. Size structures for all species are good. However, the average size for Black Crappies has been declining over time, and an 11-inch minimum size limit has been established; this will be evaluated through 2005 to see if it improves the Crappie size structure. Lake is not stocked by the DNR.

FISHING INFORMATION: Big Lake Lida is located a few miles east of Pelican Rapids and is widely regarded as one of the finer year around fisheries in central Minnesota. Ciscoes in the winter and Walleye in the summer are what most anglers seem to be after, but the lake also offers good populations of panfish, Largemouth Bass and Northerns. There seems to be unlimited structure in the main lake for spring Walleye. Check out the humps and bars; there are roughly a dozen good ones, most of them lying not too far offshore on all sides of the lake. Kansas and Matson's Points offer good opportunities along the south shore, as does Clay Point at the north shore. There are also several smaller points around the lake. The humps and points are mostly sand-bottomed, and you'll do well early in the season fishing a bottom rig and shiner minnow, putting it in deep and retrieving it up the sloping sides of the bars where Walleye are feeding. Don't overlook the south end of the lake which has deep holes and some good points for Walleyes. There aren't a lot of Smallmouth in Lida, but your chances of running across them are good in the same areas where the Walleyes are feeding. Head for the weeds, though, if you're after early Bass and Crappies; offer pork rinds on a bright marabou jig. Those weeds also are where Northern Pike prowl. Troll just off the weedlines with live baits, spoons or spinnerbaits.

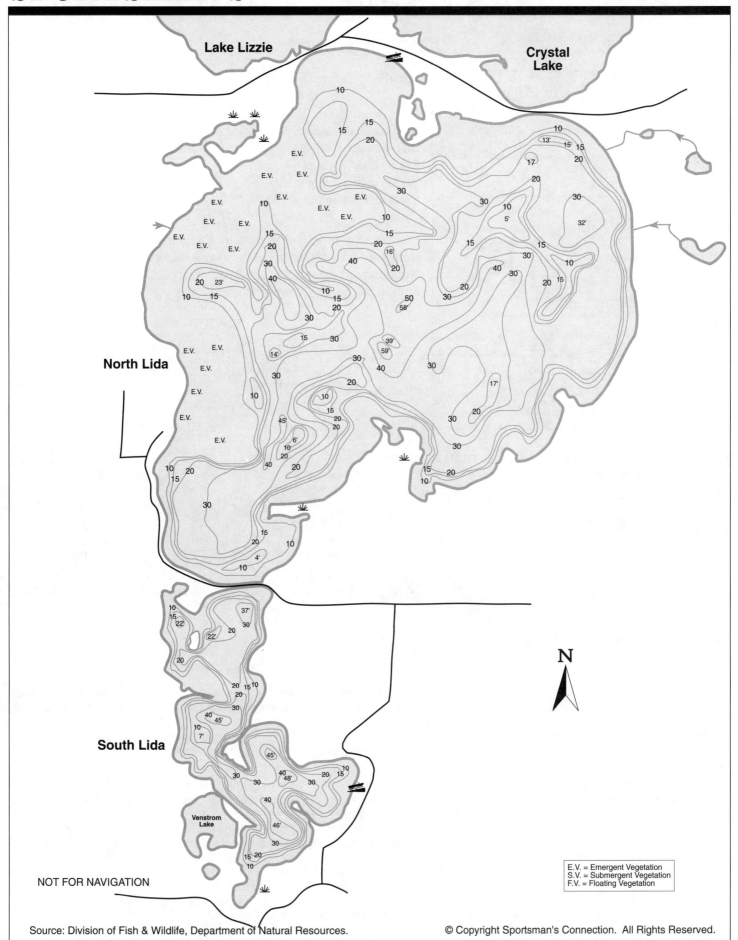

Lake Lizzie

Crystal Lake

North Lida

South Lida

Venstrom Lake

N

E.V. = Emergent Vegetation
S.V. = Submergent Vegetation
F.V. = Floating Vegetation

NOT FOR NAVIGATION

EAST SPIRIT LAKE
Otter Tail County

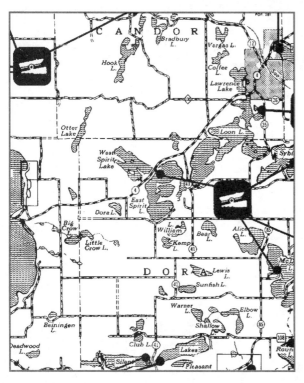

Location: Township 136
Range 41
Watershed: Otter Tail
Surface Water Area: 544 Acres
Shorelength: 6.6 Miles
Secchi disk (water clarity): 15 Ft.
Water color: Light green
Cause of water color: Algae

Maximum depth: 38 Ft.
Median depth: NA
Accessibility: Public access on southwest shore off Cty. Road 4
Boat Ramp: Concrete
Accommodations: NA

Shoreland zoning classification: Recreational Development
Dominant forest/soil type: Deciduous/Loam
Management class: Walleye-Centrarchid
Ecological type: Centrarchid

FISH STOCKING DATA

year	species	size	# released
93	Walleye	Fingerling	14,508
95	Walleye	Fingerling	10,959
97	Walleye	Fry	246,000

NET CATCH DATA

survey date: 7/10/95

| | Gill Nets | | Trap Nets | |
| | | avg fish | | avg fish |
species	# per net	wt. (lbs.)	# per set	wt. (lbs.)
Black Bullhead	0.1	1.36	0.2	1.04
Black Crappie	0.3	0.07	0.9	0.42
Bluegill	7.0	0.18	131.9	0.24
Brown Bullhead	0.2	0.72	0.3	0.13
Hybrid Sunfish	0.1	0.14	0.2	0.07
Largemouth Bass	-	-	0.8	0.57
Northern Pike	13.2	1.45	1.2	1.16
Pumpkin. Sunfish	1.8	0.21	3.6	0.21
Rock Bass	0.3	0.39	3.2	0.34
Walleye	5.1	1.56	0.8	2.70
White Sucker	0.1	2.76	-	-
Yellow Bullhead	4.1	0.68	10.9	0.59
Yellow Perch	7.7	0.12	-	-

LENGTH OF SELECTED SPECIES SAMPLED FROM ALL GEAR

Number of fish caught for the following length categories (inches):

species	0-5	6-8	9-11	12-14	15-19	20-24	25-29	>30	Total
Black Bullhead	-	-	-	3	-	-	-	-	3
Black Crappie	2	2	7	-	-	-	-	-	11
Bluegill	58	238	-	-	-	-	-	-	296
Brown Bullhead	2	1	2	-	-	-	-	-	5
Hybrid Sunfish	3	-	-	-	-	-	-	-	3
Largemouth Bass	2	1	3	1	-	-	-	-	7
Northern Pike	-	-	9	19	63	28	7	2	128
Pumpkin. Sunfish	19	29	-	-	-	-	-	-	48
Rock Bass	1	31	-	-	-	-	-	-	32
Walleye	-	1	11	12	17	12	-	-	53
Yellow Bullhead	-	13	114	8	-	-	-	-	135
Yellow Perch	14	41	-	-	-	-	-	-	55

DNR COMMENTS: Northern Pike population up substantially and above normal range for lake class; size structure stable, as 9 percent of sample reached at least 24 inches; natural reproduction appears stable. Walleye abundance up slightly and within normal range; average size 15.6 inches and 1.5 lb. Largemouth Bass and Black Crappie numbers within normal ranges for lake class. Bluegill population and size structure improved; 32 percent of fish reaching at least 7 inches. Yellow Perch numbers up slightly and within normal range; Perch are reaching 6.4 inches by age 4.

FISHING INFORMATION: The Department of Natural Resources has stocked Walleye in East Spirit for a long time, but the marble eyes still aren't as abundant as anglers would like. The ones to be found, though, are of good size. A large Bluegill population seems to be the primary forage base in the lake, though many of these panskis grow to be larger than 7 inches. There are also good numbers of Rock Bass, as well as a few Crappies. For spring Walleyes you'll want to fish the numerous points on the lake , especially the long ones along the east side. The water is quite clear, so you can do well offering shiner minnows or leeches along the bottom, retrieving your bait slowly up the slopes where the marble eyes are feeding. Of course, you'll have to troll deep for Wally in summer. Fish the outside of weedlines, especially where the bulrushes are emerging, for Northerns. They are fairly good-size, and you can slow troll or still-fish for them with lip hooked leeches early in the season, then troll the flats with spoons or spinnerbaits in warm weather. Panfish are in the weeds early and, because of the clarity of the water, you won't need much more than worms or smaller minnows on a bare hook to get their attention. Bobber fishing in deeper water, 10 to 12 feet down, is your best bet during hot summer days.

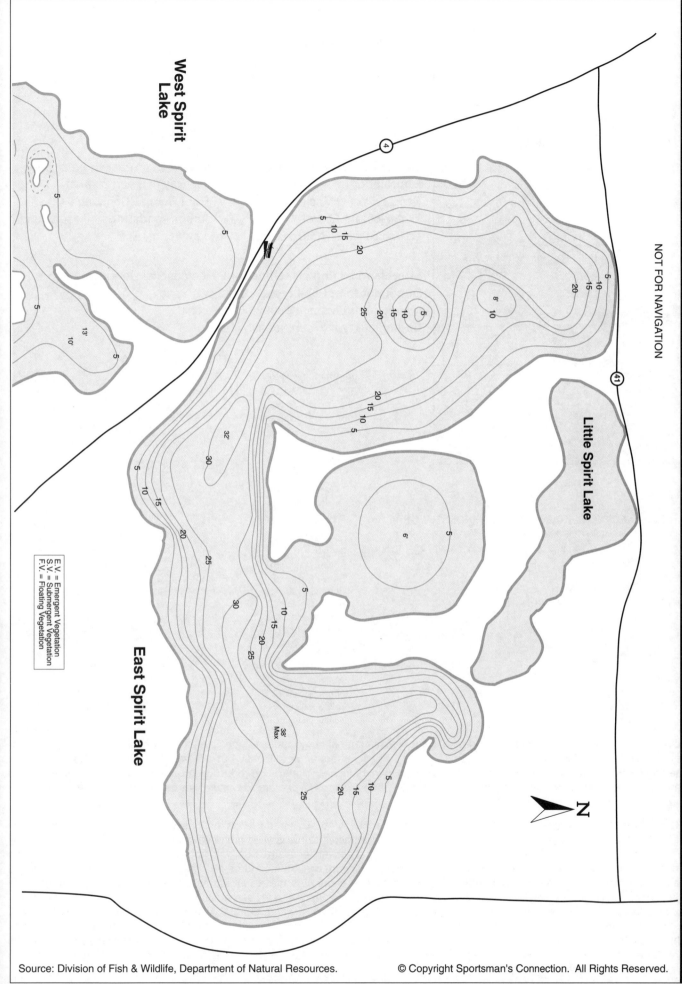

West Spirit Lake

East Spirit Lake

Little Spirit Lake

NOT FOR NAVIGATION

E.V. = Emergent Vegetation
S.V. = Submergent Vegetation
F.V. = Floating Vegetation

N

SPORTSMAN'S Connection®

LOON LAKE
Otter Tail County

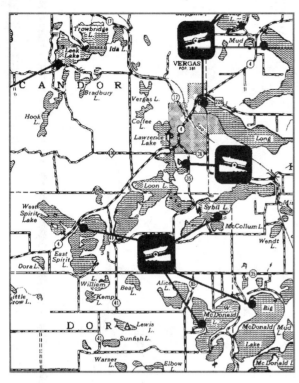

Location: Township 136, 137 Range 41
Watershed: Otter Tail
Surface Water Area: 1,048 Acres
Shorelength: 14.9 Miles
Secchi disk (water clarity): 8.8 Ft.
Water color: Green
Cause of water color: Algae

Maximum depth: 105 Ft.
Median depth: NA
Accessibility: State-owned public access on east shore of Sperling Bay (NE part of lake)
Boat Ramp: Concrete
Accommodations: Resorts and campgrounds

Shoreland zoning classification: Recreational Development
Dominant forest/soil type: Deciduous/Sand
Management class: Walleye-Centrarchid
Ecological type: Centrarchid-Walleye

FISH STOCKING DATA

year	species	size	# released
90	Walleye	Fry	1,184,000
94	Walleye	Fry	592,000
96	Walleye	Fry	592,000
98	Walleye	Fry	592,000

NET CATCH DATA

survey date: 7/26/93

	Gill Nets		Trap Nets	
		avg fish		avg fish
species	# per net	wt. (lbs.)	# per set	wt. (lbs.)
Black Bullhead	7.2	0.33	2.8	0.38
Black Crappie	trace	0.62	1.4	0.34
Bluegill	11.1	0.16	39.4	0.18
Bowfin (Dogfish)	-	-	0.5	5.54
Brown Bullhead	1.2	0.57	3.8	0.57
Common Carp	trace	8.38	0.9	6.04
Hybrid Sunfish	0.4	0.33	4.6	0.24
Largemouth Bass	0.5	0.87	0.6	1.10
Northern Pike	14.1	1.17	0.9	0.73
Pumpkin. Sunfish	1.8	0.19	7.3	0.17
Rock Bass	0.3	0.34	trace	0.24
Tullibee (Cisco)	1.0	1.10	-	-
Walleye	2.0	3.03	0.2	3.43
White Sucker	trace	2.65	-	-
Yellow Bullhead	7.2	0.46	7.8	0.49
Yellow Perch	2.7	0.12	-	-

LENGTH OF SELECTED SPECIES SAMPLED FROM ALL GEAR

Number of fish caught for the following length categories (inches):

species	0-5	6-8	9-11	12-14	15-19	20-24	25-29	>30	Total
Black Bullhead	50	19	48	3	-	-	-	-	120
Black Crappie	1	9	8	-	-	-	-	-	18
Bluegill	209	283	-	-	-	-	-	-	492
Brown Bullhead	-	9	47	4	-	-	-	-	60
Hybrid Sunfish	21	39	-	-	-	-	-	-	60
Largemouth Bass	-	2	5	5	1	-	-	-	13
Northern Pike	-	1	6	31	119	16	6	1	180
Pumpkin. Sunfish	56	54	-	-	-	-	-	-	110
Rock Bass	-	5	-	-	-	-	-	-	5
Tullibee (Cisco)	-	-	1	7	4	-	-	-	12
Walleye	-	-	-	2	8	16	-	-	26
Yellow Bullhead	2	40	119	3	-	-	-	-	164
Yellow Perch	8	23	1	-	-	-	-	-	32

DNR COMMENTS: Walleye population down slightly but still within normal range for lake type; sample sizes ranged from 14 to 23 inches; little or no natural reproduction for this species. Northern Pike numbers up significantly but well within normal range; size structure dominated by small fish, with 83 percent of sample being less than 19 inches. Natural reproduction consistent for Largemouth Bass and Black Crappie. Bluegill numbers down considerably and within normal range; 13 percent of sample was larger than 7 inches. Carp numbers up and above normal range for lake class.

FISHING INFORMATION: Loon is 1,048 acres with a shoreline of nearly 15 miles and five distinct basins. Two eastern bays are weedy shallows of less than 10 feet in depth, and, while Bass anglers are attracted to the islands in the southern bay, most of Loon's gamefish are found in the other sections. The southern basin contains the most conventional structure, with shoals and shoreline vegetation giving way to dropoffs and sharp breaks into holes of 98 and 105 feet. In spring, cast surface lures and shallow crankbaits into the emerging weeds along the southern shore and around the point on the eastern shore. As the water warms, move to the western and northern shore and, given Loon's water clarity of almost nine feet, trail live bait rigs at the weed breaks around 15 to 20 feet deep along the shoreline around to the channel to Loon's middle basin. This basin is generally shallow with a gradual drop to about 20 feet and a small hole of 32 feet. It's good territory for Largemouth Bass. Stand off in, say, 15 feet of water and cast to the edges of the weedbeds. Try leeches on a light line and shallow-running spinners. The far northern and last section is small and irregular, but its western weedlines, around the point, are home to sizable Largemouth and Northerns. On your way back out of this section, trail a live bait rig about 20 yards out from the eastern shore. You'll find some nice fish.

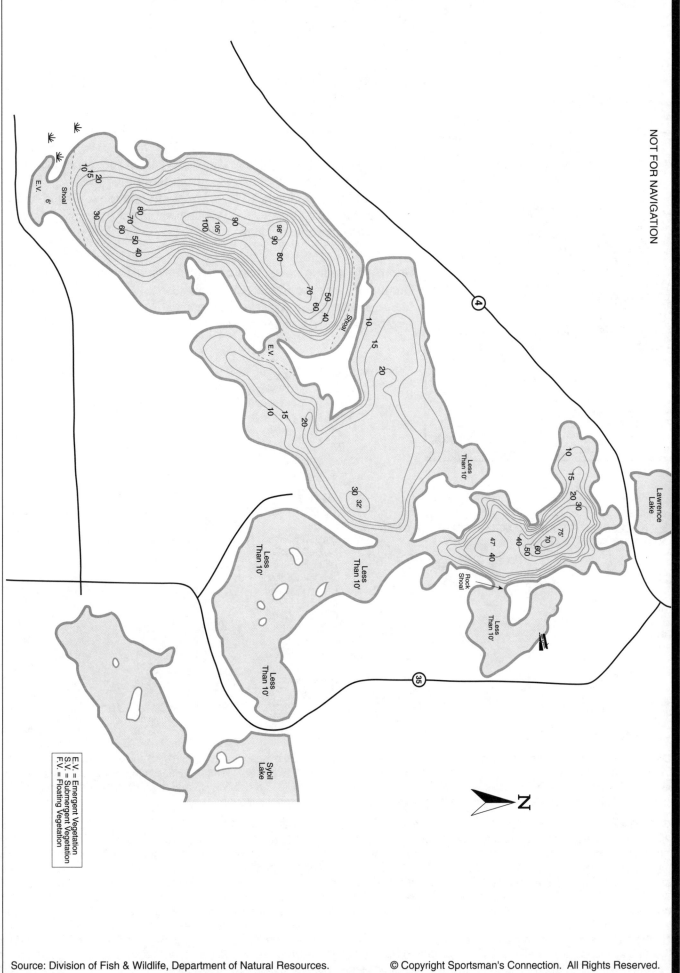

E.V. = Emergent Vegetation
S.V. = Submergent Vegetation
F.V. = Floating Vegetation

N

SYBIL LAKE
Otter Tail County

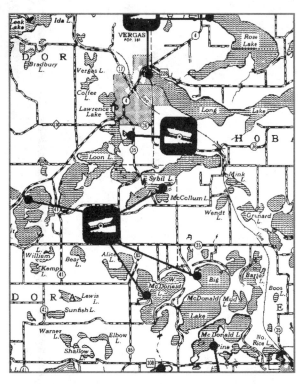

Location: Township 136, 137
Range 40, 41
Watershed: Otter Tail
Surface Water Area: 618 Acres
Shorelength: 7.2 Miles
Secchi disk (water clarity): 13 Ft.
Water color: Light green
Cause of water color: Algae

Maximum depth: 74 Ft.
Median depth: 29 Ft.
Accessibility: State-owned public access on south shore of lake
Boat Ramp: Gravel
Accommodations: Resort and campgrounds

Shoreland zoning classification: Recreational Development
Dominant forest/soil type: Deciduous/Sand
Management class: Walleye-Centrarchid
Ecological type: Centrarchid-Walleye

FISH STOCKING DATA

year	species	size	# released
90	Walleye	Fingerling	2,645
90	Walleye	Yearling	1,014
94	Walleye	Fingerling	16,746
96	Walleye	Fry	423,000
97	Walleye	Fingerling	27,747

NET CATCH DATA

survey date: 8/14/95

species	Gill Nets # per net	Gill Nets avg fish wt. (lbs.)	Trap Nets # per set	Trap Nets avg fish wt. (lbs.)
Black Bullhead	0.3	0.75	-	-
Black Crappie	0.4	0.39	1.1	0.64
Bluegill	10.3	0.24	109.2	0.23
Bowfin (Dogfish)	-	-	0.2	4.59
Brown Bullhead	2.3	1.19	0.4	0.93
Burbot	trace	2.54	-	-
Common Carp	-	-	0.3	7.90
Hybrid Sunfish	trace	0.07	1.3	0.29
Largemouth Bass	0.6	0.73	0.8	0.40
Northern Pike	5.8	1.51	0.8	1.28
Pumpkin. Sunfish	1.2	0.27	1.4	0.22
Rock Bass	1.1	0.53	-	-
Walleye	5.2	1.03	0.3	0.82
White Sucker	0.3	0.77	-	-
Yellow Bullhead	14.4	0.66	3.5	0.60
Yellow Perch	10.2	0.18	0.5	0.21

LENGTH OF SELECTED SPECIES SAMPLED FROM ALL GEAR

Number of fish caught for the following length categories (inches):

species	0-5	6-8	9-11	12-14	15-19	20-24	25-29	>30	Total
Black Bullhead	-	-	3	1	-	-	-	-	4
Black Crappie	5	1	9	3	-	-	-	-	18
Bluegill	64	344	-	-	-	-	-	-	408
Brown Bullhead	-	-	3	29	-	-	-	-	32
Hybrid Sunfish	1	15	-	-	-	-	-	-	16
Largemouth Bass	-	13	1	2	1	-	-	-	17
Northern Pike	-	-	-	11	43	20	6	-	80
Pumpkin. Sunfish	3	28	-	-	-	-	-	-	31
Rock Bass	4	12	7	-	-	-	-	-	23
Walleye	-	10	11	20	14	3	1	-	59
Yellow Bullhead	1	7	141	14	-	-	-	-	163
Yellow Perch	7	85	4	-	-	-	-	-	96

DNR COMMENTS: Northern Pike numbers stable and within normal range for lake class; mean length 19.1 inches. Walleye population up and within normal range; mean length 13.6 inches; natural reproduction limited. Largemouth Bass numbers about what can be expected for lake class; 18 percent of Bass had reached at least 14 inches. Bluegill abundance up and above normal; 31 percent of fish reaching at least 7 inches. Black Crappies present in normal numbers; mean length 9.5 inches.

FISHING INFORMATION: Sybil is the clearest lake in the Otter tail area so, plan your angling strategy accordingly. Light line and an electric motor tend to keep from spooking the fish. Canoe anglers, of course, will have an edge, but if you're in a boat, some caution will ensure success. Sybil is a long, skinny lake of 618 acres with a shoreline of 7.2 miles. Although there are three holes, whose depths range from 62 to 74 feet, there is also a sizable marsh at the western end with a depth of around five feet. This is a haven for Bluegills. The best fishing is found in the main lake. In spring, you can sit just off the narrows heading to the western marsh in about 15 feet of water and cast into the reeds for Largemouth Bass and Crappies. Or, if you prefer, move about 50 yards due east to a sunken hump that should be visible at about five feet. Jig the sides of the hump at about 15 to 20 feet with shiners or night crawlers, and then move northeast to a bar that drops down from the northern shore and do the same. You can also cast deep-running lures off both the hump and the bar for Northerns. In summer, drop leeches on a light line just off the deep weedbreaks. In the spring, the weedbeds at the far eastern end of the lake are productive, and there is a rapid drop off to a 62-foot hole which is productive. The western slope is a good bet for summer jigs and live bait. In a favorable wind, drift the entire north shore with live bait rigs at 10 to 15 feet.

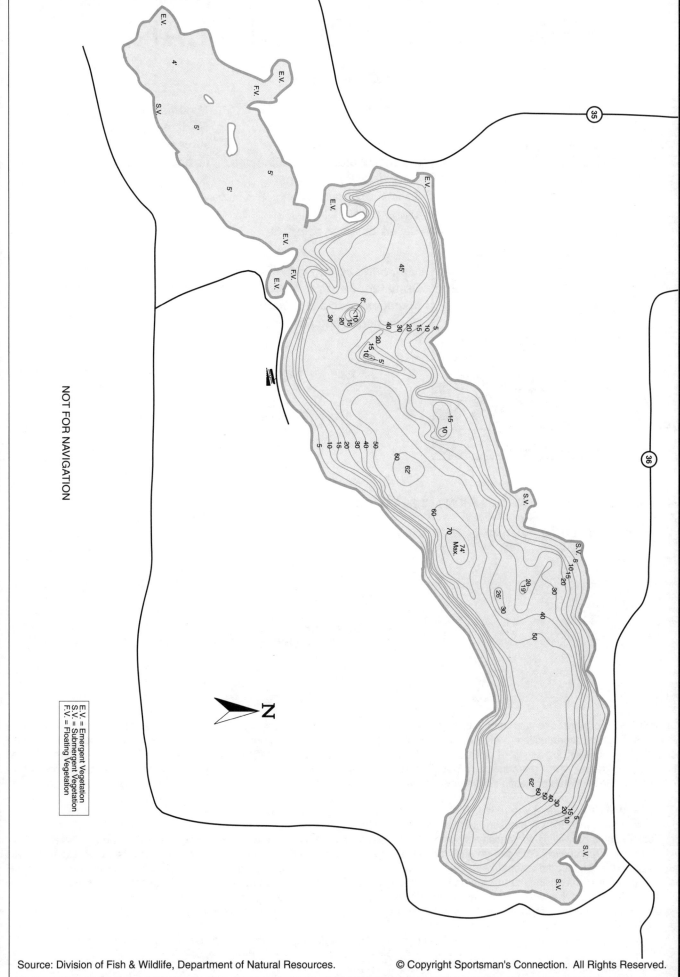

NOT FOR NAVIGATION

N

E.V. = Emergent Vegetation
S.V. = Submergent Vegetation
F.V. = Floating Vegetation

LEEK (TROWBRIDGE) LAKE

Otter Tail County

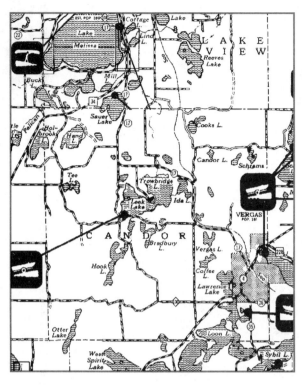

Location: Township 137
Range 41
Watershed: Otter Tail
Surface Water Area: 609 Acres
Shorelength: 7.9 Miles
Secchi disk (water clarity): 9.8 Ft.
Water color: Clear
Cause of water color: NA

Maximum depth: 76 Ft.
Median depth: NA
Accessibility: State-owned public access on southwest corner
Boat Ramp: Concrete
Accommodations: NA

Shoreland zoning classification: Recreational Development
Dominant forest/soil type: Deciduous/Loam
Management class: Walleye-Centrarchid
Ecological type: Centrarchid

FISH STOCKING DATA

year	species	size	# released
93	Walleye	Fry	272,000
95	Walleye	Fry	272,000
96	Walleye	Fry	272,000
98	Walleye	Fry	272,000

NET CATCH DATA

survey date: 8/1/94

species	Gill Nets # per net	Gill Nets avg fish wt. (lbs.)	Trap Nets # per set	Trap Nets avg fish wt. (lbs.)
Black Bullhead	1.0	0.48	0.6	0.90
Black Crappie	0.2	0.32	2.2	0.29
Bluegill	4.7	0.10	98.8	0.08
Bowfin (Dogfish)	-	-	0.2	9.92
Brown Bullhead	trace	1.32	0.1	0.62
Green Sunfish	-	-	0.5	0.11
Hybrid Sunfish	0.3	0.18	8.8	0.32
Largemouth Bass	-	-	0.6	1.08
Northern Pike	9.1	1.77	1.3	1.11
Pumpkin. Sunfish	0.2	0.33	3.4	0.33
Walleye	0.3	4.57	0.4	3.35
White Sucker	trace	7.28	0.1	6.28
Yellow Bullhead	5.4	0.89	8.6	0.58
Yellow Perch	0.6	0.08	0.2	0.16

LENGTH OF SELECTED SPECIES SAMPLED FROM ALL GEAR

Number of fish caught for the following length categories (inches):

species	0-5	6-8	9-11	12-14	15-19	20-24	25-29	>30	Total
Black Bullhead	-	13	6	-	-	-	-	-	19
Black Crappie	-	18	8	-	-	-	-	-	26
Bluegill	292	49	-	-	-	-	-	-	341
Brown Bullhead	-	1	1	-	-	-	-	-	2
Green Sunfish	6	-	-	-	-	-	-	-	6
Hybrid Sunfish	58	43	-	-	-	-	-	-	101
Largemouth Bass	-	1	4	1	1	-	-	-	7
Northern Pike	1	-	2	8	67	36	8	1	123
Pumpkin. Sunfish	27	12	-	-	-	-	-	-	39
Walleye	-	-	1	1	-	4	2	-	8
Yellow Bullhead	1	67	90	2	-	-	-	-	160
Yellow Perch	7	2	-	-	-	-	-	-	9

DNR COMMENTS: Northern Pike abundance up slightly and above normal range for lake class; 9 percent of sample reaching at least 24 inches; consistent natural reproduction. Walleye numbers down and below normal; natural reproduction inconsistent. Anglers report that Largemouth Bass fishing can be excellent at times. Black Crappie numbers within normal range; 31 percent of sample had reached at least 9 inches; consistent natural reproduction. Bluegill abundance up and above expected range; only 2 percent of fish sampled had reached 7 inches. Yellow Perch population still below normal for lake class.

FISHING INFORMATION: Leek Lake (a.k.a. Trowbridge) is located west of Vergas in northern Otter Tail County. The deep, double-basin lake doesn't get much fishing pressure except from those who know best – local anglers. Leek holds populations of Largemouth Bass and Black Crappie as well as some nice Northern Pike and Walleyes. The Bass and Crappies will be found in the weedlines early in the season following their spawn. You can go after them along the north side of the east basin, where the bulrushes offer excellent protection and food. You can also find them in the south side bays of the west basin. Use a jig and pig for Bass and small minnows for the Crappies. Northerns will be cruising the outside edges of those same weeds looking for supper. Try the north and south sides of the east basin and the west shore of the west basin. The water is fairly clear early in the season, and you can troll the weed edges with spinner-baits or spoon plugs. Walleye angling tends to be better in the west basin, where there are several good points along the south side as well as a nice hump near mid-lake. Because of the shallow shorelines, the lake's fish will head for the dark, cool water in the west basin during the hot months. Use your electronics to locate them, or search for with a slip bobber over a lip hooked shiner minnow.

Leek (Trowbridge) Lake

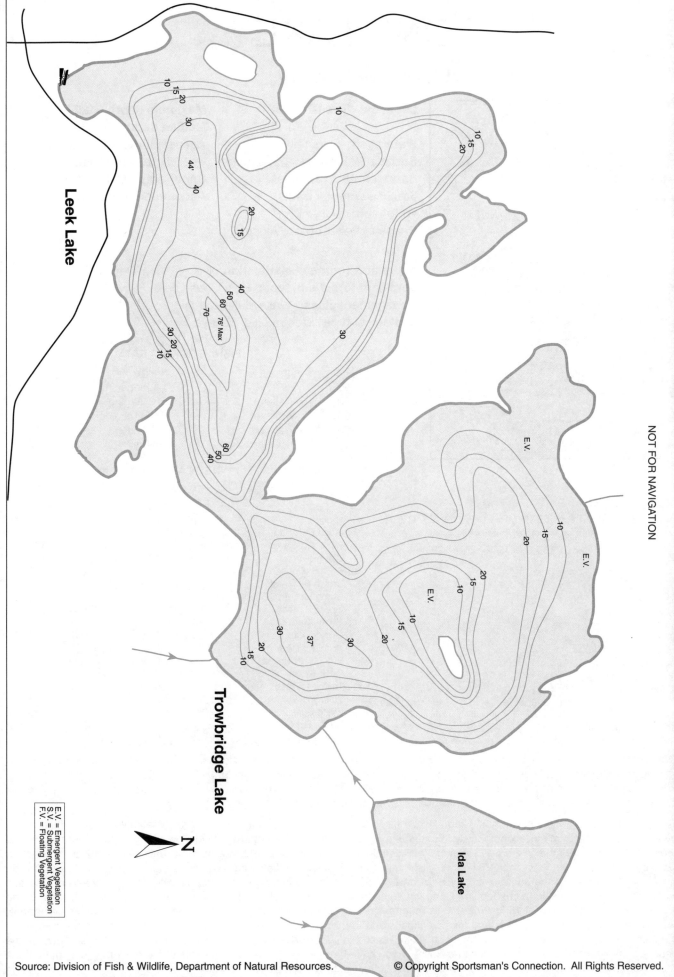

Leek Lake

Trowbridge Lake

Ida Lake

44'

76' Max

37'

N

E.V. = Emergent Vegetation
S.V. = Submergent Vegetation
F.V. = Floating Vegetation

Source: Division of Fish & Wildlife, Department of Natural Resources.

LONG LAKE
Otter Tail County

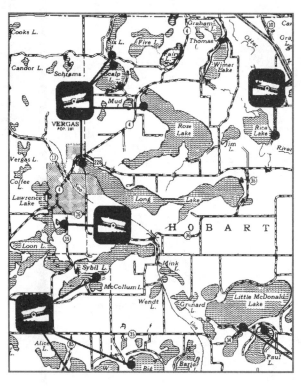

Location: Township 137
Range 40, 41
Watershed: Otter tail
Surface Water Area: 1,273 Acres
Shorelength: 10.3 Miles
Secchi disk (water clarity): 14.0 Ft.
Water color: Green tint
Cause of water color: Algae

Maximum depth: 128 Feet
Median depth: NA
Accessibility: Public access on
west shore, off Cty. Hwy. 4
Boat Ramp: Concrete
Accommodations: NA

Shoreland zoning classification: Recreational Development
Dominant forest/soil type: Deciduous/Loam
Management class: Walleye-Centrarchid
Ecological type: Centrarchid-Walleye

FISH STOCKING DATA

year	species	size	# released
90	Walleye	Fingerling	3,609
90	Walleye	Yearling	1,757
93	Walleye	Fingerling	9,788
95	Walleye	Yearling	4,304
97	Walleye	Fry	530,000

NET CATCH DATA

survey date: 6/19/95

	Gill Nets		Trap Nets	
species	# per net	avg fish wt. (lbs.)	# per set	avg fish wt. (lbs.)
Black Bullhead	0.3	0.93	-	-
Black Crappie	trace	0.77	0.1	0.78
Bluegill	3.3	0.27	90.5	0.19
Bowfin (Dogfish)	-	-	0.3	4.40
Brown Bullhead	-	-	0.3	0.89
Common Carp	-	-	0.3	8.12
Green Sunfish	-	-	0.2	0.10
Hybrid Sunfish	trace	0.30	3.7	0.22
Largemouth Bass	trace	0.10	0.8	0.13
Northern Pike	14.6	2.10	-	-
Pumpkin. Sunfish	0.3	0.26	3.8	0.20
Rock Bass	1.1	0.38	3.8	0.33
Tullibee (Cisco)	2.3	0.98	-	-
Walleye	7.3	1.46	0.1	6.28
White Sucker	3.8	2.15	0.1	0.19
Yellow Bullhead	1.8	0.86	3.5	0.79
Yellow Perch	33.8	0.12	1.4	0.11

LENGTH OF SELECTED SPECIES SAMPLED FROM ALL GEAR

Number of fish caught for the following length categories (inches):

species	0-5	6-8	9-11	12-14	15-19	20-24	25-29	>30	Total
Black Bullhead	-	1	-	2	-	-	-	-	3
Black Crappie	-	-	2	-	-	-	-	-	2
Bluegill	77	193	3	-	-	-	-	-	273
Brown Bullhead	-	-	1	2	-	-	-	-	3
Green Sunfish	2	-	-	-	-	-	-	-	2
Hybrid Sunfish	13	25	-	-	-	-	-	-	38
Largemouth Bass	6	3	-	-	-	-	-	-	9
Northern Pike	-	-	-	6	69	81	13	6	175
Pumpkin. Sunfish	16	25	-	-	-	-	-	-	41
Rock Bass	6	42	3	-	-	-	-	-	51
Tullibee (Cisco)	-	-	5	21	2	-	-	-	28
Walleye	-	-	21	26	28	13	1	-	89
Yellow Bullhead	-	1	38	18	-	-	-	-	57
Yellow Perch	56	179	-	-	-	-	-	-	235

DNR COMMENTS: Cisco numbers in normal range for lake class; mean length 13 inches. Northern Pike abundance up and above normal; mean length 20.1 inches. Walleye population up but normal for lake class; mean length 15.3 inches; natural reproduction occurring. Largemouth Bass numbers normal; only immature fish sampled. Black Crappie scarce, but trapnetting may not adequately sample this species. Bluegills abundant and above normal for lake class; average size small at 6.1 inches.

FISHING INFORMATION: Long Lake, at 1,273 acres, has a length of nearly five and a half miles. Wintertime anglers are advised to use a snowmobile to reach the prime locations handily. Long has a clarity reading of 14 feet and a layout you will want to study before your first time out. Although there are some broad areas of 10-foot shallows, the water drops sharply off the shoals, particularly in the western section where maximum depth can reach 128 feet. So fishing Long means you fish flats and dropoffs. Long is an excellent panfish lake, a very good Walleye lake and the home of trophy Bass and an above-average Northern Pike population. The lake's western section leans to panfish and Pike, with Northerns feeding along the southern weeds and Walleyes hanging out on the deep weed breaks in the far west. Troll or drift both shores at 15 to 20 feet with spoons, spinners or live bait rigs. Cast the edges of the shallows in the narrows leading to the eastern section of the lake, and toss crankbaits and leeches around the marsh on the north shore of the narrows. Just before the point on the northern shore, at mid-lake is a sunken island to jig for Bass and Walleye. The breaks along the shallows on the eastern end are favorite locations for both Pike and Bass. If you have time, you might also try the foot of the deep bay just south of the narrows for Bass. There's a lot of distance to cover on Long, but the rewards are worth your effort.

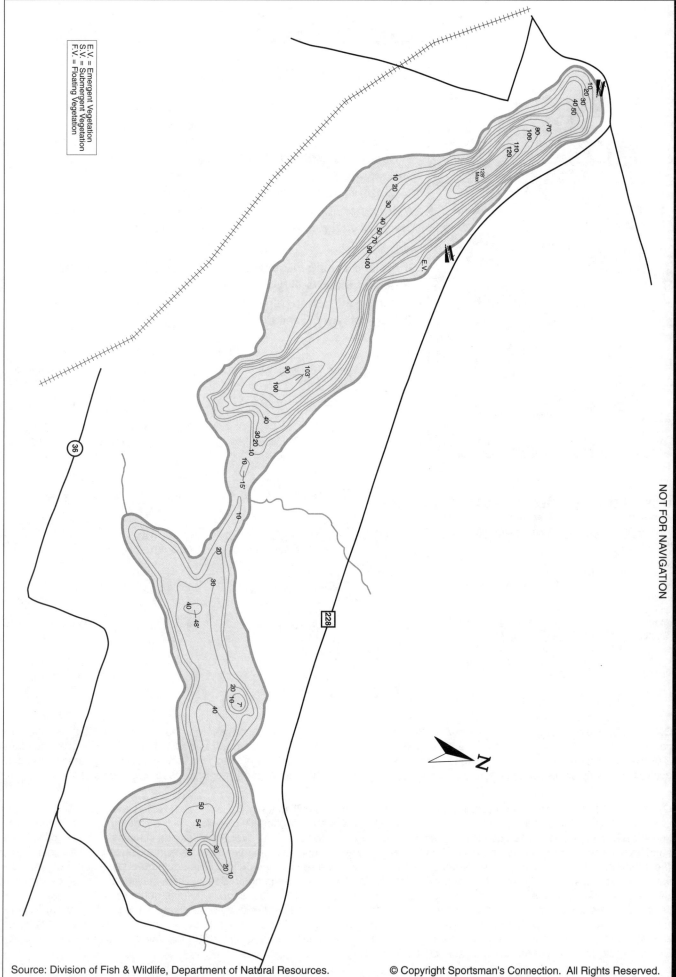

NOT FOR NAVIGATION

E.V. = Emergent Vegetation
S.V. = Submergent Vegetation
F.V. = Floating Vegetation

E.V.

128'
Max.

103'

48'

54'

N

Source: Division of Fish & Wildlife, Department of Natural Resources.

ROSE LAKE
Otter Tail County

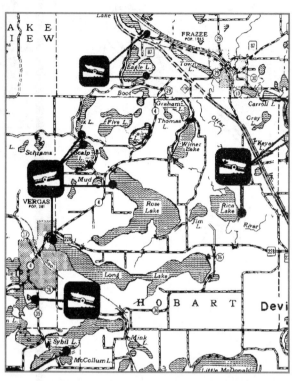

Location: Township 137
Range 40
Watershed: Otter Tail
Surface Water Area: 1,190 Acres
Shorelength: 9.4 Miles
Secchi disk (water clarity): 13.0 Ft.
Water color: Clear
Cause of water color: NA

Maximum depth: 137 Ft.
Median depth: 26 Ft.
Accessibility: State-owned access on northwest shore, off County Road 4
Boat Ramp: Earth
Accommodations: Resort and campgrounds

Shoreland zoning classification: Recreational Development
Dominant forest/soil type: Deciduous/Loam
Management class: Centrarchid
Ecological type: Centrarchid

FISH STOCKING DATA

year	species	size	# released
90	Walleye	Fingerling	3,889
90	Walleye	Yearling	795
93	Walleye	Fingerling	11,402
95	Walleye	Fry	465,000
96	Walleye	Fingerling	10,935

NET CATCH DATA

survey date: 8/18/97

species	Gill Nets # per net	Gill Nets avg fish wt. (lbs.)	Trap Nets # per set	Trap Nets avg fish wt. (lbs.)
Black Bullhead	0.8	0.88	-	-
Black Crappie	0.5	0.29	0.2	0.33
Bluegill	6.1	0.14	32.9	0.15
Brown Bullhead	0.1	0.66	-	-
Hybrid Sunfish	0.7	0.11	1.1	0.33
Largemouth Bass	1.1	1.10	0.3	0.08
Northern Pike	6.2	1.57	0.2	0.69
Pumpkin. Sunfish	4.8	0.16	2.8	0.14
Rock Bass	2.4	0.31	2.1	0.07
Walleye	2.4	2.34	0.2	3.69
White Sucker	0.6	2.65	0.1	1.47
Yellow Bullhead	3.4	0.85	1.1	0.68
Yellow Perch	2.4	0.17	0.8	0.13

LENGTH OF SELECTED SPECIES SAMPLED FROM ALL GEAR

Number of fish caught for the following length categories (inches):

species	0-5	6-8	9-11	12-14	15-19	20-24	25-29	>30	Total
Black Bullhead	-	-	5	3	-	-	-	-	8
Black Crappie	1	4	2	-	-	-	-	-	7
Bluegill	155	113	-	-	-	-	-	-	268
Brown Bullhead	-	-	1	-	-	-	-	-	1
Hybrid Sunfish	6	11	-	-	-	-	-	-	17
Largemouth Bass	2	1	6	4	1	-	-	-	14
Northern Pike	-	-	2	7	39	11	4	1	64
Pumpkin. Sunfish	48	24	-	-	-	-	-	-	72
Rock Bass	27	10	6	-	-	-	-	-	43
Walleye	-	3	-	-	17	4	2	-	26
Yellow Bullhead	-	2	25	17	-	-	-	-	44
Yellow Perch	12	15	4	-	-	-	-	-	31

DNR COMMENTS: Cisco present. Northern Pike abundant; about 8 percent of population is larger than 24 inches. Walleye numbers below the expected-level for lake class; average size good at 17.6 inches and 2.3 lb.; natural reproduction limited. Bluegills abundant; about 18 percent of fish reaching 7 inches. Largemouth Bass population good; size range 4 to 18.3 inches; consistent natural reproduction. Black Crappie numbers likewise good; size range 4.3 to 13.7 inches; consistently good year classes for this species.

FISHING INFORMATION: It shouldn't be surprising that somebody's always pulling a big Walleye out of Rose Lake. The DNR manages the lake for Walleyes, panfish and Bass and the structure is ideal. This is an exceptionally clear lake with a reading of over 13 feet. The deepest hole is 128 feet. Rose is 1,190 acres, in the shape of a rough "T" that stretches over 9.4 miles and contains a good supply of forage fish and wide variety of drops, bars and bays. If Walleyes are all you want, you can spend the season mostly around the joint of the "T". At the center of this area is a large, 20-foot-deep flat surrounded by reeds and weedbeds. The southern and western bottoms contain sunken inlets and points. Jig these at the deep weedlines for Walleyes and Largemouth Bass. Then, staying at 20 feet, head west, and you will find a sunken island standing off from the large point that juts from the south shore. Drift the northern drop off here with live bait rigs using crawlers and leeches. Move south along that sunken island and along the deep breaks just off the point. You'll also find a hump in the same area that is another good Walleye hangout. In spring, go farther down the base of the "T" and cast for Bass in the emergent weed beds. Do the same in similar structure at the far northwestern end of the lake. In late summer, troll or drift the steep drops along the north shore where fish are caught at 20 to 25 feet deep.

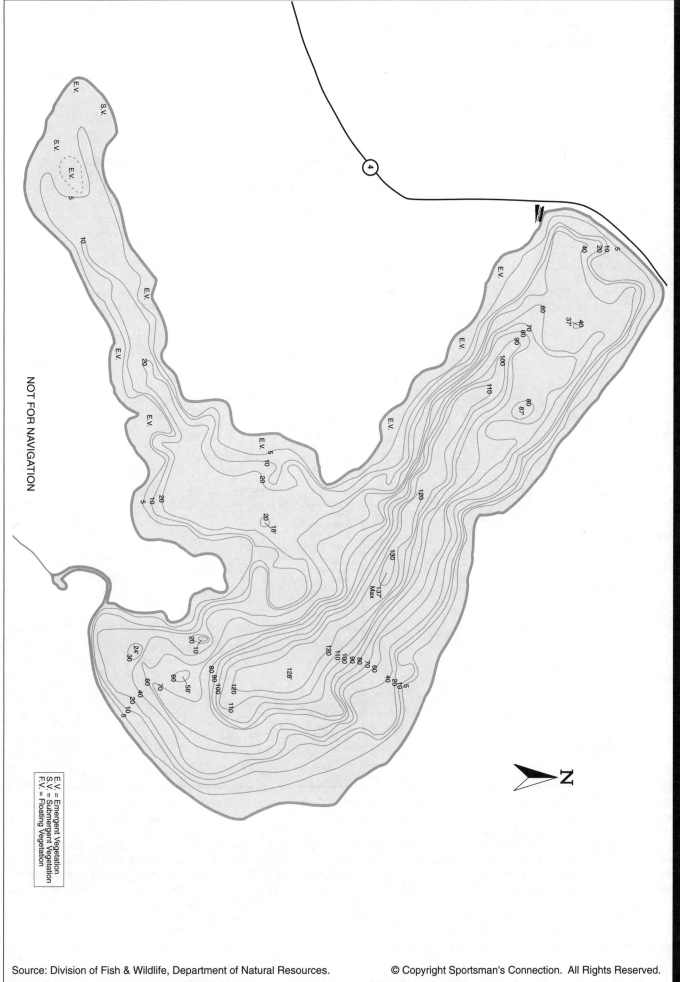

NOT FOR NAVIGATION

E.V. = Emergent Vegetation
S.V. = Submergent Vegetation
F.V. = Floating Vegetation

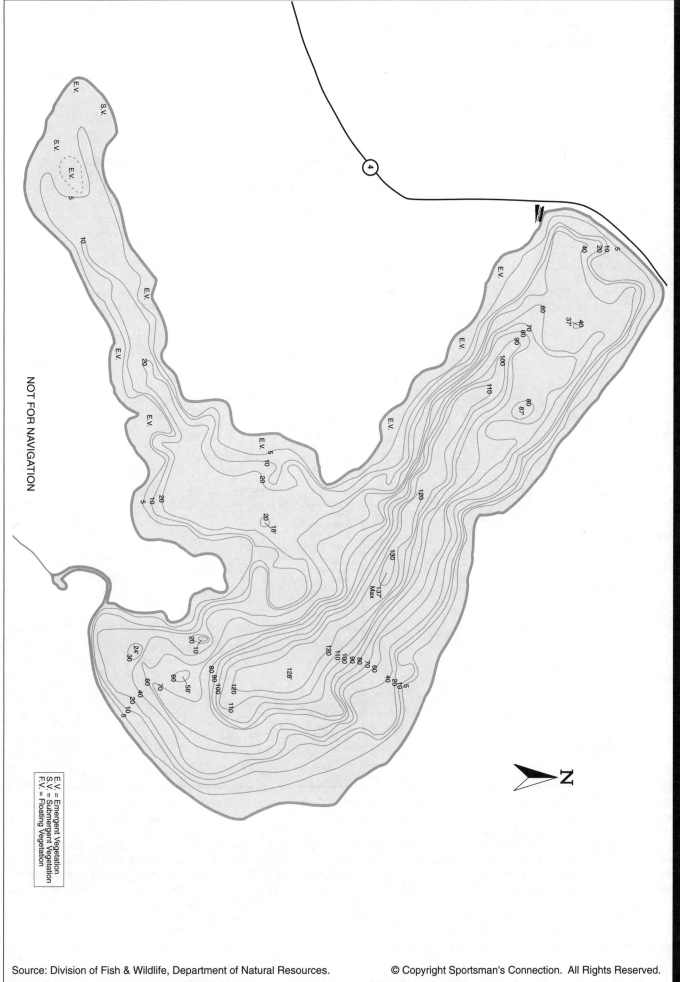

Rose Lake

SCALP (SEVEN) LAKE

Otter Tail County

LAKE SIX

Location: Township 137 Range 40
Watershed: Otter Tail
Surface Water Area: 243 Acres
Shorelength: 2.4 Miles
Secchi disk (water clarity): 17.0 Ft.
Water color: Clear
Cause of water color: NA
Maximum depth: 90 Ft.
Median depth: NA
Accessibility: State-owned public access on north shore
Boat Ramp: Concrete
Accommodations: NA
Shoreland zoning classif.: Rec. Dev.
Dominant forest/soil type: Decid/Loam
Management class: Walleye-Centrarchid
Ecological type: Centrarchid-Walleye

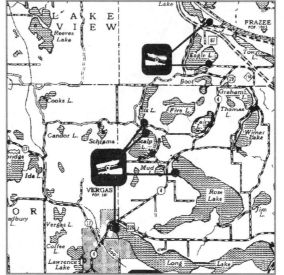

Location: Township 137 Range 40
Watershed: Otter Tail
Surface Water Area: 188 Acres
Shorelength: 3.3 Miles
Secchi disk (water clarity): 13.2 Ft.
Water color: NA
Cause of water color: NA
Maximum depth: 140 Ft.
Median depth: NA
Accessibility: State-owned public access on south shore
Boat Ramp: Earth
Accommodations: NA
Shoreland zoning classif.: Rec. Dev.
Dominant forest/soil type: NA
Management class: Walleye-Centrarchid
Ecological type: Centrarchid

DNR COMMENTS:
Walleye abundance up slightly and well above average for lake class; 50 percent of sample exceeded 16 inches; fish to 28 inches sampled; natural reproduction substantial. Northern Pike numbers low due to lack of spawning habitat; 33 percent of Pike exceed 24 inches. Bluegill numbers down, but size structure has improved; 11 percent of Bluegills exceed 7 inches, compared to 3 percent in 1988. Yellow Perch population has increased steadily and is above average. Water quality in this lake remains very good.

FISH STOCKING DATA

year	species	size	# released
90	Walleye	Fry	134,000
93	Walleye	Fry	134,000
95	Walleye	Fingerling	3,880
96	Walleye	Fry	134,000

survey date: 8/3/93

NET CATCH DATA

	Gill Nets		Trap Nets	
species	# per net	avg fish wt. (lbs)	# per set	avg fish wt. (lbs)
Bluegill	1.5	0.22	7.9	0.14
Hybrid Sunfish	0.5	0.22	13.2	0.13
Largemouth Bass	-	-	0.1	2.78
Northern Pike	1.5	2.97	-	-
Pumpkin. Sunfish	0.7	0.24	0.4	0.28
Rock Bass	8.3	0.33	10.9	0.12
Shorthead Redhorse	0.2	4.89	-	-
Walleye	11.8	1.56	0.7	2.57
White Sucker	3.5	1.21	0.1	0.08
Yellow Perch	62.3	0.17	1.7	0.12

LENGTH OF SELECTED SPECIES SAMPLED FROM ALL GEAR
Number of fish caught for the following length categories (inches):

species	0-5	6-8	9-11	12-14	15-19	20-24	25-29	>30	Total
Bluegill	44	36	-	-	-	-	-	-	80
Hybrid Sunfish	65	15	-	-	-	-	-	-	80
Largemouth Bass	-	-	-	-	1	-	-	-	1
Northern Pike	-	-	-	-	2	4	2	1	9
Pumpkin. Sunfish	3	5	-	-	-	-	-	-	8
Rock Bass	85	61	2	-	-	-	-	-	148
Walleye	-	5	2	27	37	3	3	-	77
Yellow Perch	17	165	16	-	-	-	-	-	198

FISH STOCKING DATA

year	species	size	# released
93	Walleye	Fingerling	2,224
95	Walleye	Fingerling	4,320
95	Walleye	Yearling	32
97	Walleye	Fingerling	1,408

survey date: 7/15/96

NET CATCH DATA

	Gill Nets		Trap Nets	
species	# per net	avg fish wt. (lbs)	# per set	avg fish wt. (lbs)
Black Crappie	-	-	0.4	0.08
Bluegill	7.5	0.10	93.9	0.14
Brown Bullhead	-	-	0.1	0.10
Green Sunfish	-	-	0.1	0.07
Hybrid Sunfish	0.8	0.11	7.1	0.23
Largemouth Bass	2.3	1.17	2.4	0.24
Northern Pike	12.7	1.18	1.0	0.55
Pumpkin. Sunfish	1.3	0.15	3.1	0.11
Rock Bass	1.2	0.37	4.8	0.25
Walleye	3.0	3.53	0.3	6.06
White Sucker	0.3	2.31	-	-
Yellow Perch	1.7	0.11	0.1	0.09

LENGTH OF SELECTED SPECIES SAMPLED FROM ALL GEAR
Number of fish caught for the following length categories (inches):

species	0-5	6-8	9-11	12-14	15-19	20-24	25-29	>30	Total
Black Crappie	2	1	-	-	-	-	-	-	3
Bluegill	193	77	-	-	-	-	-	-	270
Brown Bullhead	-	1	-	-	-	-	-	-	1
Green Sunfish	1	-	-	-	-	-	-	-	1
Hybrid Sunfish	20	42	-	-	-	-	-	-	62
Largemouth Bass	1	17	6	8	1	-	-	-	33
Northern Pike	-	-	4	21	38	16	1	-	80
Pumpkin. Sunfish	25	8	-	-	-	-	-	-	33
Rock Bass	13	29	3	-	-	-	-	-	45
Walleye	-	-	-	4	5	4	6	1	20

DNR COMMENTS:
Cisco sampled in small numbers; average length 6.8 inches. Northern Pike abundance up and above expected range for lake class; average size 17.3 inches and 1.2 lb.; natural reproduction stable. Walleye numbers stable; average size 19.9 inches and 3.5 lb.; natural reproduction limited. Largemouth Bass numerous; good 1994 year class; Bass reaching 11.1 inches by age 4. Bluegill population down but still high; only 7 percent of fish reaching 7 inches. Yellow Perch numbers normal; average 6.3 inches at age 4.

FISHING INFORMATION: **Scalp** (also known as #7) is a good lake for Walleyes, panfish and Largemouth Bass. Close to the community of Vergas, it is deep and clear, with good Walleye habitat. The submerged island at the north end is a good spot to look for marble eyes early in the season; so are the quick dropoffs at the east side and the point on the west side. Fish along the bottom in spring with a shiner minnow or leech. By summer, the Walleyes will spend bright days suspended in deep water at mid lake. Largemouth Bass can be found along the north shore where much of the lake's vegetation is located. You can also find them on the west side wherever you spot weedlines. And the same weeds hold plenty of Rock Bass and Bluegills. **Lake Six** is clear and deep (as much as 140 feet), and holds good populations of panfish, Largemouth Bass and Walleyes. There are also some good Northerns. Several points on the west and east sides are good places to look for the alligators early in the season, as is the 10-foot hump at the north end of the lake. In summer, you can troll the length of the lake over deep water for Northerns during the day, but you should return to shallower water where they feed after sundown and early in the morning. Walleyes are stocked by the DNR and are well above the region's average size. Largemouth and Crappies hang out in the lake's limited weeds. Local anglers tell us you can do well using worms and smaller minnows on a bare hook or a pig and jig. Some years ago, Rainbow Trout were stocked by the DNR. They have rarely been seen, so don't count on them.

Scalp, Six & Five Lakes

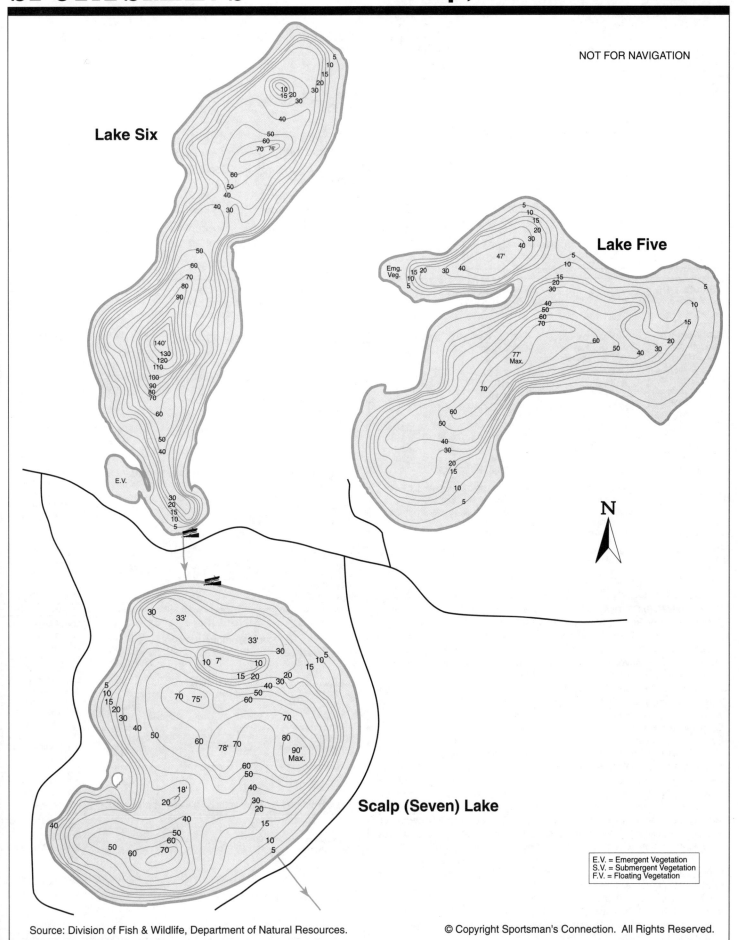

Lake Six

Lake Five

Scalp (Seven) Lake

E.V. = Emergent Vegetation
S.V. = Submergent Vegetation
F.V. = Floating Vegetation

Source: Division of Fish & Wildlife, Department of Natural Resources.

Location: Township 137, 138 Range 37, 38
Watershed: Otter Tail, Redeye

Otter Tail County

	BEAR LAKE	MURPHY LAKE	SILVER LAKE
Size of lake:	181 Acres	310 Acres	247 Acres
Shorelength:	3.7 Miles	2.5 Miles	2.5 Miles
Secchi disk (water clarity):	7.5 Ft.	6.0 Ft.	2.6 Ft.
Water color:	Green	Light green	NA
Cause of water color:	Algae	Algae	NA
Maximum depth:	32 Ft.	30 Ft.	34 Ft.
Median depth:	11 Ft.	NA	NA
Accessibility:	Public access on northwest shore, off County Road 148	Public access on south shore	Public access on north shore
Boat Ramp:	Earth	Concrete	Concrete
Accommodations:	NA	NA	NA
Shoreland zoning classif.:	Nat. Env.	Nat. Env.	Nat. Env.
Dominant forest/soil type:	Decid/Loam	Decid/Wet	Decid/Wet
Management class:	Centrarchid	Centrarchid	Centrarchid
Ecological type:	Centrarchid	Centrarchid	Centrarchid

Bear Lake

DNR COMMENTS:
Lake is subject to periodic winterkill. Northern Pike abundance within expected range for lake class; average size 19.7 inches and 1.7 lb. Walleye numbers above expected range; average size 14 inches and 1 lb.; natural reproduction limited. Black Crappie numbers within expected range; average length 8.8 inches. Yellow Perch numbers within normal range for lake class; average length 5.8 inches.

FISH STOCKING DATA

year	species	size	# released
93	Walleye	Fry	120,000
94	Walleye	Fry	120,000
96	Walleye	Fry	120,000
97	Bluegill	Adult	836

survey date: 7/15/96

NET CATCH DATA

	Gill Nets		Trap Nets	
		avg fish		avg fish
species	# per net	wt. (lbs)	# per set	wt. (lbs)
Black Crappie	0.6	1.27	-	-
Golden Shiner	-	-	0.1	0.06
Northern Pike	5.8	1.72	0.6	1.99
Pumpkin. Sunfish	-	-	0.1	0.04
Walleye	4.4	0.96	0.1	0.51
Yellow Perch	2.2	0.08	1.5	0.09

LENGTH OF SELECTED SPECIES SAMPLED FROM ALL GEAR
Number of fish caught for the following length categories (inches):

species	0-5	6-8	9-11	12-14	15-19	20-24	25-29	>30	Total
Black Bullhead	159	363	-	-	-	-	-	-	522
Black Crappie	1	2	2	4	-	-	-	-	9
Brown Bullhead	-	1	3	-	-	-	-	-	4
Northern Pike	-	-	2	20	10	1	1	34
Pumpkin. Sunfish	1	-	-	-	-	-	-	-	1
Walleye	-	-	1	18	4	-	-	-	23
Yellow Bullhead	-	9	4	-	-	-	-	-	13
Yellow Perch	12	3	-	-	-	-	-	-	15

Murphy Lake

FISH STOCKING DATA

year	species	size	# released
98	Walleye	Fry	163,000

survey date: 7/31/95

NET CATCH DATA

	Gill Nets		Trap Nets	
		avg fish		avg fish
species	# per net	wt. (lbs)	# per set	wt. (lbs)
Black Crappie	0.1	0.52	0.9	0.62
Bluegill	1.0	0.24	13.8	0.26
Northern Pike	4.4	1.00	1.3	0.81
Pumpkin. Sunfish	-	-	0.9	0.27
Tullibee (Cisco)	6.4	1.55	-	-
Walleye	5.8	0.83	0.2	3.57
Yellow Perch	1.6	0.18	0.3	0.17

LENGTH OF SELECTED SPECIES SAMPLED FROM ALL GEAR
Number of fish caught for the following length categories (inches):

species	0-5	6-8	9-11	12-14	15-19	20-24	25-29	>30	Total
Black Bullhead	1	55	72	-	-	-	-	-	128
Black Crappie	-	9	-	-	-	-	-	9
Bluegill	11	122	-	-	-	-	-	-	133
Brown Bullhead	-	-	66	2	-	-	-	-	68
Northern Pike	-	-	-	10	39	1	2	-	52
Pumpkin. Sunfish	2	6	-	-	-	-	-	-	8
Tullibee (Cisco)	-	1	6	22	29	-	-	-	58
Walleye	-	5	-	41	3	5	-	-	54
Yellow Bullhead	-	-	27	6	-	-	-	-	33
Yellow Perch	1	13	1	-	-	-	-	-	15

DNR COMMENTS:
Northern Pike numbers down but within normal range; average size 16.8 inches; only 4 percent of population exceeding 24 inches.. Walleye population up and above normal range; average size 13.4 inches.; natural reproduction limited. No Largemouth Bass sampled. Black Crappie numbers down but within normal range; average length 10.1 inches. Yellow Perch abundance up but still below normal range; average length 7.2 inches.

Silver Lake

FISH STOCKING DATA

year	species	size	# released
89	Walleye	Fry	250,000

survey date: 7/31/95

NET CATCH DATA

	Gill Nets		Trap Nets	
		avg fish		avg fish
species	# per net	wt. (lbs)	# per set	wt. (lbs)
Black Crappie	0.2	0.04	0.1	0.37
Bluegill	-	-	25.0	0.17
Largemouth Bass	0.2	0.18	0.8	0.19
Northern Pike	1.7	0.97	1.7	0.87
Pumpkin. Sunfish	0.2	0.18	5.2	0.18
Walleye	1.0	1.17	0.6	4.66
Yellow Perch	1.0	0.18	1.0	0.15

LENGTH OF SELECTED SPECIES SAMPLED FROM ALL GEAR
Number of fish caught for the following length categories (inches):

species	0-5	6-8	9-11	12-14	15-19	20-24	25-29	>30	Total
Black Bullhead	5	187	1	-	-	-	-	-	193
Black Crappie	1	1	-	-	-	-	-	-	2
Bluegill	99	92	-	-	-	-	-	-	191
Brown Bullhead	-	1	15	-	-	-	-	-	16
Largemouth Bass	-	8	-	-	-	-	-	-	8
Northern Pike	-	-	-	2	20	3	-	-	25
Pumpkin. Sunfish	24	24	-	-	-	-	-	-	48
Walleye	-	1	1	-	5	2	2	-	11
Yellow Bullhead	-	5	13	2	-	-	-	-	20
Yellow Perch	-	-	-	-	-	-	-	-	13

DNR COMMENTS:
Lake is subject to winterkill; the most recent of which was in 1992-93. No. Pike numbers down and below normal range; avg. size 17 inches. Walleye fry stocking discontinued; natural reproduction limited; avg. size 14.2 inches at age 3. LM Bass population about normal; successful natural reproduction. Bluegill abundance within normal range; 17 percent of fish reaching 7 inches. Yellow Perch scarce.

FISHING INFORMATION: Lying east of Frazee and well off the beaten path on County Road 148, smallish **Bear Lake** offers very good Largemouth Bass and Black Crappie fishing as well as good action for Bullheads and Sunfish. There are a few Northern Pike in Bear, too, and those few are well over average size. There's a good weedline for bucketmouth fishing. Go after the Bass early in the season with a pig-and-jig combination, drawing your bait slowly through weed openings. As the weeds thicken, you'll want to switch to weedless gear and live baits. Topwater lures flipped into openings in the bulrushes also will be effective. Crappies are also in the weeds early following the spawn. They will be off their feed for a while then, and your best bet is small minnows on a bare hook. A bit later, the bigger Crappies and Sunfish will spend the day in deeper water. **Silver Lake**, meanwhile, is dark, almost murky, and heavily weeded along most of the shoreline. You'll find bulrushes, too, at mid lake. Early-season fishing for Bluegills and Crappies is good around most of the weeds, though the west side beds may be best. You also have a fair chance of boating a Largemouth Bass there. You'll find Northerns outside the weedlines. Use silver spoons and other flashy lures. **Murphy Lake** is immediately north of Silver and contains a similar fish population. Black Bullheads are dominant, but there are also some decent Bluegills and Northern Pike. The heavy weeds on the east and south sides are panfish strongholds, and the flats at their outer edges are where the Northerns roam early in the season. The north end of the lake is relatively deep at 30 feet; this is the place to fish during those long, hot summer days. Murphy has been stocked with Walleyes without great success.

Bear, Murphy & Silver Lakes

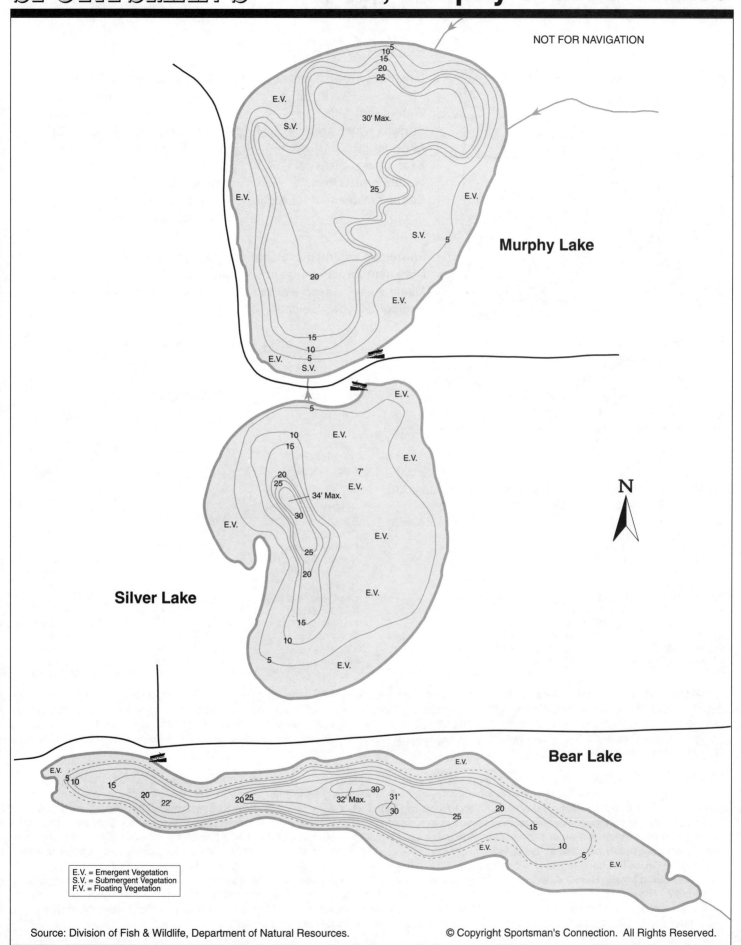

NOT FOR NAVIGATION

Murphy Lake

30' Max.

E.V. S.V. E.V. E.V. E.V. E.V.

5 10 15 20 25

25

5

20

15 10 5

Silver Lake

34' Max.

7'

E.V. E.V. E.V. E.V. E.V. E.V. E.V.

5 10 15 20 25 30 25 20 15 10 5

N

Bear Lake

E.V. E.V.

5 10 15 20 22' 20 25 30 32' Max. 31' 30 25 20 15 10 5

E.V. E.V.

E.V. = Emergent Vegetation
S.V. = Submergent Vegetation
F.V. = Floating Vegetation

Source: Division of Fish & Wildlife, Department of Natural Resources.

BIG PINE LAKE
Otter Tail County

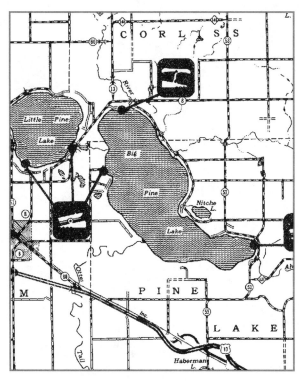

Location: Township 136, 137 Range 38
Watershed: Otter Tail
Surface Water Area: 4,730 Acres
Shorelength: 14.1 Miles
Secchi disk (water clarity): 4.5 Ft.
Water color: Green
Cause of water color: Algae bloom

Maximum depth: 75 Ft.
Median depth: 16 Ft.
Accessibility: On northwest shore, on north shore (off Cty. Road 8), on southeast shore (off Cty. Road 53)
Boat Ramp: 2 concrete; 1 earth (carry down)
Accommodations: Resort and campground

Shoreland zoning classification: General Development
Dominant forest/soil type: Deciduous/Sand
Management class: Walleye-Centrarchid
Ecological type: Centrarchid-Walleye

FISH STOCKING DATA
No record of stocking since 1988.

NET CATCH DATA

survey date: 7/8/96

species	Gill Nets # per net	Gill Nets avg fish wt. (lbs.)	Trap Nets # per set	Trap Nets avg fish wt. (lbs.)
Black Bullhead	0.7	1.02	0.6	0.82
Black Crappie	0.5	0.89	0.3	0.02
Bluegill	-	-	0.2	0.12
Bowfin (Dogfish)	-	-	0.4	4.88
Brown Bullhead	-	-	0.6	0.88
Burbot	0.2	1.78	-	-
Common Carp	0.5	9.92	0.2	7.31
Freshwater Drum	0.3	5.80	0.1	14.00
Northern Pike	2.4	4.07	0.3	1.95
Pumpkin. Sunfish	trace	0.10	5.0	0.09
Rock Bass	0.3	0.64	2.1	0.46
Shorthead Redhorse	trace	1.98	0.3	2.43
Tullibee (Cisco)	1.3	0.39	-	-
Walleye	13.3	1.24	0.4	3.74
White Sucker	5.7	1.40	6.7	2.04
Yellow Bullhead	0.3	1.09	1.0	1.08
Yellow Perch	50.3	0.19	13.4	0.11

LENGTH OF SELECTED SPECIES SAMPLED FROM ALL GEAR
Number of fish caught for the following length categories (inches):

species	0-5	6-8	9-11	12-14	15-19	20-24	25-29	>30	Total
Black Bullhead	-	-	8	9	-	-	-	-	17
Black Crappie	5	-	2	3	-	-	-	-	10
Bluegill	1	1	-	-	-	-	-	-	2
Brown Bullhead	-	-	3	3	-	-	-	-	6
Northern Pike	-	-	-	-	8	21	7	3	39
Pumpkin. Sunfish	39	6	-	-	-	-	-	-	45
Rock Bass	8	6	11	-	-	-	-	-	25
Tullibee (Cisco)	-	10	2	2	1	-	-	-	15
Walleye	-	24	58	8	94	13	6	-	203
Yellow Bullhead	-	1	6	8	-	-	-	-	15
Yellow Perch	140	551	18	-	-	-	-	-	709

DNR COMMENTS: Northern Pike abundance unchanged from 1992 level and at the lower end of the expected range for lake class; average size 23.5 inches and 4.1 lb. Common Carp numbers unchanged and at the lower end of the expected range. Walleye numbers well above expected range; average length 13.5 inches at age 4; population is self-sustaining. Bluegill numbers stable and below expected range. Yellow Perch numbers down but still at upper level of expected range; size structure good for this species, with 31 percent of Perch reaching 8 inches.

FISHING INFORMATION: Big Pine Lake at Perham, just north of Highway 10, is one of the premier walleye fisheries in Central Minnesota. The population runs well above the regional average and many times greater than the state mean. And, not only are there a lot of Walleye, but the lake's structure is diverse and fun to fish. Big Pine has good, long points with bars running off them and humps that have gravel and rubble surfaces. Aside from the obvious points, especially those along the southwest side, there are the inlet and outlet of the Otter tail River. These are often early-season hotspots. Looking at the southeast shore, you'll find steep breaks right off the shoreline, good spots both early and late in the season. There are also good breaks off the west shore that can be slow-trolled. Shiner minnows and Fuzzy Grubs are good for early season fishing. When the water warms, Walleyes head for deeper water, 15 to 20 feet, where they'll be taken with a leech. Big Pine isn't noted for its Northern Pike, but there are decent numbers of them, and average size is good, around 4 pounds. They will be found between the outer weed edges and deeper water. The flats at the northeast end are good places to find them, as is the southeast corner of the lake. Panfish, although not abundant, can be found in the weeds in June, especially where you see emerging vegetation. Offer them a variety of baits, including worms and smaller minnows.

NOT FOR NAVIGATION

Little Pine Lake

Ottertail River

Ottertail River

Nitche Lake

75'
Max

E.V. = Emergent Vegetation
S.V. = Submergent Vegetation
F.V. = Floating Vegetation

LITTLE PINE LAKE
Otter Tail County

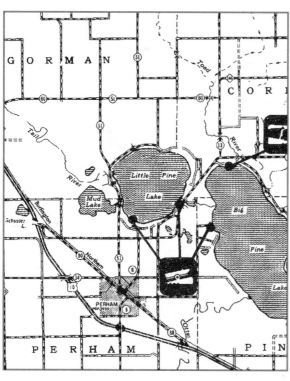

Location: Township 136, 137
Range 38, 39
Watershed: Otter Tail
Surface Water Area: 1,969 Acres
Shorelength: 7.0 Miles
Secchi disk (water clarity): 6.6 Ft.
Water color: Greenish
Cause of water color: Light algae bloom

Maximum depth: 78 Ft.
Median depth: 28 Ft.
Accessibility: Public access near outlet, off Cty. Road 8 and another on south shore, off Cty. Road 51
Boat Ramp: Concrete (both)
Accommodations: Resorts

Shoreland zoning classification: General Development
Dominant forest/soil type: Deciduous/Sand
Management class: Walleye-Centrarchid
Ecological type: Centrarchid-Walleye

FISH STOCKING DATA
No record of stocking since 1988.

NET CATCH DATA

survey date: 6/24/96

species	Gill Nets # per net	Gill Nets avg fish wt. (lbs.)	Trap Nets # per set	Trap Nets avg fish wt. (lbs.)
Black Bullhead	-	-	2.9	0.86
Black Crappie	-	-	trace	0.02
Bluegill	-	-	1.6	0.30
Bowfin (Dogfish)	-	-	0.3	4.34
Brown Bullhead	-	-	2.1	0.83
Burbot	0.3	2.54	-	-
Common Carp	-	-	0.4	8.76
Hybrid Sunfish	-	-	0.1	0.35
Northern Pike	1.6	2.96	0.2	1.51
Pumpkin. Sunfish	-	-	0.5	0.12
Rock Bass	-	-	2.2	0.66
Shorthead Redhorse	0.7	2.10	3.1	2.10
Tullibee (Cisco)	13.0	0.74	-	-
Walleye	6.9	1.54	0.8	1.67
White Sucker	5.9	2.00	6.8	2.01
Yellow Bullhead	-	-	2.1	0.89
Yellow Perch	59.4	0.20	6.1	0.12

LENGTH OF SELECTED SPECIES SAMPLED FROM ALL GEAR
Number of fish caught for the following length categories (inches):

species	0-5	6-8	9-11	12-14	15-19	20-24	25-29	>30	Total
Black Bullhead	-	-	23	21	-	-	-	-	44
Black Crappie	1	-	-	-	-	-	-	-	1
Bluegill	5	19	-	-	-	-	-	-	24
Brown Bullhead	-	-	16	16	-	-	-	-	32
Hybrid Sunfish	-	2	-	-	-	-	-	-	2
Northern Pike	-	-	-	-	3	16	5	3	27
Pumpkin. Sunfish	6	2	-	-	-	-	-	-	8
Rock Bass	3	9	21	-	-	-	-	-	33
Tullibee (Cisco)	-	40	38	105	8	-	-	-	191
Walleye	-	2	53	9	23	17	9	-	113
Yellow Bullhead	-	1	16	14	-	-	-	-	31
Yellow Perch	47	368	21	-	-	-	-	-	436

DNR COMMENTS: Cisco numbers exceed upper level of expected range for lake class; average size 11.5 inches and .8 lb. Northern Pike abundance unchanged and below expected range; average size 23.8 inches and 3 lb. Common Carp numbers unchanged and within expected range. Walleye abundance down but within expected range; average size 14.7 inches and 1.7 lb.; strong 1994 year class should afford good angling; species is self-sustaining. Bluegill numbers below expected range; size structure very good, with 58 percent of Bluegills reaching 7 inches. Yellow Perch numbers up and within expected range; 33 percent of Perch reaching 8 inches.

FISHING INFORMATION: Fishing Little Pine Lake means fishing for Walleyes and Northerns. The lake, immediately west of Perham, has a sand bottom and lots of structure, as well as a strong Yellow Perch forage base. According to a veteran angler we spoke with, the spot on the southwest side where the Otter Tail River enters the lake, is hot. Another general area for Walleyes is the north end of the lake, where you can work the flats with a bottom rig and shiner minnow. Humps in the northwest and southwest corners also deserve attention early. Walleye fingerlings and fry have been stocked biennially for many years, and there is also migration into the lake from Big Pine to the east and Mud Lake to the west where there also is natural reproduction. Northerns are usually found prowling the flats just outside the weedlines. The north-end flats are good spots, as are most areas where weeds are visible. Use those shiner minnows (or a leech) with a spoon, and you won't be disappointed. There are some nice Rock Bass in the lake as well; fish the entrance and exit of the Otter Tail River.

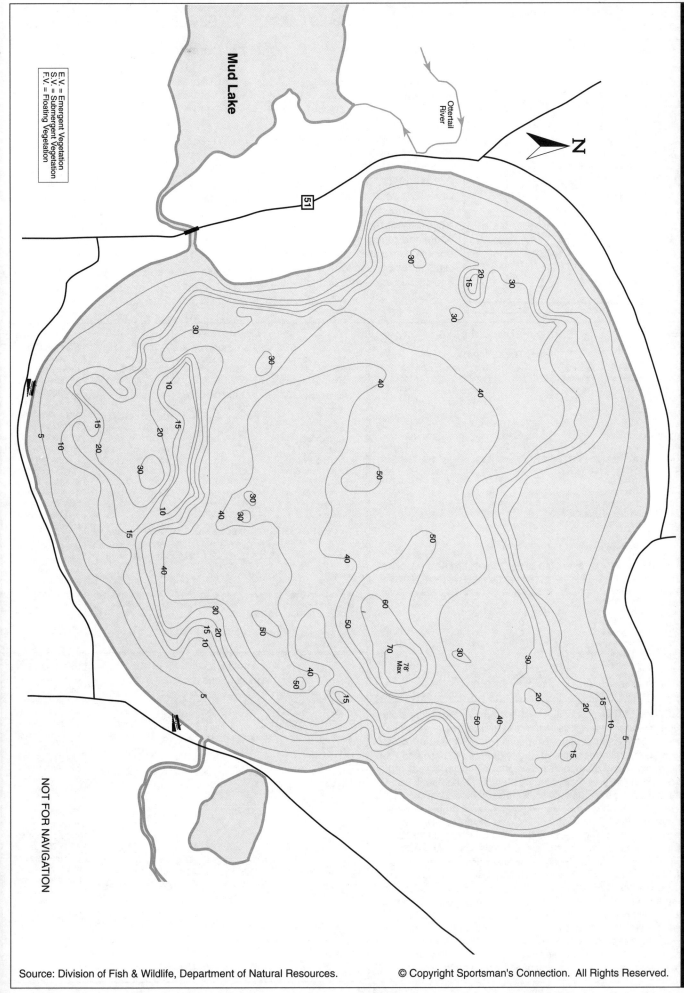

Little Pine Lake

Mud Lake

Ottertail River

N

51

E.V. = Emergent Vegetation
S.V. = Submergent Vegetation
F.V. = Floating Vegetation

NOT FOR NAVIGATION

78' Max

Location: Township 136 Range 40
Watershed: Otter Tail

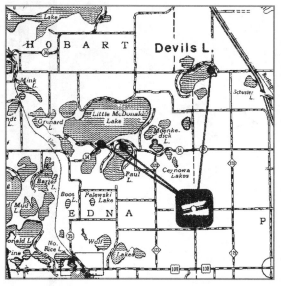

Otter Tail County

	LITTLE McDONALD LAKE	DEVILS LAKE	PAUL LAKE
Size of lake:	1,174 Acres	314 Acres	319 Acres
Shorelength:	6.1 Miles	3.1 Miles	3.0 Miles
Secchi disk (water clarity):	10.0 Ft.	15.0 Ft.	22.0 Ft.
Water color:	Light green	Clear	Clear
Cause of water color:	Algae	NA	NA
Maximum depth:	109 Ft.	67 Ft.	81 Ft.
Median depth:	33 Ft.	9 Ft.	NA
Accessibility:	State-owned public access on south shore, off Hwy. 34	Public access on northeast shore	Public access on north shore
Boat Ramp:	Concrete	Concrete	Concrete
Accommodations:	NA	NA	NA
Shoreland zoning classif.:	Gen. Dev.	Gen. Dev.	Rec. Dev.
Dominant forest/soil type:	Decid/Sand	Decid/Sand	NA
Management class:	Walleye-Centrarchid	Walleye-Centrarchid	Walleye-Centrarchid
Ecological type:	Centrarchid-Walleye	Centrarchid	Centrarchid

DNR COMMENTS:
Northern Pike numbers about normal for lake class; avg. size 20.7 inches and 2 lb.; 11 percent of population over 24 inches; natural reproduction consistent. Walleye numbers within normal range; mean size 18.7 inches and 2.7 lb.; fish to 28.8 inches sampled in gill nets. LM Bass numbers near upper limit of normal range for lake class; avg. size 12.4 inches at age 5. Black Crappie numbers normal. Bluegill population down but normal; size structure good, with 50 percent of Bluegills reaching 7 inches.

Little McDonald Lake

FISH STOCKING DATA

year	species	size	# released
94	Walleye	Fingerling	17,909
95	Walleye	Fingerling	13,180
97	Walleye	Fingerling	7,434

survey date: 8/26/96

NET CATCH DATA

	Gill Nets		Trap Nets	
		avg fish		avg fish
species	# per net	wt. (lbs)	# per set	wt. (lbs)
Black Crappie	trace	0.06	1.3	0.19
Bluegill	2.8	0.13	61.1	0.20
Largemouth Bass	0.3	1.78	1.2	0.37
Northern Pike	5.4	1.90	0.5	1.63
Pumpkin. Sunfish	1.9	0.12	1.4	0.19
Rock Bass	0.3	0.30	0.5	0.17
Walleye	6.8	2.68	0.3	2.20
Yellow Perch	0.5	0.09	0.1	0.08

LENGTH OF SELECTED SPECIES SAMPLED FROM ALL GEAR
Number of fish caught for the following length categories (inches):

species	0-5	6-8	9-11	12-14	15-19	20-24	25-29	>30	Total
Black Crappie	5	9	1	-	-	-	-	-	15
Bluegill	92	178	-	-	-	-	-	-	270
Brown Bullhead	-	-	70	18	-	-	-	-	88
Largemouth Bass	3	7	2	4	-	-	-	-	16
Northern Pike	-	-	1	1	31	23	5	2	63
Pumpkin. Sunfish	29	9	-	-	-	-	-	-	38
Rock Bass	5	3	-	-	-	-	-	-	8
Walleye	-	1	13	5	26	32	5	-	82
Yellow Bullhead	-	59	320	2	-	-	-	-	381
Yellow Perch	1	2	-	-	-	-	-	-	3

Devils Lake

FISH STOCKING DATA

year	species	size	# released
93	Walleye	Fry	211,000
95	Walleye	Yearling	2,954

survey date: 6/20/94

NET CATCH DATA

	Gill Nets		Trap Nets	
		avg fish		avg fish
species	# per net	wt. (lbs)	# per set	wt. (lbs)
Black Crappie	0.1	0.67	0.8	0.27
Bluegill	0.6	0.11	197.0	0.23
Hybrid Sunfish	0.1	0.85	1.8	0.81
Largemouth Bass	0.4	0.41	5.3	0.19
Northern Pike	10.2	1.75	0.9	1.29
Pumpkin. Sunfish	0.2	0.24	3.4	0.48
Walleye	0.6	1.68	0.1	1.32
Yellow Perch	0.8	0.05	0.3	0.06

LENGTH OF SELECTED SPECIES SAMPLED FROM ALL GEAR
Number of fish caught for the following length categories (inches):

species	0-5	6-8	9-11	12-14	15-19	20-24	25-29	>30	Total
Black Crappie	2	2	3	-	-	-	-	-	7
Bluegill	51	196	-	-	-	-	-	-	247
Hybrid Sunfish	-	15	-	-	-	-	-	-	15
Largemouth Bass	-	41	5	-	-	-	-	-	46
Northern Pike	-	-	6	12	49	17	7	4	95
Pumpkin. Sunfish	10	19	-	-	-	-	-	-	29
Walleye	-	1	-	-	5	-	-	-	6
Yellow Bullhead	-	9	84	-	-	-	-	-	93
Yellow Perch	2	3	-	-	-	-	-	-	5

DNR COMMENTS:
Northern Pike numbers above expected range for lake class; average length 19 inches. Walleye population below normal range; population sustained by stocking; average length 15 inches at age 4. Largemouth Bass numbers above normal; good natural reproduction. Population of Black Crappies within normal range. Yellow Perch numbers below normal. Bluegill abundance above expected range.

Paul Lake

FISH STOCKING DATA

year	species	size	# released
90	Walleye	Yearling	888
94	Walleye	Fingerling	3,961
96	Walleye	Fingerling	2,360

survey date: 8/18/97

NET CATCH DATA

	Gill Nets		Trap Nets	
		avg fish		avg fish
species	# per net	wt. (lbs)	# per set	wt. (lbs)
Bluegill	5.3	0.22	3.3	0.10
Largemouth Bass	1.8	0.80	0.1	0.71
Northern Pike	7.0	1.12	1.1	0.67
Pumpkin. Sunfish	3.7	0.15	0.2	0.19
Rock Bass	-	-	0.1	0.26
Walleye	4.7	2.08	0.3	4.76
Yellow Perch	0.2	0.10	-	-

LENGTH OF SELECTED SPECIES SAMPLED FROM ALL GEAR
Number of fish caught for the following length categories (inches):

species	0-5	6-8	9-11	12-14	15-19	20-24	25-29	>30	Total
Black Bullhead	-	-	5	8	-	-	-	-	13
Bluegill	27	46	-	-	-	-	-	-	73
Brown Bullhead	-	-	1	3	-	-	-	-	4
Largemouth Bass	-	4	8	5	-	-	-	-	17
Northern Pike	-	-	-	23	36	7	1	1	68
Pumpkin. Sunfish	18	13	-	-	-	-	-	-	31
Rock Bass	-	1	-	-	-	-	-	-	1
Walleye	-	4	3	7	16	13	2	-	45
Yellow Perch	-	1	-	-	-	-	-	-	1

DNR COMMENTS:
Northern Pike averaging around 17 inches in length, but Pike up to 36.6 inches have been sampled. Largemouth Bass and Bluegill numbers down, but fish of both species in acceptable sizes are present. Walleye population worth fishing; lengths range from 7.1 to 25.9 inches; both stocking and natural reproduction contributing to the population of this species.

FISHING INFORMATION: Located west of Perham, these lakes offer anglers good opportunities. **Little McDonald** is deep, clear, and has a good weedline. In addition, it has a big population of Northern Pike and panfish, as well as decent numbers of Largemouth Bass. Bass and Panfish can be found easily enough in the weeds, particularly west of the access point and in the small bay at the west end. Northerns will also be in these areas, cruising over the flats at the edge of the weeds. Your best bets for Walleyes are around the east end on the quick dropoffs or in the northwest corner. **Paul Lake** also is deep and exceptionally clear. Its best spots for Walleye fishing are around the bar off the south shore, the point on the southeast side and the steep breaks near the north-side access point. The weeds aren't heavy, but you will find Northerns outside them, particularly along the southeast and southwest shore. **Devils Lake** holds very nice Largemouth, as well as Northerns, Walleyes, and a huge Bluegill population. The lake is very clear and has good weedbeds. Bass anglers should head for the lake's west end, where the water is shallow and the weeds fairly heavy. To find Northerns early in the season, just work the weed edges and keep your eyes peeled for schools of forage fish. Walleyes are stocked, and you can do fairly well with them at the lake's east end, where dropoffs start fairly close to the shore.

NOT FOR NAVIGATION

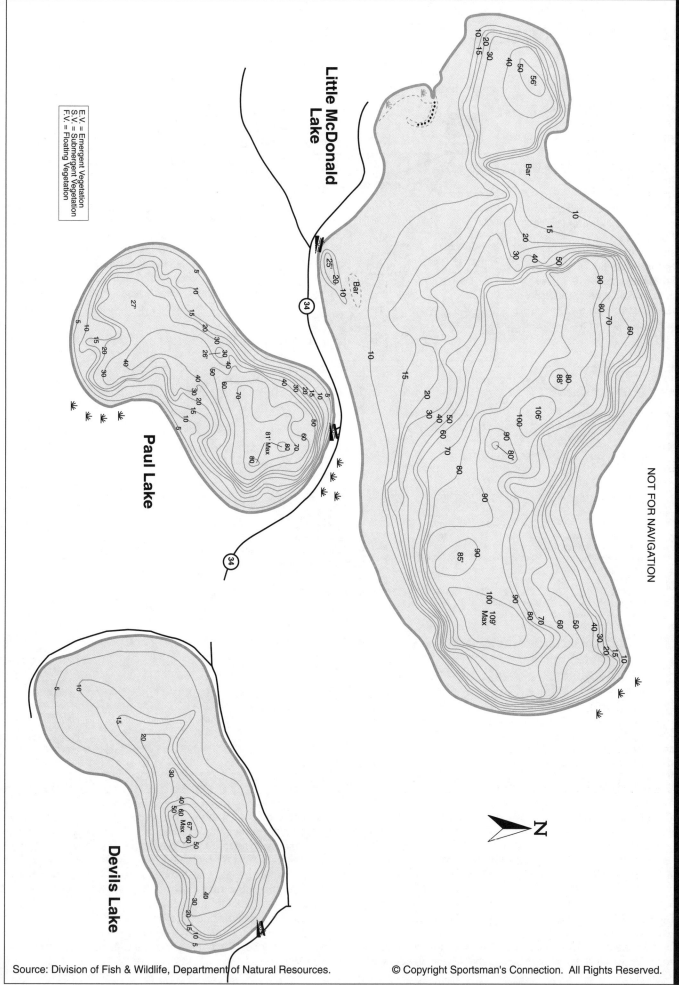

Little McDonald Lake

Paul Lake

Devils Lake

E.V. = Emergent Vegetation
S.V. = Submergent Vegetation
F.V. = Floating Vegetation

N

BIG McDONALD LAKE   WEST McDONALD LAKE
Otter Tail County

Location: Township 136 Range 40, 41
Watershed: Otter Tail
Surface Water Area: 935 Acres
Shorelength: 4.5 Miles
Secchi disk (water clarity): 11.5 Ft.
Water color: Light green
Cause of water color: Light algae bloom
Maximum depth: 46 Ft.
Median depth: NA
Accessibility: State-owned public access on northwest shore; also south shore of Lake Two
Boat Ramp: Concrete
Accommodations: NA
Shoreland zoning classif.: Rec. Dev.
Dominant forest/soil type: Decid/Sand
Management class: Walleye-Centrarchid
Ecological type: Centrarchid-Walleye

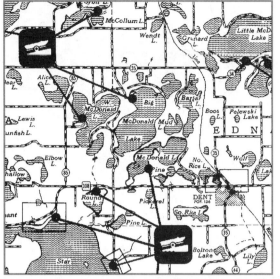

Location: Township 136 Range 40, 41
Watershed: Otter Tail
Surface Water Area: 573 Acres
Shorelength: NA
Secchi disk (water clarity): 17.1 Ft.
Water color: Clear
Cause of water color: NA
Maximum depth: 62 Ft.
Median depth: NA
Accessibility: State-owned public access on west shore
Boat Ramp: Concrete
Accommodations: NA
Shoreland zoning classif.: Rec. Dev.
Dominant forest/soil type: Decid/Sand
Management class: Walleye-Centrarchid
Ecological type: Centrarchid-Walleye

DNR COMMENTS: Northern Pike population up but within normal range for lake class; average size 17.6 inches and 1.2 lb.; 10 percent of Pike exceed 24 inches. Walleye numbers down and below normal range for lake class; some natural reproduction occurring; mean size 19.8 inches and 3 lb. Largemouth Bass numbers down but within normal range; average length only 7.9 inches. Black Crappies sampled for first time since 1977; average length 8.3 inches. Bluegill numbers above normal range; average length 6.4 inches. Yellow Perch numbers below normal; average length 6.6 inches.

FISH STOCKING DATA

year	species	size	# released
90	Walleye	Fingerling	8,924
95	Walleye	Fingerling	11,049
96	Walleye	Fry	368,000
97	Walleye	Fingerling	13,454

survey date: 8/7/95

NET CATCH DATA

species	Gill Nets # per net	avg fish wt. (lbs)	Trap Nets # per set	avg fish wt. (lbs)
Black Bullhead	7.6	0.74	0.7	0.65
Black Crappie	-	-	0.3	0.41
Bluegill	34.9	0.17	137.9	0.19
Brown Bullhead	0.8	1.04	trace	1.14
Largemouth Bass	3.9	0.67	1.1	0.30
Northern Pike	6.3	1.32	0.4	1.64
Pumpkin. Sunfish	2.6	0.19	1.8	0.18
Rock Bass	3.6	0.36	4.0	0.30
Walleye	2.4	1.77	0.9	3.04
White Sucker	trace	4.06	-	-
Yellow Bullhead	10.0	0.60	6.1	0.67
Yellow Perch	0.6	0.13	0.8	0.11

LENGTH OF SELECTED SPECIES SAMPLED FROM ALL GEAR
Number of fish caught for the following length categories (inches):

species	0-5	6-8	9-11	12-14	15-19	20-24	25-29	>30	Total
Black Bullhead	-	4	87	8	-	-	-	-	99
Black Crappie	1	1	2	-	-	-	-	-	4
Bluegill	173	373	-	-	-	-	-	-	546
Brown Bullhead	-	-	2	8	-	-	-	-	10
Largemouth Bass	3	21	26	10	-	-	-	-	60
Northern Pike	-	-	5	14	45	7	5	2	78
Pumpkin. Sunfish	24	24	-	-	-	-	-	-	48
Rock Bass	1	88	2	-	-	-	-	-	91
Walleye	-	-	2	10	14	11	1	-	38
Yellow Bullhead	-	2	183	8	-	-	-	-	193
Yellow Perch	6	9	1	-	-	-	-	-	16

FISH STOCKING DATA

year	species	size	# released
93	Walleye	Fingerling	3,792
94	Walleye	Fingerling	11,513
96	Walleye	Fingerling	5,780

survey date: 8/21/95

NET CATCH DATA

species	Gill Nets # per net	avg fish wt. (lbs)	Trap Nets # per set	avg fish wt. (lbs)
Black Bullhead	1.8	0.61	0.6	0.47
Bluegill	8.8	0.18	75.4	0.20
Brown Bullhead	3.3	0.72	0.6	0.59
Hybrid Sunfish	0.4	0.12	0.1	0.25
Largemouth Bass	3.0	0.76	0.9	0.24
Northern Pike	0.7	2.31	-	-
Pumpkin. Sunfish	0.1	0.44	2.4	0.28
Rock Bass	2.7	0.45	1.3	0.37
Walleye	16.8	0.89	0.6	2.06
White Sucker	1.0	2.43	0.4	2.46
Yellow Bullhead	2.6	0.68	2.3	0.93
Yellow Perch	3.2	0.14	0.6	0.16

LENGTH OF SELECTED SPECIES SAMPLED FROM ALL GEAR
Number of fish caught for the following length categories (inches):

species	0-5	6-8	9-11	12-14	15-19	20-24	25-29	>30	Total
Black Bullhead	-	-	20	-	-	-	-	-	20
Bluegill	99	150	1	-	-	-	-	-	250
Brown Bullhead	-	-	24	10	-	-	-	-	34
Hybrid Sunfish	3	2	-	-	-	-	-	-	5
Largemouth Bas	-	7	18	8	-	-	-	-	33
Northern Pike	-	-	1	1	3	1	-	6
Pumpkin. Sunfish	4	14	-	-	-	-	-	-	18
Rock Bass	2	20	11	-	-	-	-	-	33
Walleye	-	19	24	71	27	10	-	-	151
Yellow Bullhead	-	1	22	16	-	-	-	-	39
Yellow Perch	-	24	1	-	-	-	-	-	25

DNR COMMENTS: Northern Pike population up slightly but below normal range for lake class; spawning habitat may be limited; mean size 21.5 inches and 2.3 lb. Walleye numbers up substantially and above normal range; natural reproduction contributing substantially to population; average length 15.6 inches at age 4. Population density of Largemouth Bass is high but dominated by fish less than 12 inches. Bluegill numbers above normal range; 18 percent of fish at least 7 inches. Yellow Perch population up slightly and within normal range; 24 percent of population reaching 8 inches.

FISHING INFORMATION: It's a good idea to study up on the McDonald lakes before you fish them. You're going to need a depthfinder to make the most of your time, and you might want to find a guide in nearby Vergas or Perham the first time out. **Big McDonald** is actually three lakes but you can concentrate on Lake One and Lake Two which are connected by a manmade boat channel and West McDonald, which is separate but near Lake One. **West McDonald**, at 573 acres, has water clarity of 17.1 feet and the kind of bottom structure that makes it a respected Walleye and Northern Pike lake. The key spots you want to identify are the bar that bends north from the point sticking out from the southwestern shore, the hump about 500 yards straight out from the public ramp just north of the point, and the dead trees along the northeastern shore. The first two spots can be fished at the deep weedlines for Walleyes, while the trees will hold Largemouth Bass. At Big McDonald Lake One, which is 935 acres and spring-fed, the larger gamefish tend to hover in the weeds at the 15- to 20-foot depths. Drift with Lindy Rigs using nightcrawlers or shiners or cast deep-running lures and spinners. For early Crappies and Walleyes, take the boat channel into the 489-acre Lake Two and head for the western lobe. Circle the shoreline with crawlers or minnows and jig the deep weed lines. In summer, jig the deeper weedbreaks in all three McDonalds.

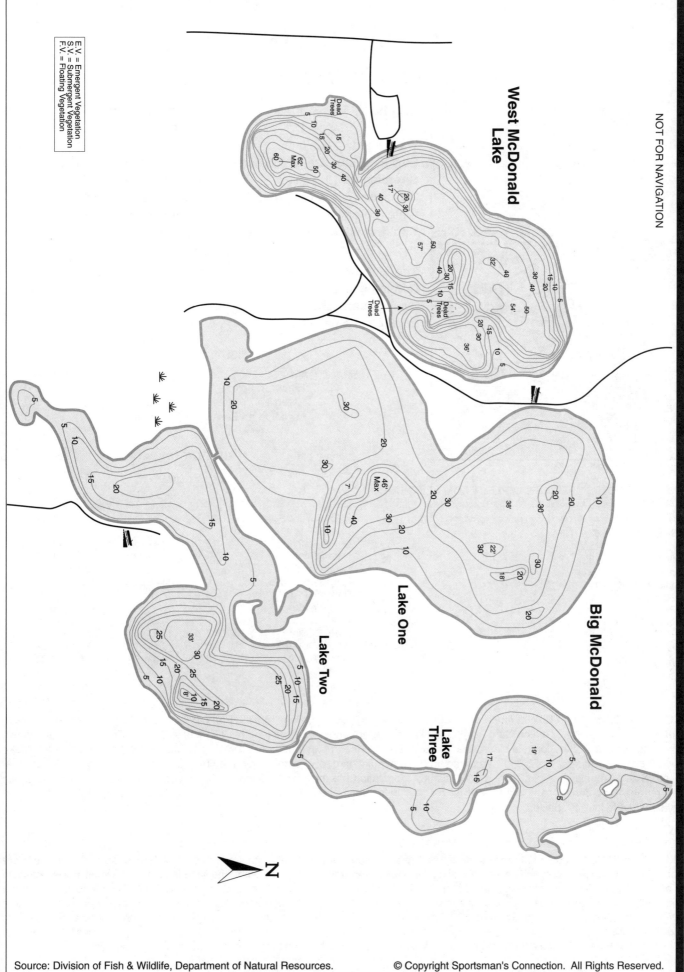

West McDonald Lake

Big McDonald

Lake One

Lake Two

Lake Three

E.V. = Emergent Vegetation
S.V. = Submergent Vegetation
F.V. = Floating Vegetation

N

ROUND LAKE
Otter Tail County

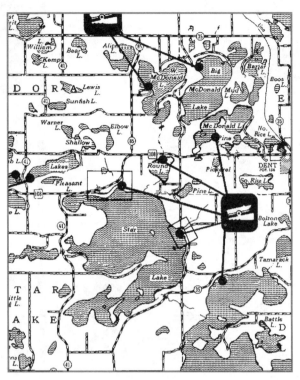

Location: Township 136
Range 41
Watershed: Otter Tail
Surface Water Area: 166 Acres
Shorelength: 1.9 Miles
Secchi disk (water clarity): 5.9 Ft.
Water color: Brownish
Cause of water color: Algae

Maximum depth: 18 Ft.
Median depth: NA
Accessibility: State-owned public access on north shore, off State Hwy. 108
Boat Ramp: Concrete
Accommodations: NA

Shoreland zoning classification: Recreational Development
Dominant forest/soil type: NA
Management class: Walleye-Centrarchid
Ecological type: Centrarchid

FISH STOCKING DATA

year	species	size	# released
97	Black Crappie	Adult	151
97	Bluegill	Adult	551
97	Largemouth Bass	Adult	1

NET CATCH DATA

survey date: 7/1/96

	Gill Nets		Trap Nets	
species	# per net	avg fish wt. (lbs.)	# per set	avg fish wt. (lbs.)
Black Bullhead	81.3	0.44	5.3	0.54
Bluegill	-	-	8.0	0.14
Brown Bullhead	5.5	0.47	0.2	0.47
Green Sunfish	-	-	0.1	0.06
Hybrid Sunfish	-	-	3.9	0.20
Largemouth Bass	0.2	0.45	0.6	0.42
Northern Pike	8.7	2.26	0.3	1.64
Pumpkin. Sunfish	-	-	2.0	0.08
Walleye	0.5	3.20	-	-
White Sucker	2.7	1.83	-	-
Yellow Bullhead	0.2	0.44	5.8	0.39
Yellow Perch	18.3	0.09	0.4	0.09

LENGTH OF SELECTED SPECIES SAMPLED FROM ALL GEAR

Number of fish caught for the following length categories (inches):

species	0-5	6-8	9-11	12-14	15-19	20-24	25-29	>30	Total
Black Bullhead	11	67	115	5	-	-	-	-	198
Bluegill	57	15	-	-	-	-	-	-	72
Brown Bullhead	-	8	27	-	-	-	-	-	35
Green Sunfish	1	-	-	-	-	-	-	-	1
Hybrid Sunfish	16	17	-	-	-	-	-	-	33
Largemouth Bass	1	2	2	1	-	-	-	-	6
Northern Pike	-	-	-	-	17	27	8	1	53
Pumpkin. Sunfish	15	1	-	-	-	-	-	-	16
Walleye	-	-	-	-	2	1	-	-	3
Yellow Bullhead	3	27	22	1	-	-	-	-	53
Yellow Perch	63	25	-	-	-	-	-	-	88

DNR COMMENTS: Northern Pike numbers up and within expected range for lake class; strong 1992 and 1993 year classes; average size 21.8 inches and 2.2 lb. Common Carp numbers below expected range; average length 10.9 inches. Black Bullhead population down but above third-quartile values for lake class; average size 9.2 inches. Walleye numbers remain low and below expected range for lake class; mean size 20.4 inches and 3.2 lb. Largemouth Bass population good; reproduction may be variable; fish average 11.3 inches at age 4. No Black Crappies sampled during 1996 survey; population has historically been cyclic. Bluegill population stable and within expected range; 10 percent of sample was at least 7 inches in length. Yellow Perch numbers down substantially; data indicate reproduction may be variable for this species.

FISHING INFORMATION: Just north of Star Lake lies a relatively obscure small body of water known as Round Lake. While there are plenty of bigger and better lakes in the area, this little lake offers a nice change of pace when the wind is blowing or when Walleye fishing is slow on the bigger lakes. Panfish are plentiful and easy to catch just about anywhere that you find weeds. They tend to run on the small side but can provide good action when the kids become impatient. The Largemouth Bass fishing can be pretty good, too. There isn't much for structure other than the weedbeds, so that's where you'll find the fish. Work the deeper edge of the weedline for the larger fish. Northern Pike are generally on the beefy side, fattening up on the numerous Yellow Perch and other forage species. Give Round Lake a try the next time you need a break from "serious" fishing. You probably won't regret it, and the kids may thank you.

NOT FOR NAVIGATION

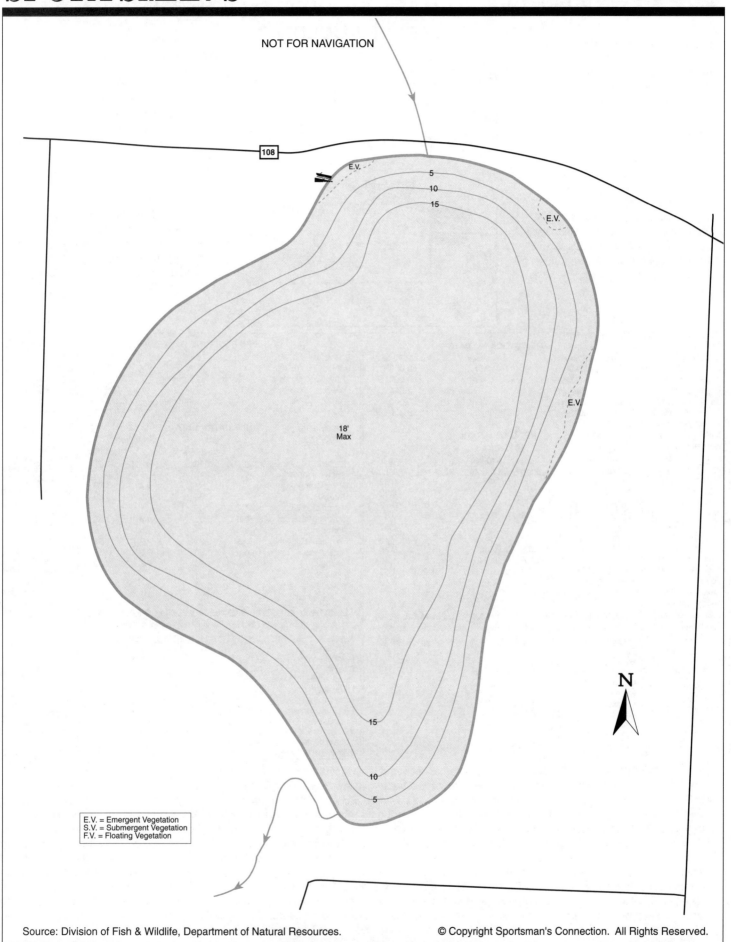

108

E.V.

5
10
15

E.V.

E.V.

18'
Max

15

10

5

N

E.V. = Emergent Vegetation
S.V. = Submergent Vegetation
F.V. = Floating Vegetation

EAST SILENT LAKE   WEST SILENT LAKE
Otter Tail County

Location: Township 136 Range 41
Watershed: Otter Tail
Surface Water Area: 310 Acres
Shorelength: 3.7 Miles
Secchi disk (water clarity): 17.0 Ft.
Water color: Clear
Cause of water color: NA
Maximum depth: 48 Ft.
Median depth: NA
Accessibility: County-owned access on south shore, off Cty. Road 41
Boat Ramp: Asphalt
Accommodations: Resort
Shoreland zoning classif.: Rec. Dev.
Dominant forest/soil type: Decid/Sand
Management class: Walleye-Centrarchid
Ecological type: Centrarchid-Walleye

Location: Township 136 Range 41
Watershed: Otter Tail
Surface Water Area: 328 Acres
Shorelength: 4.4 Miles
Secchi disk (water clarity): NA
Water color: Clear
Cause of water color: NA
Maximum depth: 58 Ft.
Median depth: NA
Accessibility: State-owned public access on north shore
Boat Ramp: Concrete
Accommodations: NA
Shoreland zoning classif.: Rec. Dev.
Dominant forest/soil type: Decid/Sand
Management class: Walleye-Centrarchid
Ecological type: Centrarchid-Walleye

DNR COMMENTS:
Northern Pike population slightly below expected range for lake class; mean size 22.4 inches and 3 lb. Walleye numbers up substantially and above the expected range; natural reproduction contributing substantially to population; average size 14.1 inches and 1.1 lb. Rock Bass numbers high. Bluegill population down and below expected range; natural reproduction inconsistent for this species. Yellow Perch numbers down but still above expected range; 30 percent of Perch exceed 8 inches.

FISH STOCKING DATA

year	species	size	# released
90	Walleye	Fry	60,000
93	Walleye	Fry	59,000
95	Walleye	Fingerling	2,594
96	Walleye	Fry	58,000
98	Walleye	Fry	58,000

survey date: 7/8/96

NET CATCH DATA

	Gill Nets		Trap Nets	
		avg fish		avg fish
species	# per net	wt. (lbs)	# per set	wt. (lbs)
Black Crappie	-	-	0.6	0.42
Bluegill	-	-	2.1	0.12
Hybrid Sunfish	-	-	0.3	0.29
Largemouth Bass	0.3	0.65	0.6	0.82
Northern Pike	1.7	3.03	0.2	0.57
Pumpkin. Sunfish	-	-	0.4	0.13
Rock Bass	3.3	0.45	16.9	0.36
Walleye	25.4	0.94	1.8	1.10
White Sucker	4.2	1.01	0.7	1.69
Yellow Bullhead	0.4	1.05	0.4	1.02
Yellow Perch	17.3	0.18	2.1	0.12

LENGTH OF SELECTED SPECIES SAMPLED FROM ALL GEAR
Number of fish caught for the following length categories (inches):

species	0-5	6-8	9-11	12-14	15-19	20-24	25-29	>30	Total
Black Crappie	-	3	2	-	-	-	-	-	5
Bluegill	15	3	1	-	-	-	-	-	19
Hybrid Sunfish	-	3	-	-	-	-	-	-	3
Largemouth Bass	1	1	5	-	1	-	-	-	8
Northern Pike	-	-	1	-	6	6	3	1	17
Pumpkin. Sunfish	3	1	-	-	-	-	-	-	4
Rock Bass	20	124	38	-	-	-	-	-	182
Walleye	-	2	16	160	61	6	-	-	245
Yellow Bullhead	-	-	3	5	-	-	-	-	8
Yellow Perch	44	106	25	-	-	-	-	-	175

FISH STOCKING DATA

year	species	size	# released
90	Walleye	Fry	119,000
93	Walleye	Fingerling	19,420
94	Walleye	Fry	119,000
96	Walleye	Fingerling	2,143
97	Walleye	Fry	119,000

survey date: 6/30/97

NET CATCH DATA

	Gill Nets		Trap Nets	
		avg fish		avg fish
species	# per net	wt. (lbs)	# per set	wt. (lbs)
Black Bullhead	0.6	1.42	-	-
Black Crappie	-	-	0.2	0.29
Bluegill	7.6	0.33	89.9	0.29
Hybrid Sunfish	0.1	0.34	-	-
Largemouth Bass	0.6	0.95	0.2	0.38
Northern Pike	8.0	1.09	0.6	0.76
Pumpkin. Sunfish	0.1	0.31	2.3	0.21
Rock Bass	0.6	0.30	9.0	0.32
Walleye	3.0	1.53	0.6	2.66
White Sucker	3.2	2.94	-	-
Yellow Bullhead	2.2	0.60	3.3	0.53
Yellow Perch	3.1	0.30	0.2	0.47

LENGTH OF SELECTED SPECIES SAMPLED FROM ALL GEAR
Number of fish caught for the following length categories (inches):

species	0-5	6-8	9-11	12-14	15-19	20-24	25-29	>30	Total
Black Bullhead	-	-	-	5	-	-	-	-	5
Black Crappie	-	2	-	-	-	-	-	-	2
Bluegill	17	248	-	-	-	-	-	-	265
Hybrid Sunfish	-	1	-	-	-	-	-	-	1
Largemouth Bass	-	-	5	2	-	-	-	-	7
Northern Pike	-	-	1	23	44	5	2	2	77
Pumpkin. Sunfish	9	13	-	-	-	-	-	-	22
Rock Bass	12	68	6	-	-	-	-	-	86
Walleye	-	-	-	7	19	6	-	-	32
Yellow Bullhead	1	5	40	4	-	-	-	-	50
Yellow Perch	1	11	16	-	-	-	-	-	28

DNR COMMENTS:
Black Crappies and Bluegills abundant, with good size structures. Walleye fry stocked biennially to supplement natural reproduction. Other gamefish species able to sustain population levels at or above management goals without stocking. Good habitat for Northern Pike, Largemouth Bass and Panfish. The west bay is an especially popular angling spot in spring for Crappies and Bluegills.

FISHING INFORMATION: These two smaller lakes about five miles west of Dent are similar in size and structure but offer anglers somewhat different fishing experiences. **East Silent** holds the better Walleye population of the two, according to both local anglers and the DNR. It also has good numbers of Largemouth Bass and panfish. Early season Walleyes are found at the steep offshore dropoffs along most of the lake's shoreline. The water is very clear and the bottom mostly sand. Use leeches or shiner minnows on a Lindy Rig, retrieving your bait slowly upwards and jigging slightly. The Walleye feed at the quick drops early but will head deeper as the water warms. The lake isn't heavily weeded, but both the east and west ends hold Largemouth Bass as well as lots of Rock Bass. Northern Pike also can be found, but in numbers well below area average. Although we have never fished East Silent in winter, local anglers say it's one of the better ice lakes for Walleyes. **West Silent**, meanwhile, has a good Northern Pike population, a fair number of Walleyes, fewer Largemouth than its neighbor and lots of Bluegills. The west bay is a good spot to look for panfish, and the flat's outer weedlines are great places to find Northerns. Offer the panskis worms and smaller minnows on a bare hook or a jig. There are no real points or bars to attract post-spawn Walleyes, but three steep breaks along the north and south shorelines are often productive. In summer, you'll have to fish Walleyes deep at mid lake during bright summer days, but the fish come back to the shorelines at night to feed.

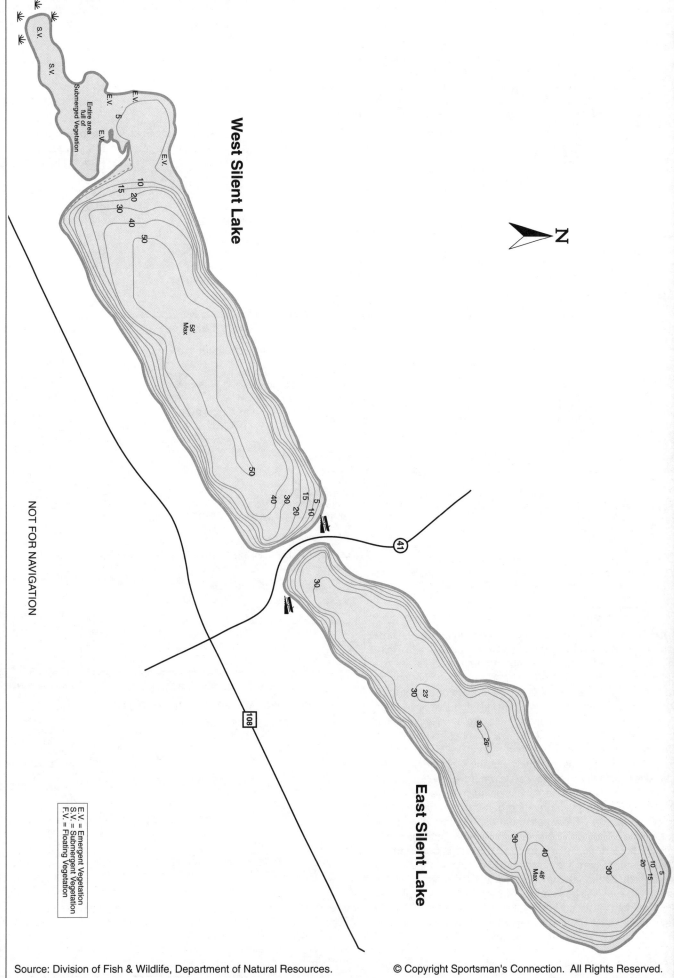

East & West Silent Lakes

N

West Silent Lake

E.V.
S.V.
S.V.

Entire area full of Submerged Vegetation

E.V.
5
E.V.
E.V.
E.V.

10
15
20
30
40
50

58' Max

50
40
30
15
20
5
10

NOT FOR NAVIGATION

41

108

30

30
23'
30

30
26'

30

40
48' Max

30

30
10
20
15
5

East Silent Lake

E.V. = Emergent Vegetation
S.V. = Submergent Vegetation
F.V. = Floating Vegetation

Source: Division of Fish & Wildlife, Department of Natural Resources.

Otter Tail County

	BASS LAKE	BEERS LAKE	LAKE TWENTY-ONE
Size of lake:	26 Acres	195 Acres	122 Acres
Shorelength:	NA	4.3 Miles	NA
Secchi disk (water clarity):	14.0 Ft.	12.0 Ft.	23.0 Ft.
Water color:	Light green	Green	Green tint
Maximum depth:	37 Ft.	60 Ft.	47 Ft.
Median depth:	NA	15 Ft.	NA
Accessibility:	Entire lake is within Maplewood State Park and is accessible for walk-in fishing	State-owned public access on the west shore	Lake is within Maplewood State Park; walk-in access
Boat Ramp:	Concrete	Gravel	None
Accommodations:	NA		Camping, picnic grounds, trails
Shoreland zoning classif.:	Nat. Env.	Nat. Env.	Nat. Env.
Dominant forest/soil type:	NA	NA	NA
Cause of water color:	Slight algae bloom	Algae bloom	Slight algae bloom
Management class:	Stream Trout	Muskie	Centrarchid
Ecological type:	Centrarchid	Centrarchid	Centrarchid

Bass Lake

DNR COMMENTS: Bass Lake was chemically treated in 1987 to eradicate Green Sunfish and Black Bullhead. The lake receives annual stocking of 2,500 yearling Rainbow Trout. Population sample in 1997 ranged in length from 7 to 16 inches; average weight .6 lb. No bullheads sampled in 1997; one hybrid Sunfish and 38 Golden Shiner minnows captured.

FISH STOCKING DATA

year	species	size	# released
90	Rainbow Trout	Yearling	2,500
93	Rainbow Trout	Yearling	2,500
94	Rainbow Trout	Yearling	2,500
95	Rainbow Trout	Yearling	2,500
96	Rainbow Trout	Yearling	2,487
97	Rainbow Trout	Yearling	2,500
98	Rainbow Trout	Yearling	2,060

NET CATCH DATA
survey date: 6/5/97

	Gill Nets		Trap Nets	
species	# per net	avg fish wt. (lbs)	# per set	avg fish wt. (lbs)
Fathead Minnow	-	-	0.1	0.02
Golden Shiner	-	-	4.8	0.05
Hybrid Sunfish	-	-	0.1	0.56
Rainbow Trout	-	-	0.8	0.57

LENGTH OF SELECTED SPECIES SAMPLED FROM ALL GEAR
Number of fish caught for the following length categories (inches):

species	0-5	6-8	9-11	12-14	15-19	20-24	25-29	>30	Total
Hybrid Sunfish	-	1	-	-	-	-	-	-	1
Rainbow Trout	-	1	4	-	1	-	-	-	6

Beers Lake

FISH STOCKING DATA

year	species	size	# released
90	Muskellunge	Fingerling	200
94	Muskellunge	Fingerling	200
96	Muskellunge	Fingerling	200

NET CATCH DATA
survey date: 8/11/97

	Gill Nets		Trap Nets	
species	# per net	avg fish wt. (lbs)	# per set	avg fish wt. (lbs)
Black Crappie	1.8	0.17	0.9	0.24
Bluegill	14.8	0.13	31.7	0.12
Hybrid Sunfish	0.7	0.20	3.6	0.15
Largemouth Bass	0.2	0.70	0.8	0.43
Northern Pike	3.7	2.47	0.2	0.71
Pumpkin. Sunfish	0.2	0.24	2.4	0.13
Walleye	0.2	3.75	-	-
Yellow Perch	0.5	0.07	0.3	0.08

LENGTH OF SELECTED SPECIES SAMPLED FROM ALL GEAR
Number of fish caught for the following length categories (inches):

species	0-5	6-8	9-11	12-14	15-19	20-24	25-29	>30	Total
Black Crappie	3	15	1	-	-	-	-	-	19
Bluegill	179	77	-	-	-	-	-	-	256
Hybrid Sunfish	18	18	-	-	-	-	-	-	36
Largemouth Bass	3	1	3	1	-	-	-	-	8
Northern Pike	-	-	1	7	11	5	-	-	24
Pumpkin. Sunfish	16	7	-	-	-	-	-	-	23
Walleye	-	-	-	-	-	1	-	-	1
Yellow Perch	4	2	-	-	-	-	-	-	6

DNR COMMENTS: Northern Pike population increasing, and size structure is good. Muskellunge numbers good; mean size 37.7 inches and 12.4 lb.; population estimate is 314 fish; fingerlings stocked biennially to bolster the population.. Walleye, White Sucker and Yellow Perch scarce. Largemouth Bass plentiful; size range 5.6 to 18.8 inches. Black Crappies numerous; size range 4.5 to 14.0 inches.

Lake Twenty-One

FISH STOCKING DATA: NO RECORD OF STOCKING

NET CATCH DATA
survey date: 6/26/95

	Gill Nets		Trap Nets	
species	# per net	avg fish wt. (lbs)	# per set	avg fish wt. (lbs)
Black Crappie	0.7	0.36	1.1	0.29
Bluegill	1.2	0.25	38.3	0.20
Green Sunfish	-	-	0.1	0.15
Hybrid Sunfish	-	-	2.3	0.22
Largemouth Bass	0.3	1.52	0.6	0.82
Northern Pike	9.8	2.28	0.8	2.00
Pumpkin. Sunfish	-	-	2.1	0.15
Yellow Perch	4.2	0.13	0.3	0.12

LENGTH OF SELECTED SPECIES SAMPLED FROM ALL GEAR
Number of fish caught for the following length categories (inches):

species	0-5	6-8	9-11	12-14	15-19	20-24	25-29	>30	Total
Black Crappie	3	7	4	-	-	-	-	-	14
Bluegill	74	104	-	-	-	-	-	-	178
Green Sunfish	1	-	-	-	-	-	-	-	1
Hybrid Sunfish	8	13	-	-	-	-	-	-	21
Largemouth Bass	3	1	1	-	2	-	-	-	7
Northern Pike	-	-	-	8	19	26	8	3	64
Pumpkin. Sunfish	14	5	-	-	-	-	-	-	19
Yellow Perch	5	21	-	-	-	-	-	-	26

DNR COMMENTS: Largemouth Bass numbers about normal for lake class; average length 11.9 inches. Northern Pike numbers up and above normal range; average size 21.2 inches and 2.2 lb.; natural reproduction appears stable. Black Crappie population about normal; average length 7.5 inches. Yellow Perch numbers up, but all fish sampled were less than 8 inches.

FISHING INFORMATION: Bass Lake is very small and is best known in the region for the fact that it has been stocked with Rainbow Trout. They provide decent fishing. Worms on a jig are the most popular bait. **Beers Lake** is bigger than its neighbor and you'll have better luck there. It holds good numbers of Largemouth Bass, Northern Pike, panfish and some Muskellunge that have been stocked by the DNR. The lake is divided into two definite parts, but boats and fish can pass through the narrow channel that divides it. Bass are found mostly in the southern part of the lake, which is shallower and has good weedbeds for spawning and protection. Northerns and Muskies are found off the weeds wherever they are thick enough to harbor panfish and forage species such as Yellow Perch. The water is fairly clear, and you may do better using live bait than lures early in the season. The weeds hold panfish, including good-size Black Crappie. They can be taken with worms and small minnows on a bare hook or jig. Walleyes can be found in both parts of the lake, but the north part is most productive. Fishing the points along the east side of the lake is your best bet for spring Walleye, though the marble eyes will be heading deeper during the daytime in July. **Lake Twenty-One** is a hike-in lake with a reputation for big Crappies and Bluegills. You'll also find good Northern and Bass fishing.

NOT FOR NAVIGATION

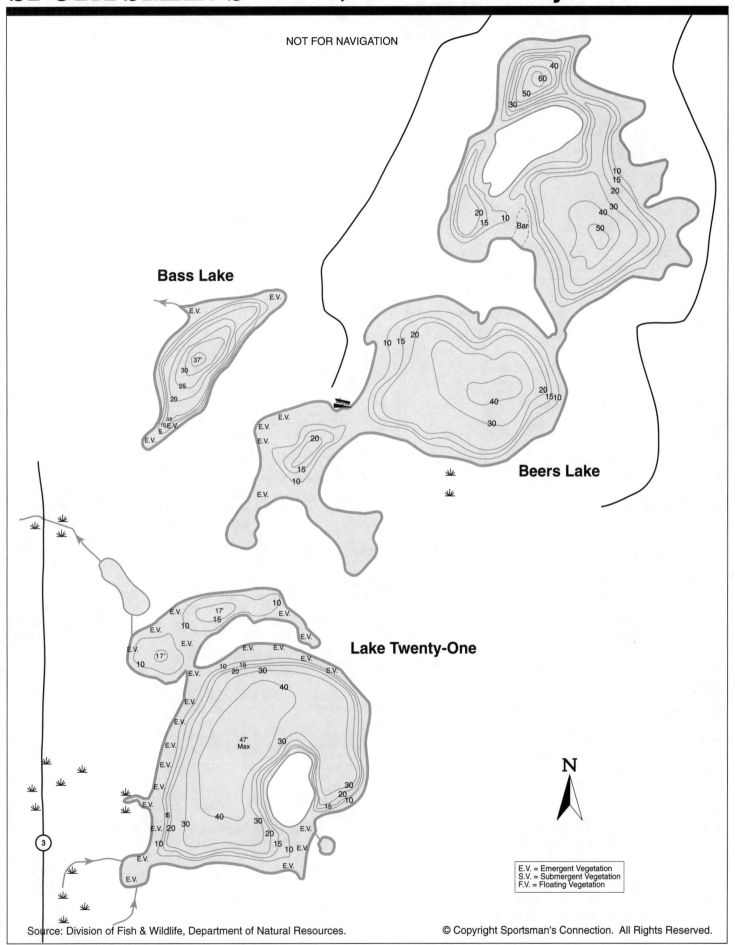

Bass Lake

Beers Lake

Lake Twenty-One

N

E.V. = Emergent Vegetation
S.V. = Submergent Vegetation
F.V. = Floating Vegetation

Source: Division of Fish & Wildlife, Department of Natural Resources.

Location: Township 134, 135   Range 42
Watershed: Otter Tail

	HEILBERGER LAKE	TONSETH LAKE	ANDERSON LAKE

Otter Tail County

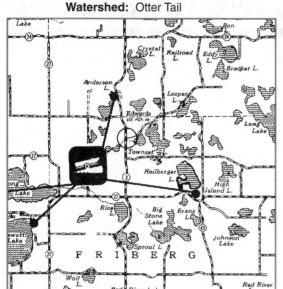

Size of lake: 224 Acres — 156 Acres — 83 Acres
Shorelength: 4.3 Miles — 3.9 Miles — NA
Secchi disk (water clarity): 10.0 Ft. — NA — NA
Water color: Light green — NA — NA
Cause of water color: Algal bloom — NA — NA
Maximum depth: 47 Ft. — 27 Ft. — 25 Ft.
Median depth: 20 Ft. — 15 Ft. — NA
Accessibility: State-owned public access located on the far south bay, off County Highway #22 — Public access located on southwest corner of lake — Public access on northeast shoreline of the lake
Boat Ramp: Concrete — Earth — Earth
Accommodations: NA — NA — NA
Shoreland zoning classif.: Rec. Dev. — Rec. Dev. — Nat. Env.
Dominant forest/soil type: Decid/Loam — Decid/Sand — NA
Management class: Walleye-Centrarchid — Centrarchid — Warm-water Gamefish
Ecological type: Centrarchid — Centrarchid — Bullhead

DNR COMMENTS:
Northern Pike numbers up but within expected range for lake class; average size 19.5 inches and 1.5 lb. Walleye population stable; and at the upper end of the normal range; average size 17.9 inches and 2.2 lb.; natural reproduction appears inconsistent. Balanced Largemouth Bass population sampled; average length 11.1 inches at age 4. Bluegill population down since 1990 sampling, but within expected range. Yellow Perch numbers remain below expected level.

Heilberger Lake

FISH STOCKING DATA

year	species	size	# released
94	Walleye	Fingerling	3,248
97	Walleye	Fingerling	4,462

survey date: 7/22/96

NET CATCH DATA

	Gill Nets		Trap Nets	
species	# per net	avg fish wt. (lbs)	# per set	avg fish wt. (lbs)
Black Crappie	0.5	0.51	0.1	0.16
Bluegill	44.8	0.23	14.1	0.14
Green Sunfish	-	-	0.1	0.01
Hybrid Sunfish	1.3	0.24	1.2	0.15
Largemouth Bass	1.0	1.11	0.6	0.38
Northern Pike	6.3	1.61	0.8	0.74
Pumpkin. Sunfish	2.2	0.18	2.3	0.12
Walleye	4.0	2.17	0.1	2.87
Yellow Perch	0.5	0.14	0.1	0.15

LENGTH OF SELECTED SPECIES SAMPLED FROM ALL GEAR
Number of fish caught for the following length categories (inches):

species	0-5	6-8	9-11	12-14	15-19	20-24	25-29	>30	Total
Black Bullhead	-	3	4	-	-	-	-	-	7
Black Crappie	-	1	3	-	-	-	-	-	4
Bluegill	91	141	-	-	-	-	-	-	232
Brown Bullhead	-	-	4	-	-	-	-	-	4
Green Sunfish	1	-	-	-	-	-	-	-	1
Hybrid Sunfish	8	11	-	-	-	-	-	-	19
Largemouth Bass	1	3	3	3	1	-	-	-	11
Northern Pike	-	-	-	3	27	12	3	-	45
Pumpkin. Sunfish	21	13	-	-	-	-	-	-	34
Walleye	-	-	2	2	14	7	-	-	25
Yellow Bullhead	-	54	45	6	-	-	-	-	105
Yellow Perch	-	4	-	-	-	-	-	-	4

Tonseth Lake

FISH STOCKING DATA

No record of stocking since 1985.

survey date: 6/6/94

NET CATCH DATA

	Gill Nets		Trap Nets	
species	# per net	avg fish wt. (lbs)	# per set	avg fish wt. (lbs)
Black Crappie	0.3	0.35	5.3	0.34
Bluegill	8.2	0.13	236.0	0.19
Green Sunfish	-	-	0.4	0.12
Hybrid Sunfish	0.7	0.34	4.4	0.46
Largemouth Bass	1.3	1.16	0.6	0.66
Northern Pike	2.8	3.66	-	-
Pumpkin. Sunfish	1.0	0.37	7.4	0.39
Walleye	0.3	3.31	-	-
Yellow Perch	41.8	0.15	0.3	0.20

LENGTH OF SELECTED SPECIES SAMPLED FROM ALL GEAR
Number of fish caught for the following length categories (inches):

species	0-5	6-8	9-11	12-14	15-19	20-24	25-29	>30	Total
Black Crappie	-	33	17	-	-	-	-	-	50
Bluegill	126	163	-	-	-	-	-	-	289
Green Sunfish	4	-	-	-	-	-	-	-	4
Hybrid Sunfish	12	32	-	-	-	-	-	-	44
Largemouth Bass	-	2	8	-	3	-	-	-	13
Northern Pike	-	-	-	2	6	7	2	-	17
Pumpkin. Sunfish	31	42	-	-	-	-	-	-	73
Walleye	-	-	-	1	1	-	-	-	2
Yellow Perch	25	141	-	-	-	-	-	-	166

DNR COMMENTS:
Northern Pike abundance stable and within normal range for lake class; mean length 25.1 inches. Walleye population below normal. Largemouth Bass numbers normal for lake class; 23 percent of sample measured 12 inches or more; natural reproduction consistent. Black Crappie numbers normal; mean length 8.5 inches; natural reproduction consistent. Yellow Perch above normal; 7.5 percent of population measured 8 inches or more.

Anderson Lake

FISH STOCKING DATA

No record of stocking since 1989.

survey date: 7/31/95

NET CATCH DATA

	Gill Nets		Trap Nets	
species	# per net	avg fish wt. (lbs)	# per set	avg fish wt. (lbs)
Black Crappie	1.5	0.34	9.1	0.31
Bluegill	52.0	0.20	67.6	0.19
Hybrid Sunfish	0.5	0.24	0.4	0.27
Largemouth Bass	-	-	0.8	0.96
Northern Pike	0.5	3.31	0.2	0.82
Pumpkin. Sunfish	0.5	0.28	1.8	0.18
Walleye	2.5	2.05	0.2	5.60

LENGTH OF SELECTED SPECIES SAMPLED FROM ALL GEAR
Number of fish caught for the following length categories (inches):

species	0-5	6-8	9-11	12-14	15-19	20-24	25-29	>30	Total
Black Crappie	5	69	11	-	-	-	-	-	85
Bluegill	58	255	1	-	-	-	-	-	314
Hybrid Sunfish	1	4	-	-	-	-	-	-	5
Largemouth Bass	1	4	-	2	-	-	-	-	7
Northern Pike	-	-	-	2	-	1	-	-	3
Pumpkin. Sunfish	7	10	-	-	-	-	-	-	17
Walleye	-	-	-	4	2	1	-	-	7

DNR COMMENTS:
Northern Pike population down and below normal for lake class; average size 25.3 inches and 3.3 lb. Walleye population stable and within normal range; average size 18.8 inches and 2.1 lb.; natural reproduction limited. LM Bass numbers up and within normal range; Bass reaching 11.5 inches at age 4. Black Crappie numbers up dramatically and 2.1 times the normal range; average lengths 8.2 inches. Yellow Perch not sampled.

FISHING INFORMATION: In normal years, **Anderson Lake** is considered a good place to fish for Walleyes, panfish and Northern Pike. Unfortunately, the lake is victimized by winterkill especially in harsh winters such as 1993-94. Many of the Walleyes seem to survive in the deepest water of the lake and panfish are able to populate, but anglers are advised to check with local bait shops before putting in boats. **Heilberger Lake** is deeper and bigger than its neighbors and is a better fishery by a long shot. Northern Pike, Bluegills and Largemouth Bass are all present as well as good numbers of stocked Walleyes. Little **Tonseth Lake** is dominated by Bullheads and has quite a few Bluegills. There is also a decent number of Black Crappies as well as a few stocked Walleyes. In addition, you'll find fair numbers of decent-size Northerns, which can be fished at the weedlines. Largemouth Bass fishing can be excellent, though average size isn't too great.

118

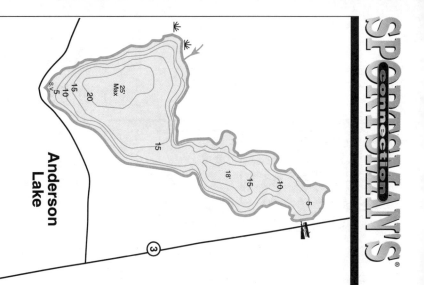

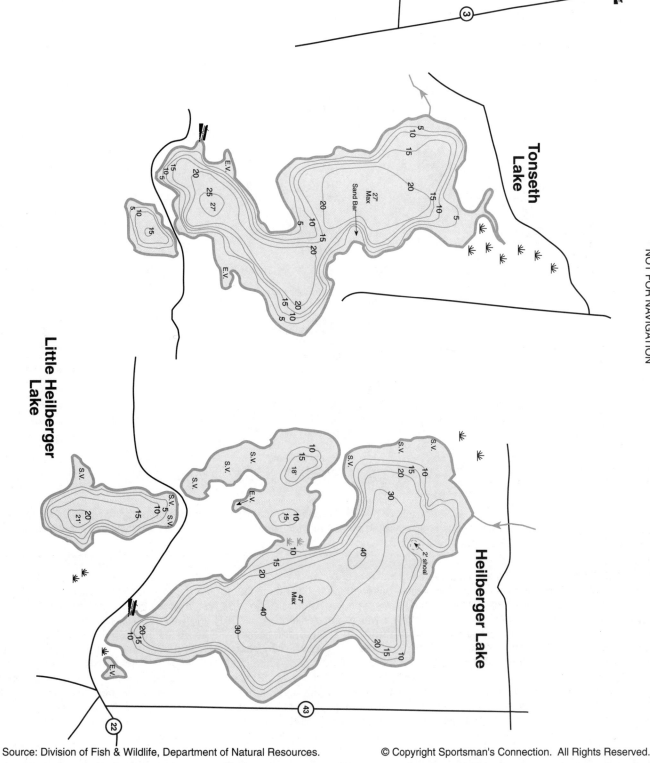

E.V. = Emergent Vegetation
S.V. = Submergent Vegetation
F.V. = Floating Vegetation

N

Anderson Lake

25' Max

Tonseth Lake

27' Max
Sand Bar

E.V.

Little Heilberger Lake

21'

Heilberger Lake

47' Max
2' shoal

Source: Division of Fish & Wildlife, Department of Natural Resources.

STAR LAKE
Otter Tail County

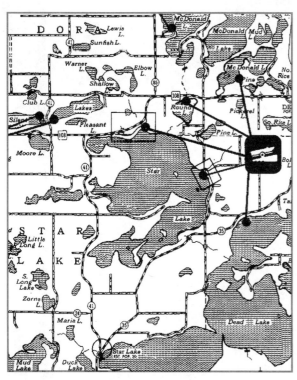

Location: Township 135, 136 Range 40, 41

Watershed: Otter Tail

Surface Water Area: 4,721 Acres

Shorelength: 29.7 Miles

Secchi disk (water clarity): 11.0 Ft.

Water color: Light green

Cause of water color: Slight algae bloom

Maximum depth: 94 Ft.

Median depth: 10 Ft.

Accessibility: State-owned public access on north shore, off Hwy. 108

Boat Ramp: Concrete

Accommodations: Resort and campground

Shoreland zoning classification: General Development

Dominant forest/soil type: No Tree/Wet

Management class: Walleye-Centrarchid

Ecological type: Centrarchid-Walleye

FISH STOCKING DATA

year	species	size	# released
90	Walleye	Fry	2,813,000
94	Walleye	Fry	2,813,000
98	Walleye	Fry	2,813,000

survey date: 7/14/97

NET CATCH DATA

	Gill Nets		Trap Nets	
		avg fish		avg fish
species	# per net	wt. (lbs.)	# per set	wt. (lbs.)
Black Bullhead	0.9	0.82	0.7	0.78
Black Crappie	trace	0.18	0.9	0.42
Bluegill	0.3	0.44	14.6	0.39
Brown Bullhead	0.5	1.00	1.9	0.48
Common Carp	-	-	trace	5.84
Green Sunfish	-	-	trace	0.05
Hybrid Sunfish	trace	0.31	1.8	0.42
Largemouth Bass	-	-	0.3	0.42
Northern Pike	10.6	1.58	1.1	0.84
Pumpkin. Sunfish	0.3	0.15	3.9	0.21
Rock Bass	4.7	0.63	5.3	0.30
Tullibee (Cisco)	0.3	0.64	-	-
Walleye	8.9	1.08	-	-
Yellow Bullhead	2.7	0.76	3.2	0.65
Yellow Perch	17.0	0.13	2.0	0.10

LENGTH OF SELECTED SPECIES SAMPLED FROM ALL GEAR

Number of fish caught for the following length categories (inches):

species	0-5	6-8	9-11	12-14	15-19	20-24	25-29	>30	Total
Black Bullhead	2	3	10	10	-	-	-	-	25
Black Crappie	1	6	7	-	-	-	-	-	14
Bluegill	34	124	13	-	-	-	-	-	171
Brown Bullhead	1	11	10	15	-	-	-	-	37
Green Sunfish	1	-	-	-	-	-	-	-	1
Hybrid Sunfish	-	26	2	-	-	-	-	-	28
Largemouth Bass	-	4	-	1	-	-	-	-	5
Northern Pike	-	-	13	19	82	49	6	3	172
Pumpkin. Sunfish	26	37	-	-	-	-	-	-	63
Rock Bass	24	62	49	-	-	-	-	-	135
Tullibee (Cisco)	-	1	-	3	-	-	-	-	4
Walleye	-	38	4	34	52	2	2	-	132
Yellow Bullhead	-	11	54	23	-	-	-	-	88
Yellow Perch	89	181	6	-	-	-	-	-	276

DNR COMMENTS: Star Lake has no known water quality or pollution problems. It is known as a good all-around fishing lake. Walleye are a popular species, and natural reproduction is supplemented by biennial stocking. Good angling also is available for Northern Pike, Largemouth Bass, Black Crappie and Sunfish.

FISHING INFORMATION: Split Star Lake's 4,721 acres in half and set aside the northern portion for anglers. That's essentially what you have here. The lake has 9.7 miles of meandering shoreline, but so much of it is marsh that for many years the DNR called Star a carry-in lake. Overall Star has a median depth of 10 feet, but the northern portion, with holes up to 94 feet, a varied bottom structure and plenty of bays and inlets makes for an interesting outing for Walleyes which are stocked by the DNR and well as naturally reproduced. In the spring, you may want to try the far eastern shoreline around the inlet at the public access and an outlet in the shallows to the south. In the same area, just off the thin point coming in from the northwest, is a good early hangout for Walleyes and Crappies. As the water warms in the main lake, jig the steep dropoffs just north of the two islands, one at about mid lake and the other toward the western narrows. About 500 yards southeast of the latter is a sunken hump that reaches within 10 feet of the surface. This is a good spot, so jig the sharp drops at 15 to 20 feet. Some anglers head right for the west arm, through the narrows and the boat channel under County Road 41. There they find Bass and Crappies in the weedy far west, Northerns at the channel narrows and Walleyes in the deep weedbreaks of a hole about a half mile into the arm from the bridge. Some anglers happily spend all summer in the west arm and all winter as well.

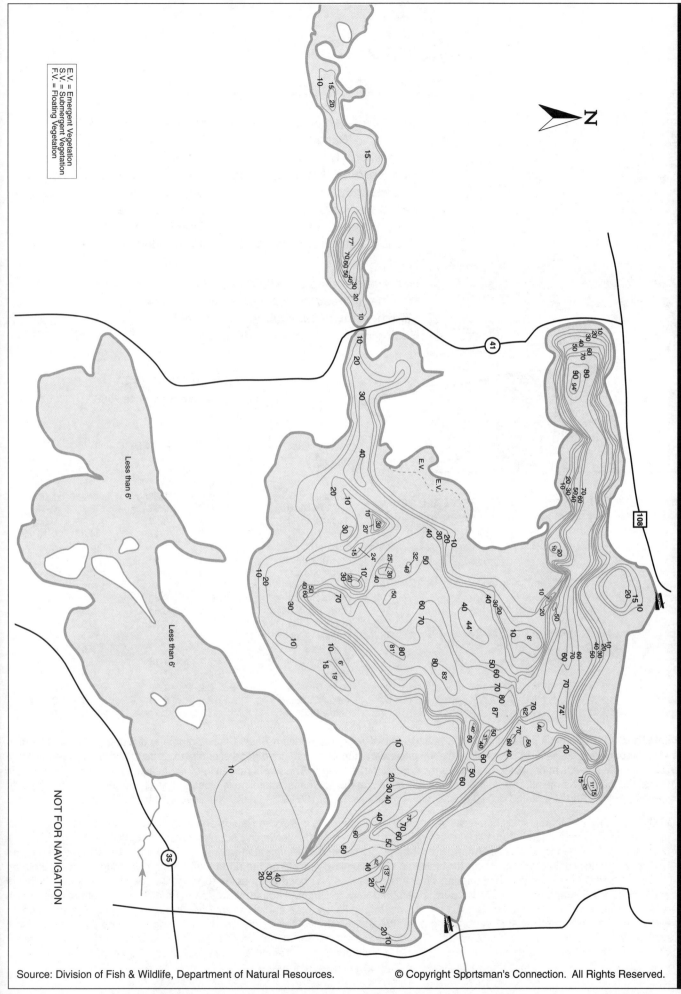

N

E.V. = Emergent Vegetation
S.V. = Submergent Vegetation
F.V. = Floating Vegetation

Less than 6'

Less than 6'

NOT FOR NAVIGATION

Source: Division of Fish & Wildlife, Department of Natural Resources.

DEAD LAKE
Otter Tail County

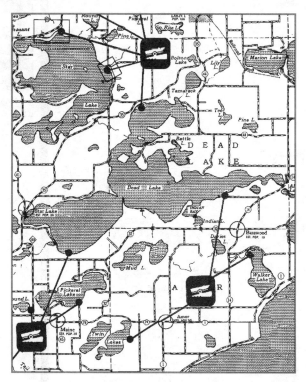

Location: Township 134, 135 Range 40, 41
Watershed: Otter Tail
Surface Water Area: 7,901 Acres
Shorelength: 36.3 Miles
Secchi disk (water clarity): 3.9 Ft.
Water color: Green
Cause of water color: Algae bloom

Maximum depth: 65 Ft.
Median depth: NA
Accessibility: Three state-owned public accesses: south shore of west arm; south shore of east arm and north shore
Boat Ramp: Concrete
Accommodations: Resorts and campground

Shoreland zoning classification: Natural Environment
Dominant forest/soil type: Deciduous/Loam
Management class: Walleye-Centrarchid
Ecological type: Centrarchid-Walleye

FISH STOCKING DATA
No record of stocking since 1988.

NET CATCH DATA

survey date: 8/11/97

species	Gill Nets # per net	Gill Nets avg fish wt. (lbs.)	Trap Nets # per set	Trap Nets avg fish wt. (lbs.)
Black Bullhead	2.7	0.95	0.2	0.44
Black Crappie	0.8	0.39	2.1	0.35
Bluegill	2.3	0.17	24.0	0.15
Bowfin (Dogfish)	-	-	0.1	4.38
Brown Bullhead	1.1	0.83	0.2	0.37
Common Carp	trace	0.74	0.2	12.80
Green Sunfish	-	-	trace	0.04
Hybrid Sunfish	0.3	0.30	0.4	0.14
Largemouth Bass	0.9	0.64	0.6	0.44
Northern Pike	7.1	1.00	0.9	0.74
Pumpkin. Sunfish	4.9	0.17	5.1	0.14
Rock Bass	-	-	0.6	0.22
Tullibee (Cisco)	0.7	1.15	-	-
Walleye	6.1	1.72	0.3	0.77
White Sucker	2.2	1.86	-	-
Yellow Bullhead	2.5	0.69	2.9	0.50
Yellow Perch	13.1	0.11	0.6	0.10

LENGTH OF SELECTED SPECIES SAMPLED FROM ALL GEAR
Number of fish caught for the following length categories (inches):

species	0-5	6-8	9-11	12-14	15-19	20-24	25-29	>30	Total
Black Bullhead	2	8	8	25	-	-	-	-	43
Black Crappie	3	21	20	-	-	-	-	-	44
Bluegill	202	140	-	-	-	-	-	-	342
Brown Bullhead	-	4	5	10	-	-	-	-	19
Green Sunfish	1	-	-	-	-	-	-	-	1
Hybrid Sunfish	3	7	-	-	-	-	-	-	10
Largemouth Bass	-	7	14	2	-	-	-	-	23
Northern Pike	-	-	29	31	34	17	1	2	114
Pumpkin. Sunfish	104	43	-	-	-	-	-	-	147
Rock Bass	8	-	1	-	-	-	-	-	9
Tullibee (Cisco)	-	2	-	4	4	-	-	-	10
Walleye	-	1	21	14	43	17	-	-	96
Yellow Bullhead	-	32	33	16	-	-	-	-	81
Yellow Perch	82	91	4	-	-	-	-	-	177

DNR COMMENTS: Dead Lake is best known for its excellent Walleye, Largemouth Bass, Black Crappie and Bluegill fishing. The data from the (1997) population assessment shows that these species are abundant and have good size distributions. The fish species present are able to sustain their levels at or above management goals without stocking. This is an indication of the quality fish habitat present. It is imperative that this habitat be maintained; therefore, Tombs Bay along the southeast shoreline is closed to angling from ice-out to June 30 each year for spawning. Partial winterkill occurs periodically – most recently in 1996-97 – in the lake's western basin.

FISHING INFORMATION: Dead Lake is northeast of Fergus Falls, closer still to Pelican Rapids and Dent, and just west of bigger, better-known Otter Tail Lake. Dead offers good Walleye fishing, with natural reproduction being supplemented with DNR stocking. Actually, Dead is two basins connected by a navigable narrows; it has plenty of good Walleye structure in spite of being fairly clouded with algae bloom. The upper (north) basin is your best bet for Walleyes. The two large points on the north side and the two long, narrow points on the south side are particularly good places for spring Walleyes. The lake has good deep holes (65-foot max depth) where the Walleyes will suspend on bright summer days. You'll have to fish deep then to reach them. Northern Pike roam the outer edges of the lake's copious weeds early in the season. Try slow-trolling the edges with bright, flashy lures and silver spoons. Weeds are where the Largemouth Bass are holed up, and you pretty well have to go right in after them with live bait or pork rinds on a bright-colored jig. As the water warms and weeds bloom and expand, you will want to switch to weedless or topwater lures. The south basin is maybe the best place for Bass, but there are good spots in the main lake too. The area around the Sunrise Resort at the far east end is highly regarded. The lake is loaded with Bluegills, most fairly small, but you'll find good Crappies in most of the weeds.

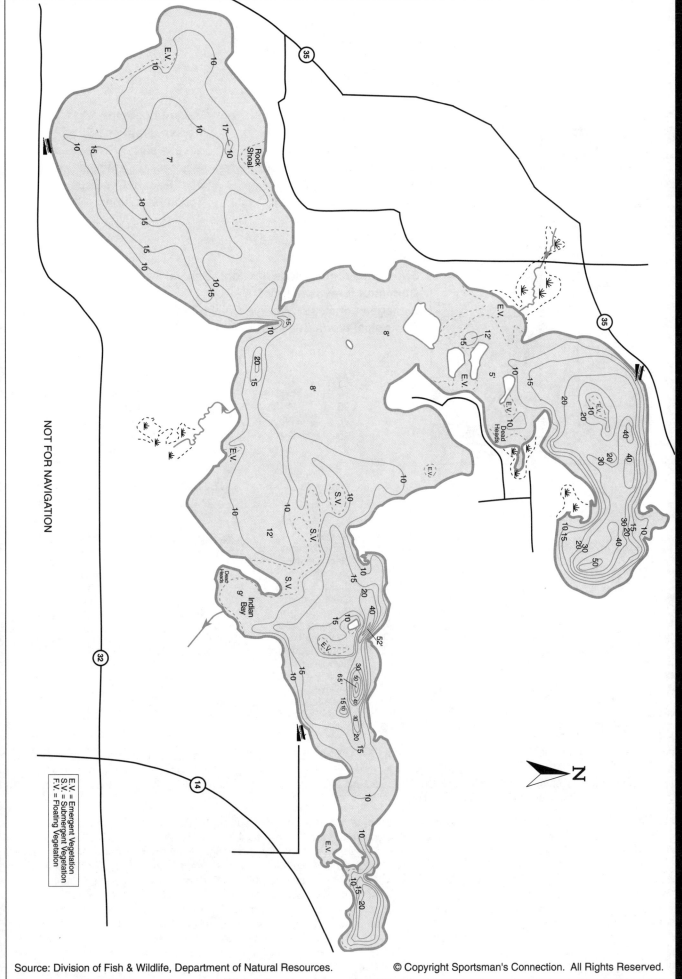

NOT FOR NAVIGATION

E.V. = Emergent Vegetation
S.V. = Submergent Vegetation
F.V. = Floating Vegetation

N

Rock Shoal

Dead Heads

Dead Heads

Indian Bay

Source: Division of Fish & Wildlife, Department of Natural Resources.

LAKE MARION
Otter Tail County

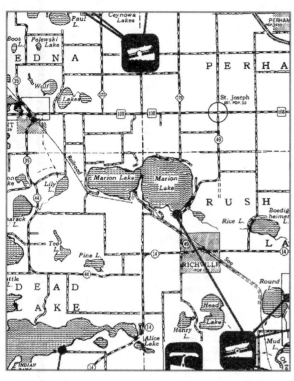

Location: Township 135
Range 39, 40
Watershed: Otter Tail
Surface Water Area: 1,664 Acres
Shorelength: 8.6 Miles
Secchi disk (water clarity): 15.0 Ft.
Water color: Greenish
Cause of water color: Algae bloom

Maximum depth: 60 Ft.
Median depth: 18 Ft.
Accessibility: State-owned public access on southeast corner
Boat Ramp: Concrete
Accommodations: Resort

Shoreland zoning classification: General Development
Dominant forest/soil type: NA
Management class: Walleye-Centrarchid
Ecological type: Centrarchid-Walleye

FISH STOCKING DATA

year	species	size	# released
90	Walleye	Fingerling	15,955
93	Walleye	Fingerling	34,567
95	Walleye	Fingerling	52,110
95	Walleye	Yearling	2,442
97	Walleye	Fingerling	32,652

NET CATCH DATA

survey date: 6/23/97

species	Gill Nets # per net	Gill Nets avg fish wt. (lbs.)	Trap Nets # per set	Trap Nets avg fish wt. (lbs.)
Black Bullhead	trace	1.48	-	-
Black Crappie	0.8	0.23	1.3	0.17
Bluegill	14.4	0.23	44.3	0.18
Brown Bullhead	-	-	0.2	1.16
Green Sunfish	-	-	1.0	0.04
Hybrid Sunfish	2.0	0.20	10.5	0.22
Largemouth Bass	1.2	0.89	6.2	0.26
Northern Pike	8.8	2.23	0.2	1.53
Pumpkin. Sunfish	0.8	0.23	9.2	0.16
Rock Bass	3.0	0.30	1.7	0.57
Tullibee (Cisco)	3.5	0.78	-	-
Walleye	4.6	2.22	0.3	3.26
White Sucker	1.4	2.72	-	-
Yellow Bullhead	6.3	0.80	11.8	0.80
Yellow Perch	72.3	0.14	1.6	0.17

LENGTH OF SELECTED SPECIES SAMPLED FROM ALL GEAR

Number of fish caught for the following length categories (inches):

species	0-5	6-8	9-11	12-14	15-19	20-24	25-29	>30	Total
Black Bullhead	-	-	-	1	-	-	-	-	1
Black Crappie	5	18	-	1	-	-	-	-	24
Bluegill	129	290	-	-	-	-	-	-	419
Brown Bullhead	-	-	1	-	1	-	-	-	2
Green Sunfish	11	-	-	-	-	-	-	-	11
Hybrid Sunfish	50	81	-	-	-	-	-	-	131
Largemouth Bass	3	61	6	4	2	-	-	-	76
Northern Pike	-	-	-	6	46	44	17	4	117
Pumpkin. Sunfish	60	51	-	-	-	-	-	-	111
Rock Bass	27	9	22	-	-	-	-	-	58
Tullibee (Cisco)	-	14	1	16	12	-	-	-	43
Walleye	-	-	5	2	40	15	1	-	63
Yellow Bullhead	1	5	145	47	1	-	-	-	199
Yellow Perch	107	404	14	-	-	-	-	-	525

DNR COMMENTS: Northern Pike abundant; 25 percent of Pike exceed 24 inches, and fish as large as 32 inches sampled in 1997 survey. Cisco numbers good. Walleye population stable and high; mean size 18.4 inches and 2.2 lb.; consistent natural reproduction supplemented by stocking. Largemouth Bass and Black Crappie numbers above normal due to strong 1995 year classes. Bluegill numbers high, with some larger fish present. Yellow Perch abundant.

FISHING INFORMATION: This lake had what it takes to be good gamefish water even before the DNR began an annual stocking program and developed a spawning reef to enhance natural Walleye reproduction. Now it's a fine year-around, all-around fishery of 1,664 acres with a shoreline of 8.6 miles. Marion is nearly split in two by Adam's Point. Each spring, anglers head for the western basin, a near-oval with a shoreline of broad weedy flats and bulrushes that drops at a gradual pace to 37 feet. In the weeds are Perch and Sunfish, and around them are Crappies, Largemouth Bass and lots of Northerns. Nobody who can fish reeds and weeds with light crankbaits and surface lures goes home empty handed. As the water warms, anglers work at 10 to 15 feet on both sides of Adam's Point for Walleyes and Crappies. Then they move to the southern shore of the eastern basin, especially around Cal's Point, to near the outlet to Rice Lake and to the east shore, casting spinners into the weedbreaks and jigging the 15- to 20-foot breaks with shiners, pork rind or leeches. They try the same technique on the deep breaks on the north shore and back over to the point again. And, along the way, they circle the a 60-foot hole, which is one of the best sources of Walleyes in the county. When the ice is in, anglers will fish the same route for a continuing supply of Crappies, Walleyes, panfish and, again, the occasional Northern.

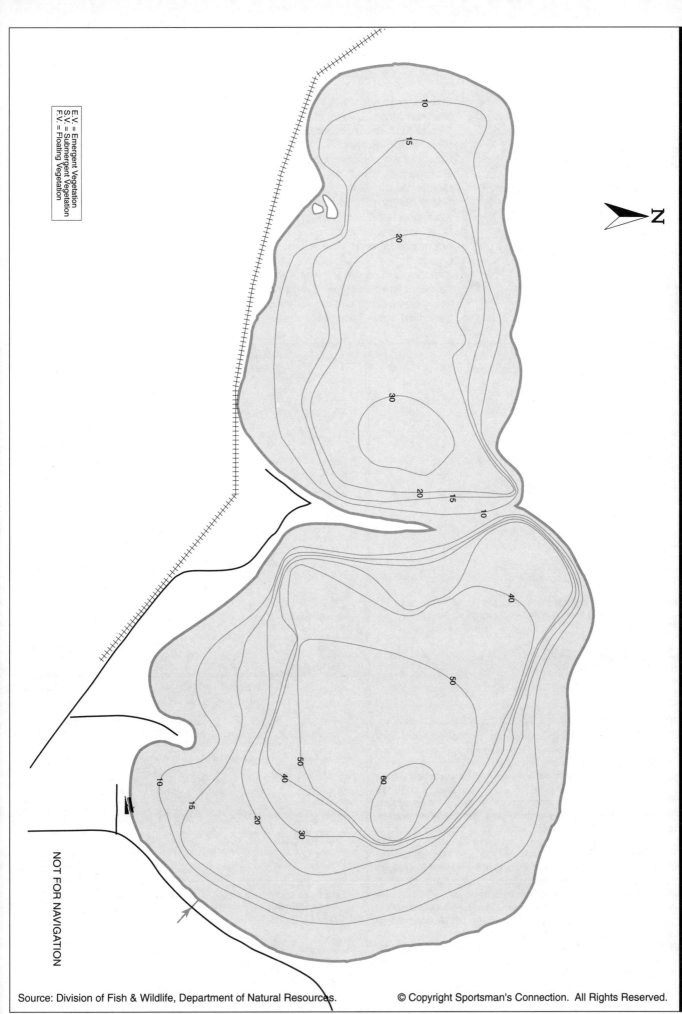

N

E.V. = Emergent Vegetation
S.V. = Submergent Vegetation
F.V. = Floating Vegetation

10
15
20
30
20
15
10
40
50
50
40
60
50
20
30
10
15

NOT FOR NAVIGATION

Location: Township 134, 135 Range 39, 40
Watershed: Otter Tail

WALKER LAKE   **BUCHANAN LAKE**   **ROUND LAKE**

Otter Tail County

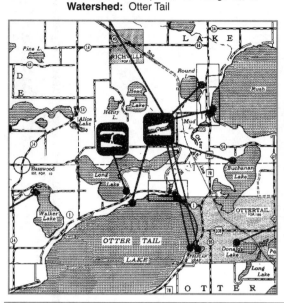

Size of lake: 540 Acres	929 Acres	262 Acres
Shorelength: 4.3 Miles	7.4 Miles	2.4 Miles
Secchi disk (water clarity): 5.5 Ft.	9.5 Ft.	9.0 Ft.
Water color: Brown	NA	Light green
Cause of water color: Bog stain	NA	Algae
Maximum depth: 29 Ft.	42 Ft.	36 Ft.
Median depth: NA	NA	NA
Accessibility: Public access on north-west shore, off County Road 14	Public access on northwest shore	Public access on east shore
Boat Ramp: Concrete	Concrete	Metal
Accommodations: Resort, campground	Resort	NA
Shoreland zoning classif.: Rec. Dev.	Gen. Dev.	Gen. Dev.
Dominant forest/soil type: Decid/Wet	Decid/Sand	Decid/Wet
Management class: Walleye-Centrarchid	Walleye-Centrarchid	Centrarchid
Ecological type: Centrarchid-Walleye	Centrarchid	Centrarchid

Walker Lake

DNR COMMENTS:
Northern Pike numbers down slightly to below expected range for lake class; average length 21 inches. Walleye numbers likewise down slightly but still within expected range; strong 1991 year class for this species. Black Crappie population within the expected range; consistent natural reproduction. Bluegill numbers up; size structure good, with 70 percent of sample at least 7 inches. Yellow Perch numbers up and above expected range; size structure poor, with only 4 percent of Perch reaching 8 inches.

FISH STOCKING DATA

year	species	size	# released
93	Walleye	Fry	2,055,000
94	Walleye	Fry	2,055,000
95	Walleye	Fry	2,100,000
96	Walleye	Fry	362,000
97	Walleye	Fry	342,000
98	Walleye	Fry	342,000

survey date: 8/22/94

NET CATCH DATA

	Gill Nets		Trap Nets	
species	# per net	avg fish wt. (lbs)	# per set	avg fish wt. (lbs)
Black Crappie	0.1	0.29	0.9	0.74
Bluegill	41.3	0.38	-	-
Hybrid Sunfish	-	-	0.6	0.69
Largemouth Bass	-	-	0.1	0.04
Northern Pike	1.9	1.93	0.7	1.07
Pumpkin. Sunfish	-	-	11.8	0.49
Tullibee (Cisco)	8.3	2.26	-	-
Walleye	3.6	0.99	0.3	2.24
Yellow Perch	94.9	0.12	5.4	0.14

LENGTH OF SELECTED SPECIES SAMPLED FROM ALL GEAR
Number of fish caught for the following length categories (inches):

species	0-5	6-8	9-11	12-14	15-19	20-24	25-29	>30	Total
Black Crappie	-	2	7	-	-	-	-	-	9
Bluegill	2	146	2	-	-	-	-	-	150
Hybrid Sunfish	-	5	-	-	-	-	-	-	5
Largemouth Bass	1	-	-	-	-	-	-	-	1
Northern Pike	-	-	-	3	9	10	1	-	23
Pumpkin. Sunfish	29	77	-	-	-	-	-	-	106
Tullibee (Cisco)	-	2	5	53	11	-	-	-	71
Walleye	-	-	3	21	10	-	1	-	35
Yellow Perch	175	191	1	-	-	-	-	-	367

Buchanan Lake

FISH STOCKING DATA

year	species	size	# released
90	Walleye	Fry	835,000
96	Walleye	Fry	837,000
98	Walleye	Fry	837,000

survey date: 7/6/95

NET CATCH DATA

	Gill Nets		Trap Nets	
species	# per net	avg fish wt. (lbs)	# per set	avg fish wt. (lbs)
Black Crappie	0.8	0.33	6.6	0.08
Bluegill	7.8	0.13	137.8	0.14
Hybrid Sunfish	0.8	0.33	1.7	0.31
Largemouth Bass	1.2	1.48	3.5	0.09
Northern Pike	12.8	1.56	0.4	1.41
Pumpkin. Sunfish	4.6	0.17	6.5	0.14
Walleye	5.7	2.84	1.3	5.04
Yellow Perch	10.8	0.17	0.1	0.20

LENGTH OF SELECTED SPECIES SAMPLED FROM ALL GEAR
Number of fish caught for the following length categories (inches):

species	0-5	6-8	9-11	12-14	15-19	20-24	25-29	>30	Total
Black Crappie	65	7	-	-	-	-	-	-	76
Bluegill	230	88	-	-	-	-	-	-	318
Hybrid Sunfish	2	20	-	-	-	-	-	-	22
Largemouth Bass	27	11	1	6	4	-	-	-	49
Northern Pike	-	1	4	33	58	44	11	1	152
Pumpkin. Sunfish	81	39	-	-	-	-	-	-	120
Walleye	-	-	2	2	36	30	11	-	81
Yellow Perch	15	67	4	-	-	-	-	-	86

DNR COMMENTS:
Northern Pike numbers up from 1991 level and above normal for lake class; avg. size 18.6 inches and 1.5 lb. Walleye numbers above normal; avg. size 19.8 inches and 2.8 lb.; natural reproduction occurring, but contribution to population appears limited. LM Bass population balanced. Black Crappie numbers normal; avg. length 7.4 inches at age 4. Bluegill numbers high; size structure poor. Yellow Perch numbers within normal range.

Round Lake

FISH STOCKING DATA

year	species	size	# released
97	Black Crappie	Adult	98
97	Bluegill	Adult	606
97	Largemouth Bass	Adult	20

survey date: 6/13/94

NET CATCH DATA

	Gill Nets		Trap Nets	
species	# per net	avg fish wt. (lbs)	# per set	avg fish wt. (lbs)
Black Crappie	1.0	0.45	0.4	0.65
Bluegill	2.0	0.16	129.1	0.17
Golden Shiner	-	-	0.1	0.08
Hybrid Sunfish	0.2	0.32	5.7	0.55
Largemouth Bass	-	-	0.1	2.06
Northern Pike	11.3	1.83	0.7	1.29
Pumpkin. Sunfish	0.3	0.19	8.8	0.47
Walleye	1.2	2.56	0.3	3.06
Yellow Perch	1.7	0.12		

LENGTH OF SELECTED SPECIES SAMPLED FROM ALL GEAR
Number of fish caught for the following length categories (inches):

species	0-5	6-8	9-11	12-14	15-19	20-24	25-29	>30	Total
Black Crappie	1	1	8	-	-	-	-	-	10
Bluegill	76	174	-	-	-	-	-	-	250
Hybrid Sunfish	11	41	-	-	-	-	-	-	52
Largemouth Bass	-	-	-	-	1	-	-	-	1
Northern Pike	-	-	1	34	33	6	-	-	74
Pumpkin. Sunfish	15	66	-	-	-	-	-	-	81
Walleye	-	-	-	5	5	-	-	-	10
Yellow Perch	5	5	-	-	-	-	-	-	10

DNR COMMENTS:
Walleye population stable and within range expected for lake class; reproduction limited; avg. length 20 inches. No. Pike numbers down considerably but above expected range; avg. length 21 inches. Black Crappie numbers stable and slightly below expected range; reproduction inconsistent. Bluegill population down but still above normal range; size structure improved. Yellow Perch population stable and at the lower end of expected range.

FISHING INFORMATION: Check tackle shops in Otter tail for current information on these lakes. Ask whether there was winterkill on Buchanan and whether the frogs are back on Round. If the report is good on Buchanan, then Walleyes and Northern Pike should be abundant. If the frogs are back, there's good late-year fishing on Round Lake. **Buchanan** has good structure for gamefish. In the spring, try casting the weedbeds along the northeast shore for Crappies and Bass. As the water warms, move out to 15 to 20 feet. A prime spot is off the long northern point in the lower lake, and there's another farther south around a 28-foot hole. Jig for Walleyes and Bass there or cast deep lures for Northerns. **Round Lake** is where you want to be in October when the frogs are trying to hibernate in the mud. Stay around the rushes at the southern end and jig nightcrawlers, shiners and frogs, moving out into deeper water until you locate Walleyes. In summer, locate the sunken island that rises to five feet just southeast of midlake and jig its sloping sides for Walleyes. **Walker**, meanwhile, is especially good the first month after Walleyes open. Try then around both the northern inlet and southern outlet areas just off the emergent reeds and weedbeds. Later, cast the weedbreaks in the marsh on the eastern shore for Largemouth and work the hole at the southeastern end for Crappie. Northerns turn up everywhere along the shoreline.

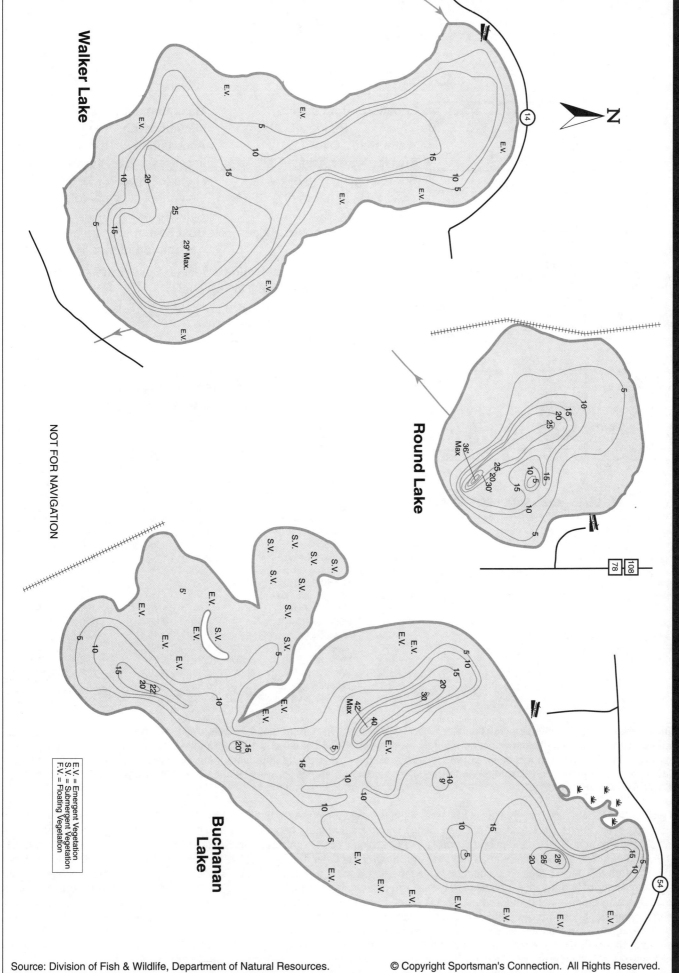

Walker Lake

29 Max.

Round Lake

36' Max

Buchanan Lake

42' Max

NOT FOR NAVIGATION

E.V. = Emergent Vegetation
S.V. = Submergent Vegetation
F.V. = Floating Vegetation

N

RUSH LAKE
Otter Tail County

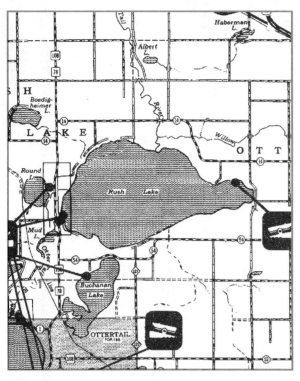

Location: Township 135
Range 38, 39
Watershed: Otter Tail
Surface Water Area: 5,337 Acres
Shorelength: 11.8 Miles
Secchi disk (water clarity): 3.5 Ft.
Water color: Green
Cause of water color: Algae
bloom

Maximum depth: 68 Ft.
Median depth: 10 Ft.
Accessibility: Two state-owned accesses-one on the southwest shore (off Hwy. 78), and one on the northeast corner (off County Road 14)
Boat Ramp: Concrete (both)
Accommodations: Resorts

Shoreland zoning classification: General Development
Dominant forest/soil type: No Tree/Wet
Management class: Walleye-Centrarchid
Ecological type: Centrarchid-Walleye

FISH STOCKING DATA
No record of stocking since 1988.

NET CATCH DATA

survey date: 8/21/95

	Gill Nets		Trap Nets	
species	# per net	avg fish wt. (lbs.)	# per set	avg fish wt. (lbs.)
Black Bullhead	trace	0.90	0.4	0.64
Black Crappie	0.9	0.64	trace	0.04
Bluegill	trace	0.25	14.6	0.24
Brown Bullhead	trace	1.12	0.2	0.65
Common Carp	-	-	1.1	9.43
Hybrid Sunfish	-	-	0.1	0.42
Largemouth Bass	-	-	1.2	0.07
Northern Pike	4.4	1.75	0.1	0.89
Pumpkin. Sunfish	1.4	0.26	3.0	0.23
Rock Bass	0.3	0.49	0.7	0.44
Tullibee (Cisco)	31.5	0.88	-	-
Walleye	13.2	1.03	0.8	1.93
White Sucker	6.4	0.78	11.6	2.14
Yellow Bullhead	0.8	1.08	1.8	0.92
Yellow Perch	21.0	0.13	3.1	0.11

LENGTH OF SELECTED SPECIES SAMPLED FROM ALL GEAR
Number of fish caught for the following length categories (inches):

species	0-5	6-8	9-11	12-14	15-19	20-24	25-29	>30	Total
Black Bullhead	-	1	5	1	-	-	-	-	7
Black Crappie	4	-	8	2	-	-	-	-	14
Bluegill	31	161	-	-	-	-	-	-	192
Brown Bullhead	-	-	2	2	-	-	-	-	4
Hybrid Sunfish	-	2	-	-	-	-	-	-	2
Largemouth Bass	14	1	-	-	-	-	-	-	15
Northern Pike	-	-	-	4	35	28	-	1	68
Pumpkin. Sunfish	11	52	-	-	-	-	-	-	63
Rock Bass	2	7	4	-	-	-	-	-	13
Tullibee (Cisco)	-	14	66	105	8	-	-	-	193
Walleye	-	3	46	47	105	8	-	-	209
Yellow Bullhead	-	-	19	16	-	-	-	-	35
Yellow Perch	73	191	6	-	-	-	-	-	270

DNR COMMENTS: Cisco numbers up substantially since 1992 and above normal range for lake class; mean size 12.3 inches and .8 lb. Northern Pike numbers up slightly and within normal range; mean size 19.6 inches and 1.7 lb. Healthy Largemouth Bass population with good size structure. Bluegill numbers down but within normal range; size structure improved at 48 percent of Bluegills exceeding 7 inches. Yellow perch numbers down but within normal range; size structure improved, with 12 percent of fish exceeding 8 inches; average length is 7.3 inches at age 5.

FISHING INFORMATION: Like many lakes in the area, Rush is fished for Walleyes but, for some, the lake's high point is reached before Walleye season even begins. In March, as soon as the ice is out, local anglers begin talking about the taste of the big, cold-water Crappies, Sunfish and Perch at Rush. One-pound Bluegills and Crappies twice that size are not uncommon. You'll find many of the boats in the western end of the lake along the edge of the shallows, around the Otter Tail River outlet and working the humps and dips scattered throughout the area at 10 to 15 feet. The common fishing method is to tip a jig with night crawler or a shiner under a slip bobber. There will be another cluster of boats early in the season in the far eastern flats for crappies, but the western end becomes a clear favorite later on because it is also a prime hangout for Walleyes. Rush is a broad 5,340-acre lake with a shoreline of 11.8 miles, and come summer you'll need to seek out the numerous sunken islands, humps and dropoffs to holes that range from 20 to 68 feet if you want to find fish. You are going to need a depthfinder for certain. Rush is a murky lake with water clarity of 3.5 fee. That means bright colors and spinners will better your chances. For summertime, the northern shore, off the shallows out from the Otter Tail River inlet, has been a steady source of Walleyes and Northern Pike. Fish the weedbeds carefully with shallow-running lures or leeches and light lines.

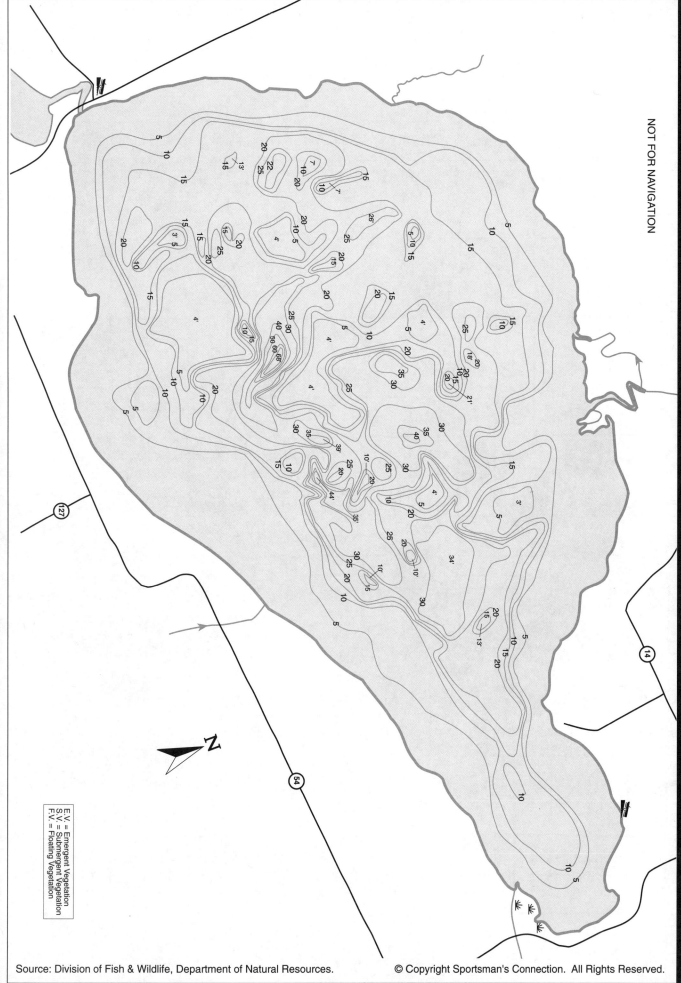

E.V. = Emergent Vegetation
S.V. = Submergent Vegetation
F.V. = Floating Vegetation

Source: Division of Fish & Wildlife, Department of Natural Resources.

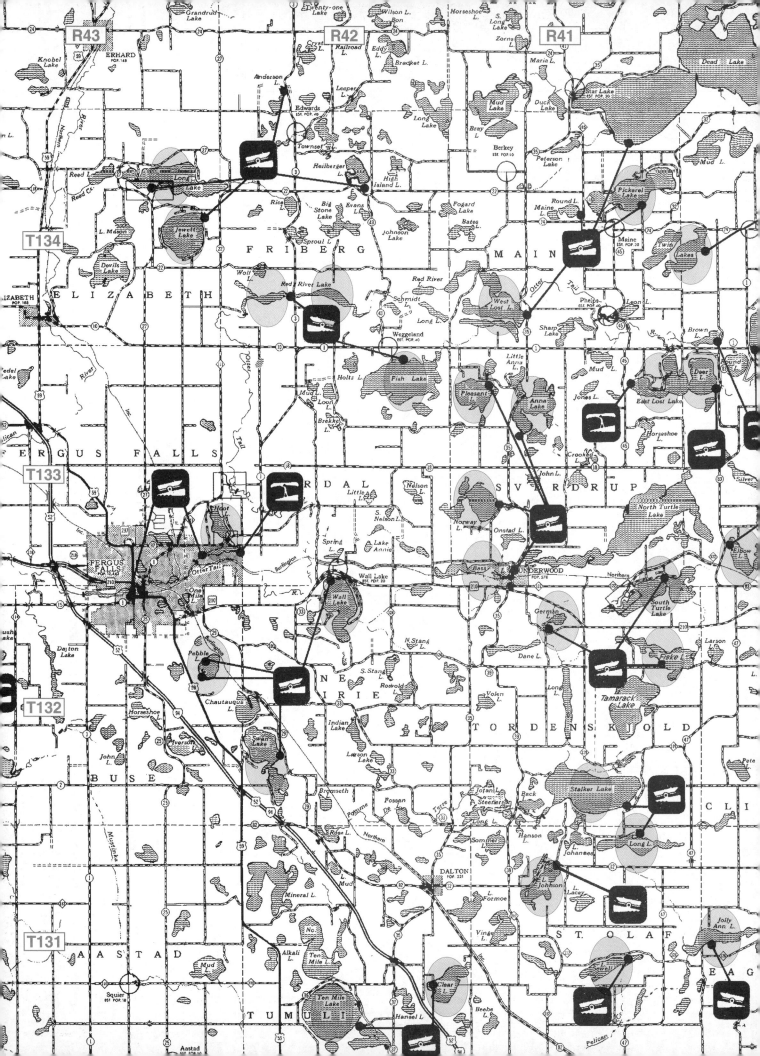

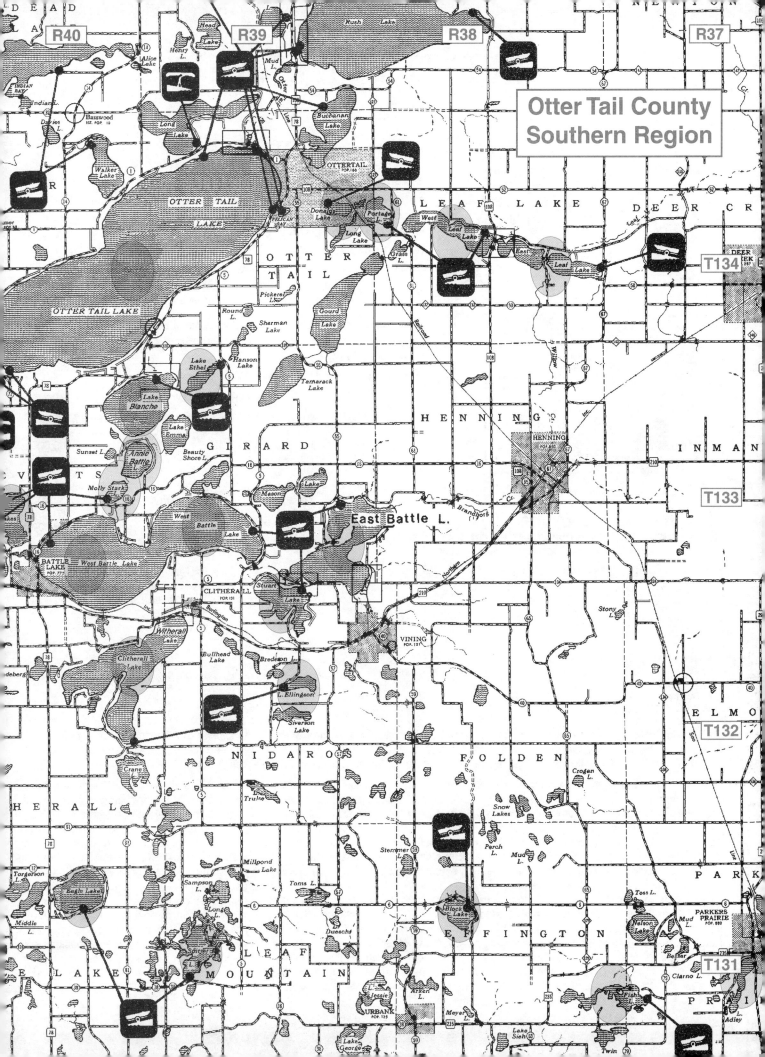

Otter Tail County
Southern Region

OTTER TAIL LAKE
Otter Tail County

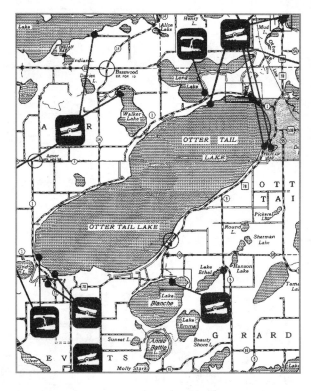

Location: Township 133, 134 Range 39, 40
Watershed: Otter Tail
Surface Water Area: 13,725 Acres
Shorelength: 21.7 Miles
Secchi disk (water clarity): 8.0 Ft.
Water color: Light green
Cause of water color: Algae

Maximum depth: 124 Ft.
Median depth: NA
Accessibility & Boat Ramp:
State-owned public access on-
- east shore (concrete) off #78
- west shore (concrete) off #72
- north shore (concrete) off #1
- also one carry-down access
Accommodations: Resorts; campground

Shoreland zoning classification: General Development
Dominant forest/soil type: Deciduous/Sand
Management class: Walleye
Ecological type: Hard-Water Walleye

FISH STOCKING DATA

year	species	size	# released
93	Walleye	Fry	14,854,000
94	Walleye	Fry	6,000,000
94	Northern Pike	Adult	12,329
95	Walleye	Fry	8,092,000
96	Walleye	Fry	5,422,000
97	Walleye	Fry	1,732,000
97	Walleye	Unknown	280,000
98	Walleye	Fry	4,448,000

LENGTH OF SELECTED SPECIES SAMPLED FROM ALL GEAR
Number of fish caught for the following length categories (inches):

species	0-5	6-8	9-11	12-14	15-19	20-24	25-29	>30	Total
Black Bullhead	-	-	-	4	-	-	-	-	4
Black Crappie	-	1	-	-	-	-	-	-	1
Bluegill	-	1	-	-	-	-	-	-	1
Brown Bullhead	-	-	1	17	-	-	-	-	18
Northern Pike	-	-	-	1	70	21	4	3	99
Pumpkin. Sunfish	1	-	-	-	-	-	-	-	1
Rock Bass	2	6	33	-	-	-	-	-	41
Tullibee (Cisco)	-	24	107	12	-	-	-	-	143
Walleye	1	59	77	75	27	7	1	-	247
Yellow Bullhead	-	-	1	6	-	-	-	-	7
Yellow Perch	56	350	69	-	-	-	-	-	475

NET CATCH DATA

survey date: 9/5/95

species	Gill Nets # per net	Gill Nets avg fish wt. (lbs.)	Trap Nets # per set	Trap Nets avg fish wt. (lbs.)
Black Crappie	trace	0.14	-	-
Bluegill	trace	0.20	-	-
Burbot	trace	2.31	-	-
Northern Pike	5.0	1.90	-	-
Pumpkin. Sunfish	trace	0.15	-	-
Rock Bass	2.1	0.85	-	-
Tullibee (Cisco)	10.1	0.47	-	-
Walleye	12.4	0.64	-	-
Yellow Perch	50.6	0.21	-	-

DNR COMMENTS: Northern Pike numbers up and above normal range; average size 19.8 inches and 2 lb. Rock Bass population like-wise above normal range; average size 9.9 inches and .9 lb. Walleye numbers down, but within normal range; average size 11.7 inches and .9 lb.; natural reproduction occurring. Yellow Perch numbers down; average size 7.5 inches.

FISHING INFORMATION: To many anglers in central Minnesota, Otter Tail Lake and Walleyes are synonymous. The reason for the close comparison is that the big lake seems to have been designed by nature as near-perfect habitat for the popular gamefish. Here's what the lake offers: a bottom that is almost all sand, interspersed with rubble; excellent sand bars; small humps rising from deeper water; a huge number of Yellow Perch (which are one of the Walleyes favorite foods), and deep holes where Walleyes can suspend on bright, summer days. Spring Walleye will be found in shallower water around bars such as those in the south end, the hump and sharp dropoffs at mid lake, the sunken island near the north shore at the middle of the lake, the steep breaks just off the flats along the southeast shore and the outlet to the Otter Tail River in the southeast corner. You are other good areas, but these are good spots to start. Use leeches, shiners, or fathead minnows on a bottom rig, bumping along the bottom slowly in front of the Walleyes until you feel that soft hit. By mid June (earlier if the weather is very warm), the marble eyes will head for deeper water and suspend in schools to avoid bright sun-light. At night, however, expect them back at the dropoffs and bars for feeding. Northern Pike are abundant and can be hooked with a lit-tle strategy. The flats just beyond the weedlines are the best place to find to find them. They cruise these areas on the lookout for Yellow Perch that emerge from the weeds, especially cabbage and other broad leafs. Jigs tipped with minnows, spoons or small bucktail spin-ners can all be productive. It's always a good idea to check bait shops for the latest information on what's working. Meanwhile, don't overlook the panfish. Crappies and 'gills are scarce, but there are plenty of Perch and Rock Bass. Look for them in the weeds early in the season. They'll be be attracted by worms or small minnows on a bare hook or jig.

NOT FOR NAVIGATION

Walker Lake

Pelican Bay

Detailed view of lake
appears on following pages

N

E.V. = Emergent Vegetation
S.V. = Submergent Vegetation
F.V. = Floating Vegetation

Source: Division of Fish & Wildlife, Department of Natural Resources.

SPORTSMAN'S connection®

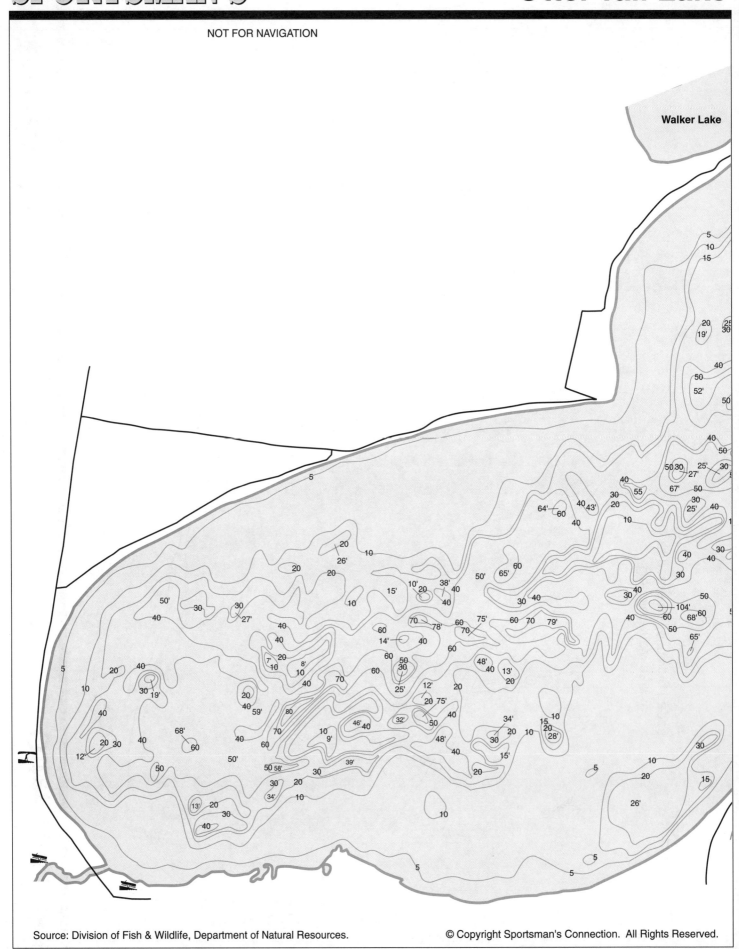

Walker Lake

Source: Division of Fish & Wildlife, Department of Natural Resources.

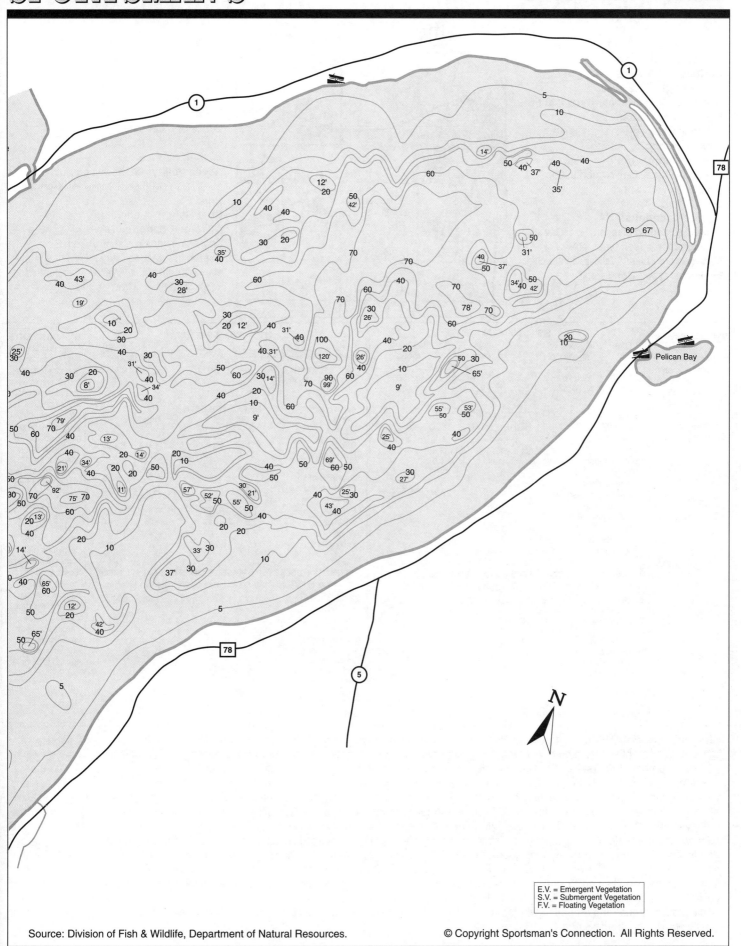

Pelican Bay

E.V. = Emergent Vegetation
S.V. = Submergent Vegetation
F.V. = Floating Vegetation

Source: Division of Fish & Wildlife, Department of Natural Resources.

DONALDS LAKE   PORTAGE LAKE
Otter Tail County

Location: Township 134 Range 3
Watershed: Redeye
Surface Water Area: 168 Acres
Shorelength: 2.2 Miles
Secchi disk (water clarity): 11.0 Ft.
Water color: Green
Cause of water color: Light algae
Maximum depth: 43 Ft.
Median depth: 18 Ft.
Accessibility: City-owned public access on west shore
Boat Ramp: Concrete
Accommodations: NA
Shoreland zoning classif.: Rec. Dev.
Dominant forest/soil type: NA
Management class: Walleye-Centrarchid
Ecological type: Centrarchid

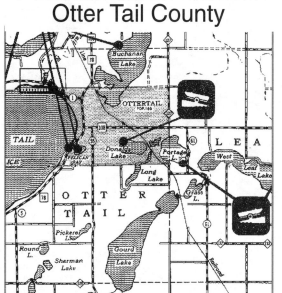

Location: Township 134 Range 38, 39
Watershed: Redeye
Surface Water Area: 265 Acres
Shorelength: 2.6 Miles
Secchi disk (water clarity): 16.0 Ft.
Water color: Light green
Cause of water color: Algae
Maximum depth: 49 Ft.
Median depth: 10 Ft.
Accessibility: State-owned public access on southeast shore, off County Road 61
Boat Ramp: Concrete
Accommodations: NA
Shoreland zoning classif.: Gen. Dev.
Dominant forest/soil type: Decid/Sand
Management class: Walleye-Centrarchid
Ecological type: Centrarchid

DNR COMMENTS:
Lake is fished for many species, including Northern Pike, Largemouth Bass, and Walleye. The most popular species are Black Crappie and Bluegill.

FISH STOCKING DATA

year	species	size	# released
93	Walleye	Fingerling	6,500
94	Walleye	Fingerling	3,270
96	Walleye	Fingerling	3,255
97	Walleye	Fingerling	1,800

survey date: 7/14/97

NET CATCH DATA

	Gill Nets		Trap Nets	
species	# per net	avg fish wt. (lbs)	# per set	avg fish wt. (lbs)
Black Crappie	1.5	0.34	1.9	0.45
Bluegill	-	-	73.7	0.12
Hybrid Sunfish	-	-	0.1	0.31
Largemouth Bass	-	-	0.1	0.11
Northern Pike	7.3	1.68	0.4	3.09
Pumpkin. Sunfish	-	-	2.3	0.16
Walleye	2.3	1.38	-	-
White Sucker	1.3	2.68	-	-
Yellow Perch	20.2	0.09	0.7	0.06

LENGTH OF SELECTED SPECIES SAMPLED FROM ALL GEAR
Number of fish caught for the following length categories (inches):

species	0-5	6-8	9-11	12-14	15-19	20-24	25-29	>30	Total
Black Bullhead	-	-	-	2	1	-	-	-	3
Black Crappie	1	14	5	2	-	-	-	-	22
Bluegill	135	21	-	-	-	-	-	-	156
Brown Bullhead	-	1	1	9	-	-	-	-	11
Hybrid Sunfish	-	1	-	-	-	-	-	-	1
Largemouth Bass	1	-	-	-	-	-	-	-	1
Northern Pike	-	-	-	1	23	16	2	1	43
Pumpkin. Sunfish	10	6	-	-	-	-	-	-	16
Walleye	-	-	3	3	4	2	-	-	12
Yellow Bullhead	-	34	106	130	-	-	-	-	270
Yellow Perch	30	10	-	-	-	-	-	-	40

FISH STOCKING DATA

year	species	size	# released
93	Walleye	Fry	153,000
95	Walleye	Fry	148,000
97	Walleye	Fry	148,000

survey date: 8/14/95

NET CATCH DATA

	Gill Nets		Trap Nets	
species	# per net	avg fish wt. (lbs)	# per set	avg fish wt. (lbs)
Black Crappie	0.3	0.99	0.2	0.92
Bluegill	7.5	0.17	73.7	0.17
Hybrid Sunfish	-	-	0.6	0.33
Largemouth Bass	1.2	1.44	0.4	0.35
Northern Pike	0.5	4.41	-	-
Pumpkin. Sunfish	1.0	0.22	0.8	0.31
Walleye	13.8	1.33	1.3	1.54
White Sucker	5.7	1.00	-	-
Yellow Perch	14.7	0.14	-	-

LENGTH OF SELECTED SPECIES SAMPLED FROM ALL GEAR
Number of fish caught for the following length categories (inches):

species	0-5	6-8	9-11	12-14	15-19	20-24	25-29	>30	Total
Black Bullhead	-	-	-	2	-	-	-	-	2
Black Crappie	-	-	2	2	-	-	-	-	4
Bluegill	97	139	-	-	-	-	-	-	236
Brown Bullhead	-	-	-	1	-	-	-	-	1
Hybrid Sunfish	-	5	-	-	-	-	-	-	5
Largemouth Bass	-	2	4	5	-	-	-	-	11
Northern Pike	-	-	-	-	-	1	1	1	3
Pumpkin. Sunfish	3	10	-	-	-	-	-	-	13
Walleye	-	1	28	27	25	11	1	-	93
Yellow Bullhead	-	-	65	66	1	-	-	-	132
Yellow Perch	2	53	1	-	-	-	-	-	56

DNR COMMENTS:
Northern Pike numbers up but below normal range for lake class; average size excellent at 27 inches and 4.4 lb. Walleye population well above normal range; abundant 1993 year class; average size 15 inches and 1.6 lb.; natural reproduction occurring. largemouth Bass numbers high; average length only 8.5 inches. Black Crappies numerous; average length good at 11.9 inches. Bluegill numbers normal; average length 6.1 inches. Yellow Perch population up but within normal range; Average length 7 inches.

FISHING INFORMATION: Northwest of Henning and southwest of New York Mills, these two smaller lakes offer some good fishing without a lot of competition from other anglers. **Donalds Lake** has good numbers of Northern Pike, panfish and Largemouth Bass as well as a decent number of Walleyes. The flats outside the weedline on both the north and south shores are where you'll find prowling Northerns. There aren't many Yellow Perch, Northerns' favorite food, so you may want to offer them a nice shiner minnow or leech. The Bass and panfish are in the same weeds waiting for worms, smaller minnows or pork rinds to come their way on a colorful jig. A good spot on Donald for early season Walleyes is the small 6-foot hump towards the northwest side which drops quickly to 20 feet. It's the sort of place Walleyes love to feed. Later, they'll head into deep water along with the larger panfish, but return after sundown. The west side of the lake, where the bottom drops quickly can also be productive. **Portage Lake** is just east of Donalds. It holds good numbers of Largemouth and Bluegills, along with very good numbers of Walleyes. Northerns are available, too. Though numbers aren't much for this species, average size is over 4 pounds – well worth the effort. The water is very clear in Portage and there's a fairly good weedline. The shallow and weed-filled north side of the lake is a good spot for Bass and panfish, as is the area below the access point in the southeast corner. Northerns are fairly well distributed in the lake. Troll the outer edges of the weeds with live bait to attract them. Early season Walleyes are around the dropoffs at the east and west sides of the lake. Later, they head for the depths at mid-lake, an area you can troll slowly starting at about 15 feet.

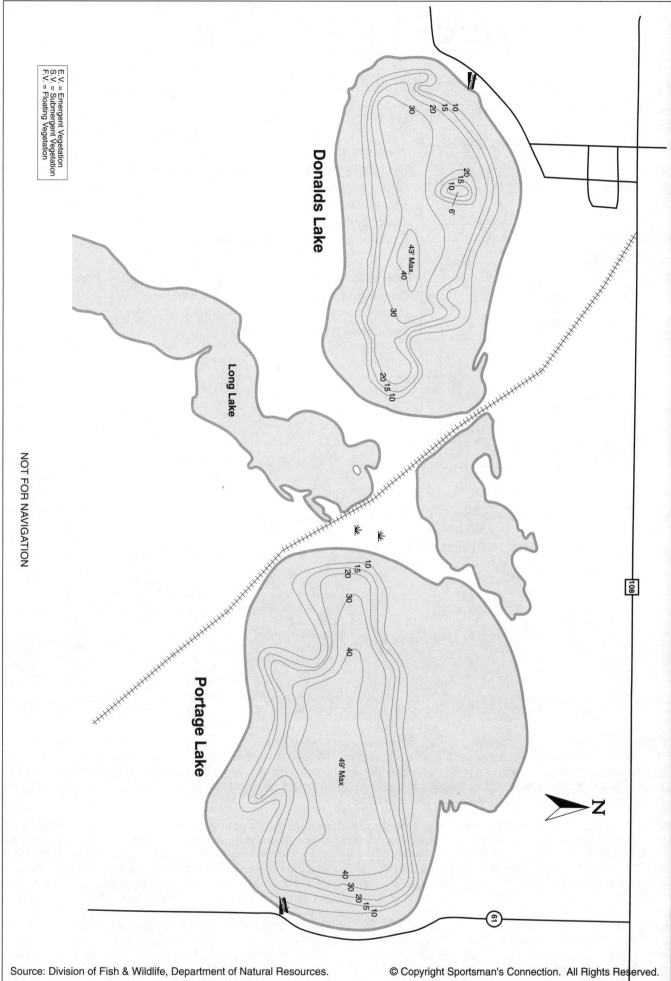

Donalds Lake

Long Lake

Portage Lake

E.V. = Emergent Vegetation
S.V. = Submergent Vegetation
F.V. = Floating Vegetation

NOT FOR NAVIGATION

N

43' Max.

49' Max

108

61

WEST LEAF LAKE
Otter Tail County

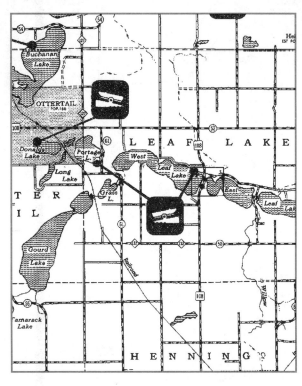

Location: Township 134 Range 3
Watershed: Otter Tail
Surface Water Area: 404 Acres
Shorelength: 6.5 Miles
Secchi disk (water clarity): 5.0 Ft.
Water color: Light green
Cause of water color: Algae bloom

Maximum depth: 55 Ft.
Median depth: 21 Ft.
Accessibility: State-owned public access on east shore, on Township Rd. off Hwy. 108
Boat Ramp: Concrete
Accommodations: NA

Shoreland zoning classification: Recreational Development
Dominant forest/soil type: Deciduous/Sand
Management class: Walleye-Centrarchid
Ecological type: Centrarchid

FISH STOCKING DATA

year	species	size	# released
90	Walleye	FIngerling	621
94	Walleye	Fingerling	10.470
96	Walleye	Fingerling	7,384

NET CATCH DATA

survey date: 7/18/94

species	Gill Nets # per net	Gill Nets avg fish wt. (lbs.)	Trap Nets # per set	Trap Nets avg fish wt. (lbs.)
Black Bullhead	12.3	1.25	0.8	1.33
Black Crappie	0.4	0.68	0.3	0.37
Bluegill	3.8	0.23	22.5	0.31
Bowfin (Dogfish)	0.3	8.88	0.7	12.38
Brown Bullhead	2.8	1.43	0.5	1.20
Common Carp	0.6	11.72	trace	8.82
Hybrid Sunfish	trace	0.33	-	-
Largemouth Bass	0.6	0.69	1.3	0.41
Northern Pike	9.1	1.55	0.5	1.06
Pumpkin. Sunfish	0.7	0.44	2.4	0.26
Rock Bass	0.2	0.75	trace	0.50
Tullibee (Cisco)	2.1	0.93	-	-
Walleye	9.2	2.06	trace	0.39
White Sucker	1.1	4.99	0.5	5.27
Yellow Bullhead	13.1	1.40	2.6	1.40
Yellow Perch	3.0	0.11	0.6	0.17

LENGTH OF SELECTED SPECIES SAMPLED FROM ALL GEAR
Number of fish caught for the following length categories (inches):

species	0-5	6-8	9-11	12-14	15-19	20-24	25-29	>30	Total
Black Bullhead	-	10	143	5	-	-	-	-	158
Black Crappie	-	2	5	1	-	-	-	-	8
Bluegill	118	87	-	-	-	-	-	-	205
Brown Bullhead	-	3	31	6	-	-	-	-	40
Hybrid Sunfish	-	1	-	-	-	-	-	-	1
Largemouth Bass	3	13	4	2	1	-	-	-	23
Northern Pike	-	1	1	13	69	25	3	1	113
Pumpkin. Sunfish	20	15	-	-	-	-	-	-	35
Rock Bass	-	3	-	-	-	-	-	-	3
Tullibee (Cisco)	2	3	13	1	2	-	-	-	21
Walleye	-	1	24	4	54	23	3	-	109
Yellow Bullhead	1	6	158	20	1	-	-	-	186
Yellow Perch	20	11	2	-	-	-	-	-	33

DNR COMMENTS: Northern Pike numbers up, but still within the normal range for lake class; size structure unchanged, with only 4 percent of Pike reaching 24 inches; good spawning areas for this species. Walleye numbers above normal range; average size 17.2 inches and 2.1 lb.; natural reproduction contributing to the population. Bluegill numbers down to within normal range for lake class; 10 percent of Bluegills reaching 7 inches. Largemouth Bass population balanced; good natural reproduction. Yellow Perch numbers up but still below normal for lake class; 9 percent of Perch reaching at least 8 inches.

FISHING INFORMATION: West Leaf is an enjoyable family lake because of its classic scenery, easy to read structure and good supply of gamefish and, especially, panfish. This slender lake with 6.5 miles of shoreline lies amid hills and marshes. There are fairly wide shelves with a depth of about 10 feet at either end. And both the north and south banks drop away sharply to holes of 40 to 55 feet. In the spring, try the weedbeds on the northwest shore and in the southwest corner, especially around the Bollands Creek inlet. Cast into the weedbreaks with surface lures for Largemouth Bass, and jig the edges of the weeds for Crappies. The inlet is also a prime early Northern Pike location. The 10-foot drop bordering the shelf at the eastern end of the lake also offers good spring fishing. As the water warms, try three other locations. For Walleyes, jig the sharp drop off at 15 to 20 feet all around the point that reaches out from the north shore at mid-lake. Use shiners, nightcrawlers and, later in the summer, leeches. About 500 feet southeast from the tip of that point, then, you'll find a hump rising from 40 feet to 9 feet. Though water clarity in West Leaf is about 5 feet, the vegetation on top of the hump is often visible. Thus you won't have much trouble spotting this Walleye haven. Jig the northern side of the hump, gradually going deeper until you find fish. Lastly, troll or, with a favorable wind, drift the northern shoreline about 25 to 50 feet out with Lindy rigs.

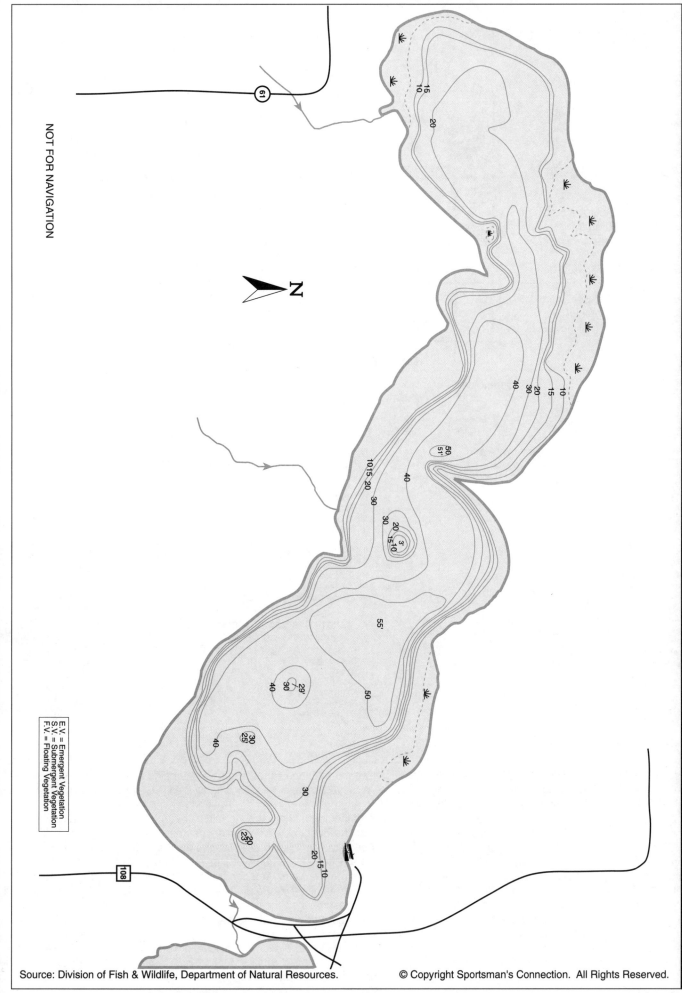

NOT FOR NAVIGATION

N

E.V. = Emergent Vegetation
S.V. = Submergent Vegetation
F.V. = Floating Vegetation

61

108

SPORTSMAN'S Connection

EAST LEAF LAKE   MIDDLE LEAF LAKE
Otter Tail County

Location: Township 134 Range 3
Watershed: Otter Tail
Surface Water Area: 398 Acres
Shorelength: 4.1 Miles
Secchi disk (water clarity): 11.0 Ft.
Water color: Light green
Cause of water color: Light algae
Maximum depth: 47 Ft.
Median depth: NA
Accessibility: Public access on northeast shore, off Cty. Road 67
Boat Ramp: Concrete
Accommodations: NA
Shoreland zoning classif.: Rec. Dev.
Dominant forest/soil type: Decid/Loam
Management class: Walleye-Centrarchid
Ecological type: Centrarchid

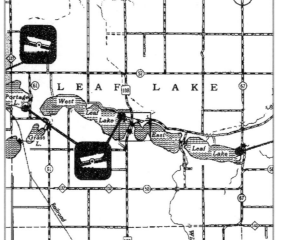

Location: Township 134 Range 3
Watershed: Otter Tail
Surface Water Area: 398 Acres
Shorelength: NA
Secchi disk (water clarity): 8.0 Ft.
Water color: NA
Cause of water color: NA
Maximum depth: 43 Ft.
Median depth: NA
Accessibility: State-owned public access on northwest shore, off Hwy. 108
Boat Ramp: Gravel
Accommodations: NA
Shoreland zoning classif.: Rec. Dev.
Dominant forest/soil type: Decid/Loam
Management class: Walleye-Centrarchid
Ecological type: Centrarchid

DNR COMMENTS:
Walleye numbers within normal range for lake class; mean length only 10 inches; natural reproduction inconsistent. Northern Pike numbers down to lower end of normal range; mean length 18.2 inches. Largemouth Bass numbers below average. Black Crappie numbers slightly below normal. Bluegill numbers down significantly. Yellow Perch numbers down but within normal range.

FISH STOCKING DATA

year	species	size	# released
90	Walleye	Yearling	828
94	Walleye	Fingerling	4,317
96	Walleye	Fingerling	3,220

survey date: 8/1/94

NET CATCH DATA

	Gill Nets		Trap Nets	
		avg fish		avg fish
species	# per net	wt. (lbs)	# per set	wt. (lbs)
Black Crappie	-	-	0.3	0.46
Bluegill	-	-	9.3	0.22
Hybrid Sunfish	-	-	0.1	0.26
Largemouth Bass	0.1	1.22	0.1	1.34
Northern Pike	3.4	1.50	0.6	1.33
Pumpkin. Sunfish	-	-	3.6	0.17
Rock Bass	-	-	0.4	0.45
Tullibee (Cisco)	0.4	1.41	-	-
Walleye	2.1	0.39	0.4	2.66
Yellow Perch	16.6	0.13	1.3	0.16

LENGTH OF SELECTED SPECIES SAMPLED FROM ALL GEAR
Number of fish caught for the following length categories (inches):

species	0-5	6-8	9-11	12-14	15-19	20-24	25-29	>30	Total
Black Crappie	-	-	3	-	-	-	-	-	3
Bluegill	17	67	-	-	-	-	-	-	84
Hybrid Sunfish	-	1	-	-	-	-	-	-	1
Largemouth Bass	-	-	-	2	-	-	-	-	2
Northern Pike	-	-	-	4	21	10	-	1	36
Pumpkin. Sunfish	20	12	-	-	-	-	-	-	32
Rock Bass	-	3	1	-	-	-	-	-	4
Tullibee (Cisco)	-	1	-	1	1	1	-	-	4
Walleye	-	9	8	2	2	2	-	-	23
Yellow Perch	44	110	5	-	-	-	-	-	159

FISH STOCKING DATA

year	species	size	# released
94	Walleye	Fingerling	7,339
96	Walleye	Fingerling	5,210

survey date: 7/25/94

NET CATCH DATA

	Gill Nets		Trap Nets	
		avg fish		avg fish
species	# per net	wt. (lbs)	# per set	wt. (lbs)
Black Crappie	0.6	0.53	-	-
Bluegill	6.8	0.17	30.1	0.10
Hybrid Sunfish	0.7	0.18	0.3	0.13
Largemouth Bass	0.6	1.10	0.1	0.91
Northern Pike	10.4	1.47	0.9	1.69
Pumpkin. Sunfish	1.6	0.14	2.9	0.09
Rock Bass	-	-	0.3	0.29
Tullibee (Cisco)	0.2	3.39	-	-
Walleye	2.9	1.23	-	-
Yellow Perch	2.1	0.14	1.1	0.36

LENGTH OF SELECTED SPECIES SAMPLED FROM ALL GEAR
Number of fish caught for the following length categories (inches):

species	0-5	6-8	9-11	12-14	15-19	20-24	25-29	>30	Total
Black Crappie	-	3	2	-	-	-	-	-	5
Bluegill	196	62	1	-	-	-	-	-	259
Hybrid Sunfish	4	4	-	-	-	-	-	-	8
Largemouth Bass	-	-	2	4	-	-	-	-	6
Northern Pike	-	-	2	18	56	16	4	3	99
Pumpkin. Sunfish	28	6	-	-	-	-	-	-	34
Rock Bass	-	2	-	-	-	-	-	-	2
Tullibee (Cisco)	-	2	-	-	-	-	-	-	2
Walleye	-	4	10	1	7	2	1	-	25
Yellow Perch	6	20	1	-	-	-	-	-	27

DNR COMMENTS:
Northern Pike abundance declined from last survey to within normal range. Mean length sampled was 18.2 inches. Bluegill abundance within normal ranges and has not fluctuated since last survey, although size has declined. Largemouth Bass numbers normal; mean length 12.5 inches. Yellow Perch numbers below normal. Walleye abundance did not change since 1989 survey and is within normal range for this lake type. Mean length of Walleyes sampled was 13.9 inches. Natural repro. and stocking maintaining numbers of this species.

FISHING INFORMATION: These smaller lakes in the drift hills of western Minnesota offer some outstanding fishing for Walleyes, Northern Pike and panfish.   **East Leaf** tends to have average or above Walleye fishing due to stocking by the DNR. And it holds good populations of Northern Pike and Largemouth Bass in its 400 acres. Veteran anglers tell us of several good spring Walleye spots. One is the breaks along the southeast shore. Another is the 8-foot hump just off the south shore around mid lake, and then there's the 9-foot hump near the northwest corner. Later in the season, as the water warms, the goggle eyes will be deeper, especially around the 47-foot hole near the middle of the lake. The west shore of the lake, near the channel into Middle Leaf, also is an excellent place much of the year and can be fished from shore with good results. The entry to the Leaf River along the north side is a good spot for Northerns; so is the east side of the lake, near the bulrushes and wild rice and the flats just to the west. You can troll the areas with spinnerbaits, spoons or live bait with good results. The east end of the lake can also produce some nice-size Bass. The water is fairly clear, and you can do well using pork rinds on a jig; topwater and weedless lures are usually necessary when the water warms and the vegetation expands. Unfortunately, the channel doesn't allow boats to move between the lakes, but **Middle Leaf** is worth the effort of transferring via the access area at the east end. Middle Leaf is best known for big Northerns and hordes of panfish, though you'll find some Walleyes and Bass, as well. Mosquito Point, on the south side, and Bellman's Point, on the north, are two excellent places to start your fishing for Walleyes and Northerns. The northwest corner close to the public access area, too, holds good Bass and panskis. Probably the best Northern Pike fishing area is way down at the southeast side, where you should fish just outside the bulrushes.

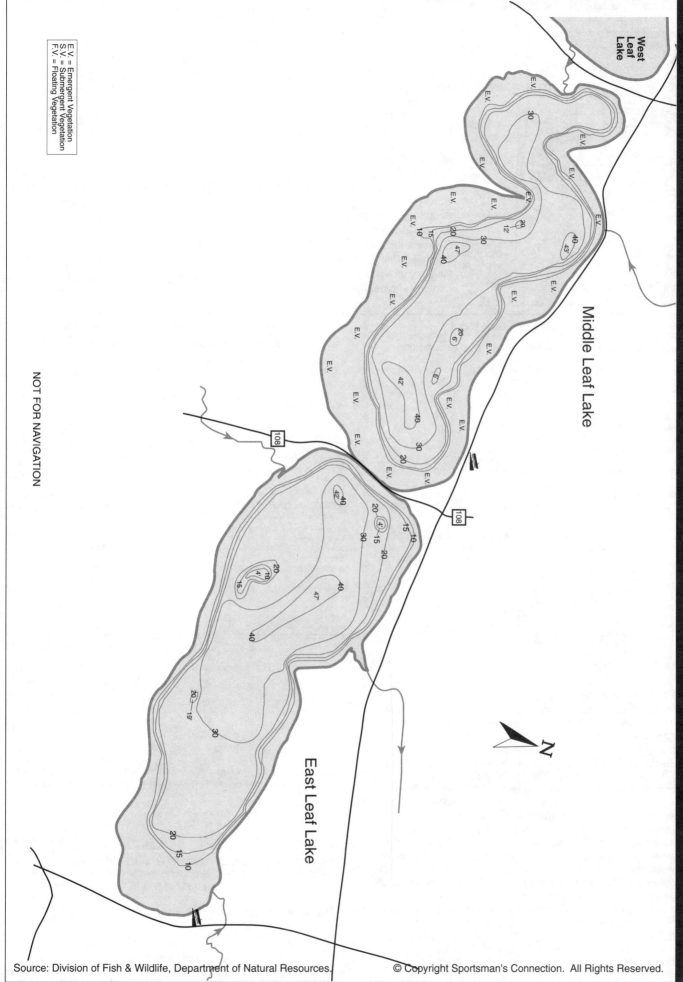

West Leaf Lake

Middle Leaf Lake

East Leaf Lake

E.V. = Emergent Vegetation
S.V. = Submergent Vegetation
F.V. = Floating Vegetation

NOT FOR NAVIGATION

N

108

108

Location: Township 133 Range 39, 40
Watershed: Otter Tail

MOLLY STARK LAKE   ANNIE BATTLE LAKE   ETHEL LAKE

Otter Tail County

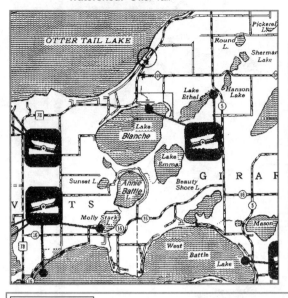

	MOLLY STARK	ANNIE BATTLE	ETHEL
Size of lake:	153 Acres	334 Acres	194 Acres
Shorelength:	1.9 Miles	NA	3.2 Miles
Secchi disk (water clarity):	16.0 Ft.	12.5 Ft.	23.0 Ft.
Water color:	Clear	Clear	Clear
Cause of water color:	NA	NA	NA
Maximum depth:	48 Ft.	51 Ft.	64 Ft.
Median depth:	NA	NA	NA
Accessibility:	State-owned public access on west shore, in Glendalough State Park	Public access on south shore in park	Public access on east shore, off Cty. Hwy. 5
Boat Ramp:	Concrete	Concrete	Concrete
Accommodations:	NA	NA	NA
Shoreland zoning classif.:	Rec. Dev.	Rec. Dev.	Rec. Dev.
Dominant forest/soil type:	Decid/Sand	Decid/Sand	Decid/Sand
Management class:	Centrarchid	Centrarchid	Walleye-Centrarchid
Ecological type:	Centrarchid	Centrarchid	Centrarchid

DNR COMMENTS:
Northern Pike numbers down but still within expected range for lake class; average size 17 inches and 1.3 lb.; growth slow. Walleye numbers likewise down but within expected range; mean size 19.7 inches and 2.6 lb.; natural reproduction appears variable. largemouth Population stable and high. Black Crappie numbers within the expected range; average length 7.4 inch Bluegills numbers down; growth slow, and only 7 percent of sampled fish had reached 7 inches.

Molly Stark Lake

FISH STOCKING DATA: NO RECORD OF STOCKING

NET CATCH DATA

survey date: 8/19/96

	Gill Nets		Trap Nets	
species	# per net	avg fish wt. (lbs)	# per set	avg fish wt. (lbs)
Black Crappie	0.5	0.30	0.9	0.21
Bluegill	11.2	0.12	18.1	0.15
Hybrid Sunfish	0.3	0.35	1.5	0.23
Largemouth Bass	2.2	0.61	0.1	0.26
Northern Pike	9.0	1.29	0.6	0.75
Pumpkin. Sunfish	4.2	0.26	1.9	0.18
Rock Bass	-	-	0.8	0.28
Tullibee (Cisco)	3.7	0.68	-	-
Walleye	1.7	2.62	0.3	4.93
Yellow Perch	4.0	0.23		

LENGTH OF SELECTED SPECIES SAMPLED FROM ALL GEAR
Number of fish caught for the following length categories (inches):

species	0-5	6-8	9-11	12-14	15-19	20-24	25-29	>30	Total
Black Crappie	-	9	1	-	-	-	-	-	10
Bluegill	109	65	-	-	-	-	-	-	174
Hybrid Sunfish	4	10	-	-	-	-	-	-	14
Largemouth Bass	-	6	6	1	1	-	-	-	14
Northern Pike	-	-	5	21	17	11	1	2	57
Pumpkin. Sunfish	10	30	-	-	-	-	-	-	40
Rock Bass	2	4	-	-	-	-	-	-	6
Tullibee (Cisco)	-	2	11	4	5	-	-	-	22
Walleye	-	-	-	-	6	4	2	-	12
Yellow Bullhead	-	5	26	6	-	-	-	-	37
Yellow Perch	-	18	4	-	-	-	-	-	22

Annie Battle Lake

FISH STOCKING DATA: NO RECORD OF STOCKING

NET CATCH DATA

survey date: 8/12/96

	Gill Nets		Trap Nets	
species	# per net	avg fish wt. (lbs)	# per set	avg fish wt. (lbs)
Black Crappie	1.6	0.70	0.2	0.60
Bluegill	5.8	0.27	16.0	0.26
Hybrid Sunfish	0.1	0.49	2.1	0.36
Largemouth Bass	3.3	1.06	0.6	0.55
Northern Pike	5.9	1.27	0.6	1.71
Pumpkin. Sunfish	1.6	0.33	1.7	0.27
Rock Bass	0.1	0.54	0.7	0.59
Walleye	1.9	2.27	0.2	4.79
Yellow Perch	1.8	0.31	0.3	0.21

LENGTH OF SELECTED SPECIES SAMPLED FROM ALL GEAR
Number of fish caught for the following length categories (inches):

species	0-5	6-8	9-11	12-14	15-19	20-24	25-29	>30	Total
Black Crappie	2	3	5	6	-	-	-	-	16
Bluegill	29	136	1	-	-	-	-	-	166
Hybrid Sunfish	2	18	-	-	-	-	-	-	20
Largemouth Bass	2	7	5	21	-	-	-	-	35
Northern Pike	-	-	3	25	12	11	6	1	58
Pumpkin. Sunfish	6	23	-	-	-	-	-	-	29
Rock Bass	-	2	5	-	-	-	-	-	7
Walleye	-	-	3	6	9	1	-	-	19
Yellow Bullhead	-	-	14	23	-	-	-	-	37
Yellow Perch	-	10	5	-	-	-	-	-	15

DNR COMMENTS:
No motors or electronics allowed. Experimental regulations in effect; check regs before fishing. Walleye numbers down but within normal range; average size 18.8 inches and 2.3 lb. Northern Pike numbers up; average size 17.5 inches and 1.3 lb.; growth slow. Largemouth Bass numbers high; average size 12.1 inches and 1.1 lb. Black Crappie numbers within expected range; good average size of 10.1 inches and .7 lb.

Ethel Lake

FISH STOCKING DATA

year	species	size	# released
94	Walleye	Fingerling	2,307
95	Walleye	Fry	69,000
97	Walleye	Fingerling	1,803
98	Walleye	Fry	69,000

NET CATCH DATA

survey date: 6/21/93

	Gill Nets		Trap Nets	
species	# per net	avg fish wt. (lbs)	# per set	avg fish wt. (lbs)
Bluegill	2.2	0.10	106.2	0.16
Green Sunfish	-	-	0.4	0.05
Hybrid Sunfish	1.7	0.12	13.2	0.15
Largemouth Bass	0.2	2.43	5.0	0.39
Northern Pike	2.8	3.37	-	-
Walleye	2.3	1.89	-	-
Yellow Perch	63.3	0.13	0.3	0.17

LENGTH OF SELECTED SPECIES SAMPLED FROM ALL GEAR
Number of fish caught for the following length categories (inches):

species	0-5	6-8	9-11	12-14	15-19	20-24	25-29	>30	Total
Bluegill	139	154	1	-	-	-	-	-	294
Green Sunfish	4	-	-	-	-	-	-	-	4
Hybrid Sunfish	67	50	-	-	-	-	-	-	117
Largemouth Bass	2	21	21	1	1	-	-	-	46
Northern Pike	-	-	-	-	9	7	1	-	17
Pumpkin. Sunfish	85	43	-	-	-	-	-	-	128
Walleye	-	-	-	2	10	2	-	-	14
Yellow Bullhead	1	94	199	8	-	-	-	-	302

DNR COMMENTS:
Northern Pike numbers normal for lake class; size good, with all sampled individuals' being larger than 21 inches. Walleye numbers about average for lake class; majority of fish are 16 to 19 inches; natural reproduction is supplemented by stocking. Largemouth Bass and Bluegill numbers very high, but fish are small; 91 percent of sampled Bass were less than 12 inches, and 97 percent of Bluegills were less than 7.1 inches.

FISHING INFORMATION: Ethel has a fair number of both Northern Pike and Largemouth Bass. There are also some Walleye, though fewer than are found in most other area lakes. The Bass patrol along the south and southwest sides, where there are bulrushes and well-defined weedlines. Toss pig-and-jig combos or plastic worms at them. early, or topwater gear later in the season. Fish the outer edges of the weedlines with live bait to attract Northerns. Or, troll spoons slowly parallel to the weedlines. You will find some Walleyes, planted as fingerlings by the DNR, at the quick dropoffs. Offer them minnows early, then switch to leeches. Located immediately south of Ethel, **Molly Stark** holds decent numbers of Northerns, Largemouth and panfish. The Bass and Crappies haunt the weeds at the north end and along the southwest shore. A pig-and-jig will attract Bass in the weeds following their spawn, and Crappies can be tempted by small minnows. Northerns will be cruising the outer edges of the weeds. Your best bet for larger panfish and Walleyes after the first of July is at the deeper waters of mid lake. In **Annie Battle**, look for Walleyes around the two mid-lake bars; jig/minnow combinations worked parallel to the weedlines should get good action. Also fish marble eyes at the steeply dropping inside turns on the northwest and southwest, off the lake's inlet and outlet. You'll find Bass and Northerns along the north and east shores.

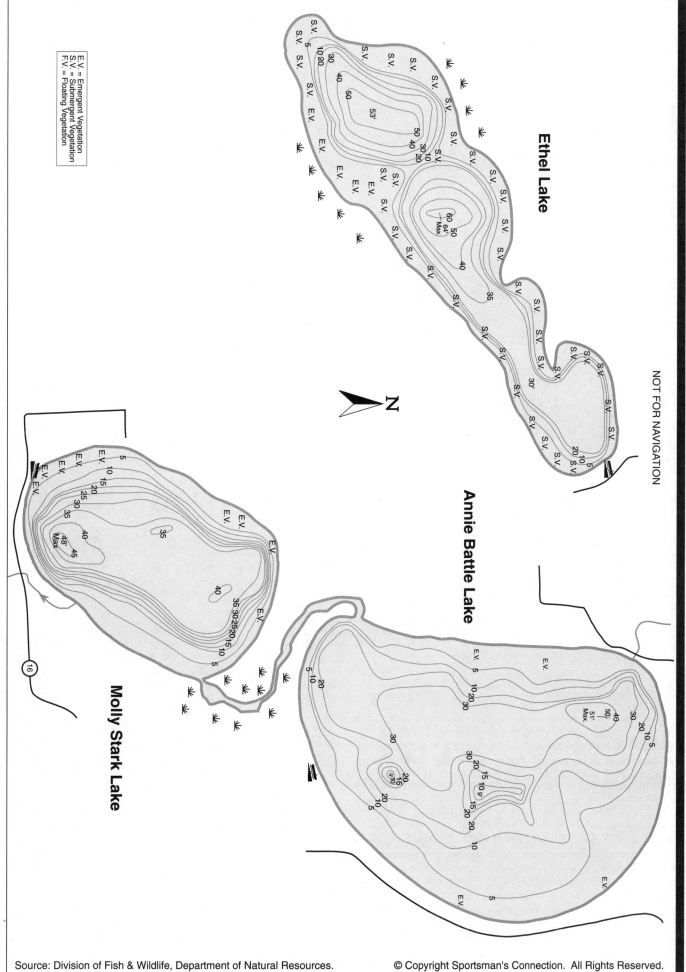

LAKE BLANCHE
Otter Tail County

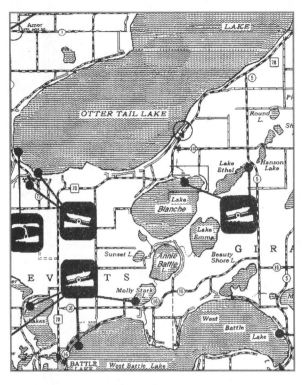

Location: Township 133 Range 39, 40
Watershed: Otter Tail
Surface Water Area: 1,268 Acres
Shorelength: 1.9 Miles
Secchi disk (water clarity): 7.0 Ft.
Water color: Green
Cause of water color: Algae

Maximum depth: 64 Ft.
Median depth: 12 Ft.
Accessibility: State-owned public access on north shore, off Hwy. 78
Boat Ramp: Concrete
Accommodations: Resort and campground

Shoreland zoning classification: Recreational Development
Dominant forest/soil type: Deciduous/Sand
Management class: Walleye-Centrarchid
Ecological type: Centrarchid

FISH STOCKING DATA

year	species	size	# released
93	Walleye	Fry	1,002,000
95	Walleye	Fry	1,002,000
97	Walleye	Fry	1,002,000

NET CATCH DATA

survey date: 7/17/95

	Gill Nets		Trap Nets	
species	# per net	avg fish wt. (lbs.)	# per set	avg fish wt. (lbs.)
Black Bullhead	0.8	1.34	trace	1.04
Black Crappie	0.2	0.78	0.2	0.45
Bluegill	4.4	0.22	57.1	0.15
Bowfin (Dogfish)	-	-	0.2	7.05
Brown Bullhead	0.3	1.42	0.2	0.84
Common Carp	0.2	2.74	-	-
Hybrid Sunfish	trace	0.28	0.5	0.29
Largemouth Bass	0.9	0.75	1.2	0.33
Northern Pike	6.2	1.07	0.6	0.72
Pumpkin. Sunfish	3.8	0.25	2.8	0.24
Rock Bass	0.2	0.57	0.4	0.51
Tullibee (Cisco)	0.9	1.02	-	-
Walleye	4.7	1.30	1.0	1.35
White Sucker	1.2	2.18	0.2	3.66
Yellow Bullhead	3.0	0.73	4.4	0.79
Yellow Perch	2.1	0.19	0.2	0.06

LENGTH OF SELECTED SPECIES SAMPLED FROM ALL GEAR

Number of fish caught for the following length categories (inches):

species	0-5	6-8	9-11	12-14	15-19	20-24	25-29	>30	Total
Black Bullhead	-	-	1	10	-	-	-	-	11
Black Crappie	-	1	3	-	-	-	-	-	4
Bluegill	147	205	-	-	-	-	-	-	352
Brown Bullhead	-	-	1	5	-	-	-	-	6
Hybrid Sunfish	1	6	-	-	-	-	-	-	7
Largemouth Bass	8	4	9	4	-	-	-	-	25
Northern Pike	-	-	2	22	49	4	3	1	81
Pumpkin. Sunfish	11	69	-	-	-	-	-	-	80
Rock Bass	1	2	4	-	-	-	-	-	7
Tullibee (Cisco)	-	2	1	6	2	-	-	-	11
Walleye	-	4	3	12	44	3	-	-	66
Yellow Bullhead	-	1	72	15	1	-	-	-	89
Yellow Perch	6	15	4	-	-	-	-	-	25

DNR COMMENTS: Walleye numbers up slightly and within normal range for lake class; average size 15.8 inches and 1.3 lb.; some natural reproduction occurring. Northern Pike population down slightly but still within normal range; average size 16.8 inches and 1.1 lb.; only 5 percent of Pike sampled had reached 24 inches. Largemouth Bass numbers up and within normal range; average length only 7.5 inches. Black Crappie numbers down and below normal range; average length 9.4 inches. Yellow Perch population below normal range; average length 7.5 inches.

FISHING INFORMATION: Located close to Fergus Falls, Blanche is a fine lake for Northern Pike, panfish, Largemouth Bass and Walleyes. The Walleyes have been stocked during alternate years, and there is evidence of reproduction. The lake itself is easy to read. Shorelines are shallow, with abundant weedlines, and large flats stretch from there out to mid lake where the water deepens quickly to 50 feet. Look for early season Walleyes at the fast dropping breaks. There are good ones in the small bay at the east end. Also use the mid-lake breaks on both the north and south sides of the deep holes. Use a minnow on a bottom rig, working the bait upwards along the bottom where Walleye feed in the spring. In summer, the marble eyes will be deep in the holes, and you can troll east to west and back effectively. The Northern Pike are on the flats at the outside edges of weedlines, where they prey on the lake's ample supply of forage fish. The wide south and west flats are your best bets. Look for schools of small forage fish, estimate their depth and direction; Northerns won't be far behind. The weeds, meanwhile, are home to Largemouth Bass, and the emerging vegetation ranging from the northeast corner south to the west side is productive in June. You will want to try your whole arsenal of bass lures and baits, including jigs tipped with worms, small minnows or pork rinds. As the vegetation blooms you'll want to go to your tackle box for weedless lures, spinnerbaits and topwater lures. Panfish start in the weeds early in the season. You can do well then with worms and minnows. By the end of June, the panskis will be suspended in deeper water near the lake's center, where bobber fishing is effective.

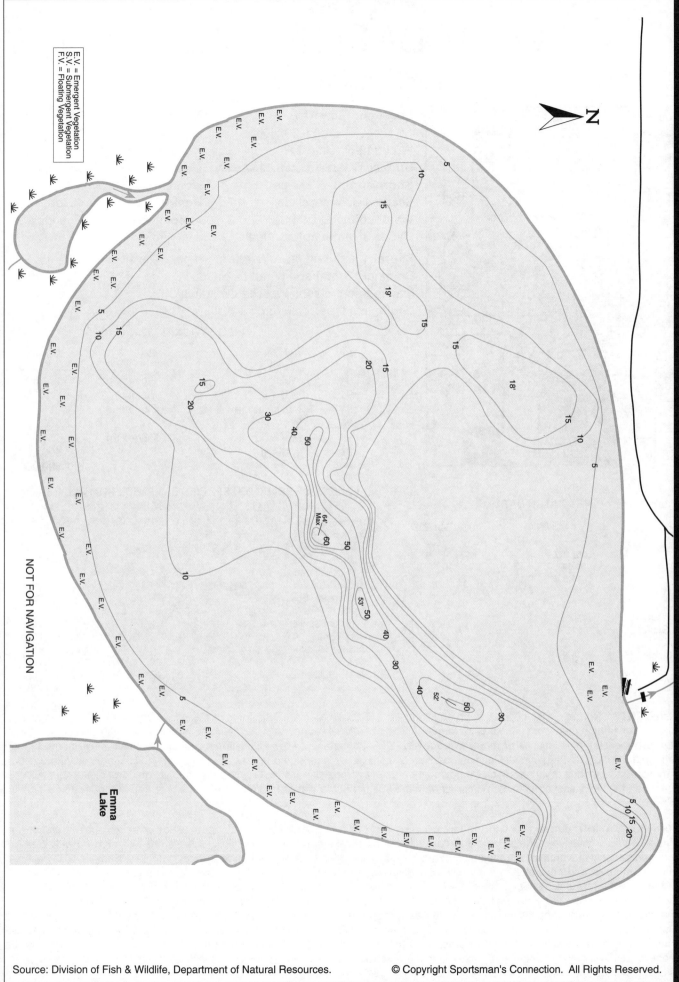

Lake Blanche

N

NOT FOR NAVIGATION

E.V. = Emergent Vegetation
S.V. = Submergent Vegetation
F.V. = Floating Vegetation

Emma
Lake

5
10
15

10

15

19'

15

15

20

15

18'

15

10

5

15

10

5

20

15

10

15

30

40

50

64'
Max.

60

50

53'
50

40

30

40

52

50

30

10

5

5
10
15
20

E.V.

WEST BATTLE LAKE
Otter Tail County

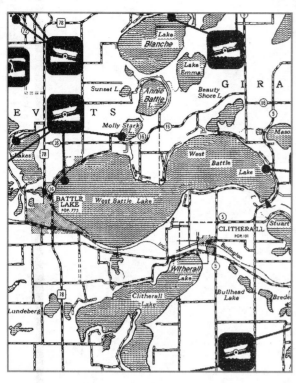

Location: Township 132, 133 Range 39, 40

Watershed: Otter Tail

Surface Water Area: 5,624 Acres

Shorelength: 5.9 Miles

Secchi disk (water clarity): 11.0 Ft.

Water color: Light green

Cause of water color: Algae

Maximum depth: 108 Ft.

Median depth: 20 Ft.

Accessibility: Access on east shore, off County Road 5 and west shore, off County Road 16

Boat Ramp: Concrete (both)

Accommodations: Resorts and campground

Shoreland zoning classification: General Development

Dominant forest/soil type: Deciduous/Sand

Management class: Walleye-Centrarchid

Ecological type: Centrarchid-Walleye

FISH STOCKING DATA

year	species	size	# released
94	Walleye	Fry	2,496,000
94	Walleye	Fingerling	41,525
94	Walleye	Yearling	399
94	Muskellunge	Fingerling	1,898
96	Walleye	Fry	7,500,000
96	Muskellunge	Fingerling	1,248
97	Walleye	Fry	7,500,000
98	Walleye	Fry	7,500,000

NET CATCH DATA

survey date: 7/10/95

species	Gill Nets # per net	Gill Nets avg fish wt. (lbs.)	Trap Nets # per set	Trap Nets avg fish wt. (lbs.)
Black Crappie	trace	0.23	1.2	0.19
Bluegill	11.0	0.15	188.9	0.20
Hybrid Sunfish	1.6	0.21	6.0	0.21
Largemouth Bass	0.4	0.56	7.2	0.17
Northern Pike	10.6	1.82	0.3	1.33
Pumpkin. Sunfish	1.6	0.25	6.0	0.24
Rock Bass	5.7	0.49	1.5	0.36
Tullibee (Cisco)	4.2	0.25	-	-
Walleye	3.5	2.05	0.4	0.11
Yellow Perch	22.2	0.15	0.2	0.15

LENGTH OF SELECTED SPECIES SAMPLED FROM ALL GEAR

Number of fish caught for the following length categories (inches):

species	0-5	6-8	9-11	12-14	15-19	20-24	25-29	>30	Total
Black Bullhead	-	-	-	4	-	-	-	-	4
Black Crappie	7	6	2	-	-	-	-	-	15
Bluegill	158	285	1	-	-	-	-	-	444
Brown Bullhead	-	-	-	7	1	-	-	-	8
Hybrid Sunfish	30	66	-	-	-	-	-	-	96
Largemouth Bass	45	27	14	2	-	-	-	-	88
Northern Pike	-	-	-	31	60	55	11	5	162
Pumpkin. Sunfish	14	82	-	-	-	-	-	-	96
Rock Bass	12	60	32	-	-	-	-	-	104
Tullibee (Cisco)	-	42	10	5	-	-	-	-	57
Walleye	-	12	4	-	29	11	2	-	58
Yellow Bullhead	-	-	13	20	-	-	-	-	33
Yellow Perch	51	189	11	-	-	-	-	-	251

DNR COMMENTS: Northern Pike population up substantially and above normal range for lake class; average size 19.5 inches and 1.9 lb.; 13 percent of sample measured 24 inches or larger. A total of 19 Muskellunge sampled; lengths from 11.5 to 46 inches sampled, with five of the fish measuring 40 inches or more; average size 37.3 inches and 14 lb. Bluegill numbers up and well above normal range; average length 5.9 inches. Largemouth Bass numbers up and still above normal range; average length only 9.8 inches; only 2 percent of sample measured 12 inches or more. Black Crappie numbers up; average size 7.4 inches. Walleye population down slightly but still within normal range for lake class; size structure improved, with 67 percent of Walleyes reaching 16 inches or larger; natural reproduction limited.

FISHING INFORMATION: Anglers coming in after trolling here or drifting for fall Walleyes talk about shadows trailing their lures now and then. Those would be Muskies. West Battle is a designated Muskie lake stocked by the DNR. It is also heavily stocked with Walleyes and has a good supply of Northerns, Crappies and Largemouth Bass. It's also a lake that needs studying. West Battle is 5,624 acres of water, divided into east and west lobes with six miles of shoreline. The bottom is full of humps, bars, drops and holes up to 113 feet. It's a good idea to visit a few tackle shops around town on the eastern edge of the lake or hire a guide the first time out. Minimally, a good depthfinder will come in handy. Failing all that, though, there is some pretty clear structure. At mid-lake, points stick out from both the north and south shores. The dropoffs there hold Walleyes all season long. In the spring and fall, head for a hole just north of the outlet to Molly Stark Lake on the north side of the western lobe. The weedbreaks there hold Pike and Bass. In the fall, try jigging frogs. The best spot in the eastern lobe, especially in the spring, tends to be just off the weedbeds at the inlet from East Battle. Summertime use that depthfinder to locate the many humps and drops along the southern and western shorelines in the western lobe and work them with live bait rigs using leeches and frogs. While you're at it, watch for those shadows in the water.

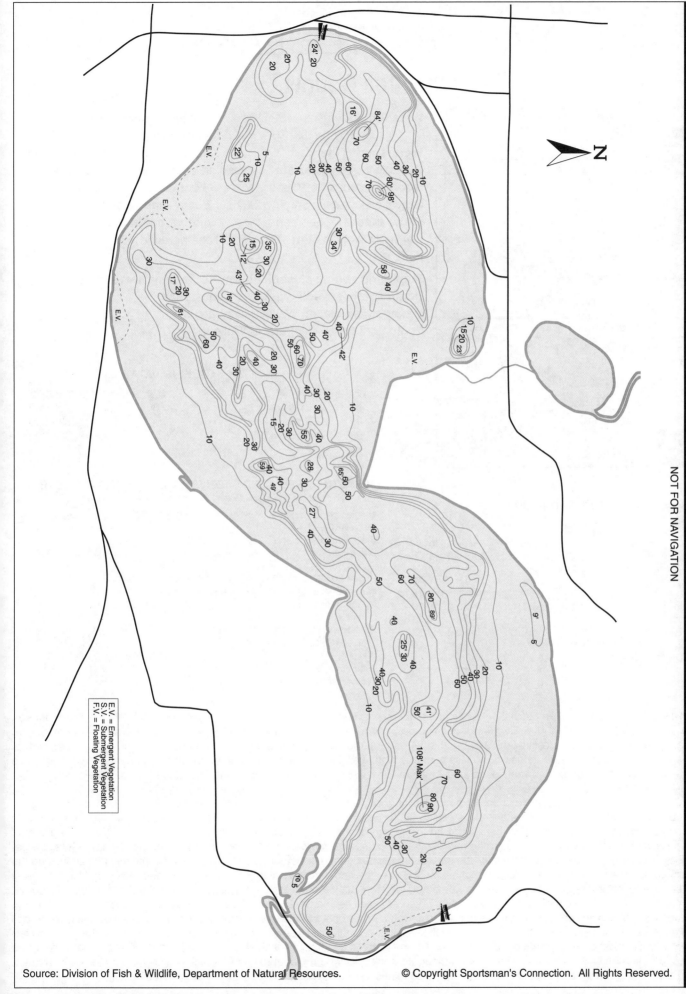

NOT FOR NAVIGATION

N

West Battle Lake

E.V. = Emergent Vegetation
S.V. = Submergent Vegetation
F.V. = Floating Vegetation

Source: Division of Fish & Wildlife, Department of Natural Resources.

EAST BATTLE LAKE
Otter Tail County

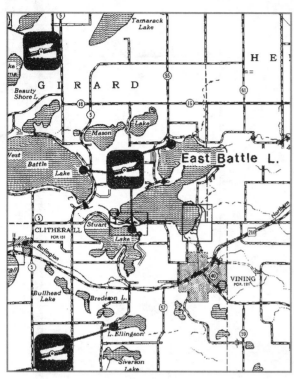

Location: Township 132, 133 Range 38, 39
Watershed: Otter Tail
Surface Water Area: 1,949 Acres
Shorelength: 14.6 Miles
Secchi disk (water clarity): 12.0 Ft.
Water color: Light green
Cause of water color: Algae bloom

Maximum depth: 87 Ft.
Median depth: NA
Accessibility: State-owned public access on northeast shore, off Hwy. 55
Boat Ramp: Earth
Accommodations: Resort and campground

Shoreland zoning classification: Recreational Development
Dominant forest/soil type: Deciduous/Sand
Management class: Walleye-Centrarchid
Ecological type: Centrarchid-Walleye

FISH STOCKING DATA

year	species	size	# released
94	Walleye	Fry	825,000
96	Walleye	Fry	825,000
98	Walleye	Fry	828,000

NET CATCH DATA

survey date: 8/5/96

	Gill Nets		Trap Nets	
species	# per net	avg fish wt. (lbs.)	# per set	avg fish wt. (lbs.)
Black Bullhead	0.1	0.97	0.1	1.24
Black Crappie	0.5	0.10	0.5	0.59
Bluegill	11.9	0.16	22.1	0.18
Hybrid Sunfish	0.9	0.23	1.9	0.20
Largemouth Bass	6.5	0.55	0.5	0.38
Northern Pike	9.5	1.01	1.0	0.77
Rock Bass	1.6	0.60	1.8	0.19
Tullibee (Cisco)	0.5	0.70	-	-
Walleye	7.5	1.62	0.2	2.25
Yellow Perch	5.9	0.22	0.2	0.13

LENGTH OF SELECTED SPECIES SAMPLED FROM ALL GEAR

Number of fish caught for the following length categories (inches):

species	0-5	6-8	9-11	12-14	15-19	20-24	25-29	>30	Total
Black Bullhead	-	-	1	3	-	-	-	-	4
Black Crappie	1	7	1	2	-	-	-	-	11
Bluegill	170	188	-	-	-	-	-	-	358
Brown Bullhead	-	-	-	11	2	-	-	-	13
Hybrid Sunfish	18	23	-	-	-	-	-	-	41
Largemouth Bass	-	32	69	2	1	-	-	-	104
Northern Pike	-	-	10	64	54	24	4	-	156
Pumpkin. Sunfish	35	55	-	-	-	-	-	-	90
Rock Bass	21	10	18	-	-	-	-	-	49
Tullibee (Cisco)	-	4	-	1	2	-	-	-	7
Walleye	-	4	20	26	44	18	3	-	115
Yellow Bullhead	-	-	9	50	-	-	-	-	59
Yellow Perch	16	51	13	-	-	-	-	-	80

DNR COMMENTS: Northern Pike population stable and high; average size 16.4 inches and 1.2 lb.; experimental 22-inch maximum size limit imposed in 1997 to improve size structure of this species. Walleye numbers within expected range for lake class; average size 16 inches and 1.6 lb.; strong year classes from 1992 and 1994; natural reproduction occurring. Cisco numbers up and in the lower level of the expected range for lake class. Largemouth Bass numbers high. Bluegill numbers down but within expected range for lake class; size structure improving, as 17 percent of sample reached 7 inches. Yellow Perch population below the expected range for lake class.

FISHING INFORMATION: East Battle is one of a number of good fisheries in Otter Tail County. It is a few miles west of Henning, on State 210, and is correctly considered a first-class fishing lake. Holding clear water and a fairly good weedline, the lake has nice little bays, good points and some deep holes that all add up to the sort of interesting structure that challenges anglers. There are plenty of Walleyes present, thanks partly to DNR stocking and partly to good natural reproduction. There are also plenty of Northern Pike, Largemouth Bass and Bluegills. Spring Walleyes will be off various points during the day. Good starting places in the west basin include the northwest corner; the point with quick drops along the south shore; the hump midway along the south shore and the channel into the east basin. In the east basin, try the drops just outside the emergent vegetation around the peninsula, as well as the drops in the east corner and on the west side. The bottoms are mostly sand, and you'll do well fishing the bottom with a shiner minnow or leech on a bottom rig. By mid June, the Walleyes will spend their days in deeper water. Your best bet then will be the west basin where you will have to troll deep. The Bass love the weeds around the island and the vegetation at the east side of the eastern basin which is quite shallow. The far-west corner of the west basin is also a good spot. Because the water is generally very clear, you can offer pork rinds or smaller minnows on a jig. You'll find Bluegills in the same spots early, though it won't take long for them to head for deeper water during the day. Try minnows on a bare hook under a slip bobber. Experimental size restrictions are in effect. Check current regs before fishing.

NOT FOR NAVIGATION

East Battle Lake

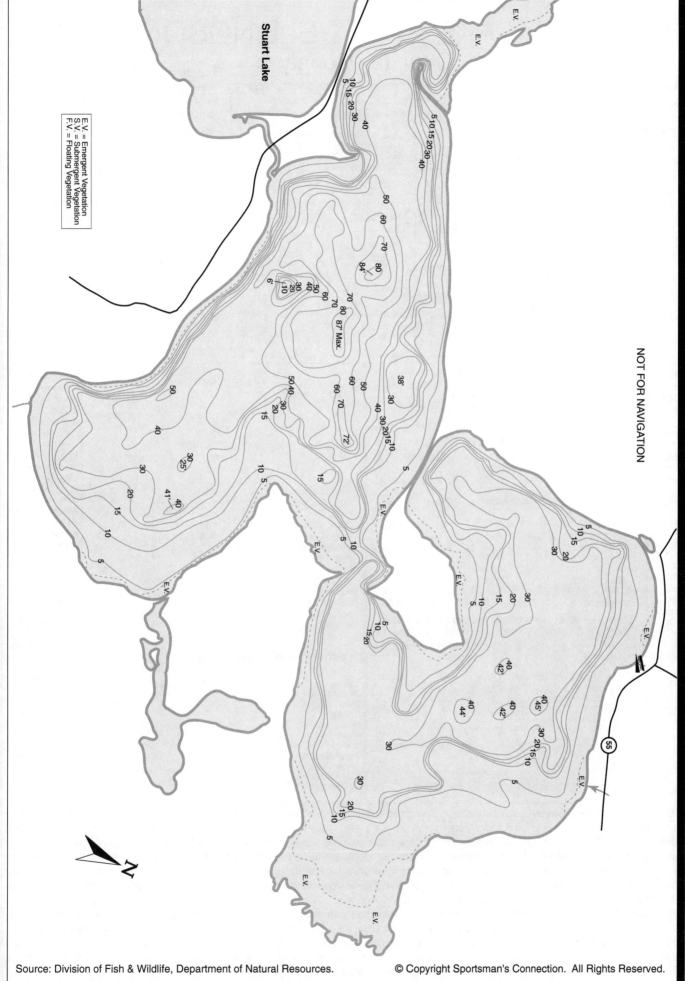

Stuart Lake

E.V. = Emergent Vegetation
S.V. = Submergent Vegetation
F.V. = Floating Vegetation

N

Source: Division of Fish & Wildlife, Department of Natural Resources.

STUART LAKE   ELLINGSON LAKE
Otter Tail County

Location: Township 132, 133 Range 3
Watershed: Otter Tail
Surface Water Area: 699 Acres
Shorelength: 8 Miles
Secchi disk (water clarity): 9.3 Ft.
Water color: NA
Cause of water color: NA
Maximum depth: 49 Ft.
Median depth: 17 Ft.
Accessibility: State-owned public access on northeast corner of the lake
Boat Ramp: Concrete
Accommodations: Resort, campground
Shoreland zoning classif.: Rec. Dev.
Dominant forest/soil type: Decid/Sand
Management class: Walleye-Centrarchid
Ecological type: Centrarchid-Walleye

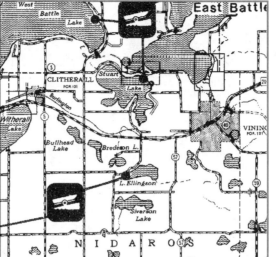

Location: Township 132 Range 39
Watershed: Otter Tail
Surface Water Area: 138 Acres
Shorelength: 2.5 Miles
Secchi disk (water clarity): 3.5 Ft.
Water color: Green
Cause of water color: Algae
Maximum depth: 19 Ft.
Median depth: NA
Accessibility: State-owned public access on northwest shore of lake
Boat Ramp: Earth
Accommodations: NA
Shoreland zoning classif.: Nat. Env.
Dominant forest/soil type: Decid/Sand
Management class: Walleye-Centrarchid
Ecological type: Centrarchid

DNR COMMENTS:
Northern Pike population above normal for lake class; mean size 16.4 inches. Walleye numbers normal; mean size 18 inches; natural reproduction and stocking contribute to population. Largemouth Bass abundant; mean size 11 inches. Black Crappie numbers about average; mean size good at 9.2 inches. Bluegill numbers above lake class average; 38 percent of sample exceeded 8 inches. Yellow Perch numerous, with 21 percent of population exceeding 8 inches.

FISH STOCKING DATA

year	species	size	# released
94	Walleye	Fingerling	15,767
95	Walleye	Fry	407,000
97	Walleye	Fingerling	7,326
98	Walleye	Fry	407,000

survey date: 6/20/94

NET CATCH DATA

	Gill Nets		Trap Nets	
		avg fish		avg fish
species	# per net	wt. (lbs)	# per set	wt. (lbs)
Black Crappie	-		0.7	0.47
Bluegill	1.4	0.11	174.8	0.23
Green Sunfish	-		2.7	0.09
Hybrid Sunfish	0.9	0.45	17.7	0.48
Largemouth Bass	trace	1.44	1.9	0.84
Northern Pike	12.3	1.02	1.9	0.77
Pumpkin. Sunfish	0.2	0.45	4.8	0.48
Rock Bass	1.3	0.76	2.4	0.62
Tullibee (Cisco)	3.7	2.91	-	-
Walleye	2.5	1.96	trace	5.03
Yellow Perch	27.8	0.15	0.8	0.25

LENGTH OF SELECTED SPECIES SAMPLED FROM ALL GEAR
Number of fish caught for the following length categories (inches):

species	0-5	6-8	9-11	12-14	15-19	20-24	25-29	>30	Total
Black Bullhead	-	-	3	6	-	-	-	-	9
Black Crappie	-	1	7	-	-	-	-	-	8
Bluegill	77	294	1	-	-	-	-	-	372
Brown Bullhead	-	-	1	4	-	-	-	-	5
Green Sunfish	28	-	-	-	-	-	-	-	28
Hybrid Sunfish	24	135	-	-	-	-	-	-	159
Largemouth Bass	-	7	8	8	-	1	-	-	24
Northern Pike	-	-	13	44	98	12	1	2	170
Pumpkin. Sunfish	8	52	-	-	-	-	-	-	60
Rock Bass	5	39	-	-	-	-	-	-	44
Tullibee (Cisco)	-	6	8	4	26	-	-	-	44
Walleye	-	1	-	-	25	4	1	-	31
Yellow Bullhead	-	1	57	17	-	-	-	-	75
Yellow Perch	112	138	27	-	-	-	-	-	277

FISH STOCKING DATA

year	species	size	# released
95	Walleye	Fry	98,000
97	Walleye	Fry	100,000

survey date: 8/15/94

NET CATCH DATA

	Gill Nets		Trap Nets	
		avg fish		avg fish
species	# per net	wt. (lbs)	# per set	wt. (lbs)
Black Bullhead	2.5	2.82	0.3	2.81
Black Crappie	2.7	0.48	14.0	0.47
Bluegill	-	-	1.4	0.66
Bowfin (Dogfish)	0.2	11.24	0.8	7.64
Brown Bullhead	1.5	3.35	0.8	2.73
Common Carp	-	-	0.2	19.18
Hybrid Sunfish	0.5	1.99	1.2	0.49
Northern Pike	6.7	1.69	0.6	1.51
Pumpkin. Sunfish	0.5	0.74	0.6	0.30
Walleye	1.0	3.81	0.1	7.05
White Sucker	0.7	7.11	0.3	6.04
Yellow Bullhead	16.5	2.04	11.0	2.19
Yellow Perch	32.7	0.25	1.2	0.23

LENGTH OF SELECTED SPECIES SAMPLED FROM ALL GEAR
Number of fish caught for the following length categories (inches):

species	0-5	6-8	9-11	12-14	15-19	20-24	>30	Total
Black Bullhead	-	-	1	17	-	-	-	18
Black Crappie	7	64	65	4	-	-	-	140
Bluegill	-	8	5	-	-	-	-	13
Brown Bullhead	-	-	-	16	-	-	-	16
Hybrid Sunfish	-	14	-	-	-	-	-	14
Northern Pike	-	1	-	3	24	11	4	43
Pumpkin. Sunfish	4	4	-	-	-	-	-	8
Walleye	-	-	-	-	2	3	2	7
Yellow Bullhead	-	2	86	110	-	-	-	198
Yellow Perch	7	83	17	-	-	-	-	107

DNR COMMENTS:
Northern Pike population has declined considerably but is still within normal range for lake class; mean length 19.4 inches. Walleye numbers below normal; mean length 22.5 inches; natural reproduction limited; all Walleye sampled were from 1989 year class. Largemouth Bass sampled by electrofishing at 15.9 fish/hr. Black Crappies much more numerous and above normal range; average length 9.3 inches. Bluegill numbers down; all fish sampled exceeded 7 inches. Yellow Perch numbers up; mean length 8 inches.

FISHING INFORMATION: Stuart Lake provides some good fishing for Northern Pike, Bass, Walleyes, and panfish. Walleyes are stocked by the DNR and have a large forage base to make them hefty. What's more, there's some good structure that seems to have been made for them. Points and bars off the west side of the main lake are two of the better places for spring Walleyes, especially those at the entrance to the two south bays. Other hotspots include humps near the northwest corner and the east side. Offer the marble eyes leeches or big minnows. The two south bays, meanwhile, are naturals for Largemouth Bass and panfish. Mallard Bay in the southeast corner has excellent weedbeds where there is early spawning and good cover and protection through most of the summer. Those weeds, as well as many other around the lake, are where you can find Northerns. They'll be hanging around the outer edges in 10 to 15 feet of water. **Ellingson Lake** is also a good producer of Northern Pike and panfish. You'll also find some big Walleyes, but numbers for this species are sub-par. Ellingson's shoreline is heavily weeded, and there's a decent number of Yellow Perch and other forage fish for cruising Northerns all around the lake. The southeast corner and the west end are probably the best places to look for them early, though the northeast corner is also very good. These are also places where you can count on some good panfishing. The middle of the south shore, where the bottom breaks downward quickly, is usually productive for Walleyes.

NOT FOR NAVIGATION

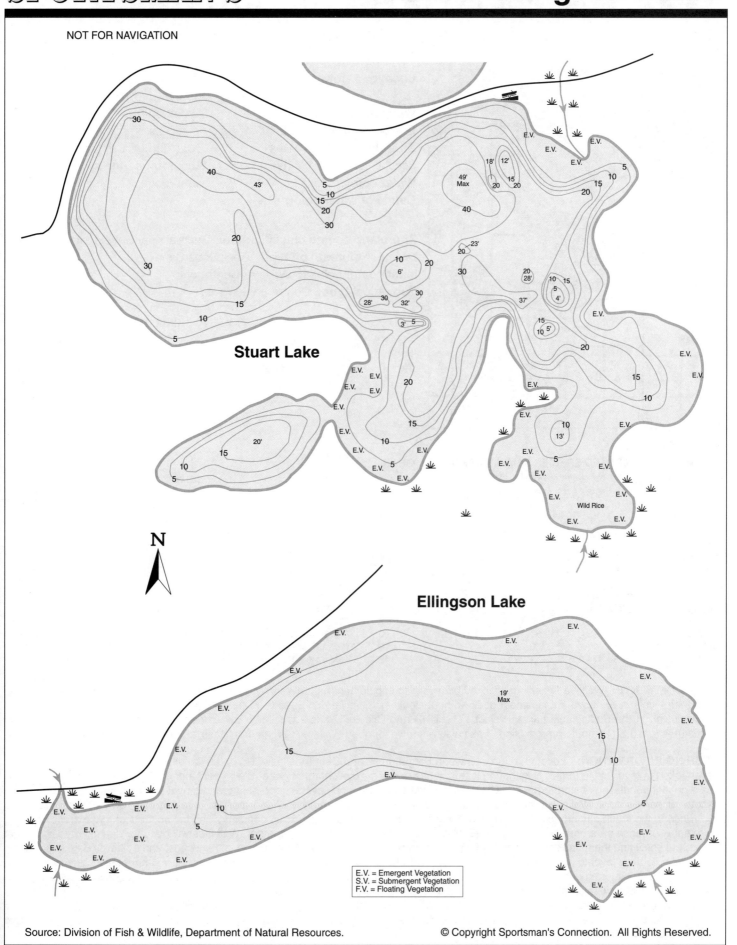

Stuart Lake

Ellingson Lake

N

E.V. = Emergent Vegetation
S.V. = Submergent Vegetation
F.V. = Floating Vegetation

Wild Rice

CLITHERALL LAKE
Otter Tail County

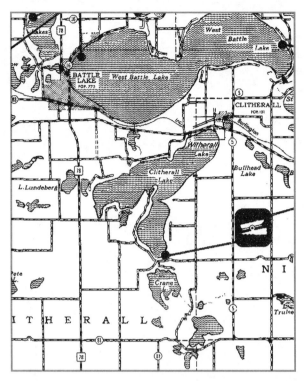

Location: Township 132 Range 39, 40
Watershed: Otter Tail
Surface Water Area: 2,493 Acres
Shorelength: 14.4 Miles
Secchi disk (water clarity): 15.0 Ft.
Water color: Clear
Cause of water color: NA

Maximum depth: 69 Ft.
Median depth: NA
Accessibility: State-owned public access on south shore of lake
Boat Ramp: Concrete
Accommodations: Resorts and campground

Shoreland zoning classification: Recreational Development
Dominant forest/soil type: Deciduous/Sand
Management class: Walleye-Centrarchid
Ecological type: Centrarchid-Walleye

FISH STOCKING DATA

year	species	size	# released
93	Walleye	Fingerling	47,485
95	Walleye	Fingerling	35,066
95	Walleye	Yearling	52
96	Walleye	Fingerling	40,869
98	Smallmouth Bass	Adult	114

LENGTH OF SELECTED SPECIES SAMPLED FROM ALL GEAR

Number of fish caught for the following length categories (inches):

species	0-5	6-8	9-11	12-14	15-19	20-24	25-29	>30	Total
Black Bullhead	-	-	-	4	-	-	-	-	4
Black Crappie	1	16	-	-	-	-	-	-	17
Bluegill	241	313	-	-	-	-	-	-	554
Brown Bullhead	-	-	-	3	-	-	-	-	3
Hybrid Sunfish	8	12	-	-	-	-	-	-	20
Largemouth Bass	6	8	26	2	1	-	-	-	43
Northern Pike	-	-	-	3	18	32	7	4	64
Pumpkin. Sunfish	36	84	-	-	-	-	-	-	120
Rock Bass	38	186	1	-	-	-	-	-	225
Tullibee (Cisco)	-	-	-	5	2	-	-	-	7
Walleye	-	2	20	33	22	10	3	-	90
Yellow Bullhead	-	-	4	6	-	-	-	-	10
Yellow Perch	28	114	3	-	-	-	-	-	145

NET CATCH DATA

survey date: 7/7/97

	Gill Nets		Trap Nets	
		avg fish		avg fish
species	# per net	wt. (lbs.)	# per set	wt. (lbs.)
Black Crappie	0.9	0.25	0.3	0.25
Bluegill	13.1	0.18	32.5	0.17
Hybrid Sunfish	1.1	0.20	0.2	0.22
Largemouth Bass	2.1	0.66	0.7	0.21
Northern Pike	4.3	2.42	trace	0.71
Pumpkin. Sunfish	6.5	0.20	1.5	0.20
Rock Bass	13.9	0.26	1.1	0.27
Tullibee (Cisco)	0.5	1.02	-	-
Walleye	5.5	1.28	0.5	2.94
White Sucker	2.4	1.52	0.4	1.96
Yellow Bullhead	trace	1.51	0.6	1.02
Yellow Perch	9.6	0.14	0.2	0.16

DNR COMMENTS: Walleye fingerlings stocked biennially to supplement natural reproduction. Other gamefish species are able to sustain their levels at or above management goals without stocking. Smallmouth Bass were to be reintroduced, and lake has been chosen for inclusion in the Sustainable Lakes Project. The DNR and Clitherall Lake Association will emplace nesting structures and rock reef structures to aid Smallmouth reproduction. Lake also is known for good Walleye, Largemouth Bass, and Black Crappie angling.

FISHING INFORMATION: Located roughly between Fergus Falls and Detroit Lakes, Clitherall is an all around fishery that shouldn't be overlooked in favor of the larger, neighboring lakes. It has good-to-excellent numbers of Walleyes, Largemouth Bass and panfish, as well as a decent population of Northern Pike. Clitherall has steeps breaks and several good points with gravel and rubble bars. Start at these spots for early season Walleyes; the long bar on the south shore of the main lake and the fast breaking point on the east side at the entrance to the south bay are excellent. The water is fairly clear in the spring, so you can fish along the bottoms of these areas, working a minnow or leech on a bottom rig up the sides where Walleyes feed. In warmer weather, Walleyes will head for deeper water on bright days, but you'll find them back on the points at night and at dawn and dusk. Largemouth are in the weeds, and Clitherall Bay, south of the main lake, is their favorite spot, especially the weedy west shore. Other good spots are the southwest and northeast sides of the main lake. The clear water means you can start the season with worms, minnows or pork rinds on a jig. Weedless and topwater lures are better when the water warms and the vegetation blooms. Panfish, including excellent populations of Rock Bass, will be in the south bay as well as other heavy weedlines early on, but you'll want to head for deeper water in July. Rockies will suspend there during the day but return to the weeds to feed when the sun goes down. Northerns, somewhat small on average, are well distributed at the weed edges and on the flats around the lake.

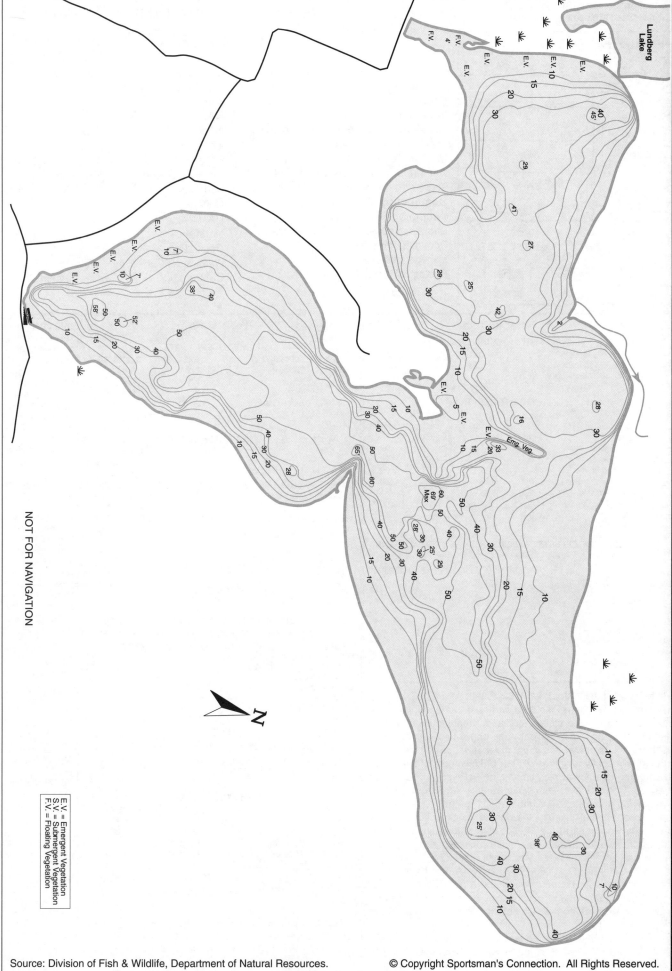

Lundberg Lake

NOT FOR NAVIGATION

N

E.V. = Emergent Vegetation
S.V. = Submergent Vegetation
F.V. = Floating Vegetation

Emg. Veg.

Clitherall Lake

Source: Division of Fish & Wildlife, Department of Natural Resources.

BLOCK LAKE   FISH LAKE   ADLEY LAKE

Otter Tail County

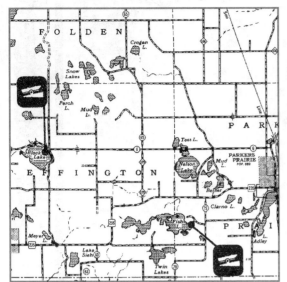

	BLOCK LAKE	FISH LAKE	ADLEY LAKE
Size of lake:	285 Acres	435 Acres	239 Acres
Shorelength:	2.8 Miles	10.2 Miles	NA
Secchi disk (water clarity):	5.0 Ft.	NA	NA
Water color:	Green	NA	NA
Cause of water color:	Algae bloom	NA	NA
Maximum depth:	23 Ft.	17 Ft.	19 Ft.
Median depth:	NA	6 Ft.	NA
Accessibility:	State-owned public access on north shore, off Cty. Rd. 6	Public access on northeast shore	Public access on east shore, in park
Boat Ramp:	Concrete	Concrete	Concrete
Accommodations:	NA	NA	NA
Shoreland zoning classif.:	Rec. Dev.	Nat. Env.	Nat. Env.
Dominant forest/soil type:	NA	Decid./Loam	NA
Management class:	Centrarchid	Warm-water Gamefish	Walleye
Ecological type:	Centrarchid	Centrarchid	Centrarchid

DNR COMMENTS:
No. Pike numbers below range expected for lake class; natural reproduction variable for this species. Walleye numbers up and above normal range for lake class; avg. length 17 inches and 1.8 lb.. Bluegill population up slightly but still below expected range; natural reproduction variable. Black Crappie numbers stable and within expected range; all fish from 1995 year class; mean length 5.6 inches. Yellow Perch numbers up sharply and above the expected range; average length 8.6 inches at age 3.

Block Lake

FISH STOCKING DATA

year	species	size	# released
93	Walleye	Fry	132,000
95	Walleye	Fry	132,000
97	Walleye	Fry	132,000

survey date: 7/22/96

NET CATCH DATA

	Gill Nets		Trap Nets	
		avg fish		avg fish
species	# per net	wt. (lbs)	# per set	wt. (lbs)
Black Crappie	1.2	0.11	1.1	0.09
Bluegill	0.5	0.04	5.8	0.08
Golden Shiner	-	-	0.1	0.08
Largemouth Bass	0.8	0.38	0.6	0.28
Northern Pike	0.3	5.95	-	-
Pumpkin. Sunfish	-	-	2.5	0.06
Walleye	5.7	1.81	-	-
Yellow Perch	119.0	0.10	9.0	0.10

LENGTH OF SELECTED SPECIES SAMPLED FROM ALL GEAR

Number of fish caught for the following length categories (inches):

species	0-5	6-8	9-11	12-14	15-19	20-24	25-29	>30	Total
Black Bullhead	215	73	19	1	-	-	-	-	308
Black Crappie	7	3	-	-	-	-	-	-	10
Bluegill	35	5	1	-	-	-	-	-	41
Brown Bullhead	-	2	13	11	-	-	-	-	26
Largemouth Bass	2	6	2	-	-	-	-	-	10
Northern Pike	-	-	-	-	-	-	1	1	2
Pumpkin. Sunfish	17	1	-	-	-	-	-	-	18
Walleye	-	-	3	5	21	5	-	-	34
Yellow Bullhead	3	5	-	1	-	-	-	-	9
Yellow Perch	120	78	10	-	-	-	-	-	208

FISHING INFORMATION: Block Lake is great to fish. The DNR has stocked Walleyes and Northern Pike here and reports a good supply of Perch for forage. Block has a simple structure, dropping steadily from the shoreline to a wide bottom at 20 feet. Use bright color and spinners to go with shiners and nightcrawlers in the murk. Cast or drift the drops, moving out gradually until you find fish. **Fish Lake** is more of the same, murky with Largemouth Bass at nine times and Walleyes at three times the area median. Fish has a surface water area of 435 acres and 10.2 miles of meandering shoreline, a maximum depth of just 17 feet and a median depth of six. The far-east bay, the western inlet leading to a dam and outlet and the weedlines at the 10-foot hole in the middle are the best bets for Largemouth and Walleyes. Again, you may need your most colorful plastics and noisy lures here. Meanwhile, Eileen Koep of Koep's Clitherall Corner, Clitherall (218) 864-8731, says **Adley Lake** offers some good opportunities for nice Northerns and a good spring bite for Walleyes. In addition, there's good winter fishing, she says, for 'gills and Crappies. Look for Wally along the sides of the "deep," 15-foot hole in the lake's south end. The Northerns, of course, will be hanging around the offshore weedlines, where they can be tempted by sucker minnows, spoons or spinnerbaits retrieved or trolled parallel to the breaks.

Fish Lake

FISH STOCKING DATA

year	species	size	# released
93	Walleye	Fry	428,000
95	Walleye	Fry	428,000
97	Walleye	Fry	428,000
97	Black Crappie	Adult	60

survey date: 6/6/94

NET CATCH DATA

	Gill Nets		Trap Nets	
		avg fish		avg fish
species	# per net	wt. (lbs)	# per set	wt. (lbs)
Black Bullhead	2.2	0.77	152.1	0.37
Black Crappie	0.1	0.16	4.8	0.22
Brown Bullhead	-	-	0.3	0.65
Golden Shiner	0.1	0.15	14.0	0.06
Largemouth Bass	-	-	0.1	0.87
Northern Pike	0.3	2.75	-	-
Pumpkin. Sunfish	-	-	0.9	0.29
Walleye	1.1	1.73	0.5	0.14
White Sucker	11.3	3.75	0.6	4.86
Yellow Perch	33.0	0.16	4.8	0.08

LENGTH OF SELECTED SPECIES SAMPLED FROM ALL GEAR

Number of fish caught for the following length categories (inches):

species	0-5	6-8	9-11	12-14	15-19	20-24	25-29	>30	Total
Black Bullhead	-	115	65	7	-	-	-	-	187
Black Crappie	5	29	4	1	-	-	-	-	39
Brown Bullhead	-	1	1	-	-	-	-	-	2
Largemouth Bass	-	-	1	-	-	-	-	-	1
Northern Pike	-	-	-	-	-	3	-	-	3
Pumpkin. Sunfish	5	2	-	-	-	-	-	-	7
Walleye	-	3	-	2	6	1	-	-	12
Yellow Perch	61	222	8	-	-	-	-	-	291

Adley Lake

FISH STOCKING DATA

year	species	size	# released
93	Walleye	Fingerling	6,426
95	Walleye	Yearling	381
95	Walleye	Fingerling	333
97	Walleye	Fingerling	4,284

NET CATCH DATA: Not Available.

LENGTH OF SELECTED SPECIES SAMPLED FROM SURVEY

Not Available.

DNR COMMENTS:
Lake is susceptible to periodic, partial winterkill. No. Pike numbers below normal for lake class; avg. length 22.4 inches. Walleye population within normal range; mean length 15.6 inches; natural reproduction is occurring. LM Bass numbers low. Black Crappie population about normal; reproduction consistent. Bluegills not sampled in this survey. Yellow Perch numbers above normal; five year classes present; 10 percent of Perch sampled reached 8 inches.

DNR COMMENTS:

NOT AVAILABLE

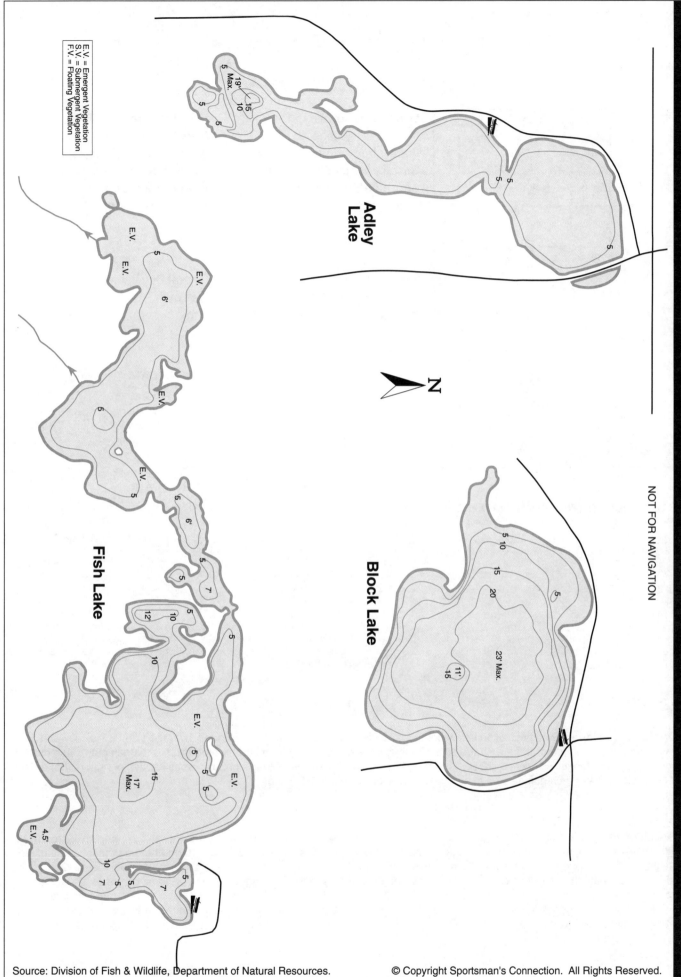

E.V. = Emergent Vegetation
S.V. = Submergent Vegetation
F.V. = Floating Vegetation

Adley Lake

19" Max.
15
10
5

N

NOT FOR NAVIGATION

Fish Lake

E.V.
E.V.
6'
E.V.
E.V.
E.V.
6'
7'
12'
10
10
17" Max.
15
E.V.
E.V.
4.5'
E.V.

Block Lake

5 10
15
20
23 Max.
11'
15
5

Block, Fish & Adley Lakes

Source: Division of Fish & Wildlife, Department of Natural Resources.

© Copyright Sportsman's Connection. All Rights Reserved.

EAGLE LAKE
Otter Tail County

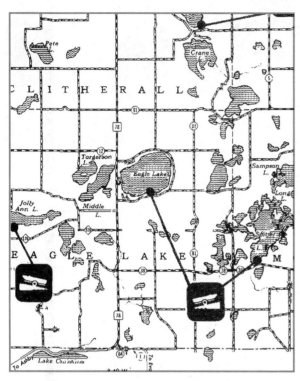

Location: Township 131
Range 40
Watershed: Pomme De Terre
Surface Water Area: 46 Acres
Shorelength: 4.3 Miles
Secchi disk (water clarity): 18 Ft.
Water color: Clear
Cause of water color: NA

Maximum depth: 46 Ft.
Median depth: NA
Accessibility: Public access on south shore, off County Hwy. 78
Boat Ramp: Concrete
Accommodations: NA

Shoreland zoning classification: General Development
Dominant forest/soil type: Deciduous/Loam
Management class: Walleye-Centrarchid
Ecological type: Centrarchid-Walleye

FISH STOCKING DATA

year	species	size	# released
90	Walleye	Fingerling	3,115
94	Walleye	Fingerling	6,746
96	Walleye	Fingerling	1,456

LENGTH OF SELECTED SPECIES SAMPLED FROM ALL GEAR

Number of fish caught for the following length categories (inches):

species	0-5	6-8	9-11	12-14	15-19	20-24	25-29	>30	Total
Bluegill	289	149	-	-	-	-	-	-	438
Green Sunfish	2	2	-	-	-	-	-	-	4
Hybrid Sunfish	94	46	-	-	-	-	-	-	140
Largemouth Bass	8	5	16	8	-	-	-	-	37
Northern Pike	-	-	-	-	-	3	5	4	12
Pumpkin. Sunfish	2	12	-	-	-	-	-	-	14
Rock Bass	-	3	4	-	1	-	-	-	8
Walleye	-	10	5	39	48	16	-	-	118
Yellow Bullhead	1	96	228	17	-	-	-	-	342
Yellow Perch	4	73	1	-	-	-	-	-	78

NET CATCH DATA

survey date: 7/24/95

	Gill Nets		Trap Nets	
species	# per net	avg fish wt. (lbs.)	# per set	avg fish wt. (lbs.)
Bluegill	14.7	0.16	237.3	0.12
Golden Shiner	-	-	trace	0.05
Green Sunfish	0.3	0.12	trace	0.20
Hybrid Sunfish	2.9	0.19	8.8	0.12
Largemouth Bass	2.0	0.80	1.3	0.13
Northern Pike	0.9	5.87	trace	2.98
Pumpkin. Sunfish	1.0	0.25	0.2	0.22
Rock Bass	0.4	0.74	0.3	0.50
Walleye	9.1	1.64	0.9	0.15
Yellow Perch	10.7	0.15	0.5	0.15

DNR COMMENTS: Northern Pike population below normal range for lake class; size structure good, average size 28.8 inches and 5.9 lb. Walleye numbers above normal range; average size 16.4 inches and 1.8 lb.; some natural reproduction . Largemouth Bass numbers above normal; average length 6.1 inches; 22 percent of Bass reaching 23 inches. Bluegill population still above normal range; average length 5.4 inches. Yellow Perch numbers up to normal range; average length 7.2 inches.

FISHING INFORMATION: Eagle is a very clear lake without many weedbeds, but you can find plenty of Largemouth Bass anyway, along with Walleyes and some Northern Pike. Eagle is also full of Bluegills. Start looking for Largemouth at the northeast end and along the south shore near the public access area. A worm, minnow or pork rind on a jig offers the best approach to June Bass. Go right into the weeds with your bait; the fish won't come to you. Several good humps of 14 and 18 feet in the northeast corner of the lake and the sharp breaks in the southeast and southwest corners are excellent places to look for Walleyes. Use live bait, and put it close to or right on the sandy bottom. The goggle eyes will spend bright summer days suspended in deeper water, but they'll be back at the humps and breaks at dawn and dusk. Northern Pike, of course, will be cruising between the weeds and deeper water. Toss spoons or spinnerbaits for them, or fish them with live sucker minnows.

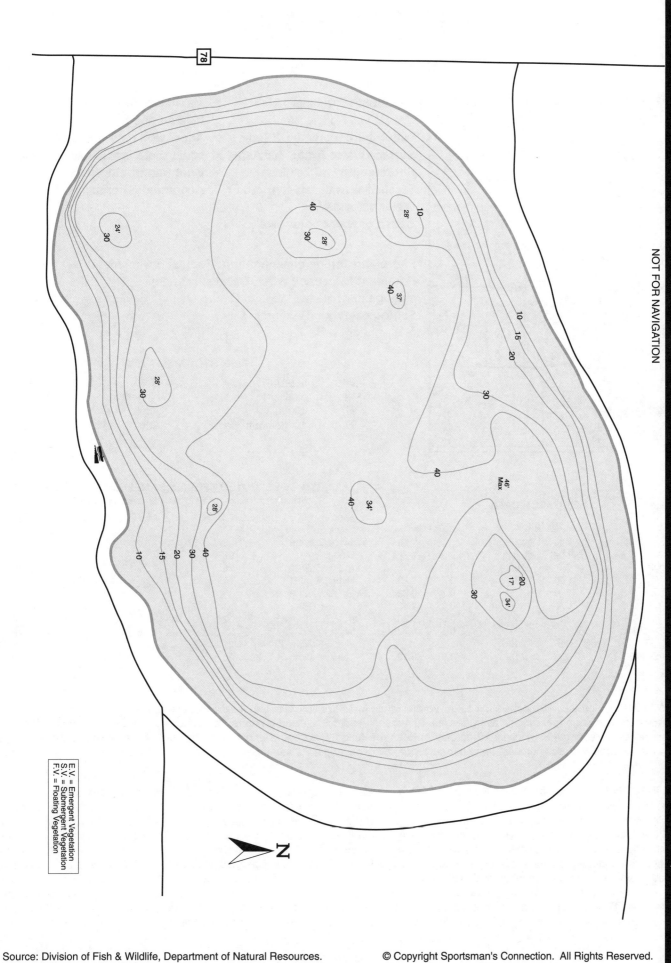

NOT FOR NAVIGATION

Eagle Lake

E.V. = Emergent Vegetation
S.V. = Submergent Vegetation
F.V. = Floating Vegetation

N

SPORTSMAN'S Connection®

SPITZER LAKE
Otter Tail County

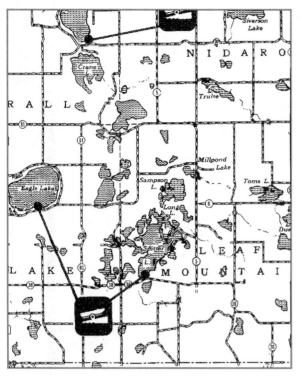

Location: Township 131
Range 39
Watershed: Pomme De Terre
Surface Water Area: 728 Acres
Shorelength: 17.7 Miles
Secchi disk (water clarity): 5.5 Ft.
Water color: NA
Cause of water color: NA

Maximum depth: 33 Ft.
Median depth: NA
Accessibility: Public access on south shore, off County Road 38
Boat Ramp: Concrete
Accommodations: NA

Shoreland zoning classification: Natural Environment
Dominant forest/soil type: Deciduous/Loam
Management class: Walleye-Centrarchid
Ecological type: Centrarchid

FISH STOCKING DATA

year	species	size	# released
94	Walleye	Fingerling	21,390
97	Bluegill	Adult	265
97	Largemouth Bass	Adult	21

NET CATCH DATA

survey date: 8/25/97

	Gill Nets		Trap Nets	
		avg fish		avg fish
species	# per net	wt. (lbs.)	# per set	wt. (lbs.)
Black Crappie	0.4	0.05	0.8	0.38
Bluegill	0.3	0.24	8.7	0.23
Hybrid Sunfish	-	-	0.3	0.22
Largemouth Bass	0.5	1.18	0.2	1.46
Northern Pike	8.8	1.10	0.9	0.73
Pumpkin. Sunfish	-	-	0.5	0.17
Walleye	0.8	1.10	-	-
Yellow Perch	9.1	0.15	0.6	0.12

LENGTH OF SELECTED SPECIES SAMPLED FROM ALL GEAR
Number of fish caught for the following length categories (inches):

species	0-5	6-8	9-11	12-14	15-19	20-24	25-29	>30	Total
Black Bullhead	-	51	-	-	-	-	-	-	51
Black Crappie	5	3	5	-	-	-	-	-	13
Bluegill	7	92	-	-	-	-	-	-	99
Brown Bullhead	-	36	4	-	-	-	-	-	40
Hybrid Sunfish	2	1	-	-	-	-	-	-	3
Largemouth Bass	-	-	2	5	-	-	-	-	7
Northern Pike	-	1	2	18	63	13	-	1	98
Pumpkin. Sunfish	3	2	-	-	-	-	-	-	5
Walleye	-	-	1	2	5	-	-	-	8
Yellow Bullhead	4	27	6	1	-	-	-	-	38
Yellow Perch	25	60	5	-	-	-	-	-	90

DNR COMMENTS: Northern Pike population below normal range for lake class; size structure good, average size 28.8 inches and 5.9 lb. Walleye numbers above normal range; average size 16.4 inches and 1.8 lb.; some natural reproduction . Largemouth Bass numbers above normal; average length 6.1 inches; 22 percent of Bass reaching 23 inches. Bluegill population still above normal range; average length 5.4 inches. Yellow Perch numbers up to normal range; average length 7.2 inches.

FISHING INFORMATION: Before fishing Spitzer, make the rounds of bait and tackle stores or the DNR offices in Fergus Falls for information on winterkill conditions. This is a lake that's fun to fish in non-winterkill years, but the unwary can lose a prop before the fun even begins. Spitzer was once a shallow mud hole until rising water created a 728-acre basin with a winding shoreline of nearly 18 miles and a dozen different bays. Some of the bays are stump-filled – good Bass territory but treacherous boating. Unless you have a penchant for exploration, you are just as well off heading due north between the large island and the slender point. At the top of that section of the lake is a hole of about 20 feet, and around it lies a shoreline which holds Largemouth Bass and Crappies. Just off the eastern shore, the submerged weed bed is a prime hangout for Walleyes and Northern Pike. Then, beyond that weedbed are a sunken point jutting from the western shore and another weedbed that forms a long, slender bar. Trail a live bait rig along the breaks at 10 to 15 feet on the northern side of the bar until just before the narrows on your left. You will then have reached the deepest hole in the lake at 33 feet and covered most of the available gamefish territory unless your pleasure is shallow, stump-filled bays. Happy angling!

NOT FOR NAVIGATION

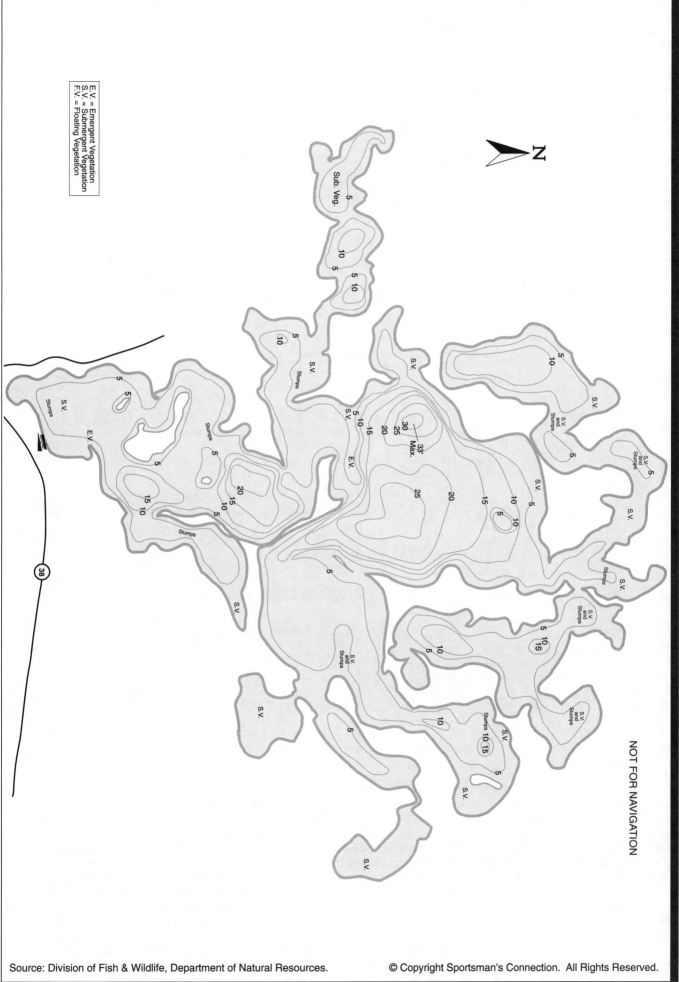

E.V. = Emergent Vegetation
S.V. = Submergent Vegetation
F.V. = Floating Vegetation

N

38

Sub. Veg.

JOLLY ANN LAKE

SEWELL LAKE

Otter Tail County

Location: Township 131 Range 40, 41
Watershed: Pomme De Terre
Surface Water Area: 256 Acres
Shorelength: NA
Secchi disk (water clarity): 8.6 Ft.
Water color: Light green
Cause of water color: Slight algae bloom
Maximum depth: 89 Ft.
Median depth: NA
Accessibility: State-owned public access on south shore of lake
Boat Ramp: Earth
Accommodations: NA
Shoreland zoning classif.: Nat. Env.
Dominant forest/soil type: NA
Management class: Walleye-Centrarchid
Ecological type: Centrarchid

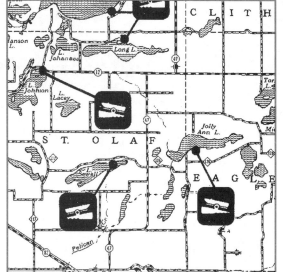

Location: Township 131   Range 41
Watershed: Pomme De Terre
Surface Water Area: 338 Acres
Shorelength: 4.5 Miles
Secchi disk (water clarity): NA
Water color: NA
Cause of water color: NA
Maximum depth: 52 Ft.
Median depth: NA
Accessibility: State-owned public access on north shore of lake
Boat Ramp: Concrete
Accommodations: NA
Shoreland zoning classif.: Rec. Dev.
Dominant forest/soil type: Decid/Loam
Management class: Walleye-Centrarchid
Ecological type: Centrarchid

DNR COMMENTS:
Walleye numbers up and within normal range for lake class; mean length 15 inches; fish up to 23.8 inches captured. Northern Pike numbers below normal; mean length 18.8 inches. Largemouth Bass population above normal; mean length 10.2 inches, but Bass up to 19.3 inches were sampled. Black Crappie numbers have fluctuated; and are now normal for lake class; mean length good at 9.9 inches. Bluegill population up but normal for lake class; only 7 percent of sample reaching 7 inches. Yellow Perch numbers within normal range; only 4 percent of fish reaching 8 inches.

FISH STOCKING DATA

year	species	size	# released
95	Walleye	Fingerling	1,220
95	Walleye	Yearling	43

survey date: 8/29/94

NET CATCH DATA

	Gill Nets		Trap Nets	
		avg fish		avg fish
species	# per net	wt. (lbs)	# per set	wt. (lbs)
Black Bullhead	0.3	1.18	-	-
Black Crappie	0.5	0.73	1.1	0.61
Bluegill	-	-	33.4	0.15
Bowfin (Dogfish)	0.3	4.59	0.6	6.46
Brown Bullhead	0.3	0.88	-	-
Common Carp	1.5	5.92	0.8	12.18
Hybrid Sunfish	-	-	0.9	0.50
Largemouth Bass	2.3	1.04	1.5	0.99
Northern Pike	2.8	1.44	0.3	1.70
Pumpkin. Sunfish	-	-	0.5	0.29
Walleye	2.5	1.21	-	-
White Sucker	0.3	0.23	0.8	4.41
Yellow Bullhead	1.0	1.40	1.4	1.56
Yellow Perch	23.7	0.13	-	-

LENGTH OF SELECTED SPECIES SAMPLED FROM ALL GEAR
Number of fish caught for the following length categories (inches):

species	0-5	6-8	9-11	12-14	15-19	20-24	25-29	>30	Total
Black Bullhead	-	-	2	-	-	-	-	-	2
Black Crappie	-	4	5	3	-	-	-	-	12
Bluegill	123	96	-	-	-	-	-	-	219
Brown Bullhead	-	-	2	-	-	-	-	-	2
Hybrid Sunfish	1	6	-	-	-	-	-	-	7
Largemouth Bass	2	5	7	8	2	-	-	-	24
Northern Pike	-	-	-	-	13	3	1	-	17
Pumpkin. Sunfish	3	1	-	-	-	-	-	-	4
Walleye	-	-	-	13	1	1	-	-	15
Yellow Bullhead	1	-	12	4	-	-	-	-	17
Yellow Perch	8	103	-	-	-	-	-	-	111

FISH STOCKING DATA

year	species	size	# released
93	Walleye	Fingerling	2,400
96	Walleye	Fingerling	3,700

survey date: 6/29/87

NET CATCH DATA

	Gill Nets		Trap Nets	
		avg fish		avg fish
species	# per net	wt. (lbs)	# per set	wt. (lbs)
Northern Pike	19.0	1.61	1.0	0.88
Yellow Bullhead	37.0	0.48	11.2	0.65
Brown Bullhead	0.8	0.68	0.7	1.25
Black Bullhead	0.2	0.80	-	-
Largemouth Bass	0.2	0.05	1.3	0.11
Black Crappie	-	-	0.2	0.80
Green Sunfish	-	-	0.2	0.10
Bluegill	1.4	0.24	55.2	0.24
Pumpkin. Sunfish	3.2	0.25	10.8	0.28
Hybrid Sunfish	3.2	0.27	8.3	0.30
Yellow Perch	73.0	0.12	0.3	0.10
Walleye	10.0	1.06	1.5	3.13

LENGTH OF SELECTED SPECIES SAMPLED FROM SURVEY

Not Available.

DNR COMMENTS:
The gill net catch of Walleye in 1987 is approximately four times the catch in 1982. Natural reproduction of Walleye in 1982, 1985 and 1986 was evident as representatives of these skip year classes were captured. Northern Pike and Bluegill numbers continue to be well above state and local medians. Yellow Perch numbers are up considerably since the 1982 test netting.

FISHING INFORMATION: These two lakes are just a few miles east of Dalton and not far off I-94. **Sewell Lake** is managed for Walleyes by the DNR, but there are plenty of Northerns and Bluegills to be found too, along with a strong forage base of Yellow Perch. There is also a decent number of Largemouth Bass. The best places to look for early Bass and panfish are at the southwest end, especially in the weedline at the mouth of the south bay. The fish there aren't very hungry while recovering from the spawn, but they are terrific just afterwards. Northerns are well distributed along the lake's weeds and you can do well trolling for them at the south end and along the north shoreline. Walleyes are located at the steep dropoffs along the north and south sides, particularly at points. The Walleyes will hang out at these same places at night during the summer, but during the day you'll find them suspended in deep water near the middle of the lake where there are 40- and 50-foot-deep holes. **Jolly Ann Lake**, just to the east of Sewell, is best known as a Largemouth Bass lake, and the reputation is well deserved. Of course, there are Northerns, Walleyes and panfish here too. The shallow, weed-filled areas at the east and west ends of the lake are the best places to start looking for Bass just after the spawn. You'll likely find Crappies in these areas, too. They're good-size in Jolly Ann.

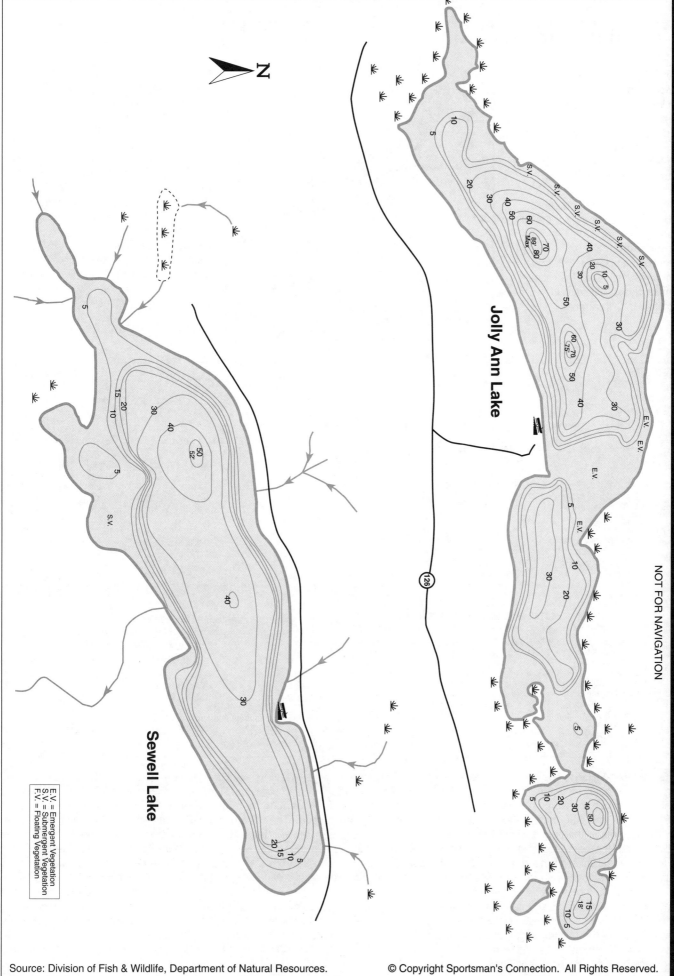

Jolly Ann & Sewell Lakes

NOT FOR NAVIGATION

N

Jolly Ann Lake

126

Sewell Lake

89' 80 Max
52'
18'

S.V.
E.V.
F.V.

E.V. = Emergent Vegetation
S.V. = Submergent Vegetation
F.V. = Floating Vegetation

CLEAR LAKE SOUTH TEN MILE LAKE

Otter Tail County

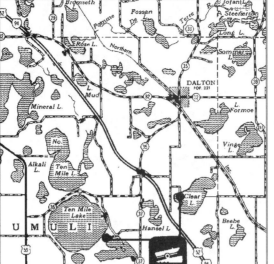

Location: Township 131 Range 41, 42
Watershed: Pomme De Terre
Surface Water Area: 352 Acres
Shorelength: 3.6 Miles
Secchi disk (water clarity): 7.0 Ft.
Water color: Green
Cause of water color: Algae bloom
Maximum depth: 29 Ft.
Median depth: NA
Accessibility: State-owned public access on northwest corner of the lake
Boat Ramp: Concrete
Accommodations: NA
Shoreland zoning classif.: Rec. Dev.
Dominant forest/soil type: Decid/Loam
Management class: Centrarchid
Ecological type: Centrarchid

Location: Township 131 Range 42
Watershed: Pomme De Terre
Surface Water Area: 1,411 Acres
Shorelength: 9.5 Miles
Secchi disk (water clarity): 7.0 Ft.
Water color: Green
Cause of water color: Slight algae bloom
Maximum depth: 51 Ft.
Median depth: 15 Ft.
Accessibility: State-owned public access on southeast shore
Boat Ramp: Concrete
Accommodations: NA
Shoreland zoning classif.: Rec. Dev..
Dominant forest/soil type: Decid/Loam
Management class: Walleye-Centrarchid
Ecological type: Centrarchid-Walleye

DNR COMMENTS:
Northern Pike numbers down and below expected range for lake class; average size 23.3 inches and 3.1 lb. Walleye population down but above the upper level of the expected range; average size 20 inches and 3 lb. Black Crappie numbers up; strong 1995 year class. Bluegill population within expected range; poor size structure for this species. Yellow Perch numbers down but still high; average length 6.5 inches. Black Bullhead numbers down but still high; average length 10.3 inches.

FISH STOCKING DATA

year	species	size	# released
93	Walleye	Fingerling	2,370
94	Walleye	Fry	155,000
96	Walleye	Fingerling	4,381

survey date: 8/12/96

NET CATCH DATA

	Gill Nets		Trap Nets	
species	# per net	avg fish wt. (lbs)	# per set	avg fish wt. (lbs)
Black Bullhead	71.9	0.62	1.9	0.56
Black Crappie	9.4	0.10	0.2	0.10
Bluegill	1.3	0.07	17.4	0.06
Golden Shiner	-	-	0.3	0.05
Largemouth Bass	-	-	0.1	0.28
Northern Pike	1.7	3.09	0.6	1.42
Pumpkin. Sunfish	7.2	0.09	4.6	0.06
Walleye	2.7	2.97	0.4	3.78
Yellow Bullhead	2.7	0.56	1.3	0.68
Yellow Perch	78.6	0.11	6.6	0.12

LENGTH OF SELECTED SPECIES SAMPLED FROM ALL GEAR
Number of fish caught for the following length categories (inches):

species	0-5	6-8	9-11	12-14	15-19	20-24	25-29	>30	Total
Black Bullhead	7	11	312	-	-	-	-	-	330
Black Crappie	71	12	-	-	-	-	-	-	83
Bluegill	159	6	-	-	-	-	-	-	165
Brown Bullhead	-	-	1	-	-	-	-	-	1
Largemouth Bass	-	1	-	-	-	-	-	-	1
Northern Pike	-	1	2	-	5	3	8	1	20
Pumpkin. Sunfish	104	-	-	-	-	-	-	-	104
Walleye	1	1	-	1	13	10	2	-	28
Yellow Bullhead	-	4	29	3	-	-	-	-	36
Yellow Perch	57	258	1	-	-	-	-	-	316

FISH STOCKING DATA

year	species	size	# released
93	Walleye	Fingerling	29,104
95	Walleye	Fingerling	23,375
95	Walleye	Yearling	1,955

survey date: 6/23/97

NET CATCH DATA

	Gill Nets		Trap Nets	
species	# per net	avg fish wt. (lbs)	# per set	avg fish wt. (lbs)
Black Crappie	1.1	0.40	2.9	0.24
Bluegill	1.0	0.19	26.5	0.13
Longnose Gar	2.1	4.33	1.7	2.29
Northern Pike	1.8	2.14	0.3	2.30
Pumpkin. Sunfish	-	-	0.1	0.17
Rock Bass	0.7	0.58	1.1	0.45
Smallmouth Bass	0.6	0.88	-	-
Walleye	18.2	1.28	0.5	1.39
Yellow Bullhead	-	-	0.3	1.21
Yellow Perch	45.9	0.12	1.9	0.09

LENGTH OF SELECTED SPECIES SAMPLED FROM ALL GEAR
Number of fish caught for the following length categories (inches):

species	0-5	6-8	9-11	12-14	15-19	20-24	25-29	>30	Total
Black Crappie	10	24	8	-	-	-	-	-	42
Bluegill	201	60	-	-	-	-	-	-	261
Brown Bullhead	-	-	1	-	-	-	-	-	1
Northern Pike	-	-	1	-	7	14	1	1	24
Pumpkin. Sunfish	1	-	-	-	-	-	-	-	1
Rock Bass	-	14	5	-	-	-	-	-	19
Smallmouth Bass	-	1	4	2	-	-	-	-	7
Walleye	-	7	11	85	108	11	-	-	222
Yellow Bullhead	-	-	1	2	-	-	-	-	3
Yellow Perch	222	175	10	-	-	-	-	-	407

DNR COMMENTS:
This lake is known for its excellent Walleye, Smallmouth Bass, and Black Crappie fishing. These species are not only abundant, but they also have good size distributions. Walleye fingerlings are stocked every three years; however, test netting indicates natural reproduction may be substantial for this species.

FISHING INFORMATION: The dominant species in **Clear Lake** are Walleye and Black Bullhead, but there's a fair number of Northern Pike thrown in for good measure. Located just off I-94, close to Dalton, Clear's Walleyes are no secret to local anglers who take a lot of 10-pounders out every season. You can catch them – the Walleyes, that is – at many spots in the lake, but the two sunken islands, one near the west side, the other toward the east at mid lake, are always productive. The bottom is mostly sand and rubble, which means you can fish these spots in the spring with a bottom rig and a leech or shiner minnow. Some fairly sharp dropoffs at the north end are also productive. Head for the deeper water at the lake's center when the water warms or on very bright days. The south end is a good place to look for Northerns most of the summer. **Ten Mile Lake** is right across I-94 from Clear and has a well-deserved reputation for good Crappie and Walleye fishing. There is very good natural reproduction among the Walleye population and, in addition, the lake is liberally stocked with fry and fingerlings. Early Walleye fishing is best on the east side, where a good-size hump and several rock piles make excellent habitat. A sunken island near the north side also produces good catches. The Crappies are in the weeds early, especially on the north side and in the northeast corner where you can do well using a bright marabou jig armed with a smaller minnow or worms. Northern Pike patrol the outside edges of the weeds, often on the south side and the entrance into the small south bay of the lake on the east side. There is an entrance into North Ten Mile Lake along the north shore. This smaller lake is very shallow and full of bulrushes, but often contains early Crappies and Bass.

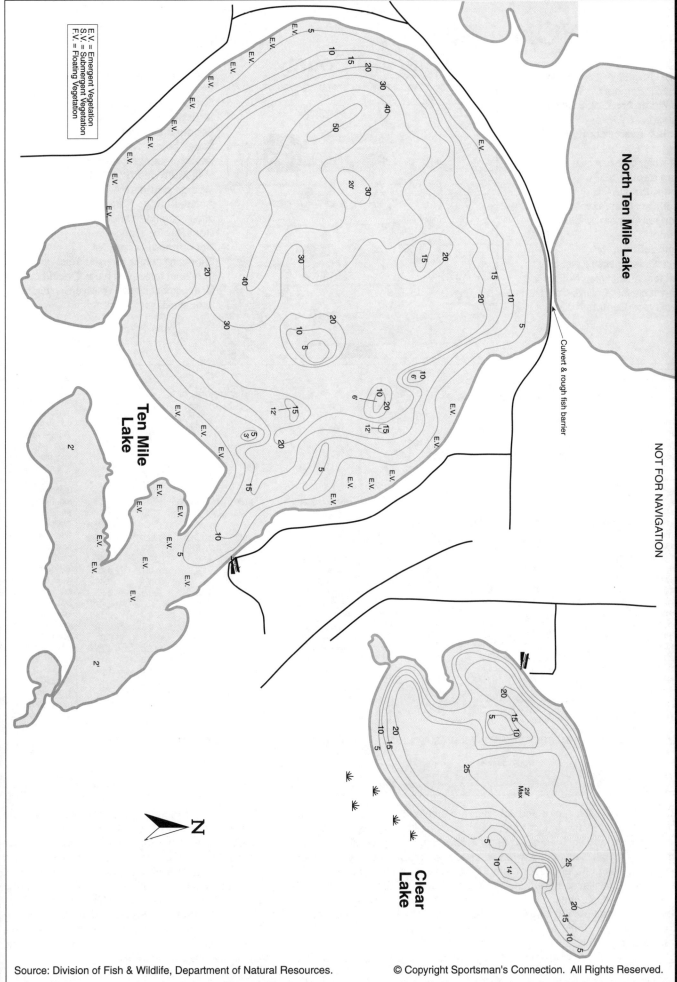

North Ten Mile Lake

NOT FOR NAVIGATION

Culvert & rough fish barrier

E.V. = Emergent Vegetation
S.V. = Submergent Vegetation
F.V. = Floating Vegetation

Ten Mile Lake

Clear Lake

N

JOHNSON LAKE

Otter Tail County

LONG LAKE

Location: Township 131 Range 41
Watershed: Pomme De Terre
Surface Water Area: 338 Acres
Shorelength: 4.7 Miles
Secchi disk (water clarity): 7.5 Ft.
Water color: Greenish
Cause of water color: Algae
Maximum depth: 33 Ft.
Median depth: NA
Accessibility: State-owned public access on north shore, off Hwy. 12
Boat Ramp: Concrete
Accommodations: NA
Shoreland zoning classif.: Nat. Env.
Dominant forest/soil type: No Tree/Wet
Management class: Walleye-Centrarchid
Ecological type: Centrarchid

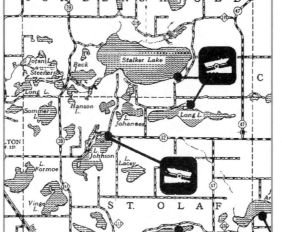

Location: Township 131 Range 41
Watershed: Pomme De Terre
Surface Water Area: 350 Acres
Shorelength: 5.8 Miles
Secchi disk (water clarity): 12.0 Ft.
Water color: NA
Cause of water color: NA
Maximum depth: 88 Ft.
Median depth: NA
Accessibility: State-owned public access on north shore of lake
Boat Ramp: Concrete
Accommodations: NA
Shoreland zoning classif.: Rec. Dev.
Dominant forest/soil type: Decid/Loam
Management class: Walleye-Centrarchid
Ecological type: Centrarchid

DNR COMMENTS:
No Bullheads were caught in the 1976 survey while many were taken in 1986. Yellow Perch numbers have increased dramatically. Sunfish captured in assessment nets were small, but angler creels that were checked contained many Sunfish greater than 7" in length. Northern Pike average weight was good. Walleye catches decreased significantly since 1976. Fry stocking seems to be unsuccessful. Average size up from 0.64 lbs. to 3.73 lbs., with none smaller than 18".

FISH STOCKING DATA

year	species	size	# released
93	Walleye	Fry	165,000
94	Walleye	Fingerling	5,431
96	Walleye	Fry	165,000
97	Walleye	Fingerling	4,950

NET CATCH DATA

survey date: 6/30/86

	Gill Nets		Trap Nets	
		avg fish		avg fish
species	# per net	wt. (lbs)	# per set	wt. (lbs)
Northern Pike	4.0	3.58	0.5	4.70
White Sucker	3.7	2.59	1.3	2.72
Black Bullhead	93.0	0.51	2.5	0.47
Hybrid Sunfish	1.7	0.24	-	-
Yellow Bullhead	-	-	0.3	1.60
Hybrid Sunfish	1.7	0.24	26.0	0.24
Pumpkin. Sunfish	1.0	0.07	5.0	0.11
Bluegill	0.7	0.10	160.3	0.14
Largemouth Bass	0.3	0.80	1.0	0.38
Yellow Perch	148.7	0.14	10.5	0.15
Walleye	6.0	3.73	0.5	3.10

LENGTH OF SELECTED SPECIES SAMPLED FROM SURVEY

Not Available.

FISH STOCKING DATA

year	species	size	# released
93	Walleye	Fingerling	8,255
96	Walleye	Fingerling	4,200

NET CATCH DATA

survey date: 8/3/87

	Gill Nets		Trap Nets	
		avg fish		avg fish
species	# per net	wt. (lbs)	# per set	wt. (lbs)
Northern Pike	12.6	2.15	0.9	1.71
Yellow Bullhead	36.8	0.80	27.8	0.85
Golden Shiner	-	-	0.1	0.10
White Sucker	-	-	0.1	3.00
Largemouth Bass	6.9	0.86	3.9	0.55
Black Crappie	1.1	0.19	2.8	0.27
Bluegill	6.9	0.15	63.0	0.14
Green Sunfish	-	-	0.2	0.10
Pumpkin. Sunfish	0.6	0.20	7.9	0.21
Hybrid Sunfish	0.3	0.15	17.0	0.25
Yellow Perch	-	-	0.3	0.13
Walleye	1.5	1.18	1.4	1.24

LENGTH OF SELECTED SPECIES SAMPLED FROM SURVEY

Not Available.

DNR COMMENTS:
Northern Pike numbers in gill nets have nearly doubled since '82 Bluegill numbers down from '82, still very high. Once again, net catches indicate good populations of Largemouth Bass & Black Crappies. Walleye numbers & average weight have fallen to nearly half of the '82 survey. There were 3 year classes missing; '83 was supplemented with fry stocking, yet none were seen. The '85 class (a skip year) may be the result of age 1+ fish stocked in '86. There was no other evidence of natural reproduction.

FISHING INFORMATION: Long and Johnson are smaller lakes just east of Dalton and southeast of Fergus Falls. **Johnson Lake**, the smaller of the two, is relatively clear and has a fair weedline hosting lots of Northern Pike and Bluegills. The panfish are in the weeds early in the season, and you can get to them with worms or smaller minnows on a bare hook. Many of the Sunfish are plump. There are also some Largemouth Bass in the weeds that you can attract with a pig-and-jig. The Northerns are cruising the weeds, and you should troll slowly along the outer edges for them. It would be smart to offer live bait, because there are a lot of Yellow Perch to compete with. There aren't many Walleyes here (they're stocked, but don't seem to make it), but you will find some along the east side points. **Long Lake**, just to the east of Johnson, also has good numbers of Northerns, Largemouth Bass and Crappie. Bass will be found in the shallow flats of the east end after they spawn as well as the small bay in the middle of the north shore. Crappies and Sunfish will be found mostly along the north shore. Later in the season, the larger ones will be at deep spots in the lake. Northerns cruise the outer edges of the weeds, and you can do well with live bait trolled slowly. On overcast days, use a spoon or spoon plug. The Walleyes most often hang around points on the south side early in the season and at night. During the summer, they will be deep at mid lake.

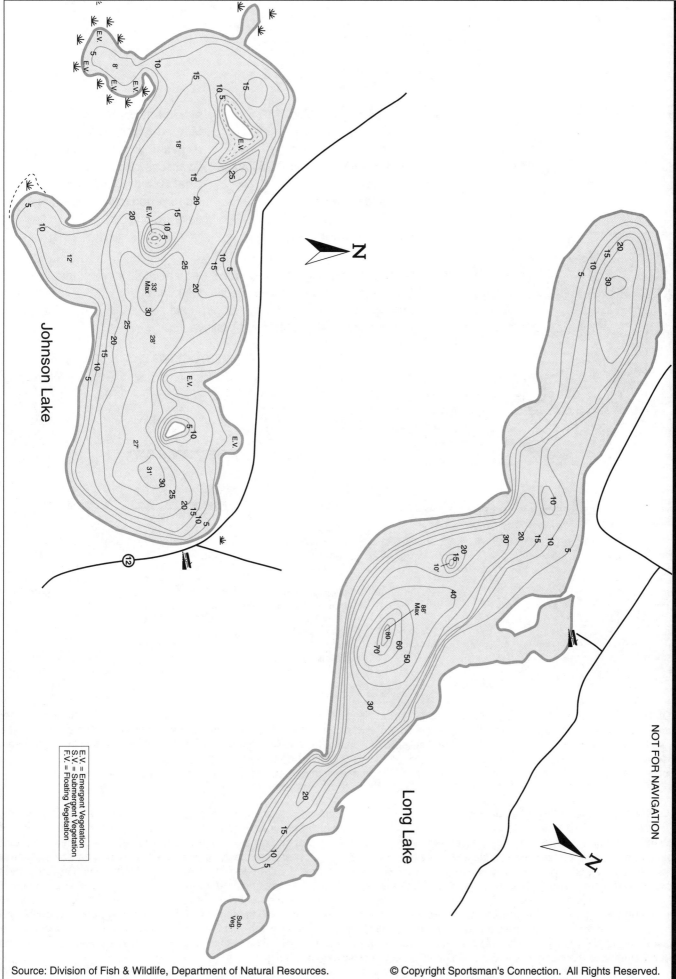

NOT FOR NAVIGATION

N

Johnson Lake

Long Lake

33'
Max

30

28'

27'

31'

18'

12'

88'
Max

80

70

60

50

40

30

20

15

10

5

Sub.
Veg.

E.V. = Emergent Vegetation
S.V. = Submergent Vegetation
F.V. = Floating Vegetation

Source: Division of Fish & Wildlife, Department of Natural Resources.

STALKER LAKE
Otter Tail County

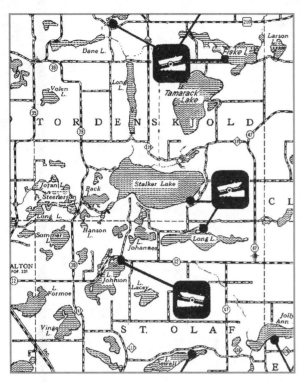

Location: Township 132 Range 41
Watershed: Pomme De Terre
Surface Water Area: 1,280 Acres
Shorelength: 7.9 Miles
Secchi disk (water clarity): 7.9 Ft.
Water color: Light green
Cause of water color: Algae

Maximum depth: 95 Ft.
Median depth: NA
Accessibility: State-owned public access on southeast shore
Boat Ramp: Concrete
Accommodations: Resorts and campground

Shoreland zoning classification: Recreational Development
Dominant forest/soil type: Deciduous/Loam
Management class: Walleye-Centrarchid
Ecological type: Centrarchid-Walleye

FISH STOCKING DATA

year	species	size	# released
93	Walleye	Fingerling	29,688
95	Walleye	Fingerling	11,787
97	Walleye	Fingerling	10,902

NET CATCH DATA

survey date: 8/22/94

species	Gill Nets # per net	Gill Nets avg fish wt. (lbs.)	Trap Nets # per set	Trap Nets avg fish wt. (lbs.)
Black Bullhead	7.3	2.35	1.0	1.98
Bluegill	2.1	0.27	41.1	0.18
Bowfin (Dogfish)	-	-	0.5	11.64
Hybrid Sunfish	trace	0.56	3.2	0.50
Largemouth Bass	-	-	1.0	0.06
Longnose Gar	2.1	6.43	0.3	5.65
Northern Pike	4.3	1.11	0.9	1.19
Pumpkin. Sunfish	trace	0.31	0.7	0.52
Rock Bass	1.0	0.88	1.7	0.72
Walleye	7.3	1.46	0.4	4.27
White Sucker	0.3	3.38	-	-
Yellow Bullhead	trace	3.83	0.8	3.26
Yellow Perch	8.9	0.14	0.4	0.13

LENGTH OF SELECTED SPECIES SAMPLED FROM ALL GEAR

Number of fish caught for the following length categories (inches):

species	0-5	6-8	9-11	12-14	15-19	20-24	25-29	>30	Total
Black Bullhead	-	-	58	40	-	-	-	-	98
Bluegill	118	128	-	-	-	-	-	-	246
Hybrid Sunfish	9	24	-	-	-	-	-	-	33
Largemouth Bass	10	-	-	-	-	-	-	-	10
Northern Pike	-	3	5	14	33	2	3	1	61
Pumpkin. Sunfish	3	5	-	-	-	-	-	-	8
Rock Bass	3	26	-	-	-	-	-	-	29
Walleye	-	5	9	19	47	8	4	-	92
Yellow Bullhead	-	-	1	8	-	-	-	-	9
Yellow Perch	17	90	4	-	-	-	-	-	111

DNR COMMENTS: Northern Pike population down slightly but still within normal range for lake class; population had been very stable; size range 10 to 29 inches, with 8 percent of sample measuring at least 24 inches. Walleye numbers up but within normal range for lake class; age 4 fish average 16.5 inches; consistent natural reproduction for this species, but stocking is improving the population. Bluegill population within normal range; size structure has improved, with 20 percent of sample reaching 7 inches; consistently good natural reproduction. Yellow Perch numbers down substantially but still within expected range; majority of fish less than 8 inches.

FISHING INFORMATION: Stalker has been a top gamefish lake for years and continues to produce in spite of heavy fishing pressure. One reason for this is DNR Walleye stocking; others are fine structure which encourages natural reproduction and a hefty population of Yellow Perch for forage. Stalker is a broad, 1,280-acre lake with a 7.9 miles of shoreline and water clarity of nearly eight feet. It has a rolling bottom, with numerous sunken islands and holes dropping to 95 feet. There are plenty of good spots to fish here, so don't linger too long in one place; keep moving until you find fish. For Bass and Crappies, try the opening of the bay to the Pomme De Terre River outlet channel and the narrows and sides of the two holes in the channel. Then locate the four-foot-deep hump just off the western end of the lake and work the edges at 10 feet. Then head up to the reedy inlets, one at the northwestern end, another at just around the small point on the north shore, and finally, one at the northwestern end of the lake. Work just off the reeds, jigging a shiner on a slip bobber. As summer arrives, switch to leeches on light line. For summer Walleyes and Largemouth Bass, focus on the sunken islands west of the river channel in mid lake. Just off these are big flats ranging from three to six feet deep. Work the edges of the flats with night crawlers and leeches, starting at the weedlines and moving out and deeper until you find fish.

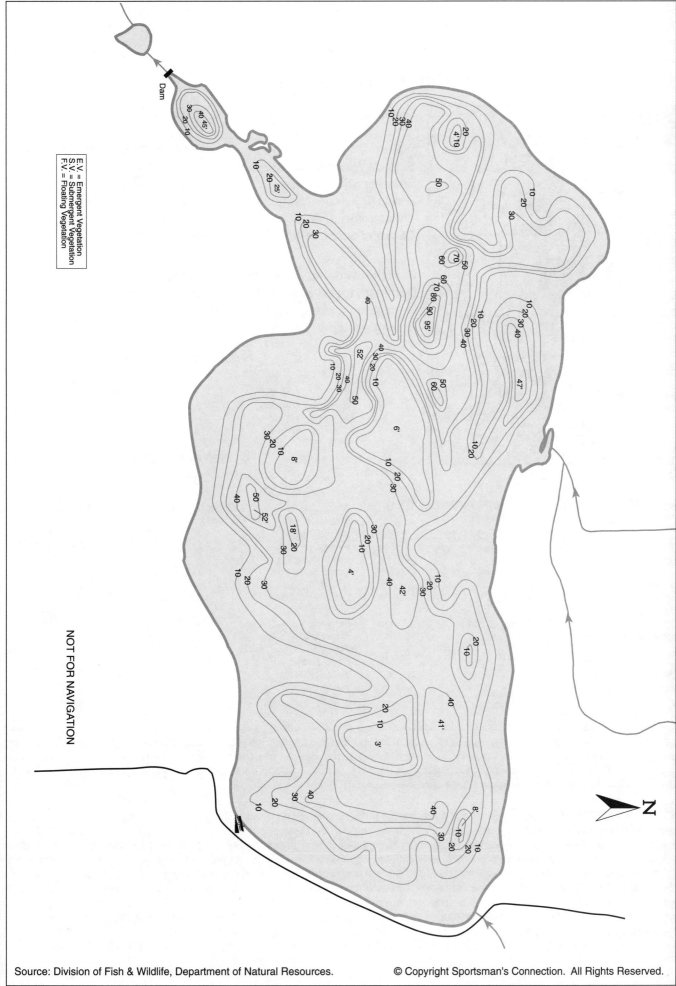

N

NOT FOR NAVIGATION

E.V. = Emergent Vegetation
S.V. = Submergent Vegetation
F.V. = Floating Vegetation

Dam

SWAN LAKE
Otter Tail County

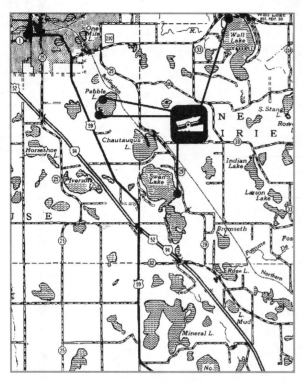

Location: Township 132
Range 42, 43
Watershed: Pomme De Terre
Surface Water Area: 689 Acres
Shorelength: 8.8 Miles
Secchi disk (water clarity): 17.0 Ft.
Water color: Clear
Cause of water color: NA

Maximum depth: 44 Ft.
Median depth: 12 Ft.
Accessibility: State-owned public access on the east shore, off County Road 29
Boat Ramp: Concrete
Accommodations: Resort and campgrounds

Shoreland zoning classification: Recreational Development
Dominant forest/soil type: Deciduous/Loam
Management class: Walleye-Centrarchid
Ecological type: Centrarchid-Walleye

FISH STOCKING DATA

year	species	size	# released
90	Walleye	Fingerling	8,690
93	Walleye	Fingerling	10,361
95	Walleye	Fry	371,000
97	Walleye	Fry	371,000

NET CATCH DATA

survey date: 7/28/97

	Gill Nets		Trap Nets	
species	# per net	avg fish wt. (lbs.)	# per set	avg fish wt. (lbs.)
Black Bullhead	14.0	0.43	0.1	0.31
Black Crappie	0.2	0.31	0.4	0.42
Bluegill	14.2	0.20	60.2	0.18
Bowfin (Dogfish)	-	-	0.1	3.02
Brown Bullhead	0.2	0.30	-	-
Hybrid Sunfish	-	-	0.2	0.26
Largemouth Bass	4.5	0.69	0.1	1.20
Northern Pike	9.5	2.46	0.8	2.42
Pumpkin. Sunfish	1.0	0.21	3.1	0.13
Rock Bass	1.7	0.30	0.7	0.41
Walleye	4.3	1.85	-	-
White Sucker	0.3	2.68	-	-
Yellow Bullhead	21.9	0.44	7.4	0.40
Yellow Perch	8.7	0.12	-	-

LENGTH OF SELECTED SPECIES SAMPLED FROM ALL GEAR

Number of fish caught for the following length categories (inches):

species	0-5	6-8	9-11	12-14	15-19	20-24	25-29	>30	Total
Black Bullhead	4	92	36	9	3	-	-	-	144
Black Crappie	1	2	3	-	-	-	-	-	6
Bluegill	163	239	-	-	-	-	-	-	402
Brown Bullhead	-	2	-	-	-	-	-	-	2
Hybrid Sunfish	1	1	-	-	-	-	-	-	2
Largemouth Bass	-	6	36	10	-	-	-	-	52
Northern Pike	-	-	1	9	38	43	24	3	118
Pumpkin. Sunfish	28	12	-	-	-	-	-	-	40
Rock Bass	5	19	2	-	-	-	-	-	26
Walleye	-	2	3	4	32	5	3	-	49
Yellow Bullhead	27	116	157	13	-	-	-	-	313
Yellow Perch	31	44	1	-	-	-	-	-	76

DNR COMMENTS: Anglers should find an abundant Northern Pike population averaging around 21 inches; there is the distinct possibility of catching a Pike over 30 inches. Walleye population typical for lake class; variety of lengths and ages present, with particularly strong 1994 year class; natural reproduction and stocking both contributing to population. Largemouth Bass numbers appear stable, but average size is down, probably because of weak year classes in the early 1990s. Strong 1994 year class should provide good angling for Black Crappies. Bluegills abundant; average size about 6 inches.

FISHING INFORMATION: You can fish Swan for Walleyes but in the process, you're also going to come up with a Northern or Largemouth Bass. Northerns abound, and there has been a recent explosion in the Bass population. Whenever that happens, the Walleye fingerlings seeded by the DNR are going to be lucky to escape those other roving gamefish. Swan's 689 acres are divided, from the southern end, into small, medium and large sections that take up 8.8 miles of shoreline. This is a very clear lake with a Secchi disk reading of 17 feet. That results in a weedline by mid-summer at 10 to 15 feet, with good cover along the breaks in the deeper holes. The deepest hole in Swan is 44 feet. This is a lake of broad shallows, however, and that's where you want to be in the early weeks, casting surface lures and crankbaits into the weedbreaks at the far northern rim or around the shoreline in the small southern section of the lake. Fishing stays good here in summer when a switch to live bait rigs and, especially, light lines and leeches, is in order along the edges of the reeds. Up until early summer, troll or drift minnows on Lindy rigs in the two narrows between lake sections for Northerns. As the water warms, locate the sunken humps and jig them and the lower weedbreaks in the deeper holes using minnows, nightcrawlers and leeches.

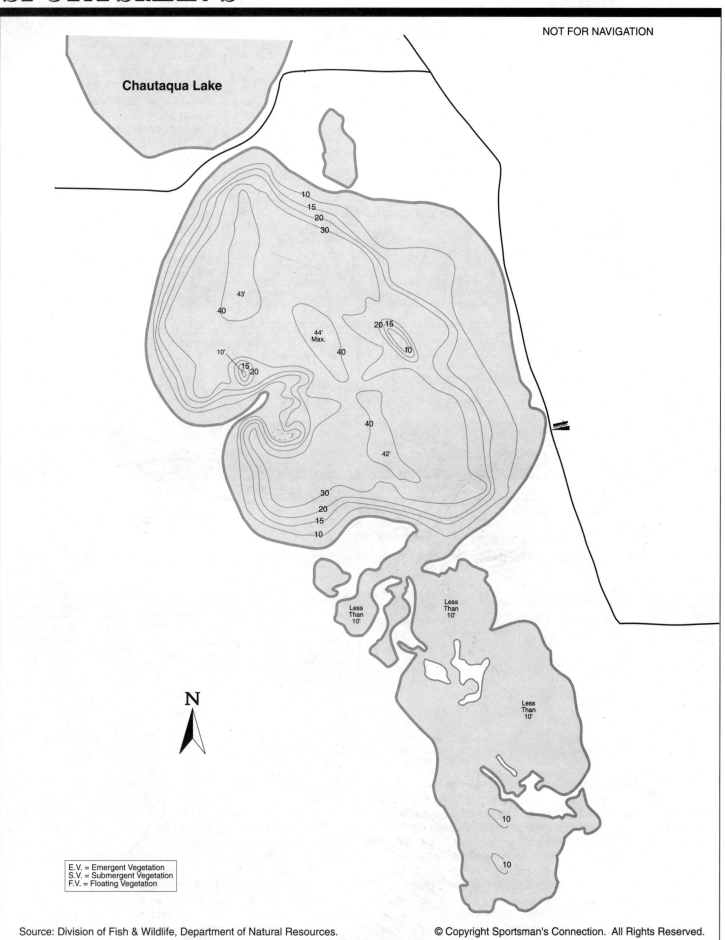

Chautaqua Lake

10
15
20
30

43'
40

44'
Max.
40

20 15
10

10'
15
20

40

42'

30
20
15
10

Less
Than
10'

Less
Than
10'

Less
Than
10'

10

10

N

E.V. = Emergent Vegetation
S.V. = Submergent Vegetation
F.V. = Floating Vegetation

Source: Division of Fish & Wildlife, Department of Natural Resources.

WALL LAKE

Otter Tail County

PEBBLE LAKE

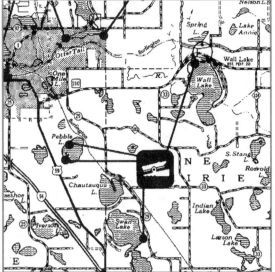

Location: Township 132, 133 Range 42
Watershed: Otter Tail
Surface Water Area: 682 Acres
Shorelength: 7 Miles
Secchi disk (water clarity): 7.5 Ft.
Water color: Light green
Cause of water color: Slight algae bloom
Maximum depth: 27 Ft.
Median depth: NA
Accessibility: State-owned access on the north side of lake, off service road
Boat Ramp: Concrete
Accommodations: NA
Shoreland zoning classif.: Gen. Dev.
Dominant forest/soil type: No tree/Wet
Management class: Walleye-Centrarchid
Ecological type: Centrarchid

Location: Township 132   Range 4
Watershed: Otter Tail
Surface Water Area: 169 Acres
Shorelength: 2 Miles
Secchi disk (water clarity): 6.5 Ft.
Water color: Light green
Cause of water color: Algae bloom
Maximum depth: 62 Ft.
Median depth: NA
Accessibility: Two public accesses, one on south shore; one on northwest shore
Boat Ramp: Asphalt
Accommodations: NA
Shoreland zoning classif.: Rec. Dev.
Dominant forest/soil type: Decid/Loam
Management class: Walleye-Centrarchid
Ecological type: Centrarchid

WALL LAKE

DNR COMMENTS:
Walleye natural reproduction sporadic, but a strong 1996 year class should offer good angling in the future; Walleye fingerlings stocked biennially. Anglers pursuing Northern Pike should find the majority of fish around 21 inches; there is a good chance at a Pike over 30 inches. Largemouth Bass population healthy, with Bass larger than 17 inches sampled. Bluegills plentiful; strong 1995 year class for this species; 1992 and 1993 year classes were poor, however.

FISH STOCKING DATA

year	species	size	# released
93	Walleye	Fingerling	5,603
95	Walleye	Fingerling	1,466
95	Walleye	Yearling	92
97	Walleye	Fingerling	3,940

survey date: 7/21/97

NET CATCH DATA

	Gill Nets		Trap Nets	
species	# per net	avg fish wt. (lbs)	# per set	avg fish wt. (lbs)
Bluegill	0.7	0.14	54.2	0.09
Bowfin (Dogfish)	-	-	0.9	4.72
Common Carp	0.3	3.24	0.2	2.72
Golden Shiner	-	-	0.2	0.06
Green Sunfish	-	-	6.1	0.04
Hybrid Sunfish	0.3	0.22	15.1	0.08
Largemouth Bass	1.0	1.21	2.0	0.44
Northern Pike	6.2	2.49	-	-
Pumpkin. Sunfish	0.4	0.11	3.4	0.09
Rock Bass	2.3	0.17	13.7	0.11
Walleye	4.3	2.26	0.1	7.03
Yellow Bullhead	2.1	1.03	1.3	0.82
Yellow Perch	60.8	0.11	3.6	0.12

LENGTH OF SELECTED SPECIES SAMPLED FROM ALL GEAR
Number of fish caught for the following length categories (inches):

species	0-5	6-8	9-11	12-14	15-19	20-24	25-29	>30	Total
Black Bullhead	11	12	2	2	2	-	-	-	29
Bluegill	212	57	-	-	-	-	-	-	269
Green Sunfish	66	-	-	-	-	-	-	-	66
Hybrid Sunfish	80	19	-	-	-	-	-	-	99
Largemouth Bass	6	13	5	7	3	-	-	-	34
Northern Pike	-	-	-	1	28	28	14	2	73
Pumpkin. Sunfish	39	3	-	-	-	-	-	-	42
Rock Bass	79	26	1	-	-	-	-	-	106
Walleye	-	-	14	1	21	12	4	-	52
Yellow Bullhead	2	4	17	16	-	-	-	-	39
Yellow Perch	111	261	-	-	-	-	-	-	372

PEBBLE LAKE

FISH STOCKING DATA

year	species	size	# released
90	Walleye	Yearling	2,157
93	Walleye	Fingerling	4,314
94	Walleye	Fingerling	1,013
94	Walleye	Yearling	4
95	Walleye	Fingerling	2,482
95	Walleye	Yearling	44
96	Walleye	Fingerling	1,965

survey date: 7/29/96

NET CATCH DATA

	Gill Nets		Trap Nets	
species	# per net	avg fish wt. (lbs)	# per set	avg fish wt. (lbs)
Black Crappie	-	-	0.1	0.03
Bluegill	2.6	0.21	14.9	0.11
Hybrid Sunfish	0.8	0.32	0.3	0.07
Largemouth Bass	0.2	0.29	0.2	0.14
Northern Pike	3.8	1.97	0.2	2.50
Pumpkin. Sunfish	2.6	0.19	1.7	0.12
Rock Bass	19.2	0.17	5.2	0.14
Tullibee (Cisco)	0.6	1.02	-	-
Walleye	18.4	0.97	0.3	1.18
Yellow Perch	98.6	0.10	3.1	0.07

LENGTH OF SELECTED SPECIES SAMPLED FROM ALL GEAR
Number of fish caught for the following length categories (inches):

species	0-5	6-8	9-11	12-14	15-19	20-24	25-29	>30	Total
Black Bullhead	-	1	25	9	1	-	-	-	36
Black Crappie	1	-	-	-	-	-	-	-	1
Bluegill	67	26	-	-	-	-	-	-	93
Brown Bullhead	-	-	2	-	-	-	-	-	2
Hybrid Sunfish	3	4	-	-	-	-	-	-	7
Largemouth Bass	1	2	-	-	-	-	-	-	3
Northern Pike	-	-	-	-	4	17	-	-	21
Pumpkin. Sunfish	17	11	-	-	-	-	-	-	28
Rock Bass	101	36	6	-	-	-	-	-	143
Tullibee (Cisco)	-	-	1	2	-	-	-	-	3
Walleye	-	3	26	32	31	3	-	-	95
Yellow Perch	40	93	-	-	-	-	-	-	133

DNR COMMENTS:
Northern Pike population up slightly to near the lower end of the expected range for lake class; average size 20.7 inches and 2 lb. Walleye numbers up slightly and well above the expected range for lake class; average size 13.9 inches and 1 lb. Largemouth Bass population balanced; Bass reaching 12.9 inches at age 3. Bluegill numbers down to within the expected range; size structure poor, with only 3 percent of fish reaching 7 inches. Yellow Perch population down but still above expected range; size structure poor, with no sampled fish exceeding 8 inches.

FISHING INFORMATION: Located five miles east of Fergus Falls, **Wall Lake** is home to Northern Pike, Largemouth Bass and Walleyes. The Northerns are in the bigger, northern bay of the lake, and the best fishing there is along the north and west sides where you'll find a distinct weedline and a lot of reeds. The weeds are home to many forage fish, so the Northerns move around waiting for them to venture out. Bass are in the weeds also, along with Bluegills and Yellow Perch. You can tempt the Bass in mid June with a pig-and-jig, but a few weeks later you may have to switch to weedless or topwater lures. Walleyes have some good places to feed in the spring, including a point off the southwest side of the main lake, the sunken island in the north part of the lake, and the sand bar that crosses the lake near the south bay. Use leeches and large minnows to attract the marble eyes. Many of the Walleyes and larger panfish will suspend in deep water at mid lake when the water is warm and the days are bright, but they'll return to shallow water again after sunset. You can cross the sandbar that separates the lake's bay most of the year. There are Walleye on the south side of the bar, as well as off two points on the bay's west side. Panfish and Bass can be found in weeds at the northwest side of the bay, but your best bet is the far south end which has copious weeds and shallow water. Fishing the outside edges of the weeds will most likely net you a decent-size Northern as well. Walleyes are stocked in **Pebble Lake,** and there are fair numbers of Northern Pike and Bullheads to be had, as well.

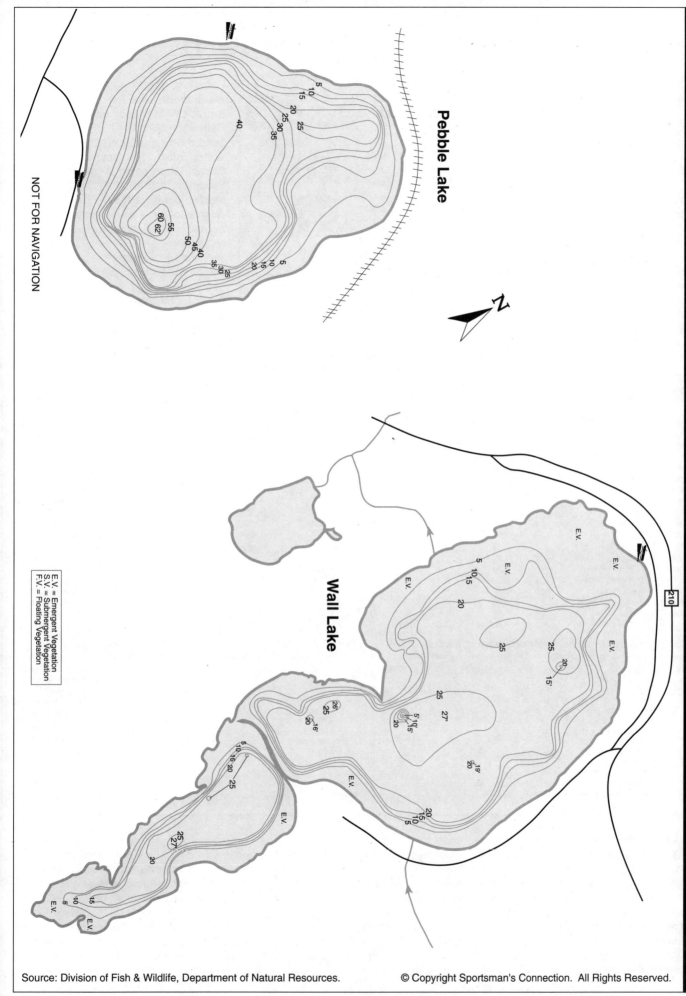

Pebble Lake

NOT FOR NAVIGATION

Wall Lake

E.V. = Emergent Vegetation
S.V. = Submergent Vegetation
F.V. = Floating Vegetation

HOOT LAKE   WRIGHT LAKE

Otter Tail County

Location: Township 133 Range 42, 43
Watershed: Otter Tail
Surface Water Area: 155 Acres
Shorelength: 2.5 Miles
Secchi disk (water clarity): 9.0 Ft.
Water color: Light green
Cause of water color: Moderate algae bloom
Maximum depth: 20 Ft.
Median depth: NA
Accessibility: City-owned public access on the south shore, off County Hwy. 1
Boat Ramp: Concrete
Accommodations: NA
Shoreland zoning classif.: Rec. Dev.
Dominant forest/soil type: Decid/Loam
Management class: Walleye-Centrarchid
Ecological type: Centrarchid

Location: Township 133 Range 42, 43
Watershed: Otter Tail
Surface Water Area: 63 Acres
Shorelength: NA
Secchi disk (water clarity): 9.6 Ft.
Water color: Light green
Cause of water color: Algae bloom
Maximum depth: 32 Ft.
Median depth: NA
Accessibility: City-owned public access on west shore, carry-down on north shore
Boat Ramp: Concrete
Accommodations: NA
Shoreland zoning classif.: Rec. Dev.
Dominant forest/soil type: Decid/Loam
Management class: Walleye-Centrarchid
Ecological type: Centrarchid

HOOT LAKE

DNR COMMENTS:
Northern Pike population down and below normal for lake class; mean length of sample 21.8 inches. Walleye numbers normal for lake class; average length 16.2 inches; natural reproduction occurring. Natural reproduction consistent for Largemouth Bass; fish reaching average of 11.9 inches in 4 years. Strong 1992 year class for Black Crappies; sample ranged from 8.3 to 9.8 inches. Bluegill population about normal for lake class; average size has increased to 7.1 inches.

FISH STOCKING DATA

year	species	size	# released
93	Walleye	Fingerling	1,449
95	Walleye	Fingerling	940
95	Walleye	Yearling	50
97	Walleye	Fingerling	1,741
97	Walleye	Yearling	10

survey date: 6/24/96

NET CATCH DATA

	Gill Nets		Trap Nets	
species	# per net	avg fish wt. (lbs)	# per set	avg fish wt. (lbs)
Black Crappie	0.5	0.30	-	-
Bluegill	6.8	0.25	21.0	0.26
Hybrid Sunfish	0.2	0.17	0.2	0.27
Largemouth Bass	0.8	1.01	-	-
Northern Pike	3.3	2.34	-	-
Pumpkin. Sunfish	7.2	0.20	3.9	0.22
Rock Bass	0.2	0.33	-	-
Tullibee (Cisco)	2.0	0.78	-	-
Walleye	2.7	1.52	-	-
Yellow Perch	86.2	0.10	2.6	0.09

LENGTH OF SELECTED SPECIES SAMPLED FROM ALL GEAR

Number of fish caught for the following length categories (inches):

species	0-5	6-8	9-11	12-14	15-19	20-24	25-29	>30	Total
Black Bullhead	-	1	27	1	-	-	-	-	29
Black Crappie	1	1	1	-	-	-	-	-	3
Bluegill	4	176	-	-	-	-	-	-	180
Brown Bullhead	-	-	6	3	-	-	-	-	9
Hybrid Sunfish	1	2	-	-	-	-	-	-	3
Largemouth Bass	-	1	2	1	1	-	-	-	5
Northern Pike	-	-	-	5	13	2	-	-	20
Pumpkin. Sunfish	17	59	-	-	-	-	-	-	76
Rock Bass	-	1	-	-	-	-	-	-	1
Tullibee (Cisco)	-	1	5	6	-	-	-	-	12
Walleye	-	1	-	5	8	2	-	-	16
Yellow Bullhead	-	-	-	2	-	-	-	-	2
Yellow Perch	85	135	-	-	-	-	-	-	220

WRIGHT LAKE

FISH STOCKING DATA

year	species	size	# released
93	Walleye	Fingerling	828
95	Walleye	Fingerling	1,001
95	Walleye	Adult	16
97	Walleye	Fingerling	1,376
97	Walleye	Yearling	40

survey date: 7/1/96

NET CATCH DATA

	Gill Nets		Trap Nets	
species	# per net	avg fish wt. (lbs)	# per set	avg fish wt. (lbs)
Black Crappie	-	-	0.4	0.10
Bluegill	1.0	0.38	15.3	0.24
Green Sunfish	-	-	0.2	0.06
Hybrid Sunfish	-	-	1.1	0.22
Largemouth Bass	1.0	1.74	0.2	0.42
Northern Pike	9.0	2.15	0.2	1.64
Pumpkin. Sunfish	1.0	0.29	3.8	0.19
Rock Bass	1.0	0.50	0.2	0.49
Walleye	3.0	1.24	-	-
Yellow Perch	6.0	0.08	2.0	0.08

LENGTH OF SELECTED SPECIES SAMPLED FROM ALL GEAR

Number of fish caught for the following length categories (inches):

species	0-5	6-8	9-11	12-14	15-19	20-24	25-29	>30	Total
Black Bullhead	-	-	24	-	-	-	-	-	24
Black Crappie	2	2	-	-	-	-	-	-	4
Bluegill	4	130	-	-	-	-	-	-	134
Brown Bullhead	-	-	-	2	-	-	-	-	2
Green Sunfish	2	-	-	-	-	-	-	-	2
Hybrid Sunfish	2	8	-	-	-	-	-	-	10
Largemouth Bass	-	-	2	2	-	-	-	-	4
Northern Pike	-	-	-	2	4	12	2	-	20
Pumpkin. Sunfish	10	22	-	-	-	-	-	-	32
Rock Bass	-	4	-	-	-	-	-	-	4
Walleye	-	-	-	2	4	-	-	-	6
Yellow Bullhead	-	-	-	2	-	-	-	-	2
Yellow Perch	18	10	-	-	-	-	-	-	28

DNR COMMENTS:
Northern Pike population highest on record for lake and within normal range for lake class; average size 21 inches and 2.1 lb. Walleye numbers up and within normal range; average size 15.6 inches and 1.2 lb.; age information indicates natural reproduction is occurring for this species. Largemouth Bass sampled by electrofishing; sample sizes 7.9 to `17.4 inches. Black Crappie numbers down and below normal; average size 9 inches. Bluegills numbers up slightly and within normal range; 51 percent of sample was larger than 7 inches.

FISHING INFORMATION: These two connected lakes are located virtually in the city of Fergus Falls and provide residents and visitors alike with some excellent panfishing, as well as some decent angling opportunities for Walleyes, Northern Pike and Largemouth Bass. **Wright Lake**, the smaller and deeper of the two, has a power plant inlet on its west side which is often a good spot to find panfish and Northerns. In fact, Northerns abound in this lake, and they aren't just snakes, either. Size isn't bad, in fact, with the average being roughly 2 pounds, give or take an ounce or two. Several points along the south side, meanwhile, offer opportunities for early-season Walleyes. The channel between the two lakes usually holds panfish, especially in the area around the bridge where County Road 1 crosses. Drop a line and see what you hook. **Hoot Lake**, meanwhile, has a heavier weedline than its neighbor. That helps make it a good place to look for Largemouth Bass and Crappies. As in Wright, you'll also find a few stocked Walleyes. The water is fairly clear, so you can attract the panskis with worm chunks or small minnows on a bare hook. A number of bait shops and anglers in Fergus Falls will be happy to give you fishing information if you ask.

NOT FOR NAVIGATION

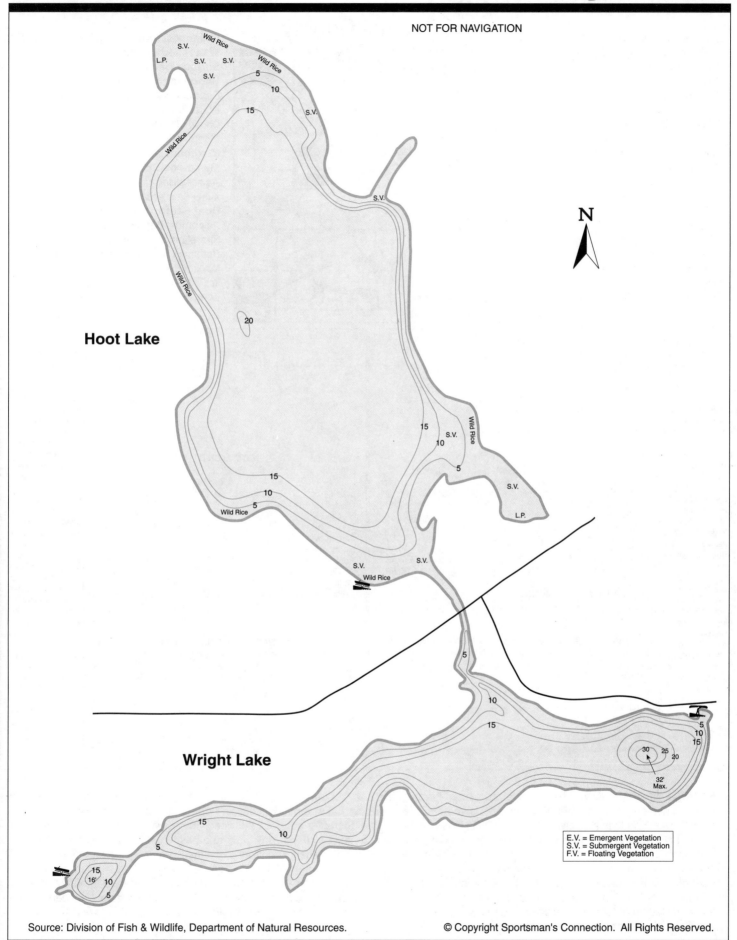

Hoot Lake

Wild Rice

S.V.

L.P.

Wild Rice

5

10

15

20

Wild Rice

15

10

5

Wild Rice

15

10

5

S.V.

S.V.

L.P.

S.V.

Wild Rice

N

Wright Lake

15

10

5

30 25 20

32' Max.

5
10
15

5

10

15

15

16'

10

5

E.V. = Emergent Vegetation
S.V. = Submergent Vegetation
F.V. = Floating Vegetation

Source: Division of Fish & Wildlife, Department of Natural Resources.

NORWAY LAKE

BASS LAKE

Otter Tail County

Location: Township 133 Range 41, 42
Watershed: Pomme De Terre
Surface Water Area: 384 Acres
Shorelength: 4.8 Miles
Secchi disk (water clarity): 4.0 Ft.
Water color: Green
Cause of water color: Heavy filamentous algae bloom
Maximum depth: 19 Ft.
Median depth: NA
Accessibility: State-owned public access on east shore
Boat Ramp: Concrete
Accommodations: NA
Shoreland zoning classif.: Rec. Dev.
Dominant forest/soil type: No Tree/Loam
Management class: Warm-Water Gamefish
Ecological type: Centrarchid

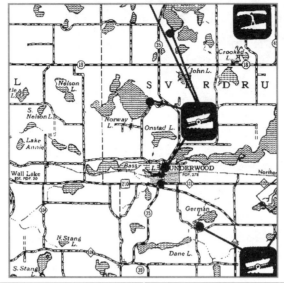

Location: Township 133 Range 41, 42
Watershed: Pomme De Terre
Surface Water Area: 292 Acres
Shorelength: 5.3 Miles
Secchi disk (water clarity): 4.5 Ft.
Water color: Green
Cause of water color: Heavy algae bloom
Maximum depth: 36 Ft.
Median depth: NA
Accessibility: City-owned public access on east shore of the lake
Boat Ramp: Concrete
Accommodations: NA
Shoreland zoning classif.: Gen. Dev.
Dominant forest/soil type: Decid/Wet
Management class: Warm-Water Gamefish
Ecological type: Roughfish-Gamefish

DNR COMMENTS:
Walleye population down and below normal range for lake class; sampled lengths 17 to 25 inches; little or no natural reproduction. Northern Pike numbers down substantially; in all previous surveys Pike numbers were above average; Pike to 29 inches sampled, and all but one was larger than 22 inches. Largemouth Bass numbers good, but population dominated by fish smaller than 9 inches. Bluegill numbers extremely low for lake class; reasons not clear; only one fish sampled. Yellow Perch numbers up substantially and well above average; 24 percent larger than 7 inches.

FISH STOCKING DATA

year	species	size	# released
90	Walleye	Fry	247,000
94	Walleye	Fry	244,000
96	Walleye	Fry	244,000
98	Walleye	Fry	242,000

survey date: 7/19/93

NET CATCH DATA

	Gill Nets		Trap Nets	
species	# per net	avg fish wt. (lbs)	# per set	avg fish wt. (lbs)
Black Crappie	0.2	0.11	0.4	0.48
Bluegill	0.1	0.45	-	-
Largemouth Bass	0.2	0.26	1.9	0.61
Northern Pike	0.4	3.55	0.4	2.55
Pumpkin. Sunfish	-	-	0.1	0.08
Walleye	1.0	3.60	0.7	4.48
White Sucker	0.4	2.52	0.1	3.80
Yellow Bullhead	-	-	0.1	1.72
Yellow Perch	107.7	0.14	17.4	0.08

LENGTH OF SELECTED SPECIES SAMPLED FROM ALL GEAR
Number of fish caught for the following length categories (inches):

species	0-5	6-8	9-11	12-14	15-19	20-24	25-29	>30	Total
Black Crappie	3	2	-	1	-	-	-	-	6
Bluegill	-	1	-	-	-	-	-	-	1
Largemouth Bass	12	4	1	-	2	-	-	-	19
Northern Pike	-	-	1	-	-	5	2	-	8
Pumpkin. Sunfish	1	-	-	-	-	-	-	-	1
Walleye	-	-	-	-	4	11	-	-	15
Yellow Bullhead	-	-	-	1	-	-	-	-	1
Yellow Perch	190	253	10	-	-	-	-	-	453

DNR COMMENTS:
Walleye catch rate within normal range for lake class; natural reproduction consistent; 27 percent of fish sampled exceeded 19 inches. Northern Pike numbers down to just below normal range; pike to 28 inches captured; 60 percent of sample larger than 23 inches. Largemouth Bass sampled for first time in this lake. Bluegill population fluctuates widely, and at last sampling numbers were low. Black Bullhead numbers down significantly but still very high.

FISH STOCKING DATA

year	species	size	# released
93	Walleye	Fry	138,000
95	Walleye	Fry	138,000
97	Walleye	Fry	138,000

survey date: 6/8/93

NET CATCH DATA

	Gill Nets		Trap Nets	
species	# per net	avg fish wt. (lbs)	# per set	avg fish wt. (lbs)
Black Bullhead	4.7	0.67	102.6	0.85
Bluegill	1.2	0.06	1.7	0.31
Brown Bullhead	1.7	0.59	5.1	0.37
Largemouth Bass	-	-	0.3	1.78
Northern Pike	1.3	2.66	0.2	3.69
Pumpkin. Sunfish	3.3	0.07	5.0	0.11
Walleye	3.5	1.84	0.1	5.29
White Sucker	1.2	2.87	-	-
Yellow Perch	3.2	0.26	-	-

LENGTH OF SELECTED SPECIES SAMPLED FROM ALL GEAR
Number of fish caught for the following length categories (inches):

species	0-5	6-8	9-11	12-14	15-19	20-24	25-29	>30	Total
Black Bullhead	-	9	170	9	3	-	-	-	191
Bluegill	5	16	-	-	-	-	-	-	21
Brown Bullhead	-	7	49	-	-	-	-	-	56
Largemouth Bass	-	-	-	2	1	-	-	-	3
Northern Pike	-	-	1	1	4	4	-	10
Pumpkin. Sunfish	62	3	-	-	-	-	-	-	65
Walleye	-	1	6	3	6	5	1	-	22
Yellow Perch	-	19	-	-	-	-	-	-	19

FISHING INFORMATION: These two lakes, east of Fergus Falls and just outside the community of Underwood, are heavy on Northern Pike, Largemouth Bass and Panfish and offer some Walleyes. **Norway Lake**, for instance, has Northerns pretty well distributed throughout its basin, and they are relatively large. Often they can be found at the outer edges of the weedlines preying on small Sunfish and Yellow Perch. Norway's water is cloudy with algae bloom, so it's a good idea to use flashy lures to attract attention as you troll the edges. The north bay of the lake is great for panfish, but beware the stumps in the shallow entrance channel; you can lose a prop easily. This shallow area is a good spot to look for Bass, however, and when the water is fairly high you can fish them with bright marabou jigs and pork rinds or minnows. You can also find some off the point in the southeast corner of the lake. There is no evidence of natural Walleye reproduction here, but this species has been stocked by the DNR. The southeast point marked by bulrushes is your best bet early. **Bass Lake**, just south of Norway, is loaded with Black Bullheads, but it offers some Walleye opportunities as well as decent fishing for Bluegills. You'll also find Northern Pike in the south end, off the weeds.

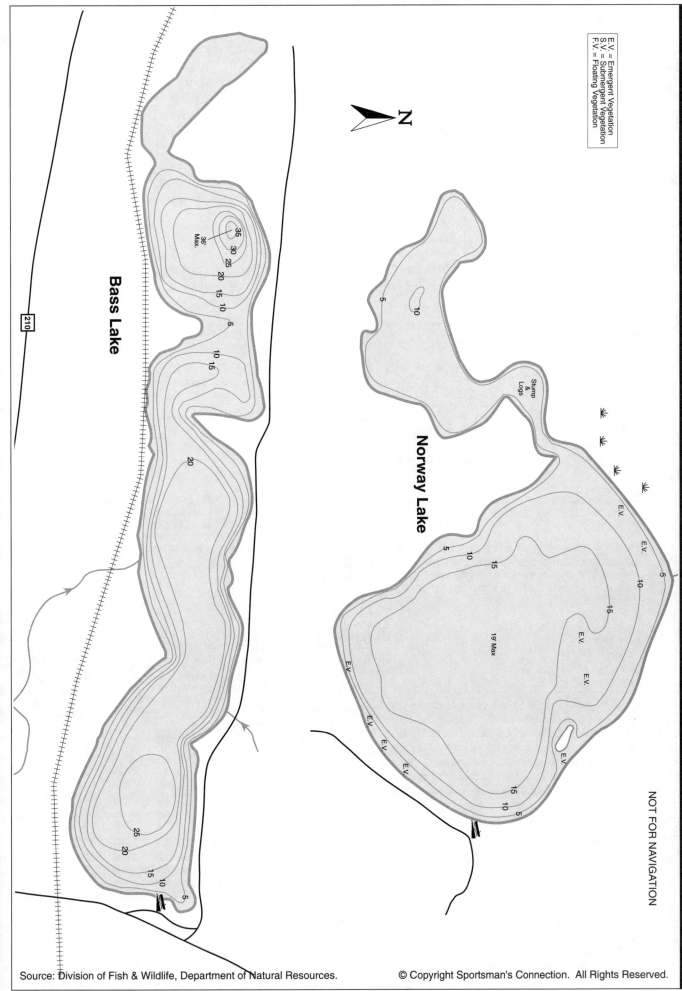

SPORTSMAN'S Connection®

E.V. = Emergent Vegetation
S.V. = Submergent Vegetation
F.V. = Floating Vegetation

N

210

Bass Lake

36'
Max.

35
30
25
20
15
10
5
10
15
20
20
25
20
15
10
5

Norway Lake

Stump
& Logs

5
10

5
10
15
15
E.V.
E.V.
10
5
15
E.V.
E.V.
E.V.
19' Max.
E.V.
E.V.
15
10
5

NOT FOR NAVIGATION

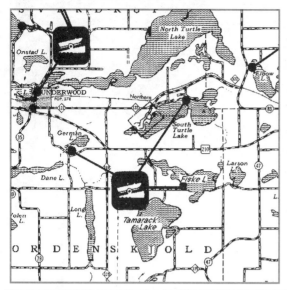

Otter Tail County

Size of lake:	630 Acres	71 Acres	250 Acres
Shorelength:	8.9 Miles	NA	5.2 Miles
Secchi disk (water clarity):	5.5 Ft.	9.0 Ft.	2.3 Ft.
Water color:	Green	Clear	Green
Cause of water color:	Algal bloom	NA	Algae bloom
Maximum depth:	35 Ft.	46 Ft.	26 Ft.
Median depth:	NA	NA	NA
Accessibility:	State-owned public access on north shore	Public access on southwest shore	Public access on south shore
Boat Ramp:	Concrete	Earth	Concrete
Accommodations:	NA	NA	NA
Shoreland zoning classif.:	Rec. Dev.	Nat. Env.	Nat. Env.
Dominant forest/soil type:	Decid/Sand	NA	Decid/Loam
Management class:	Walleye-Centrarchid	Walleye-Centrarchid	Walleye-Centrarchid
Ecological type:	Centrarchid-Walleye	Centrarchid	Centrarchid-Walleye

South Turtle Lake

DNR COMMENTS:
Northern Pike numbers down and below normal for lake class; average size 18.9 inches and 1.4 lb. Walleye population up and above normal; mean size 16.7 inches and 1.7 lb.; stocking supplementing natural reproduction for this species. Largemouth Bass numbers about normal; average size 13.1 inches; good 1990 and 1991 year classes. Black Crappie population below normal; average size 8.5 inches. Bluegill population normal; average length 6.5 inches.

FISH STOCKING DATA

year	species	size	# released
94	Walleye	Fry	120,000
95	Walleye	Yearling	5,278
95	Walleye	Fingerling	735

NET CATCH DATA

survey date: 8/12/96

	Gill Nets		Trap Nets	
species	# per net	avg fish wt. (lbs)	# per set	avg fish wt. (lbs)
Black Crappie	0.4	0.54	trace	0.37
Bluegill	4.1	0.23	13.9	0.21
Hybrid Sunfish	-	-	trace	0.13
Largemouth Bass	0.6	1.11	0.5	0.47
Northern Pike	2.7	1.37	1.4	1.45
Pumpkin. Sunfish	2.0	0.22	0.5	0.14
Walleye	6.5	1.67	0.4	4.10
Yellow Perch	0.8	0.09	0.2	0.25

LENGTH OF SELECTED SPECIES SAMPLED FROM ALL GEAR
Number of fish caught for the following length categories (inches):

species	0-5	6-8	9-11	12-14	15-19	20-24	25-29	>30	Total
Black Crappie	3	1		2					6
Bluegill	55	155							210
Hybrid Sunfish	1								1
Largemouth Bass	3	1	3	6					13
Northern Pike				4	30	10	3		47
Pumpkin. Sunfish	6	18							24
Walleye			8	10	53	10	2		83
Yellow Bullhead		20	99	46					165
Yellow Perch	7	4	1						12

German Lake

FISH STOCKING DATA

No record of stocking since 1985.

NET CATCH DATA

survey date: 6/23/97

	Gill Nets		Trap Nets	
species	# per net	avg fish wt. (lbs)	# per set	avg fish wt. (lbs)
Black Crappie	-	-	0.9	0.14
Bluegill	-	-	21.1	0.15
Green Sunfish	-	-	0.9	0.10
Hybrid Sunfish	-	-	14.3	0.18
Largemouth Bass	0.5	1.68	0.8	0.58
Northern Pike	8.5	1.80	0.1	0.49
Pumpkin. Sunfish	-	-	6.6	0.19
Walleye	0.5	7.94	-	-
Yellow Perch	2.0	0.17	0.2	0.19

LENGTH OF SELECTED SPECIES SAMPLED FROM ALL GEAR
Number of fish caught for the following length categories (inches):

species	0-5	6-8	9-11	12-14	15-19	20-24	25-29	>30	Total
Black Crappie	4	4							8
Bluegill	81	58							139
Green Sunfish	7	1							8
Hybrid Sunfish	51	54							105
Largemouth Bass		1	5	2					8
Northern Pike				2	10	4	2		18
Pumpkin. Sunfish	26	33							59
Walleye							1		1
Yellow Perch	2	3	1						6

DNR COMMENTS:
Northern Pike population healthy with average length of about 20 inches. Largemouth Bass very healthy, but average size small at roughly 10 inches. Bluegill and other Panfish average around 6 inches, but some exceed 8 inches. Longnose Gar offer a bonus fishery for anglers and bowfishers.

Fiske Lake

FISH STOCKING DATA

year	species	size	# released
90	Walleye	Fry	190,000
93	Walleye	Fry	186,000

NET CATCH DATA

survey date: 6/26/95

	Gill Nets		Trap Nets	
species	# per net	avg fish wt. (lbs)	# per set	avg fish wt. (lbs)
Black Crappie	4.2	0.21	1.0	0.22
Bluegill	2.2	0.21	9.9	0.21
Golden Shiner	4.5	0.08	-	-
Hybrid Sunfish	0.2	0.46	1.0	0.31
Largemouth Bass	0.5	0.98	0.6	0.89
Northern Pike	20.7	1.79	2.0	1.43
Pumpkin. Sunfish	2.7	0.19	2.9	0.17
Walleye	1.2	2.90	0.1	5.40
Yellow Perch	64.2	0.11	1.7	0.11

LENGTH OF SELECTED SPECIES SAMPLED FROM ALL GEAR
Number of fish caught for the following length categories (inches):

species	0-5	6-8	9-11	12-14	15-19	20-24	25-29	>30	Total
Black Crappie	3	28	1						32
Bluegill	7	75							82
Hybrid Sunfish	1	7							8
Largemouth Bass		4	3						7
Northern Pike			2	21	71	25	13	4	136
Pumpkin. Sunfish	20	16							36
Walleye					4	4			8
Yellow Perch	68	79							147

DNR COMMENTS:
This lake has been subject to severe winterkill in past years. Northern Pike numbers above normal; mean length 19.1 inches. Walleye population normal; mean length 20.1 inches; stocking discontinued for lack of success. Largemouth Bass abundance normal; mean length 11.8 inches. Black Crappie numbers normal; mean length 6.6 inches. Bluegill population down but within normal range; mean length 6.6 inches.

FISHING INFORMATION: South Turtle Lake is home to decent populations of Largemouth Bass and Bluegills. It also holds a few bigger-than-average Northern Pike and good numbers of Walleyes. There are abundant weeds, as well as good points and coves on the lake's east side. In addition, There bays to the north and west and some holes in excess of 30 feet. The north and west bays can both produce fine Largemouth following the spawn, though you can do fairly well at any of the weedlines much of the year. The water is somewhat cloudy, so you'll want to use bright jigs with pork rinds. Northerns will be prowling the outer edges of the weeds. You can find Walleyes early in the season along the east side near the points there, also at the northwest corner of the lake. Fish these spots with live bait. **German Lake** offers good numbers of panfish and Yellow Bullheads, and also holds lots of small-to-decent Northern Pike. The lake is relatively clear and has a good weedline full of Bluegill and Perch. Northerns roam the edges of those same weeds; troll there with spoons and live bait. **Fiske Lake** is heavily weeded and subject to partial winterkill during harsh winters. It's a good idea to check at area bait shops for a report before putting your boat in.

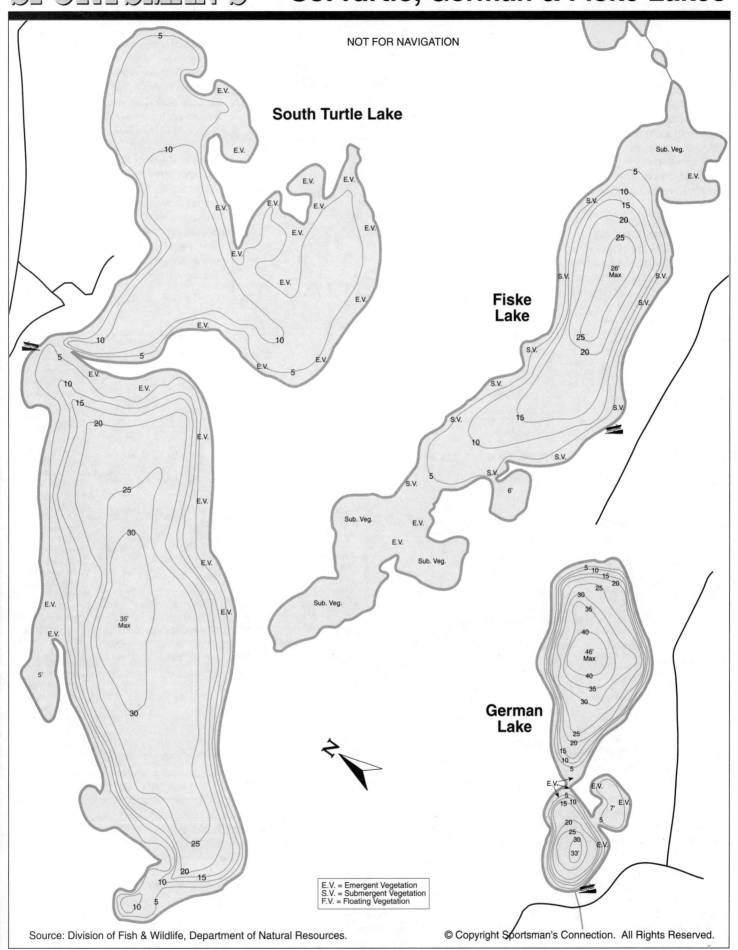

So. Turtle, German & Fiske Lakes

NOT FOR NAVIGATION

South Turtle Lake

Fiske Lake

German Lake

E.V. = Emergent Vegetation
S.V. = Submergent Vegetation
F.V. = Floating Vegetation

Source: Division of Fish & Wildlife, Department of Natural Resources.

ELBOW LAKE   SILVER LAKE
Otter Tail County

Location: Township 133 Range 30
Watershed: Pomme De Terre
Surface Water Area: 189 Acres
Shorelength: 4.2 Miles
Secchi disk (water clarity): 18.0 Ft.
Water color: Clear
Cause of water color: NA
Maximum depth: 46 Ft.
Median depth: NA
Accessibility: State-owned public access on northwest shore, just off Highway 83
Boat Ramp: Concrete
Accommodations: NA
Shoreland zoning classif.: Nat. Env.
Dominant forest/soil type: NA
Management class: Walleye-Centrarchid
Ecological type: Centrarchid

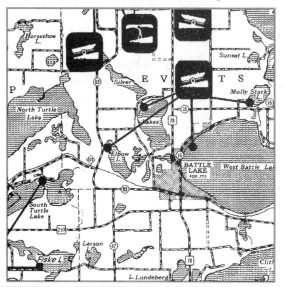

Location: Township 133 Range 40
Watershed: Pomme De Terre
Surface Water Area: 547 Acres
Shorelength: 4.2 Miles
Secchi disk (water clarity): 9.3 Ft.
Water color: Greenish
Cause of water color: Algae bloom
Maximum depth: 45 Ft.
Median depth: 16 Ft.
Accessibility: Public access on northwest shore
Boat Ramp: Concrete
Accommodations: NA
Shoreland zoning classif.: Rec. Dev.
Dominant forest/soil type: NA
Management class: Walleye-Centrarchid
Ecological type: Centrarchid-Walleye

DNR COMMENTS:
Northern Pike abundance down but within expected range for lake class; average length 24 inches. Walleye numbers down but within expected range; average 18 inches and 2.6 lb.; natural reproduction limited for this species. Largemouth Bass numbers near upper end of expected range; growth slow, with Bass reaching only 9 inches at age 4. Black Crappie population normal; reproduction inconsistent. Bluegill numbers up and above expected range; 14 percent of Bluegills reaching 7 inches.

FISH STOCKING DATA

year	species	size	# released
94	Walleye	Fingerling	2,672
96	Walleye	Fingerling	2,550

NET CATCH DATA
survey date: 6/13/94

| | Gill Nets | | Trap Nets | |
| | | avg fish | | avg fish |
species	# per net	wt. (lbs)	# per set	wt. (lbs)
Black Bullhead	0.5	1.72	2.3	2.14
Black Crappie	0.2	0.59	0.6	0.48
Bluegill	13.5	0.12	366.8	0.20
Green Sunfish	-	-	0.9	0.08
Hybrid Sunfish	2.3	0.30	23.4	0.40
Largemouth Bass	1.7	0.99	1.7	0.21
Northern Pike	3.3	3.21	-	-
Pumpkin. Sunfish	1.5	0.46	3.0	0.43
Walleye	1.2	2.63	-	-
White Sucker	2.2	3.50	-	-
Yellow Bullhead	-	-	0.1	2.28
Yellow Perch	23.2	0.20	0.2	0.32

LENGTH OF SELECTED SPECIES SAMPLED FROM ALL GEAR
Number of fish caught for the following length categories (inches):

species	0-5	6-8	9-11	12-14	15-19	20-24	25-29	>30	Total
Black Bullhead	-	-	10	14	-	-	-	-	24
Black Crappie	-	-	6	-	-	-	-	-	6
Bluegill	144	248	-	-	-	-	-	-	392
Green Sunfish	6	-	-	-	-	-	-	-	6
Hybrid Sunfish	50	143	-	-	-	-	-	-	193
Largemouth Bass	1	12	8	3	1	-	-	-	25
Northern Pike	-	-	-	-	4	8	7	1	20
Pumpkin. Sunfish	9	25	-	-	-	-	-	-	34
Walleye	-	-	3	1	2	1	-	-	7
Yellow Bullhead	-	-	-	1	-	-	-	-	1
Yellow Perch	8	116	13	-	-	-	-	-	137

FISH STOCKING DATA

year	species	size	# released
94	Walleye	Fingerling	10,265
96	Walleye	Fingerling	7,209
96	Walleye	Fry	2,813,000
98	Black Crappie	Adult	509

NET CATCH DATA
survey date: 7/8/96

| | Gill Nets | | Trap Nets | |
| | | avg fish | | avg fish |
species	# per net	wt. (lbs)	# per set	wt. (lbs)
Black Bullhead	0.4	1.35	-	-
Black Crappie	0.1	1.09	-	-
Bluegill	0.1	0.45	1.9	0.20
Hybrid Sunfish	0.1	0.39	-	-
Northern Pike	1.0	4.09	-	-
Pumpkin. Sunfish	0.6	0.22	0.9	0.17
Rock Bass	7.0	0.40	5.1	0.25
Walleye	8.6	1.81	0.5	1.95
White Sucker	7.9	1.55	0.9	1.97
Yellow Bullhead	2.1	1.10	4.9	1.09
Yellow Perch	10.7	0.11	0.3	0.05

LENGTH OF SELECTED SPECIES SAMPLED FROM ALL GEAR
Number of fish caught for the following length categories (inches):

species	0-5	6-8	9-11	12-14	15-19	20-24	25-29	>30	Total
Black Bullhead	-	-	1	3	-	-	-	-	4
Black Crappie	-	-	-	1	-	-	-	-	1
Bluegill	6	10	-	-	-	-	-	-	16
Hybrid Sunfish	-	1	-	-	-	-	-	-	1
Northern Pike	-	-	-	-	-	2	5	2	9
Pumpkin. Sunfish	6	6	-	-	-	-	-	-	12
Rock Bass	33	48	23	-	-	-	-	-	104
Walleye	-	-	3	6	64	8	-	-	81
Yellow Bullhead	-	-	12	46	-	-	-	-	58
Yellow Perch	30	37	1	-	-	-	-	-	68

DNR COMMENTS:
Northern Pike numbers up slightly but still below the expected range for lake class; population may be limited by lack of suitable spawning habitat; average size 27.2 inches and 4.1 lb. Walleye numbers high; average size 17.2 inches and 1.9 lb.; natural reproduction limited by lack of spawning habitat; stocking may be supplementing limited reproduction. Bluegill numbers down and below expected range; reproduction variable; fish reaching 5.7 inches at age 5. Yellow Perch population also down but within normal range; reproduction variable.

FISHING INFORMATION: These lakes west of Fergus Falls and three miles southwest of Battle Lake are both fine places to fish, though for different reasons. **Silver Lake** is an excellent Walleye lake which also holds good numbers of Largemouth Bass and Crappies. The lake seems to have been designed as Walleye habitat; a sand bottom, good forage base, points, humps and deep water provide a fine setting for natural reproduction. In addition, regular stocking of fingerlings by the DNR bolsters the Walleye population. Early season Walleye are found at the small points off the southeast and southwest shores. There is also a good hump in the middle of the south end of the lake. And the quick dropoffs along the north end can also be productive. Fish the bottoms at these areas with leeches or minnows. Bass are in the weeds here, especially in the shallow water in the northeast corner and along the northwest shore. Crappies are in the weeds early and will go for smaller minnows on a bare hook or small marabou jig. When the water warms, the Crappies and Walleyes will go deep during the day, most often at the north end. **Elbow Lake** does not have as many Walleyes as its neighbor, but there are still enough to be interesting. A point on the east side is an excellent place to start looking for them, but many areas with quick dropoffs are also productive. For Largemouth and panfish, try the weeded areas at the north and south ends. The water is extremely clear, so you will do well using live bait: shiner minnows for the Walleyes; worms, smaller minnows and pork rinds for panfish and Bass.

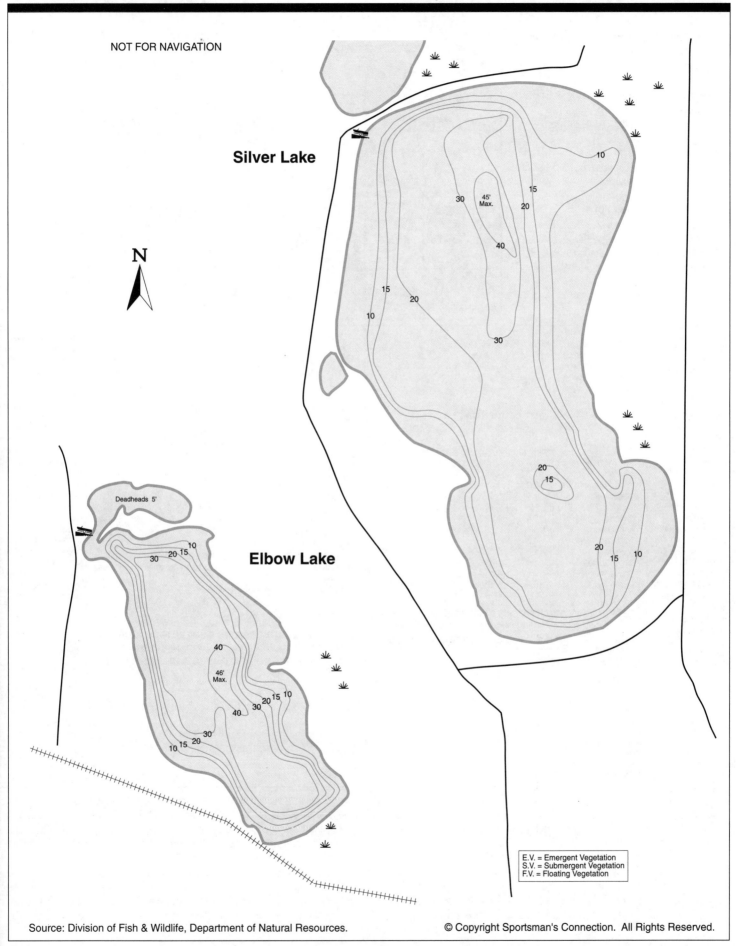

NOT FOR NAVIGATION

Silver Lake

N

30   45' Max.   15   10
20
40

15
20
10

30

20
15

20   10
15

Deadheads 5'

10   15
30   20
20

Elbow Lake

40
46' Max.
40   30   20   15   10
30
30   20
10   15   20

E.V. = Emergent Vegetation
S.V. = Submergent Vegetation
F.V. = Floating Vegetation

Source: Division of Fish & Wildlife, Department of Natural Resources.

DEER LAKE

EAST LOST LAKE

Otter Tail County

Location: Township 133 Range 40
Watershed: Otter Tail
Surface Water Area: 457 Acres
Shorelength: 3.8 Miles
Secchi disk (water clarity): 5.5 Ft.
Water color: Greenish
Cause of water color: Algae bloom
Maximum depth: 26 Ft.
Median depth: 7 Ft.
Accessibility: Public access on southeast shore, off Hwy. 83
Boat Ramp: Concrete
Accommodations: NA
Shoreland zoning classif.: Rec. Dev.
Dominant forest/soil type: Decid/Wet
Management class: Walleye-Centrarchid
Ecological type: Centrarchid-Walleye

Location: Township 133 Range 40, 41
Watershed: Otter Tail
Surface Water Area: 501 Acres
Shorelength: 6.5 Miles
Secchi disk (water clarity): 6.2 Ft.
Water color: Green
Cause of water color: Algae bloom
Maximum depth: 36 Ft.
Median depth: 8 Ft.
Accessibility: Southwest shore (carry-in); via navigable channel from Deer Lake
Boat Ramp: Concrete ramp on Deer Lake
Accommodations: NA
Shoreland zoning classif.: Rec. Dev.
Dominant forest/soil type: Decid/Sand
Management class: Walleye-Centrarchid
Ecological type: Centrarchid-Walleye

DEER LAKE

DNR COMMENTS: Walleye numbers down but within normal range for lake class; natural reproduction limited, and stocking contributes heavily to population of this species. Northern Pike numbers down slightly but within normal range; only 4 percent of Pike exceeded 23 inches in length. Bluegill population stable; size structure improved, as 17 percent of fish are reaching 7 inches. Consistent natural reproduction for Black Crappie.

FISH STOCKING DATA

year	species	size	# released
93	Walleye	Fry	306,000
95	Walleye	Fry	306,000
97	Walleye	Fry	306,000

NET CATCH DATA

survey date: 8/30/93

	Gill Nets		Trap Nets	
species	# per net	avg fish wt. (lbs)	# per set	avg fish wt. (lbs)
Black Crappie	0.9	0.67	1.4	0.41
Bluegill	9.7	0.18	54.2	0.20
Hybrid Sunfish	0.2	0.35	0.4	0.33
Largemouth Bass	1.4	1.40	0.7	0.95
Northern Pike	5.9	1.44	-	-
Pumpkin. Sunfish	6.4	0.22	2.0	0.21
Rock Bass	0.7	0.32	0.3	0.12
Tullibee (Cisco)	0.2	0.93	-	-
Walleye	2.6	1.16		
White Sucker	1.6	2.00	0.3	2.04
Yellow Bullhead	4.1	0.31	0.4	0.93
Yellow Perch	13.6	0.13	0.1	0.14

LENGTH OF SELECTED SPECIES SAMPLED FROM ALL GEAR

Number of fish caught for the following length categories (inches):

species	0-5	6-8	9-11	12-14	15-19	20-24	25-29	>30	Total
Black Bullhead	-	-	2	1	-	-	-	-	3
Black Crappie	-	6	15	-	-	-	-	-	21
Bluegill	132	220	-	-	-	-	-	-	352
Brown Bullhead	-	1	1	6	-	-	-	-	8
Hybrid Sunfish	-	6	-	-	-	-	-	-	6
Largemouth Bass	-	2	7	7	3	-	-	-	19
Northern Pike	-	-	-	3	33	17	-	-	53
Pumpkin. Sunfish	20	56	-	-	-	-	-	-	76
Rock Bass	3	6	-	-	-	-	-	-	9
Tullibee (Cisco)	-	-	-	2	-	-	-	-	2
Walleye	-	-	12	3	4	4	-	-	23
Yellow Bullhead	-	3	36	2	-	-	-	-	41
Yellow Perch	52	70	1	-	-	-	-	-	123

EAST LOST LAKE

FISH STOCKING DATA

year	species	size	# released
93	Walleye	Fry	327,000
95	Walleye	Fry	327,000
97	Walleye	Fry	327,000

NET CATCH DATA

survey date: 8/30/93

	Gill Nets		Trap Nets	
species	# per net	avg fish wt. (lbs)	# per set	avg fish wt. (lbs)
Black Bullhead	1.0	1.04	-	-
Black Crappie	0.3	0.17	0.6	0.54
Bluegill	9.1	0.13	58.2	0.22
Bowfin (Dogfish)	-	-	0.6	4.61
Brown Bullhead	0.1	0.89	0.2	0.89
Common Carp	-	-	0.4	11.28
Hybrid Sunfish	0.2	0.18	0.7	0.27
Largemouth Bass	1.0	0.77	0.7	0.47
Northern Pike	7.2	1.04	1.1	0.46
Pumpkin. Sunfish	4.0	0.16	2.8	0.23
Rock Bass	0.1	0.33	0.4	0.33
Walleye	1.4	1.40	-	-
White Sucker	0.9	2.20	0.9	2.75
Yellow Bullhead	9.1	0.73	6.3	0.78
Yellow Perch	2.1	0.15	-	-

LENGTH OF SELECTED SPECIES SAMPLED FROM ALL GEAR

Number of fish caught for the following length categories (inches):

species	0-5	6-8	9-11	12-14	15-19	20-24	25-29	>30	Total
Black Bullhead	-	-	4	5	-	-	-	-	9
Black Crappie	2	1	5	-	-	-	-	-	8
Bluegill	103	200	-	-	-	-	-	-	303
Brown Bullhead	-	-	1	2	-	-	-	-	3
Hybrid Sunfish	1	7	-	-	-	-	-	-	8
Largemouth Bass	-	4	8	3	-	-	-	-	15
Northern Pike	-	6	-	16	43	10	-	-	75
Pumpkin. Sunfish	28	33	-	-	-	-	-	-	61
Rock Bass	1	3	1	-	-	-	-	-	5
Walleye	-	-	4	1	8	-	-	-	13
Yellow Bullhead	-	5	106	26	2	-	-	-	139

DNR COMMENTS: Walleye population down but still within normal range for lake class; natural reproduction limited; 54 percent of sample exceeded 16 inches in length. Northern Pike numbers up and above normal range; population dominated by fish less than 22 inches in length. Largemouth Bass and Black Crappies sampled by electrofishing. Bluegill population stable; little change in numbers and sizes for this species since 1988. Aquatic habitat conditions in this lake remain good; bulrush, cattail and wild rice beds prevalent.

FISHING INFORMATION: While Otter Tail Lake receives the most attention in the area and deservedly so, these two relatively small lakes produce some decent fishing of their own. Both are heavily stocked with Walleye fry which, along with good natural reproduction and some migration from Otter Tail, produce decent numbers of catchable-size fish. Work the sunken islands and steep shoreline drops with minnows switching to leeches and nightcrawlers as the water warms during summer. **Deer** is the better Walleye lake of the two while **East Lost** harbors a better Largemouth Bass population. Typical Bass fishing techniques work here as well as in Deer - spinnerbaits, crankbaits, plastic worms and topwaters are all productive at different times. Fish primarily in and around the shoreline weedbeds and the sunken islands. The panfish tend to run on the small side although we have heard some reports of good-size Crappies' being pulled out by anglers who know the lake. Northern Pike fishing is basically a waste of time unless you are into hammerhandles. Again, there are exceptions to this rule too, as an occasional lunker is caught, probably migrating along the river. The next time you are out on Otter Tail and maybe feeling a little overwhelmed, give these lakes a try. They're worth the side trip.

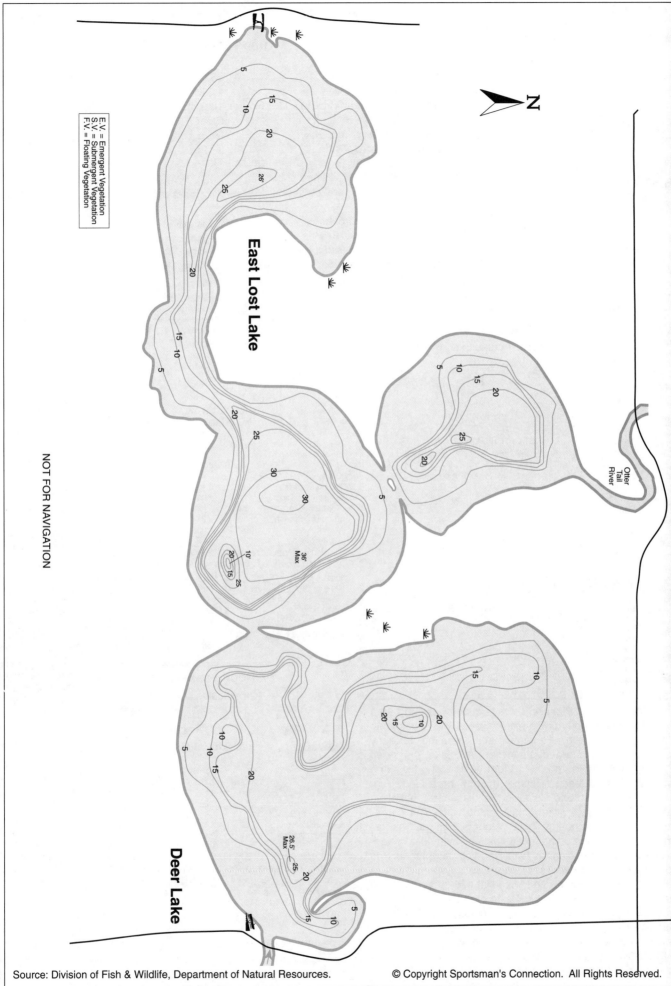

East Lost Lake

Deer Lake

Otter Tail River

N

NOT FOR NAVIGATION

E.V. = Emergent Vegetation
S.V. = Submergent Vegetation
F.V. = Floating Vegetation

Source: Division of Fish & Wildlife, Department of Natural Resources.

Otter Tail County

	PICKEREL LAKE	TWIN LAKE	ROUND LAKE
Size of lake:	829 Acres	333 Acres	83 Acres
Shorelength:	6.3 Miles	4.3 Miles	NA
Secchi disk (water clarity):	14.0 Ft.	14.0 Ft.	6.5 Ft.
Water color:	Clear	Clear	NA
Cause of water color:	NA	NA	NA
Maximum depth:	78 Ft.	50 Ft.	34 Ft.
Median depth:	28 Ft.	15 Ft.	NA
Accessibility:	State-owned public access on south-central shore, off County Road 74	Public access on southeast shore	Public access on east shore, off Cty. Road 11
Boat Ramp:	Concrete	Concrete	Gravel
Accommodations:	Resorts, campground	Resort, campground	NA
Shoreland zoning classif.:	Rec. Dev.	Rec. Dev.	Nat. Env.
Dominant forest/soil type:	Decid/Sand	Decid/Sand	Decid/Sand
Management class:	Walleye-Centrarchid	Walleye-Centrarchid	Walleye-Centrarchid
Ecological type:	Centrarchid-Walleye	Centrarchid	Centrarchid-Walleye

DNR COMMENTS:
Walleye population above expected range for lake class; avg. size 16.2 inches and 1.4 lb. No. Pike population small; avg. size is good, however; spawning habitat limited. SM Bass popular with anglers; spawning structures emplaced in 1997 to supplement natural spawning habitat. LM Bass, Black Crappies and Bluegills scarce; due to lack of suitable spawning areas. Cisco population thriving, and this species is popular with winter anglers. Yellow Perch and White Suckers present.

Pickerel Lake

FISH STOCKING DATA

year	species	size	# released
94	Northern Pike	Fingerling	2,064
94	Walleye	Fry	274,000
94	Northern Pike	Yearling	40
94	Northern Pike	Adult	2
95	Walleye	Fingerling	9,711
97	Walleye	Fry	274,000

survey date: 8/25/97

NET CATCH DATA

	Gill Nets		Trap Nets	
species	# per net	avg fish wt. (lbs)	# per set	avg fish wt. (lbs)
Bluegill	-	-	10.5	0.11
Largemouth Bass	-	-	2.2	0.21
Northern Pike	0.8	3.34	-	-
Rock Bass	-	-	4.1	0.20
Smallmouth Bass	0.7	1.53	4.7	0.37
Tullibee (Cisco)	0.2	0.92	-	-
Walleye	10.6	1.43	0.2	1.00
Yellow Perch	26.3	0.17	2.1	0.16

LENGTH OF SELECTED SPECIES SAMPLED FROM ALL GEAR
Number of fish caught for the following length categories (inches):

species	0-5	6-8	9-11	12-14	15-19	20-24	25-29	>30	Total
Bluegill	92	14	-	-	-	-	-	-	106
Largemouth Bass	-	26	-	-	-	-	-	-	26
Northern Pike	-	-	-	-	-	5	4	-	9
Rock Bass	32	13	4	-	-	-	-	-	49
Smallmouth Bass	3	41	9	9	2	-	-	-	64
Tullibee (Cisco)	-	1	-	-	1	-	-	-	2
Walleye	-	-	12	24	92	1	-	-	129
Yellow Perch	6	310	6	-	-	-	-	-	322

DNR COMMENTS:
No. Pike population stable but below expected range for lake class; avg. size 23.3 inches and 3.5 lb. Walleye numbers up and above expected range; avg. size 17.5 inches and 1.9 lb.; natural reproduction; stocking is supplementing spawning; Walleye reaching avg. length of 15.9 inches at age 4. LM Bass abundant; avg. length 10.3 inches at age 4. Bluegill numbers down substantially but within expected range. Yellow Perch scarce; average length 6.5 inches at age 4.

Twin Lake

FISH STOCKING DATA

year	species	size	# released
93	Walleye	Fry	190,000
94	Walleye	Fry	189,000
96	Walleye	Fry	189,000
98	Walleye	Fry	189,000

survey date: 8/5/96

NET CATCH DATA

	Gill Nets		Trap Nets	
species	# per net	avg fish wt. (lbs)	# per set	avg fish wt. (lbs)
Black Crappie	-	-	0.1	0.26
Bluegill	4.6	0.21	44.0	0.19
Golden Shiner	-	-	0.3	0.06
Hybrid Sunfish	0.4	0.10	-	-
Largemouth Bass	1.1	1.05	0.4	0.39
Northern Pike	2.0	3.41	0.1	3.75
Pumpkin. Sunfish	3.5	0.21	2.3	0.11
Walleye	6.4	1.89	0.8	4.49
Yellow Perch	2.8	0.09	0.3	0.31

LENGTH OF SELECTED SPECIES SAMPLED FROM ALL GEAR
Number of fish caught for the following length categories (inches):

species	0-5	6-8	9-11	12-14	15-19	20-24	25-29	>30	Total
Black Crappie	-	1	-	-	-	-	-	-	1
Bluegill	100	126	1	-	-	-	-	-	227
Hybrid Sunfish	-	1	-	-	-	-	-	-	1
Largemouth Bass	1	4	6	-	2	-	-	-	13
Northern Pike	-	-	-	-	12	4	1	-	17
Pumpkin. Sunfish	23	26	-	-	-	-	-	-	49
Walleye	-	-	-	18	16	17	3	-	54
Yellow Perch	3	15	1	-	-	-	-	-	19

Round Lake

FISH STOCKING DATA

year	species	size	# released
95	Walleye	Fingerling	1,225
97	Walleye	Fingerling	770

survey date: 7/20/94

NET CATCH DATA

	Gill Nets		Trap Nets	
species	# per net	avg fish wt. (lbs)	# per set	avg fish wt. (lbs)
Bluegill	24.0	0.17	81.7	0.15
Hybrid Sunfish	7.7	0.28	19.3	0.26
Largemouth Bass	-	-	0.6	0.25
Northern Pike	1.7	6.62	0.1	0.14
Pumpkin. Sunfish	1.0	0.19	1.8	0.40
Walleye	2.3	1.95	0.7	1.42
Yellow Perch	25.7	0.14	2.1	0.15

LENGTH OF SELECTED SPECIES SAMPLED FROM ALL GEAR
Number of fish caught for the following length categories (inches):

species	0-5	6-8	9-11	12-14	15-19	20-24	25-29	>30	Total
Bluegill	218	143	-	-	-	-	-	-	361
Hybrid Sunfish	63	60	-	-	-	-	-	-	123
Largemouth Bass	1	3	1	-	-	-	-	-	5
Northern Pike	-	1	-	-	1	1	3	-	6
Pumpkin. Sunfish	10	9	-	-	-	-	-	-	19
Walleye	-	-	4	1	5	3	-	-	13
Yellow Bullhead	-	34	149	4	-	-	-	-	187
Yellow Perch	8	66	-	-	-	-	-	-	74

DNR COMMENTS:
Walleye numbers down but still within expected range for lake class; fish 10 to 22 inches sampled; limited natural reproduction. Northern Pike population below expected range; average size 30.5 inches and 6.6 lb. Balanced Largemouth Bass population present. Bluegill numbers down but still above expected range; 8 percent of Bluegills exceed 8 inches. Yellow Perch numbers up; small Perch dominated sample.

FISHING INFORMATION: Pickerel Lake is quite clear and has a limited weedline. It has good numbers of Walleyes and Smallmouth Bass and is loaded with Yellow Perch. Good spots to look for early Walleyes include the submerged island near mid lake, the steep dropoffs off the south shore and the 15-foot hump along the north side. Fish with either a leech or shiner minnow on a Lindy Rig. Smallmouth Bass can be found earlier in the season at rubble bottomed areas. Fish for them with small spinnerbaits. The Largemouth Bass population of nearby **Twin Lakes** is high, and almost all of them are concentrated at the lake's east end in the heavy vegetation. The water is fairly clear in Twin, and you can probably do well using a pig-and-jig combo. There are also a good number of Walleyes in the lake. A submerged island at mid lake and steep dropoffs at the east end are good spots to start looking for them. Eileen Koep of Koep's Clitherall Corner, Clitherall (218) 864-8731, says **Round Lake** offers good Bass fishing and some nice Walleyes and Northerns. The lake's west bay is essentially a slough, and the Bass concentrate there, she says. Otherwise, fish the weedlines around the lake.

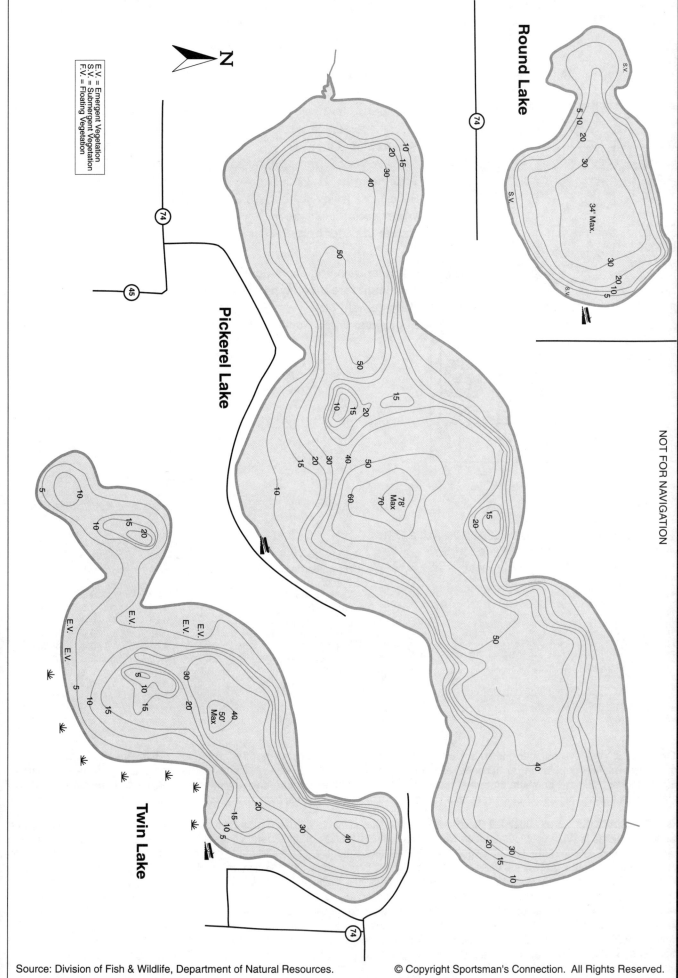

N

E.V. = Emergent Vegetation
S.V. = Submergent Vegetation
F.V. = Floating Vegetation

Round Lake

74

S.V.
5 10
20
30
34' Max.
30
20 10
5
S.V.
S.V.

Pickerel Lake

74

45

50

40
30
10 15
20

50

15
10 15 20
30
40 50
60
70
78' Max.
20
15

50

40

50

20
30
15
10

Pickerel Lake

Twin Lake

5
10
15 20
15
10

E.V.
E.V.
E.V.
E.V.
E.V.
E.V.

5
10
30
20
40
50' Max.
15
10 15
20

20
15
10 5
30
40

74

NOT FOR NAVIGATION

Pickerel, Twin & Round Lakes

Source: Division of Fish & Wildlife, Department of Natural Resources.

WEST LOST LAKE
Otter Tail County

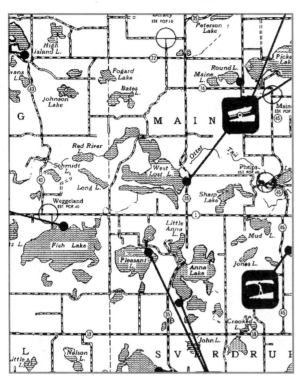

Location: Township 134
Range 41
Watershed: Otter Tail
Surface Water Area: 586 Acres
Shorelength: 11.3 Miles
Secchi disk (water clarity): 7.0 Ft.
Water color: Light green
Cause of water color: Algae

Maximum depth: 16 Ft.
Median depth: 8 Ft.
Accessibility: County-owned public access on east shore, off Hwy. 35
Boat Ramp: Asphalt
Accommodations: Resort and campground

Shoreland zoning classification: Natural Environment
Dominant forest/soil type: Deciduous/Loam
Management class: Walleye-Centrarchid
Ecological type: Centrarchid-Walleye

FISH STOCKING DATA

year	species	size	# released
93	Walleye	Fry	694,000
95	Walleye	Fry	692,000
97	Walleye	Fry	692,000

NET CATCH DATA

survey date: 8/23/93

	Gill Nets		Trap Nets	
species	# per net	avg fish wt. (lbs.)	# per set	avg fish wt. (lbs.)
Black Bullhead	0.8	0.70	0.1	trace
Black Crappie	0.6	0.11	1.1	0.39
Bluegill	7.8	0.17	17.8	0.25
Bowfin (Dogfish)	1.2	3.82	1.4	5.14
Brown Bullhead	0.1	1.14	0.1	1.03
Burbot	0.1	2.93	-	-
Common Carp	0.2	4.25	0.6	7.05
Greater Redhorse	0.1	3.09	0.5	2.94
Hybrid Sunfish	0.6	0.24	0.3	0.24
Largemouth Bass	0.8	0.46	0.4	0.58
Northern Pike	7.3	1.64	0.4	2.85
Pumpkin. Sunfish	4.0	0.20	0.9	0.19
Rock Bass	0.1	0.59	-	-
Shorthead Redhorse	0.4	3.42	-	-
Walleye	1.9	1.74	0.4	3.72
White Sucker	5.8	1.72	1.4	2.49
Yellow Bullhead	5.8	0.68	4.1	0.83
Yellow Perch	2.3	0.19	0.1	0.11

LENGTH OF SELECTED SPECIES SAMPLED FROM ALL GEAR

Number of fish caught for the following length categories (inches):

species	0-5	6-8	9-11	12-14	15-19	20-24	25-29	>30	Total
Black Bullhead	-	-	-	8	-	-	-	-	8
Black Crappie	5	4	5	-	-	-	-	-	14
Bluegill	64	146	2	-	-	-	-	-	212
Brown Bullhead	-	-	-	2	-	-	-	-	2
Hybrid Sunfish	2	5	-	-	-	-	-	-	7
Largemouth Bass	1	2	6	1	-	-	-	-	10
Northern Pike	-	-	-	4	37	19	9	-	69
Pumpkin. Sunfish	17	26	-	-	-	-	-	-	43
Rock Bass	-	-	1	-	-	-	-	-	1
Walleye	-	-	2	6	7	3	2	-	20
Yellow Bullhead	1	6	66	12	-	-	-	-	85
Yellow Perch	10	7	5	-	-	-	-	-	22

DNR COMMENTS: Walleye numbers down but within normal range for lake class; natural reproduction is being supplemented by fry stocking. Northern Pike population up and above normal range for first time; size structure unchanged, with 22 percent of sample exceeding 23 inches. Bluegill numbers in normal range for lake class; size structure down, with only 18 percent of sample exceeding 7 inches. West Lost Lake continues to enjoy reputation as good Bass water. Good spawning habitat for centrarchids.

FISHING INFORMATION: As the Otter Tail River heads for the North Dakota border, it runs through a series of lakes, bringing fish with it. One of benefitting lakes is West Lost, 586 surface water acres with 11.3 miles of meandering shoreline. It's a shallow lake with one hole of just 16 feet and a median depth of 8 feet. The good part is that, given the river current from the eastern shoreline to the far end of a north-western bay and the overall shallowness, West Lost is open earlier than most lakes, and fish are on the move to spawning grounds. There are four good spots here for early Northern Pike, Largemouth Bass and Walleyes. First are the two Otter Tail River inlet channels on the eastern shore. Stay off to the side of the channel and cast crankbaits into the pools and weedbreaks or use shiners with a slip bobber just off the reeds. The second spot is across the lake at the edge of the western weedbed and marsh. Cast there for Largemouth and Crappies. Third is the narrows heading into the northern section of West Lost. Cast shallow running baits or spinners in the channel, which is the lake's prime early Pike location. Lastly, move around the weedlines in the northern bay, especially in the channel leading to the bridge at the river outlet. Spring is the prime time for the larger migrating gamefish here. By summer, they have largely moved to the larger lakes. West Lost, however, remains a good panfish source all season.

NOT FOR NAVIGATION

E.V. = Emergent Vegetation
S.V. = Submergent Vegetation
F.V. = Floating Vegetation

Source: Division of Fish & Wildlife, Department of Natural Resources.

Location: Township 133, 134 Range 41, 42
Watershed: Otter Tail

Otter Tail County

	Anna Lake	Pleasant Lake	Fish Lake
Size of lake:	538 Acres	370 Acres	888 Acres
Shorelength:	6.6 miles	4.7 Miles	8.2 Miles
Secchi disk (water clarity):	5.5 Ft.	8.5 Ft.	4.0 Ft.
Water color:	Green	Light green	Green
Cause of water color:	Algae, silt	Slight algae bloom	Algae bloom
Maximum depth:	55 Ft.	38 Ft.	14 Ft.
Median depth:	NA	NA	5 Ft.
Accessibility:	State-owned public access on southwest shore	Public access on northeast shore	Public access on north shore
Boat Ramp:	Concrete	Concrete	Concrete
Accommodations:	NA	NA	NA
Shoreland zoning classif.:	Nat. Envir.	Rec. Dev.	Nat. Env.
Dominant forest/soil type:	Decid-Wet	Decid./Loam	Decid/Loam
Management class:	Walleye-Centrarchid	Walleye-Centrarchid	Warm-water Gamefish
Ecological type:	Centrarchid	Centrarchid	Unclassified

Anna Lake

DNR COMMENTS:
Walleye population up but within normal range for lake class; no evidence of natural reproduction. Northern Pike numbers up to normal range; 95 percent of sample under 23 inches. Black Crappie numbers up, but only 9 percent of fish exceeded 10 inches. Bluegill population down but still within the normal range. Carp population has declined substantially from 47.8/gillnet set in 1988 to 4.1/set; all Carp sampled less than 19 inches, indicating poor recruitment.

FISH STOCKING DATA

year	species	size	# released
94	Northern Pike	Fingerling	128
94	Walleye	Fingerling	12,586
95	Walleye	Fry	373,000
97	Walleye	Fingerling	11,084
98	Walleye	Fry	373,000

survey date: 8/9/93

NET CATCH DATA

	Gill Nets		Trap Nets	
species	# per net	avg fish wt. (lbs)	# per set	avg fish wt. (lbs)
Black Crappie	2.9	0.12	6.0	0.28
Bluegill	0.1	0.25	7.0	0.24
Hybrid Sunfish	-	-	0.4	0.16
Largemouth Bass	0.3	0.75	0.1	0.58
Northern Pike	5.6	1.27	0.6	1.35
Walleye	2.7	1.36	0.9	1.36
Yellow Perch	3.2	0.13	-	-

LENGTH OF SELECTED SPECIES SAMPLED FROM ALL GEAR
Number of fish caught for the following length categories (inches):

species	0-5	6-8	9-11	12-14	15-19	20-24	25-29	>30	Total
Black Bullhead	1	187	31	-	-	-	-	-	219
Black Crappie	13	52	15	-	-	-	-	-	80
Bluegill	10	54	-	-	-	-	-	-	64
Brown Bullhead	-	7	23	2	-	-	-	-	32
Hybrid Sunfish	3	1	-	-	-	-	-	-	4
Largemouth Bass	-	-	3	1	-	-	-	-	4
Northern Pike	-	-	2	7	27	19	-	-	55
Walleye	-	-	2	9	20	1	-	-	32
Yellow Perch	9	20	-	-	-	-	-	-	29

Pleasant Lake

FISH STOCKING DATA

year	species	size	# released
94	Walleye	Fingerling	9,976
96	Walleye	Fingerling	7,920

survey date: 6/16/97

NET CATCH DATA

	Gill Nets		Trap Nets	
species	# per net	avg fish wt. (lbs)	# per set	avg fish wt. (lbs)
Black Crappie	1.8	0.15	1.8	0.13
Bluegill	28.2	0.10	79.4	0.14
Green Sunfish	-	-	0.3	0.06
Hybrid Sunfish	2.7	0.08	6.1	0.15
Largemouth Bass	0.8	0.64	0.8	0.32
Northern Pike	12.4	1.89	0.3	0.89
Pumpkin. Sunfish	11.2	0.06	11.3	0.10
Walleye	2.2	2.57	-	-
Yellow Perch	0.8	0.18	0.3	0.05

LENGTH OF SELECTED SPECIES SAMPLED FROM ALL GEAR
Number of fish caught for the following length categories (inches):

species	0-5	6-8	9-11	12-14	15-19	20-24	25-29	>30	Total
Black Bullhead	-	288	70	-	-	-	-	-	358
Black Crappie	14	13	1	-	-	-	-	-	28
Bluegill	302	111	-	-	-	-	-	-	413
Brown Bullhead	-	5	32	1	-	-	-	-	38
Green Sunfish	2	-	-	-	-	-	-	-	2
Hybrid Sunfish	44	29	-	-	-	-	-	-	73
Largemouth Bass	-	5	7	-	1	-	-	-	13
Northern Pike	-	-	4	17	33	44	13	1	112
Pumpkin. Sunfish	165	5	-	-	-	-	-	-	170
Walleye	-	-	3	11	6	-	-	-	20
Yellow Bullhead	1	9	54	-	-	-	-	-	64
Yellow Perch	3	4	2	-	-	-	-	-	9

DNR COMMENTS:
Sunfish and Northern Pike abundant but tend to be small. Walleye, Largemouth Bass and Black Crappie popular with anglers. Common Carp documented in the lake for the first time in 1997. Neascus, the "black spot" disease of fish, was observed in 86 percent of bluegill and in 8 percent of Northern Pike. This parasite normally infects the skin of fish and does not affect edibility.

Fish Lake

FISH STOCKING DATA

year	species	size	# released
93	Walleye	Fingerling	14,013
96	Walleye	Yearling	1,952

survey date: 6/18/92

NET CATCH DATA

	Gill Nets		Trap Nets	
species	# per net	avg fish wt. (lbs)	# per set	avg fish wt. (lbs)
Yellow Perch	0.5	0.35	-	-
White Sucker	1.8	1.87	-	-
Yellow Bullhead	-	-	1.5	0.30
Walleye	3.5	2.31	0.3	2.10
Northern Pike	2.5	3.27	0.2	3.70
Brown Bullhead	21.5	0.24	51.7	0.33
Black Bullhead	524.3	0.24	1335.0	0.22
Black Crappie	3.8	0.63	-	-

LENGTH OF SELECTED SPECIES SAMPLED FROM SURVEY

Not Available.

DNR COMMENTS:
NOT AVAILABLE

FISHING INFORMATION: These lakes are north of Underwood. **Pleasant** is managed for Walleyes by the DNR and also has good numbers of Northern Pike and Crappies. Bass and panfish are present, too, in the weedy south and northeast parts of the lake. The outer edges of the weedlines are good places to troll slowly for Northerns. And a point coming off the middle of the north shore is an early season Walleye hot spot, as well as a good place to night-fish for Wallies throughout the season. **Fish Lake**, meanwhile, is very shallow and can be affected by winterkill some years. Even so, it often holds remarkable numbers of Walleyes and Northern Pike. There are weeds all around the lake for Northerns and Panfish. Two humps at mid lake, both marked by reeds, offer fine Walleye fishing, too. Check with local anglers and bait shops to see how well Fish Lake survived the winter. If it came out well, some fine fishing awaits you. **Anna Lake** is a fishery just returning from the dead, according to Ken Grewe of Ken's Tackle, RR2, Battle Lake (218) 495-2895. The lake had become overrun with Carp, but this species seems to be dying off on its own, says Grewe. Which, of course, leaves room for Walleyes, Northerns, and other species. Numbers and sizes weren't ideal at this writing, but they may become so. Try your luck around the mid-lake hump and off the steeply dropping east shore.

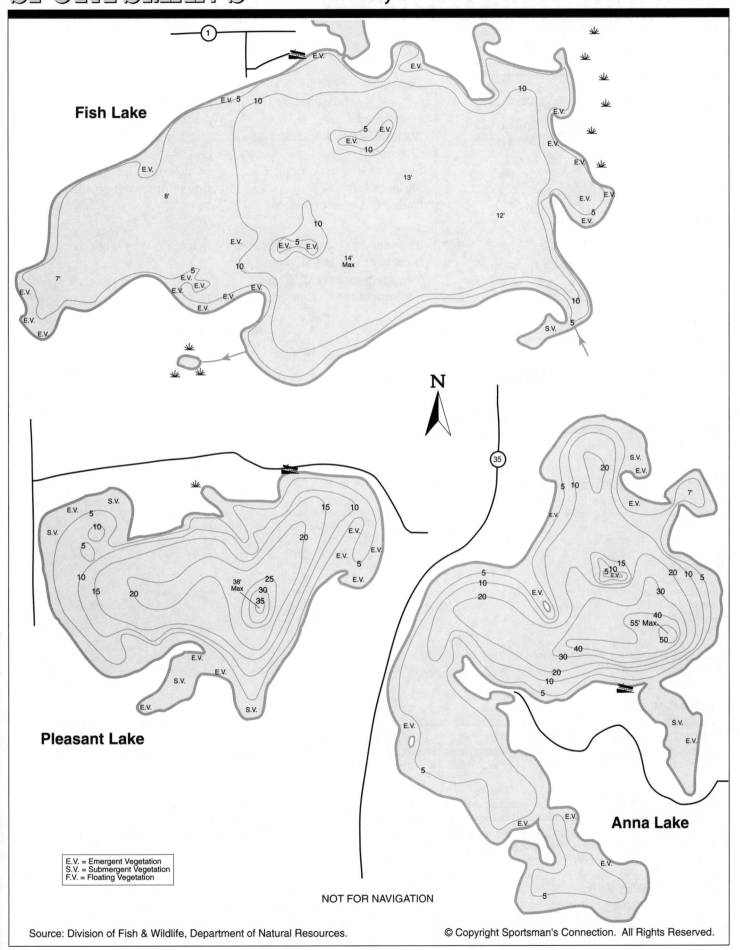

Fish Lake

Pleasant Lake

Anna Lake

N

E.V. = Emergent Vegetation
S.V. = Submergent Vegetation
F.V. = Floating Vegetation

NOT FOR NAVIGATION

RED RIVER LAKE
Otter Tail County

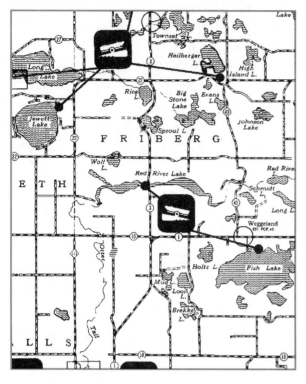

Location: Township Range

Watershed:

Surface Water Area: 305 Acres

Shorelength: NA

Secchi disk (water clarity): NA

Water color: NA

Cause of water color: NA

Maximum depth: 55 Ft.

Median depth: NA

Accessibility: County-owned public access on north shore, off Hwy. 3

Boat Ramp: Concrete

Accommodations: NA

Shoreland zoning classification: Natural Environment
Dominant forest/soil type:
Management class: Walleye
Ecological type: Centrarchid-Walleye

FISH STOCKING DATA

year	species	size	# released
93	Walleye	Fingerling	4,806
94	Walleye	Fry	138,000
96	Walleye	Fingerling	3,366
97	Walleye	Fry	138,000

NET CATCH DATA

survey date: 6/6/94

	Gill Nets		Trap Nets	
species	# per net	avg fish wt. (lbs.)	# per set	avg fish wt. (lbs.)
Black Bullhead	0.2	2.12	0.6	1.62
Black Crappie	0.2	0.25	1.0	0.43
Bluegill	2.8	0.20	18.8	0.20
Green Sunfish	-	-	0.3	0.28
Hybrid Sunfish	-	-	1.8	0.33
Largemouth Bass	0.6	1.48	0.3	0.80
Northern Pike	9.3	2.34	0.9	0.78
Pumpkin. Sunfish	1.8	0.30	8.8	0.29
Rock Bass	-	-	0.4	1.21
Walleye	2.2	1.20	0.5	4.56
White Sucker	1.7	1.85	0.9	5.88
Yellow Bullhead	0.9	1.48	3.1	1.88
Yellow Perch	19.7	0.08	0.6	0.08

LENGTH OF SELECTED SPECIES SAMPLED FROM ALL GEAR

Number of fish caught for the following length categories (inches):

species	0-5	6-8	9-11	12-14	15-19	20-24	25-29	>30	Total
Black Bullhead	-	1	3	3	-	-	-	-	7
Black Crappie	-	4	6	-	-	-	-	-	10
Bluegill	75	96	2	-	-	-	-	-	173
Green Sunfish	2	-	-	-	-	-	-	-	2
Hybrid Sunfish	9	5	-	-	-	-	-	-	14
Largemouth Bass	-	-	1	6	-	-	-	-	7
Northern Pike	-	-	2	5	25	45	9	3	89
Pumpkin. Sunfish	68	18	-	-	-	-	-	-	86
Rock Bass	-	2	1	-	-	-	-	-	3
Walleye	-	-	8	5	5	5	1	-	24
Yellow Bullhead	-	1	19	13	-	-	-	-	33
Yellow Perch	99	29	-	-	-	-	-	-	128

DNR COMMENTS: Walleye population up and within normal range for lake class; mean length 14.4 inches; natural reproduction is contributing to population. Northern Pike numbers down slightly but still above normal range for lake class; size structure improved, with 21 percent of Pike reaching at least 24 inches; mean length 21.4 inches. Largemouth Bass numbers normal; mean length 11.6 inches. Black Crappie abundance within normal range; mean length 9.2 inches. Bluegill numbers stable and within normal range; size structure has deteriorated, however, as only 24 percent of fish are reaching 7 inches; in 1988 survey this figure was 56 percent.

FISHING INFORMATION: OK; we admit it: we don't know a whole lot about this lake. We haven't fished it ourselves, and our contacts in the area either don't know – or aren't telling – much about it either. The "lake" is basically a couple of wide spots in the Otter Tail River, which, for some obscure reason, bear the same name as that of another, more famous area waterway, the Red River. The DNR says there are decent numbers of decent-size Walleyes in this double-basin lake. And this isn't surprising, given that there's fairly good natural habitat for this species and good forage, as well. The shorelines in both basins offer steep drops which should hold fish. And there's a good, deep pool with steep sides, as well, in the lake's western basin that should get some action. Try your luck, too, at the drops around the bridge, and off the points in the lake's western basin. Northerns in Red River average slightly above hammerhandle-size, and you'll want to try for them with sucker minnows fished just off the weedlines. Of course, you can troll in the same places with bright spoons or spinnerbaits. Fish the Crappies with minnows, of course, and the 'gills with worm chunks. Pig your jig for the Largemouth.

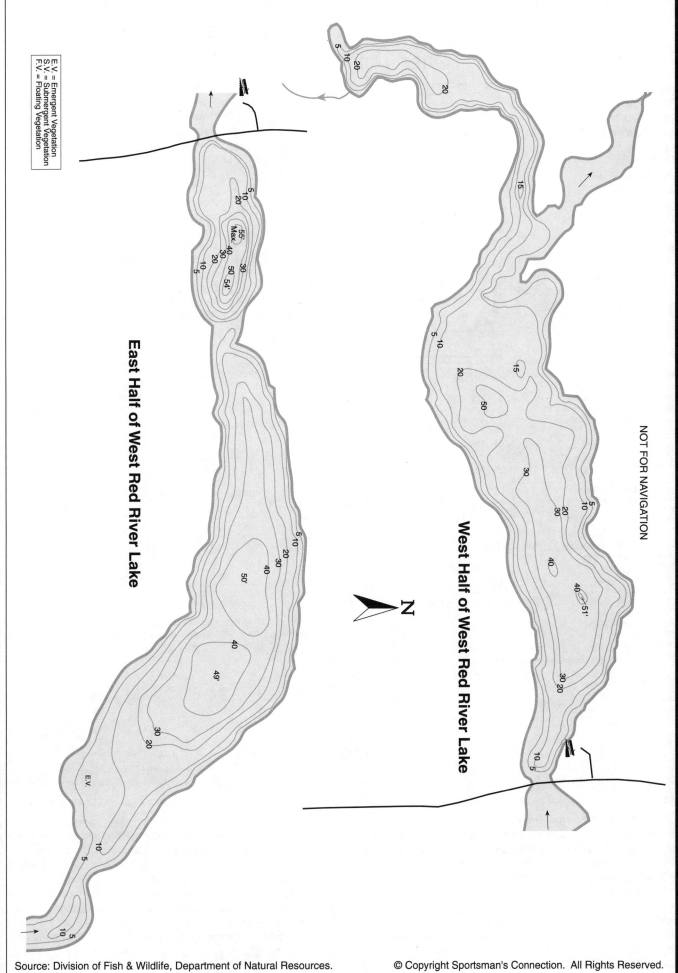

E.V. = Emergent Vegetation
S.V. = Submergent Vegetation
F.V. = Floating Vegetation

East Half of West Red River Lake

West Half of West Red River Lake

NOT FOR NAVIGATION

N

55' Max.

54'

50'

49'

40'

51'

E.V.

JEWETT LAKE

Otter Tail County

LONG LAKE

Location: Township 134 Range 43
Watershed: Otter Tail
Surface Water Area: 737 Acres
Shorelength: 4.1 Miles
Secchi disk (water clarity): 11.0 Ft.
Water color: Light green
Cause of water color: Algae bloom
Maximum depth: 75 Ft.
Median depth: 30 Ft.
Accessibility: State-owned public access on the northeast shore
Boat Ramp: Concrete
Accommodations: NA
Shoreland zoning classif.: Gen. Dev.
Dominant forest/soil type: Decid/Wet
Management class: Walleye-Centrarchid
Ecological type: Centrarchid-Walleye

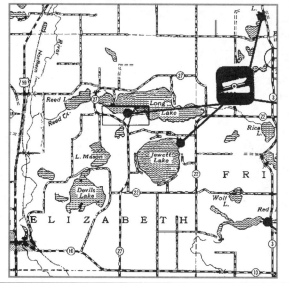

Location: Township 134 Range 42, 43
Watershed: Otter Tail
Surface Water Area: 756 Acres
Shorelength: 8.6 Miles
Secchi disk (water clarity): 6.9 Ft.
Water color: Light green
Cause of water color: Algae
Maximum depth: 72 Ft.
Median depth: NA
Accessibility: State-owned public access on the south shore, off County Hwy. 27
Boat Ramp: Concrete
Accommodations: NA
Shoreland zoning classif.: Rec. Dev.
Dominant forest/soil type: Decid/Sand
Management class: Walleye-Centrarchid
Ecological type: Centrarchid-Walleye

DNR COMMENTS:
Northern Pike numbers down slightly and below expected range for lake class; mean size 25.1 inches and 3.4 lb. Walleye numbers down, but within expected range; average size 17.7 inches and 2.1 lb.; natural reproduction limited. Largemouth Bass population balanced; average length 13.1 inches at age 3. Bluegill numbers within expected range; 16 percent of population at least 7 inches, up from 2 percent in 1992. Yellow Perch numbers down and below normal range for lake class; average size 5.6 inches at age 3.

FISH STOCKING DATA

year	species	size	# released
93	Walleye	Fingerling	6,388
95	Walleye	Fry	262,000
96	Walleye	Fingerling	7,567

survey date: 8/19/96

NET CATCH DATA

	Gill Nets		Trap Nets	
species	# per net	avg fish wt. (lbs)	# per set	avg fish wt. (lbs)
Black Bullhead	-	-	0.1	0.82
Black Crappie	1.5	0.16	0.4	0.24
Bluegill	6.8	0.18	42.0	0.20
Brown Bullhead	trace	1.58	0.1	1.34
Hybrid Sunfish	4.3	0.17	10.4	0.17
Largemouth Bass	0.8	1.01	0.8	0.32
Northern Pike	0.8	3.47	0.1	2.87
Pumpkin. Sunfish	5.1	0.25	7.6	0.24
Rock Bass	trace	0.40	0.2	0.37
Walleye	7.4	2.06	0.4	4.71
White Sucker	0.7	2.54	0.3	2.67
Yellow Bullhead	13.8	0.84	8.7	0.79
Yellow Perch	2.8	0.10	0.1	0.06

LENGTH OF SELECTED SPECIES SAMPLED FROM ALL GEAR
Number of fish caught for the following length categories (inches):

species	0-5	6-8	9-11	12-14	15-19	20-24	25-29	>30	Total
Black Bullhead	-	-	-	1	-	-	-	-	1
Black Crappie	3	17	2	-	-	-	-	-	22
Bluegill	90	205	-	-	-	-	-	-	295
Brown Bullhead	-	-	-	2	-	-	-	-	2
Hybrid Sunfish	63	79	-	-	-	-	-	-	142
Largemouth Bass	2	3	5	5	-	-	-	-	15
Northern Pike	-	-	-	-	5	5	1	-	11
Pumpkin. Sunfish	19	108	-	-	-	-	-	-	127
Rock Bass	-	3	-	-	-	-	-	-	3
Yellow Bullhead	1	5	147	89	-	-	-	-	242
Yellow Perch	3	19	1	-	-	-	-	-	23

FISH STOCKING DATA

year	species	size	# released
96	Walleye	Fry	305,000
97	Walleye	Fingerling	6,688

survey date: 7/24/95

NET CATCH DATA

	Gill Nets		Trap Nets	
species	# per net	avg fish wt. (lbs)	# per set	avg fish wt. (lbs)
Black Bullhead	3.3	0.75	0.6	0.65
Black Crappie	-	-	0.2	0.03
Bluegill	5.6	0.14	64.5	0.12
Green Sunfish	-	-	0.1	0.04
Hybrid Sunfish	0.5	0.22	4.0	0.13
Largemouth Bass	0.8	0.85	0.3	0.43
Northern Pike	9.3	1.46	0.8	1.46
Pumpkin. Sunfish	3.5	0.24	1.0	0.14
Rock Bass	-	-	1.1	0.33
Tullibee (Cisco)	0.3	0.70	-	-
Walleye	3.0	2.23	0.2	3.30
Yellow Bullhead	8.2	0.66	8.6	0.67
Yellow Perch	4.4	0.18	0.4	0.14

LENGTH OF SELECTED SPECIES SAMPLED FROM ALL GEAR
Number of fish caught for the following length categories (inches):

species	0-5	6-8	9-11	12-14	15-19	20-24	25-29	>30	Total
Black Bullhead	-	1	39	6	-	-	-	-	46
Black Crappie	2	-	-	-	-	-	-	-	2
Bluegill	226	100	-	-	-	-	-	-	326
Brown Bullhead	-	-	5	3	-	-	-	-	8
Green Sunfish	1	-	-	-	-	-	-	-	1
Hybrid Sunfish	33	17	-	-	-	-	-	-	50
Largemouth Bass	-	3	2	5	-	-	-	-	10
Northern Pike	-	-	1	19	64	21	9	1	115
Pumpkin. Sunfish	10	29	-	-	-	-	-	-	39
Rock Bass	-	12	-	-	-	-	-	-	12
Tullibee (Cisco)	-	-	3	1	-	-	-	-	4
Walleye	-	-	-	7	15	11	1	-	34
Yellow Bullhead	-	12	161	20	-	-	-	-	193
Yellow Perch	5	27	5	-	-	-	-	-	37

DNR COMMENTS:
Northern Pike population stable and normal for lake class; mean size 18.5 inches; 10 percent of sample larger than 24 inches. Walleye numbers down and below normal; mean length 18.6 inches; natural recruitment is occurring. Largemouth Bass population normal for lake class; mean length 11.4 inches. Black Crappies sampled by electrofishing; mean length 9.5 inches; all fish age 3-plus. Bluegill numbers down slightly but population is normal for lake class; mean length 5.3 inches. Yellow Perch numbers below normal; mean length 7.6 inches.

FISHING INFORMATION: Nine miles north of Fergus Falls, these lakes provide decent fishing for regional anglers. **Jewett Lake** is a long-time producer of nice Walleyes, both through natural reproduction and DNR stocking of fingerlings. Three sunken islands, two at the north end, and one in the south, are hotspots early in the season. There are some steep banks on the west side which can also be productive. The lake bottom is mostly sand and rubble and can be fished with a leech or shiner minnow bounced along to attract attention. The lake is fairly deep in several areas, and that's where the Walleyes head on summer days. There aren't too many Northerns in the lake, but they are bigger than average. You'll find them on the north and south flats. **Long Lake** provides decent fishing for Northerns and Largemouth Bass, and there are a few Walleyes which might be worth your while. Early season Walleyes hang around the nice points on the lake: the long point at the northwest corner; two good ones at the northeast corner and three smaller ones on the south shore. There is a lot of deep water in this lake, which is where the Walleyes head during summer days. They'll return to the points after sundown, however. Largemouth Bass can be found around the east end. The northeast and southeast shores are good for panfish as well as Bass. The flats off the east end weeds are also excellent for Northern Pike.

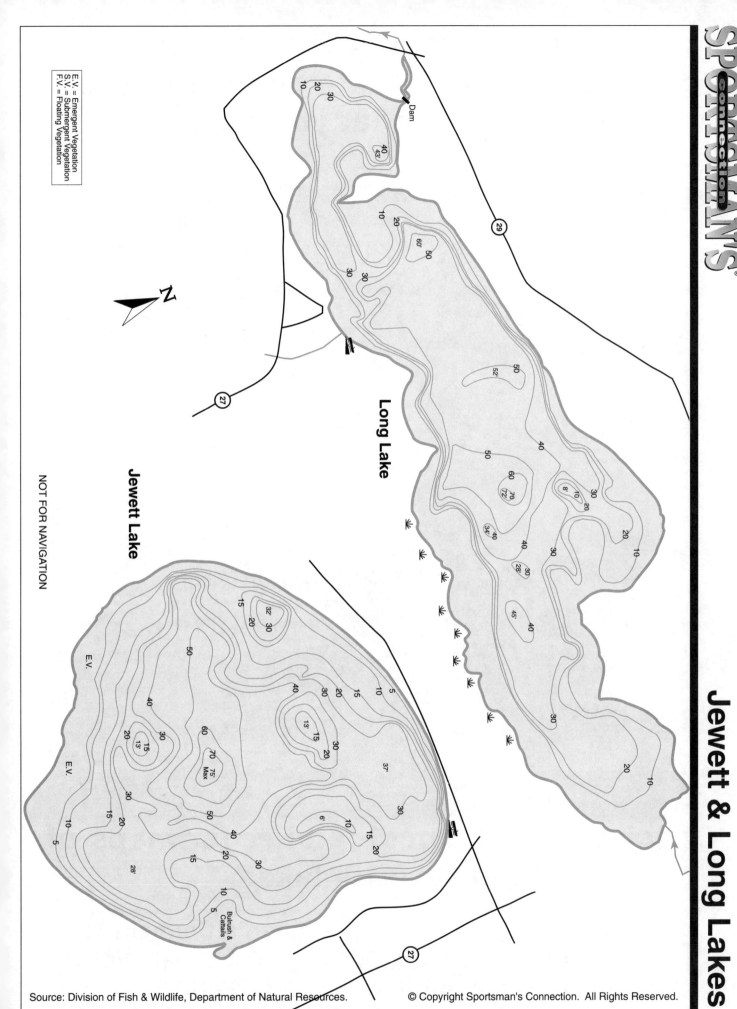

E.V. = Emergent Vegetation
S.V. = Submergent Vegetation
F.V. = Floating Vegetation

N

NOT FOR NAVIGATION

Long Lake

Jewett Lake

Dam

29

27

27

Source: Division of Fish & Wildlife, Department of Natural Resources.

E.V.

E.V.

Bulrush & Cattails

Sportsman's Connection publishes a complete line of fishing map guides for the areas that *you* fish

Check with your local retailer for maps of <u>your</u> favorite lakes.

For a complete list, write Sportsman's Connection, 1423 North Eighth Street, Superior, Wisconsin 54880 or phone toll free: 1-800-777-7461